The Highest
Meaning of Life

The Highest Meaning of Life

(The Complete Love of Truth)

Sukhdev Singh

ISBN: Softcover   978-1-5434-8794-7
             eBook   978-1-5434-8793-0

Print information available on the last page.

Rev. date: 06/20/2018

To order additional copies of this book, contact:
Xlibris
800-056-3182
www.Xlibrispublishing.co.uk
Orders@Xlibrispublishing.co.uk
769543

CONTENTS

III — Philosophy

Ontology-The Nature of the universe

Epistemology

Ethics

Religion is a Search for Devatma

IV — Survival of the Sublime Species

(The Poetry of suffering, agony, torture and sacrifice)

Acknowledgements

I dedicate this work to my dear parents – Bhai Gurmukh Singh ji and Mata Kaushlya Devi ji – my Birth-giver, Nurturer, Protector, Educator and the only safe anchor in the unsympathetic world! They gave me the invaluable gift of human consciousness and human destiny.

Without their love, I would be unable to develop my emotional health, thus placing me in a hopeless situation. With only a limited means to service my needs, they always fed me better, clothed me better, spent more on my entertainment, sent me to a better school. Living a modest life, they took great satisfaction in being able to care for me. With their unconditional love, our home at Kesupura was glorious beyond comparison – the crumbs of food they gave me were more satisfying than the most exquisite dishes of London's top luxury hotels, and the rags in which they put me were more valuable than a prince's garments.

My parents are unique beings and foundational benefactors. Without providing me with an atmosphere of love, concern, sincerity, love and service, even Devatma's blessings would be meaningless.

They provided me with the best psychological conditions of love, companionship, concern, identity, love and appreciative teaching, thus providing invaluable support to develop maturity. Through this acknowledgement, I extend my sincere appreciation of their virtues and noble traditions, which have enriched my life and strengthened my life-force infinitely.

Foreword

It is with immense pleasure and consummate gratification that I detail the structural Principles of goodness and truth, the structural principles of the new species and the psychology of new class and new variety. Developing a complete love of Truth, Goodness and Beauty can prosper through the progress of an innovative and progressive future population. The psychology of such a personality does represent a clean slate; rather, building upon this new slate provides humanity with a new sphere in which we can build unique and true values.

I am overwhelmingly blessed to have the light of the Sublime Master in enabling me to describe such a life and philosophy that is far beyond my understanding of a complete love of truth, goodness and beauty. Value is an essential part of natural existence for the unique species an essential condition for persistence in existence. There is a casual relationship between value and existence, in such a way that VALUE represents an inevasible stage which furthers existence, while DISVALUE is an imminent level that reduces further existence, leading to stagnation, degeneration, and death.

To come into existence of such a personality does not require a supernatural or transcendental sphere – it can evolve within our natural bodies as a repercussion of evolution. Also, this personality cannot disembody itself and transmigrate from one body to another. The soul works positively to build the body through physical health, exercise, and the development of consciousness in the pursuit of the Highest values, culminating in DEVAT (Trinity of Truth, Goodness and Beauty). Complete love of Truth, Goodness and Beauty is welcomed, duly accompanying the soul living in its body.

The love of truth is a new element of urges. These urges are under the command of the truth principle; therefore, they do not have a disposition to untruth and evil.

Where only a complete attraction and love for Truth, Goodness and Beauty exists, there is no ground to query the reason or purpose of human life. If such a sublime life comes into existence, the pleasure principle loses its aura, which surrounds the Psychology and Philosophy of the sublime life, where there is no chance to deviate into untruth and evil, and where only the Trinity principle is the character of complete love for Truth, Goodness and Beauty.

Similarly, in the human world, humanity is still in the process of evolution, and thus continues the quest in attaining higher values, all of which culminate in altruism. Hence, humankind is still bound by low-hates and low-loves and has the tendency to deviate into untruth and evil, thus lowering the survival rate of such a sublime species.

In light of this, to what extent and to which level of depth must sublime species suffer and sacrifice themselves to attain sublime values. This is the greatest challenge faced by Nature at the present moment for the survival of these species.

Before describing the structural Principles of Truth, Goodness and Beauty, let me caution the readers when I use the word "Devatma", "sublime-life", "the psychology of Devatma", and "Philosophy of Devatma" humble request lies not to fall into the error that I present the life-sketch or philosophy of a great man, an extraordinary philosopher and a noble social reformer who encapsulates a truly perfect human being. It is the life-sketch of a new sublime species that has the character of the Trinity (complete love of Truth, Goodness and Beauty).

We offer a new spurt to religious evolution, which is wholly committed to using scientific methods to discover human nature and its destiny. His findings of evolutionary naturalism offer no loopholes for easy deliverance from human slavery to passions and freedom into the life of light and salvation. His scriptures can be taken as books in science. Philosophy and life are concave and convex to a person. Such a sublime philosophy of absolute excellence is a reflection of his unique life. It invites utmost curiosity to read about his matchless existence and to revel in the most valuable fulfilment of one's destiny.

Secondly, the readers are requested to understand "soul" to mean "life principle" or "life-force", which is entirely biological in its origin and evolution. The soul is biological in its origin, thus embracing intrinsic higher values, such as compassion, love, justice, benevolence, reverence, gratitude and disinterested service. Such values also include a love for ideal, ethical values, which are as much products of natural conditions as they are intrinsic evils, such as feeling of cruelty, low-hatred, injustice, selfishness, irreverence, and ingratitude.

Here, the soul has no supernatural meaning or, "The spiritual or immaterial part of a human being or animal, which is regarded as immortal."

It is difficult for Western readers to understand how Religionless Religion (or Religion without God or supernaturalism) is possible, and how the word "soul" is synonymous with the term life-force.

The soul (life-force) has a biological origin. It is the product of the evolutionary process and transmutations in the natural world, and exists in a state ceaseless metamorphosis, for better and worse. It can stay alive under certain physical and psychological conditions and has a dependent origination.

The biological origin of the human soul has the power of construction in it to build, sustain, protect, develop, repair and reproduce its own kind.

The fundamental characteristics common to all organized life forces are:

- To build one or another kind of body.
- To maintain or nurture that living body.
- To living body alive
- To multiply itself.

The soul, or life-force, grows under certain conditions, much in the same way as our body grows under certain conditions. It also decays under certain conditions as the human body decays under certain conditions. The soul gains vitality and vigour when it develops altruistic motivations, and loses vitality and health when it develops low loves and low hates, which makes it think and cultivate harm to others. Spiritual knowledge is the knowledge of the laws of the life and death of the soul. Good and evil in the soul have as much natural origin as health and disease have. This view breaks from all other religious studies of the human soul.

The soul is not identical with God, nor is it his essence or his breath. The soul is neither creature nor child, as certain theologians assert, and it is not a mere combination of sensations and perceptions that disappear at the dissolution of its gross body, as many materialists would allege.

The Religion of Devatma (Dev-Dharma) is the science of the soul, which is currently undergoing investigation using the scientific method. The greatest discovery in the field of knowledge is the scientific method. The scientific method must be employed in the domain of religion, and religion can be experienced as a science, much like other sciences. Therefore, in this book, religion is defined within the category of science.

Dev Dharma is the only religion that can claim to be scientific in spirit, for it alone openly accepts the scientific method as necessary for truth discovery and verification in the field of religion.

We need a philosophy of life that is scientific by nature. It is through Devatma that the Science of Religion replaces mythological religion, just as the scientific mind needs a non-theistic and non-absolutist scientific religion. As Julian Huxley, the great biologist stated: "The beliefs of this religion ——are not revelations in the supernatural sense, but are the revelations that science and learning have given us about humans and the universe."

Such a moral conviction creates an intellectual and ethical climate in the light of truth, in which the hunter of transcendental philosophies can fall from the neck of Eastern and Western thought. This universal philosophy of Devatma can open up new vistas of truth. Devatma asserts that values, which can be studied by the empirical method and human ideal, are part of the empirical life of humans and can well be accommodated in the naturalistic worldview.

The philosophy of Devatma is scientific, evolutionary and altruistic. The goal of Devatma is a life-service in which low-loves and low-hates are held to a lower-point, while the individual endeavours in high loves and high hates to remove the presence of evil in life, wherever he may find it. Devatma also heralds and establishes a religion on this Earth that is destructive of all sins and evils, and which will produce men of trust and character through whom human relations will be caressed in sweet and blessed colours. Furthermore, Davatma gives true salvation to human souls, and thus fashions a high character in them. This allows them to attain Devatma's complete blessings, not only for fellow human beings, but for all living beings with whom they have a beneficial relationship.

The word "Dev-dharma" connotes a sublime life, rather than any reference to Supernaturalism. Invariably, the word 'Devatma' is a sublime life-force, which is neither all-powerful nor all-knowing; however, he is the sublime life, which is liberal from all of the weaknesses of human souls. There is no evil passion that touches his life and conduct, and there is no altruistic feeling that is lacking in him. He is the soul with new psychology, and his urges are governed by the principles of truth and goodness. Every thought and act of his life is processed by these principles, and they bear the charm of unique quality. It is this combination of an all-sided love of truth and goodness that nourished Devatma so completely, thus making him eligible to open windows towards them for their worship. Rightfully, goodness awaits humankind to prove their faith in Devatma. Only then humans can be liberated, fully evolved, and attain the highest level of spiritual being.

Devatma could not have had a greater value for contemplation, except his sublime life. In his self-consciousness of sublime life, in the ecstatic appreciation of it, he touched the noblest and highest throne of uniqueness. In fact, the sublime life, which lacked the appreciation of itself, would have been an incomplete sublime life, for it would have lacked the appreciation of one of the greatest truths of the sublime life, which must be an integral part of the sublime life itself. One of the greatest virtues of the sublime life is its absolute capacity to behold and appreciate the completeness the aestheticism and the glory of sublime life.

Hence, greater than his sublime life was his contemplation and his appreciation of it in a language unto his own. Since the sublime life is the noblest thing to understand, its knowledge is highest.

I wish I could find the right phrase to measure my gratitude to all of the well-wishers who helped me both directly and indirectly.

In this foreword, I would like to extend my special thanks and place flowers at the pious feet of the Spiritual Master Devatma, whom I value most. In this book, there is not a single word that is not in the light of the spiritual master Devatma and his scholars.

This book is nothing but my excursion from the last twenty years. The books I loved, are mentioned in the end, invariably bless me pearls of thought in my voyage of self-discovery. All eye-beaming thoughts are either visual fields of Master Himself or His scholars where references and brief notes could possible hitherto. For detailed Notes and index scholars can either download or order from the website "www. Devatma.org".

Without the matchless contribution of Prof. S. P. Kanal in Dev Dharma, this book loses the significance in itself, although his books are also in the light of Devatma, whom I highly indebted to. Through the study of this book, if readers rejoice in the rainbow of delight and illumination, they should be grateful to Master Devatma, his scholars, and all his life workers, who helped me in turn.

For this book, Dr. Ramanpreet Kaur has played a vital role. Without her regular efforts, this book would not be possible, and my sincere appreciation extends to her. May the evolutionary process of nature bless her forever with purposeful life!

Also, I would like to state my gratitude to Shriman Baldev Singh ji (Former Secretary General of Dev Samaj), who introduced me to this light and philosophy. It is difficult to express my gratitude to him for all that he has done for me.

Despite quoting many people here, I must give all my credit to Prof. S.P. Kanal, the marvellous scholar of Devatma, whose every text on Devatma has provided me with long-term memory, which can never be forgotten. I am permanently influenced and inspired by his writings, which made it impossible for me to go out of that boundary of his writings.

Therefore, it is the benediction of our Master, who enabled me to go beyond the limits of my capacity and energy, to commit myself to the service of such universal thought, which holds the promise of bringing the next evolutionary leap of humankind into scientific soul-illumination and soul-evolution.

In spite of the low-loves and low hates, which are very much in me, I draw on his mercy to keep my faith, determination, enthusiasm, and energy to serve through writings of the master as much as my strength will permit me. In this relay race of evolution, I will pursue my goals until life asks me to pass the torch to the next participant in the race. May I run as fast as possible in the relay race, and dance ecstatically before the beauty of the master until the last unit of heat in my body exhales. I pray to the master to instil some spark of his genius in my life to assist me to keep some of my ethical promises to him to write about the many aspects of his philosophy and life.

To understand the highest meaning of life, one needs unshakable faith, unconquerable determination, ever-replenishing enthusiasm and exhaustible patience in order to be devoted and dedicated to the service of evolution (i.e. Truth, Goodness and Beauty), which basks in the tangible peace, amazing grace, majestic glory and divine compassion. Let us all join hands and hearts to reach the latest call of evolution to the largest number of human beings so that mankind touches the next leap in evolution.

Thanks to evolution for the emergence of Devatma where humankind leaps forward in evolution and obtains the meaning of life under the light and power — the embodiment of truth, goodness and beauty.

I cannot offer anything to the Master except my bondage of low-loves and low hates with pleasurable tendencies. My life is a flame of evil passions that not only stand in the way of life of truth, fairness and freedom, but also miss the intrinsic beauty of the sublime life, which can never be expressed in words. Alas! It burns me like the hatred of the pandemonium-fire. They strangulate even glimpses of the sublime beauty, the aspect of intrinsic beauty which will be hidden to humanity except, except for those of the Devatma species.

Therefore, my words for sublime Master are as follows:

Oh, Master!
Your sublime life is marvellous;
too splendid to describe.
Oh, my Monarch!
You are the shop-holder of the
Authentic love of complete Truth
and Goodness.
The world of mere individuals
cannot pay the debt of such selfless
and benevolent psalms that
knit sublime life in nature.
We are deformed persons
to the core.
To behold,
Through and through,
The glimpses of your 'twinkling loyalty'
Though, in full swing,
You provide us a huge bestowal
of sublime light.
Oh, my worshipful being!
Oh, my brook of goodness!
We are creeping identities on
the highway of your truthfulness
Even, you offer us
A 'full torch-house of illumination'.
The amalgamation of all goodness
(Moral values) cannot nourish sublime life,
Whether or not the enhancement of goodness
May be in full swing.

Oh, Sublime life!
On your pious feet,
We are not capable to bow.

Unable to have your obeisance,
Unable to pen the pains of your contours,
And tongue also incapable of utterance.
You show me life's path.
Retort us the precious genuine truths of soul.
We too, imprisoned in lower melodies.
Not even eligible to step ahead,
The path of lower life
is completely carcinogenic.
We traversed that path carelessly for our entire lives.
Lower movements degenerated us to such an extent
that
We are not able to wail over this.
Knowing your sublime wailing,
devoid of its genuineness,
We are unable to move even hands and legs.
For the support of your MISSION,
Thou hast been very supportive of us.
We too are too innocent to understand
In this 'innocent stage'.
We are not able to pay your debt,
The grandeur of sublime life
and truthful knowledge.
A person harshly needed
is a regretful condolence.
Hitherto, in the world
We are incapable of
reciting it comprehensively.

If the readers of this book can benefit from the writing contained herein, may they receive the blessings of the Master with his light and power, for having faith in and love for Devatma.

Finally, if the reading of this book provokes some philosophic scholars to examine the original texts of Devatma, it would justify that its production and universal philosophy can work to open up new vistas of truth.

Let us realize this blissfulness through the perusal of such philosophy and owe our immeasurable gratitude to our Master – the discoverer of these truths.

Service with a Grin — A Note from Editor

It is my amiable and honoured privilege to examine the book 'The Highest Meaning of Life—Complete Love of Truth' for proof-reading where I am blessed with the mind-alluring thought of the Master and his scholars! I am bountifully conscious that my own role has been nothing more than a 'pauper-lowest-point.'

If I am not 'on false track', this book wraps up the whole perspectives of the philosophy of the Master. It is an urgent requirement of the time where research scholars can achieve the book with all approaches including, ontology, evolution, epistemology, ethics, religion and psychology of the sublime life.

Undoubtedly, it is a filament of rigorous—misfortune for us that only limited scholars have completed research on Devatma hitherto. I provoke research scholars for further research on Devatma with the prayer where Nature can bless us more ideal life workers and scholars of Devatma and humanity can touch its zenith. Question is there in my mind; Will not thousands of research scholars come to research on Devatma's life and Teaching? Will Devatma be unknown, Ignored, disrespected, hated and rejected in future too? It is my humble request that innumerable research scholars should 'come forward' to emerge and enhance the stream of sublimity, aesthetically appreciated by Devatma which is the purpose of evolution.

Devatma's philosophy is based on humanist principles and scientific truths. It is appropriate that this branch of philosophy is separate from all religions or mono-theistic faiths. Based upon this school of thought, the book opens its delicate petals to present a series of scientific truths upon which Devatma School was founded. This book details the full-fledged philosophy and history of Devatma, interpreting how it can reward human existence not only on an individual level but also on a global level.

The text is organized into chapters, within which numbered lists and bullet -points summarize the major ideas, discoveries, and truths detailed in the Devatma school of thought. History and traditional arguments are initially presented, followed by a series of explanations based on scientific truths and information on whatever Devatma's philosophy teaches, as well as its similarities and differences in regards to other world religions and faiths. There is a particular focus on religion, the human mind, the evolution of human life and a discussion on the various existing theories of evolution and creation, the soul and it's life-force, the existence of the Earth and Human Life and their relationship with the animal world and the entire Universe, also existential ideas that discuss the origins of the Universe and Human life.

The text is presented as a series of sections. Within each section, each separate element of Devatma philosophy's is settled down into a set of principles, which are outlined in numbered lists. This assists the reader to summarize the philosophy based on the points and numbered lists detailed within.

Although the writing is presented clearly to the modest extent using lucid, logical, convincing and elevating style but language has also been simplified with modern stylish pattern. Thence, this book is directed at those who are serious about looking into Devatma. Therefore, it is recommended that the reader has some experience, serious interest or knowledge of humanist philosophy and is inclined towards recognizing more about the human psyche, the meaning and purpose of life, heretofore, how human existence came into being.

The contents of the book are well fed with suspense and dilemma. The forward and the introduction (Sublime Journey untouched by the Time) comprise the whole theme of the Devatma school of thought.

I am on the seven heaven of serendipity to endorse superiorly having 'one in a million' to the opportunity for the translation of the book of Devatma Ka Parichey. (Introduction to Devatma). After the translation of the book, proof-reading of this book and future coming book 'The Highest Meaning of life Part II' (Sublime Species) which is on the final stage, I feel blessed. Hats off to all the geniuses who contributed in the evolution of Sublime life and until now who participated in the relay race. When I did come to know that The Highest meaning of life-Part 1, is all credited to Prof. S.P. Kanal, the great scholar of the Master; I could not control my emotions, as it is my ethical responsibility to vocalize something about the Rev. Kaka ji (Prof S.P. Kanal) and his contribution on Devatma; even if it is outside of the border of the Book.

Prof. Kanal was the rarest natural pearl in the world with the blessing of the Spiritual Master, inherited noble virtues of high character and the pen to propagate the teachings of Devatma by Birth. He joined the philanthropic work after completing his study from the University college London with third rank, even though was permitted to take up Ph. D course without going through Master. He retired as Head of the senior-most readers, the Department of Philosophy and Dean, Delhi University after teaching 42 years. The Altruistic was KAKA Ji who stayed loyal towards Master till his last drop of energy.

This was the man who fulfilled the wish of His Rev. Father i.e. "Nothing else, O Master! but he will write your literature."

He was the great prolific writer as a pillar of Dev Samaj Literature Department, a veteran Educationist, the unique philosopher, a missionary zeal, best devotee in every perspective, pioneering social worker, an impressive orator, an ideal son, wonderful husband and blessed teacher, a true altruistic and noble soul who blessed the world invariably ever on the aspiration to get and spend every moment in the light of the Master to serve humanity. His remarkable personality was the mirror for ideal relations. He was the role model. There is fragrance of altruism in his books. Let us keep his fragrance flowing and spreading by following his noble ideas. His altruistic life proved that the depth of life is more important that its length. He was the rare gem that the world produces only once in a while who devoted his time and all resources to print Devatma's teachings. His SGR for 44 years provided countless articles and essays of perennial value which will inspire and elevate the forthcoming generations. He lived a purposeful and exemplary life. He was the priceless jewel whose every words on Devatma would be 'a life rescuing panacea' for Research scholars. He spread the literature of Devatma in hundreds of libraries in India and Abroad.

He joins the Galaxy of the stars shining on the Filament of Dev Dharma. His altruistic life was the gem that shines with the example of entire sacrifice in the lighthouse of Master who left behind a bright trail of services to humanity. I regret I never met such a Noble Personality.

His texts on Devatma are knitted with altruistic roses which bless its fragrance of sublime influences to the readers. His books on Master can fill enough fire in us to follow the path of love and responsibility towards one and all.

His literature is an icon of a rare kind and truly wore a crown of humility and would continue to motivate the boundless spirits.

I am not confident whether I will be able to do justice to the greatness of this personage, therefore, His memorable and beautiful words could express better:

"I have complete self-fulfillment in sharing my understanding with the student community. I have no desire for Paradise or Moksha. It was Moksha, it was heaven to share love with the best part of the community, the student community, the community of innocence and laughter."

"Let Philosophy Live through you".

"I place with utmost humility your kind words and sentiments as an offering at the feet of my Master, Bhagwan Devatma, and mentors who shaped my clay. Every appreciation of me is a tribute to the influences that have made me what I am."

I refer to the reader don't miss his Master-piece books —The Ethics of Devatma and Devatma Ka Parichey (Introduction to Devatma), after reading his Master piece Ethics of Devama and Introduction to Devatma, readers will realize they missed the books in the purposeful voyage in the past. Therefore, it is still not too late. I am also preparing for D.Litt on Devatma.

Finally, the efforts would be purposeful if readers could be excited to read the Master Scriptures of Devatma - i.e., Mujh Mein Dev Jiwan Ka Vikas-Part 1 (The evolution of sublime life in Devatma- volume 1) and Dev Shastra Volume III.

Dr. Ramanpreet Kaur
(Research Scholar)
M.A. (English), M. Phil & Ph.D (English),
Ph.D in Hindi (honorary, sahitya vachaspati and sahitya varidhi),
D. Litt, honorary.

Sublime journey untouched by time

There is no doubt that most religions, if not all, are primarily centred on the soul-life of man. Religion also deals with the nature of the soul, as well as its health and diseases, while it also gives guidance on salvation, provides a disputed history of evolution and places reverence on Divine life. Hence, religious teachings are foundational for those seeking a truly religious life.

The philosophy of Devatma claims to be in a league of its own in terms of the world's religions. One of the bases of this claim is its discussion of the philosophy of the soul. Devatma interprets the origin and nature of the human soul in both evolutionary and biological terms, while it also raises many interesting points regarding the evolutionary origin of the human entity. For example, Devatma's philosophy asserts that humans emerged as a species from the animal world. Since its process of origin is no different from the process of millions of other species in animal and plant worlds, it is, therefore, like all other species, a product of natural conditions. Thus, the history of humankind's evolution from the animal world posits that the theory of creation is wholly false.

Such an evolutionary history is evidenced in the vestigial tail found at the bottom of the spine—a reminder that the first and last home of all human beings is in nature, thus holding true to the biological account of the birth of a human entity. The human entity is a new entry, an emergent entity, from the ovum of a female and the sperm of a male, and its characteristics are the result of the interaction between these two cells and environments. Therefore, to understand the human entity-soul body organism, we first need to understand the laws of heredity-environments.

When we accept this scientific account of the process of birth, we must assert that every human soul is a new entity unknown to the previous history of existence. When we admit this, we must reject transmigration, which holds that the human soul, which is born, is, in fact, say, a crocodile, who, through good actions, has managed to place itself into a woman's womb in order to take on a human form. The ridiculousness of the transmigration theory becomes apparent once we grasp the evolutionary process of the origin of the human species, the biological process of the birth of a human child and the laws of heredity. When an evolutionary account of the origin of the human entity is true, it follows that the human entity is both structurally and functionally connected with the inanimate world, the vegetable world, the animal world and the human world. In addition, when the origin of humankind is in nature and the conditions of his continued existence are in nature, his entity is inseparable from it. When this is so, his destiny is inseparable from nature; hence, the human ideal cannot be salvaged in the sense of deliverance from body or mergence with the super-sensibility of a Brahman.

Humans are part of nature. Hence, the human ideal is to seek and realize true harmony with existence in nature—what stands in the way of this is a love of pleasure, which humans inherit, together with pain, from the animal world. However, new powers of ideation, thinking and imagination help to develop an attraction, and ultimately, their love for pleasure. For instance, when one is selfish and seeks pleasure at all costs, he or she harms others and deprives them of their just claims, and in turn, produces disharmony. Also, when there is an obstacle standing in the way of the satisfaction of any of his low-loves of pleasure, he reacts with low-hates, which take the form of ill-will, revenge and vindictiveness. Humans must seek moksha in order to disband himself from these low-loves and low-hates, which put him in disharmony with other existences in nature. However, harmony with others does not merely concern refraining from doing harm to them — humans must be serviceable to others to achieve the ideal of harmony. This is possible if they develop higher feelings of disinterested service of others.

This is the evolution of humankind, and these are some of the truths about soul-life which differentiate Devatma from the world Religions. Since these truths are founded on scientific verification, there is a moral obligation to accept a number of truths, as detailed in the following summary:

- Humans are evolute from the animal world – not a special creation.

- Each human soul is a new entity unknown to the previous history of the universe. Hence, transmigration is false. The human soul is neither a substance nor a pure cognition – it is a nutritive organism, a motor and a sensory instrument with affective, conative and cognitive functions. As such, it is the doer, affecting change and changing itself. Thus, the human soul is under the law of change and subject to growth, decay and death under certain conditions.

- The origin and condition of the continued existence of each human entity is in nature. He is inseparable from Nature – his first and last home. His destiny is to establish harmony with other existences in nature on an evolutionary basis (i.e. truth and goodness and beauty).

- The human ideal is to eliminate the low-loves and low-hates in one's life and develop higher feelings of disinterested service, both of which are key to moksha and vikas. The universal religious philosophy will be scientific and not merely founded on science. Again, continuity with scientific knowledge in other fields characterizes these religious teachings, which, in turn, produces solidarity and integrity in knowledge, both of which are reflected in the solidarity and integrity of the individual. When we hold both to the natural and the supernatural origin of the soul, we are divided within, harbouring repulsive disharmony, and are condemned to live a lie in the core of our personality, which thus leads to our ultimate extinction. The universal religious philosophy of Devatma is a 'saving knowledge', for it saves us from fabricating our own personalities and experiencing such torturous disintegration.

- A religion that fails to eliminate the low-loves and low-hates that harm others does not contribute to evolution. On the other hand, a religion that develops a scientific mode of thinking in religious matters is a true religion. Further, this true religion helps one to see the ugliness of evil conduct and develop a hatred for it, in addition to giving strength to eliminate it and helping one to see the beauty of altruistic feeling by awakening and developing an affinity for it, for it fosters a scientific mode of thinking on religious matters and aids human beings in eliminating their evils and developing altruistic feelings. Therefore, true religion offers a scientific view of universe and man and an evolutionary interpretation of man's morality and spirituality. Moreover, true religion delivers humans from evil and forms the complete embodiment of truth and goodness for love.

- An ideal society needs ideal men as well as ideal institutions – neither can bring about the ideal society alone. Humanism has played a noble part in changing the institutions of society, and true religion specializes in encouraging humans to be more altruistic. Thus, humanism and true religion need to work together to create a society of altruistic love and justice for all; a society void of untruth and evil, and where altruistic loves are capable of walking the path of Truth, goodness and Beauty. In Devatma, humanism will find its best companion, its highest guide and its noblest fulfillment.

- Human beings need to develop a super-altruistic character to eliminate the reign of evil and untruth in social life – it is not enough to simply follow a religious leader with altruistic virtues, such as compassion or non-violence. It is necessary to train our intellect and refine our super-altruistic character, whose virtues are not under the bewitchment of the pleasure principle nor impaired by evil and untruth, but are, instead, under the principle of truth and goodness. These altruistic virtues are free from partiality and prejudice, and our vision is wide awake to the total field of values. Such a religious genius strives to live a life of truth and goodness and despises all untruth and evil in the world. Equipped with an absolute love of truth and goodness, we are able to gain truthful satisfaction from our virtues, and through sharing an absolute hatred for untruth and evil, we are able to see the ugliness of vice, create a desire to abjure it and give strength to get rid ourselves of it. Moreover, such a religious genius will create a culture that helps us to isolate and learn to consider our vices and superstitions as diseases of the soul that must be freed. This culture helps man to consider virtues as indicators of our soul's condition and to actively cultivate a healthy soul.

- Devatma's philosophy is inclusive of Comté's religion of humanity, Dewey's all-inclusive ideal and Huxley's creative act or evolutionary humanism. Through communication with Devatma, we can all service humanity to best of our ability. In addition, we can acquire a superior vision of the all-inclusive ideals or ends of life and develop an ecstatic perception of the evolutionary process to the limits of its altruistic strength. With Devatma, religion gains its highest truth and humans reach their highest destiny.

- Dev Dharma is the true religion and its worshipful being is Devatma – the perfect embodiment of Truth, Goodness and Beauty, whose light helps the devotee to see the beauty of his altruistic potentialities and whose power gives us the strength to develop them. Over and above this, Devatma's light helps a devotee to see the ugliness of attachment to the evil pleasures of the body and ego, and whose power gives the strength to reduce one's attachment to low-loves and low hates. Devatma can enlighten a disciple to see his duties in relation to all the four orders of existences and to discharge them according to his capacity. Devatma offers the greatest blessings to a devotee by offering his sublime life as an object of love. The feeling of devotional love helps the devotee to realize its dream of becoming a perfect being in Devatma, and, in turn, finds the complete satisfaction of its love in this embodiment of Truth, Goodness and Beauty, the Devatma.

- A life of perfect commitment to evolution alone can inspire and inspirit man to reduce the influence of disposition to become fixated at some stage of its development to human destiny. This entity must have life, which does not allow the balance of goodness and pleasure to be tipped in the favour of pleasure. It is this life that determines its conduct through the principle of Truth, Goodness and Beauty. Such a life can claim to be the Guru or spiritual Master. Devatma is a perfectly committed evolutionist in thought and deed, who knows no fixation in his destiny to evolve an absolute love of Truth, Goodness and Beauty, and an unending hatred for untruth and evil. His influences can help us to reduce the influences of fixation and the pleasure principle and remove the hurdles to human destiny. We need to communicate with Devatma and his philosophy in order to frame the law of justice and welfare in society. We can achieve this by observing the existent just and benevolent laws and assimilating his light and strength to promote the human destiny of developing knowledge, appreciating beauty and harnessing altruistic feelings.

- We live a higher life when:

  - we know how to control the evil motivations that threaten the very existence of our life and the life of others.
  - we know our aptitude and abilities and engage ourselves in their development.

-   we utilize our development aptitude and abilities in the service of the family of man
-   we develop a vision and love for the sublime life, a complete love of Truth, Goodness & Beauty and a complete hatred of untruth and evil.

-   For religion, Devatma can build a science of the soul, since he has both internal and external conditions for investigation. The religion of Devatma is a unity of religions, for it is not only inclusive of all elements of truths about nature, knowledge and the values that have evolved from different religions; it also completes the science of soul, for it contains the scientific knowledge of the origin and nature of soul, the law of health and disease and the ability to rid the soul of its diseases, and the evolution of the health of the soul; on top of this, the devotee is granted Devatma's complete soul for worship. It is not only the unity and completion of all religions, but it is the fulfillment of all religions and the future of all religions, because it is the product of the application of the scientific method to the discovery of the moral and spiritual constitution of human soul.

-   The scientific method, scientific knowledge and the development of technology – three factors will affect the institute of religion. In addition, if we carry the life and light of Devatma within us, religion has a very bright future.

-   An ideal human soul is one who:

    -   is illumined with the scientific truth of the philosophy of Devatma;
    -   rises above his low loves and low hates;
    -   cultivates higher loves and higher hates; and through them lives a dedicated life of innocence and service of the four orders of existences; and who

- is in complete rapport with Devatma through the redevelopment of the feelings of faith, reverence, gratitude and love for him, to the extent a person achieves this ideal four-fold life.

- The philosophy of Devatma, as the science of moral and spiritual life, discharges a two-fold function for a new society in order to conserve old values by building a new scientific foundation for them, and to discover new values through the scientific study of nature and the laws of health and disease of human soul. In this way, Devatma contributes to the emotional development of a new society.

- The universal religion of Devatma is the only complete humanistic religion which places the origin of the human personality, both the body and soul, in human society. It also places the human ideal in human society by developing a system of meditation to reshape and refine the interpersonal relationships through the development of appreciation, gratitude, compassion, altruistic love and service in various interpersonal relationships. Its founder's life has been illumined with ideal interpersonal relationships, and in its uniqueness, Devatma's philosophy and the founder has the permanent capacity to help us build interpersonal relationships on the basis of altruism of appreciation, gratitude, love and service. In this way, Devatma is the religion for a civilization of sweetness and light in interpersonal relationships. It is too great in its excellences and achievements in human relations to justify despair about its future service in interpersonal relationships. As long as Devatma lives, the future of humanity will be preserved through maintaining ideal interpersonal and infra-personal relationships.

- The nature-based altruistic educational philosophy of Devatma contributes to the intellectual perspective for teachers under training. However, teachers must be altruistic if they are to educate the young on the feelings of altruism, since morality is not taught, but caught. Devatma is the highest form of altruism in relation to the four kingdoms of nature. There is no religious leader in the history of the world who has sung of his connection to humans, animals, plants and the physical worlds with the same intensity as a mystic sings in praise of a deity. His contemplation is not on a supernatural power, but on his gratitude towards the four kingdoms and how best he can serve them. His life gives inspiration to those seeking the all-out altruism of understanding, as well as the appreciation of, gratitude for, and service to the four kingdoms. When education unites under the philosophy of Devatma in a close and warm embrace, a new, golden future beckons for this industrialized society – a future where we can recognize our interpersonal and infra-personal relations on the basis of altruism, and thus enjoy the best intellectual and emotional satisfactions open to human life.

- There are four kinds of suffering: physical, mental, social and personal. Suffering is the truth of life. 'Suffering must be removed' is the voice of compassion. Suffering deserves to be removed because it devitalizes life. The absence of suffering is in accordance with the law of evolution or ideal state of things. The direction of evolution is towards individual health and social and cosmic harmony, and accordingly, towards a reduced state of suffering. Much of the suffering in this world arises through an unjust social structure. In addition, unjust social discrimination has condemned large sections of humanity to a life of ignorance, poverty, disease, denial and deprivation, and consequently, immeasurable suffering. Moksha from all suffering is not desirable. Though suffering can be reduced, it is not known that it can be completely eliminated, so vast, varied, deep and subtle is the coverage of suffering. The elimination of suffering as a means may be desirable, but not the elimination of suffering when it is part of the definition of an altruistic feeling. If life cannot be without suffering, the ideal man cannot feel an inner pain when knowing this and it is this pain that remains a constituent of the highest life practical and possible for man.

- Evolution is the central or key concept of Devatma.

This universe of embodied existences in ceaseless change, for better or worse, which perpetually develops higher and higher life on earth, is the only self-existent, self-explanatory reality. Hence, evolution is reality, for change is real, time is real, and the history of the planet is real. What is the highest is the product of time, change, and evolution. Dev Dharma provides the highest evolute in Devatma to grow in humans.

- Scientific attitude to seek and accept facts;
- To develop society-centred, altruistic feelings of justice and benevolence as decisive values;
- To awaken man to his soul welfare;
- To create faith in the reality and inevitability of evolution and make humankind fit to be the managing directors of evolution, and thus, to usher in world peace.

• It is a mistake to think that an altruistic life of service is the ultimate end for human life. The highest life open to man is to open communication with the supreme life force.

An altruistic life does not guarantee freedom from untruth and evil. An altruistic life is not sufficient unto itself. Man needs to communicate with the supreme life force with the feeling of faith, reverence, and love so that he can learn to control his dispositions for untruth and evil and enjoy the maximum freedom from evil conduct. Evil tendencies and evil conduct are diseases of our soul; as such, when liberate ourselves from them, our health and happiness benefit.

Man is not just a beast of prey: rapacious, lustful and aggressive. He has in him some capacity for good life, and hence, goodness is not foreign to man's nature. There are good tendencies in man, too, and he has the capacity to unite with Devatma, which can develop a hatred of and freedom from beastly tendencies and develop love and character for an altruistic life.

Human reason and will are a blessing, as they allow us to contemplate the beauty of what is good and the ugliness of what is evil under the light of truth and goodness, and how to cultivate the former and get rid of the latter, and thus, be a blessing to ourselves and to society.

- Mystic experience reveals something about the totality of things, to which humans have always placed a great importance on, and on which one's ultimate well-being or salvation wholly depends. Mystic experience of the sublime life of Devatma is the truest response towards the universe. In such mystic experiences, the beatitude of the evolutionary process in Devatma stands revealed, and man's relation to the universe in the way of vairagya and satvikta stands illumined.

The life of vairagya is free from jealousy, hatred and vindictiveness, while it is also full of compassion and forgiveness.

In addition, vairagya cultivates inattention, indifference and a non-possessiveness toward things, as well as positions and praises in life.

A vairagya devotee lives the truth that the attention, attraction and accumulation of powers and positions are deadly poisons for the soul, for they can easily lead to dishonourable conduct just to maintain these things, corrupting the purity of soul in turn. Further, they deviate the soul from its chief occupation with divinity. The devoted vairagyi sees to it that if he or she is called upon to accept a position, they would only accept it if, and only if, it is linked to the exercise of their best and highest aptitude and his training, which can alone antidote the subtle, incessant intoxication of the power that the position confers. It is as abhorrent for the devotee to accept a position outside the exercise of his highest aptitude and training, as it is repulsive for a chaste wife to think of a man other than her husband. Lastly, a vairagyi will not cross the line laid by one's primary aptitude and role so as to be indifferent to things outside one's chief exercise of aptitude in the service of knowledge, social good or aesthetic values.

11

- The highest principle of the universe

From single cell organisms to human beings and from human beings to Devatma is a story of the gradual explicitness of the spiritual principle.

The spiritual principle is the best manifested in the sublime powers (DEV SHAKTIES), sublime life (DEV JIWAN) and sublime beauty (DEV ROOP) of Devatma.

His observation is in possession of the most sublime object for reporting – himself. In knowing himself, he knows the spiritual principle in its full explicitness. His true experience has a unique quality, and Devatma's knowledge is his own in the way in which it cannot belong to others. He is heir to a truth of the highest sublimity that the human genius cannot even approach. Here is this dimension to his knowledge, which makes truth as virtue in him at its best.

His true experience is the ideal for all who wish to develop the virtue of truth in them. Through a faith and love for Devatma, men bask in the light of the spiritual principle made explicit in him at its best.

When we can observe the spiritual principle in Devatma and express it truly, we observe and speak of it in the noblest manner.

- Altruistic conduct can occur at two levels: in a person-to-person relationship, and in a person-to-institutional relationship. When we seek our own good at the cost of the good of others, this is considered exploitation. When we seek our good along with others, this is co-operation. When we seek the good of others, which is not a perfect duty, this is altruism. Hence, we should either choose to do well to others or be altruist due to different motivations.

The nature of being is related to all the four kingdoms. I cannot emotionally recognize, accept and appreciate this relationship if I believe that the soul or psyche in me is uncreated, indestructible, eternal and an unchanging entity; therefore, the four kingdoms of Nature must not influence or enter into my psychology. I can unconditionally and wholeheartedly recognize, accept and appreciate that the four kingdoms of Nature are the breath of my breath, the blood of my blood and the being of my being. My entire being is to be with them – I am inseparable from them, I am nothing without them and I am everything with them. To segregate myself from any kingdom is to tear me apart. Therefore, the nature of existence is to feel related, to feel concerned, to respect others' existence, to accept others as people, to wish well to others and to be affectionate. Also, to be good is to have reverence, to make amends, to seek harmony, to cultivate altruistic feelings of appreciation, gratitude, justice, compassion, mudita and love, among others, in interpersonal relationships.

- The philosophy of Devatma is not founded on science alone; its religious teachings are characterized by consistency and continuity with scientific knowledge other fields. Devatma fosters solidarity and integrity within the individual. When we hold both the natural and supernatural origin of the soul, we are divided within, harbouring repulsive disharmony, and are condemned to live a lie in the core of our personality, which corridors us, thus leading to our ultimate extinction. The unique philosophy of Devatma is a 'saving knowledge', for it saves us from such disintegration and lies. Dev Dharma avoids conflicts between science and religion, because it accepts that scientific verification is necessary for a belief to be true. This is Dev Dharma's first offering to modern man in search of a religion that does not compromise his scientific makeup. Devatma brought the field of religion under investigation through scientific methods and therefore founded the science of religion. The scientific method must be employed in the field of religion and religion can be made into a science, like other sciences.

- Devatma was forcefully drawn towards the scientific evolutionism of Darwin and Spencer and he built a new religion based on the facts and laws of Nature. He is the only light in world religion to openly accept the use of scientific methods in his study of the nature of man, together with his role and destiny in the universe. The principles of experimental interrogation, alongside the laws of logic, possessed Devatma completely, and became such an integral part of his mind that it became impossible for him to accept any belief merely on the basis of speculation or tradition. Dev Dharma awakens humankind to the truth that his fulfillment and highest evolution is in the service of the four kingdoms. This religious perspective can be possible in an evolutionary religion, because only an evolutionary religion can give this paramount importance and respect to the physical, biological and social environments of man.

• The law of evolution is the name for the processes of changes in entities, which are conducive in bringing about the reign of Truth, Goodness and Beauty on earth. The various species of mammals, which led to the emergence of man, are the concrete manifestations of evolutionary forces. The birth of Devatma from among the altruistic section of humankind is the highest concrete manifestation of the evolutionary forces. In this highest concrete embodiment of the evolutionary process, Devatma is a finite being but not the omniscient, all powerful and all-good God of theism. His excellence encompasses a complete love for truth and goodness. He has no disposition to entertain falsehood and evil.

Since Devatma, the highest concrete manifestation of the evolutionary forces is the embodiment of truth, goodness and beauty. It is on him the power to help human beings who establish rapport with him and adjust all the four orders of existence for mutual good. Faith in him as the supreme and sublime highest power in Nature is the truth of religious faith.

• Our experiences are Cognitive, affection, conative, as they concern knowing, feeling and willingness.

The categories of the experiences are stated as:

- Sensory experience
- Aesthetic experience
- Moral conduct experience
- Religious experience

Though it is practical and useful to divide these experiences into four categories, each is not necessarily experienced in isolation from others.

All the four values of knowledge, goodness, beauty and divinity unite and dissolve in the highest experience of some rare geniuses.

As such, an experience cannot be true or false. Our beliefs about experiences can be either true or false. All knowledge concerns the interpretation of facts. Logic is a discipline that helps us to understand the conditions under which it is correct or incorrect to draw conclusions from certain facts or propositions. Aesthetics shows us the standards by which we can correctly differentiate between a genuine and a spurious work of art.

By these standards, most of the hymns, though inspiring to devotees, lack artistic qualities and are poor works of poetry. Ethics, for example, is a discipline that tries to discover the ideal of life in the light of which we can determine the rightness of conduct. Religious experience covers moral experience, while moral experience is primarily concerned with conduct in interpersonal relationships. Lastly, the moral life of integrity, chastity and disinterested service to others, is essential to religious life but it does not cover the entire religious life.

- Man is religious when he delights in the contemplation of the Deva-rupa of Devatma, dances in joy of it and loves it with all his soul and with all his might. In communion with Devatma, man realizes his utter insignificance before the effulgence of his excellences and his eternal dependence on him for his salvation and evolution. Further, he lives to share his experiences with fellow human beings.

- A true worshipful being must:

  - Be an embodied being; that is, a historical character who has the capacity to deliver man from his evil dispositions;
  - Cultivate altruistic dispositions;
  - Illumine themselves with the truth about soul life.

Only a worshipful being possesses these qualifications and is a complete lover of Truth, Goodness and Beauty.

- Dev Jiwan (sublime life) is the life of complete love of Truth, goodness and Beauty. It is a super altruistic life that is beyond the pleasure principle. It is a sublime life in which there is not even a disposition to deviate into untruth and evil; a life for which it is psychologically impossible to think or do evil and knowingly entertain falsehood. Dev Jiwan is also an illumined life, which shines with truth and goodness – a life which cherishes and cultivates whatever is true, good and beautiful, with an unconditional and absolute commitment to the service of all the four kingdoms of nature. When the feeling of reverence and gratitude in a man ascends to the appreciation of Dev Jiwan having both faith and love for Devatma, it touches its zenith, which is the highest meaning of life.

What Type of Heaven Is This?

May the unbound and true Nature,
defender and promoter of the
evolutionary processes,
be always helpful in future, too,
in the fulfilment of the Sublime
Mission of Devatma
which is really Nature's own Mission!

May true Nature help the realization of
the truths propounded in this book,
to the greatest possible extent,
in the life force of all eligible persons
by conveying the sublime light of
Devatma!

May it also reveal
the teaching of all
false truths in
this world, which tend towards
sins and crimes;
because
the path of the soul-welfare
of the people belonging to any creed,
society, nation, or country

cannot open without getting
rid of such teachings,
and for the opening and widening
of the path,
Nature has given birth to Devatma!

A panacea of warmth!
A melody of truth!
May the authentic and
grand Nature
fructify the unique and
sublime object of Devatma!

May the prime object or 'life-vow'
of Devatma be fulfilled!
May this world achieve a new birth!
May the kingdom of truth be established
in this world as far as possible!
May whatever is false or untrue be destroyed!
May all that is auspicious in the world prosper!
Thereby, may evil be destroyed!
May all falsehoods which are
rampant in human beliefs,
in religious exercises or worship,
and all the fears and pains based on falsehood
Disappear!

May all the low-loves for
different brands of pleasures
and the low-hates in various relations
which dominate the human soul,
be destroyed along with life-destroying
low feelings
and heinous hates!

May the highway of prosperity be established!

May the consciousness and love
for whatever is pious
with regard either to their bodies or their souls,
awaken in people and whatever
is truly impure or defiling disappear!

May the consciousness and love
for whatever is true,
Pure, and beautiful,
awaken in people!
Similarly,
May higher hatred for all kinds
of ugliness sprout in them!
MAY HUMANITY INHALE THIS
AROMATIC SCENT!

May the consciousness and love for
whatever is based
on justice in accordance
with Nature's true laws,
emerge in people,
and on the contrary
May all that is based on injustice
and cruelty, vanish from this earth!

May the feeling of true regularity
spring up in people's lives,
and whatever class of irregularity is found in them,
whether in relation to themselves or to others,
may disappear!

May all the higher order or
concord in different relations

of this world
be evolved, and all that is
disorder in them
may vanish!

May all the improper quarrels so
rampant in this world,
and all the unjust
wars taking place in it disappear!
May higher peace reign over it!

May the true knowledge of the soul,
and the true consciousness of its welfare,
develop in people!
May their 'soul welfare'
triumph over their low-pleasures!
May people bathe in the pious
water of truth and goodness!

May all the disharmony that prevails
in the living and non-
living worlds
be destroyed as far as possible!
For the establishment
of true harmony in them -
May the concord of sublime light live forever...

May my life-vow be fulfilled in 'every respect'
among Nature's entire departments!
May higher forces and transformations be cycled!
May low-force be destroyed into pieces day by day!
May higher meeting be fixed!
May the lighthouse of life vow be flourished!
May the recipe of flavour and strength of life
be rejoiced all around

Along with all 'eligible persons'!
And
The reign of grandeur of development be celebrated!
For all teachings of Dev Shastras
For all,
This will be auspicious –genuine-source,
In country to country,
Town to town,
There will be the recitation of supreme sentence,
May Dev Samaj touch the glory of progress day by day!
May the domain of religion be established
Continuously,
Hence, whatever irreligion prevails
May all be declined!
May the recitation of the melody
Of the triumph of Dev Dharma be celebrated!

A Glimpse of Your Own Future

A 'full swing' module marks
a new age of humankind,
whose 'coming into being'
was inevitable
in consonance with the
process of evolution in
Nature.

To the gateway of
a new and blessed age,
the emergence of Devatma spawns
higher transformations to eradicate
the darkest, most ignorant, degraded
and harmful state of mankind,
thereby,
embodying genuine
and unique sublime forces.

In this RAINBOW - LIGHTHOUSE,
true and unique sublime forces
are produced
with Devatma's initial step.

There will be a Paradise on Earth
The pitch of Pandemonium will never touch
the 'route' of continuous evolution.

This milieu will frame
humanity – all
people will be trustworthy.

The sublime species will 'take to court'
The glimpses of your own future
Where
The sweeter life 'before death and after'
Certainly
Will be compelled to realize
how sweet this life is
Towards a new - brand Humanity!

The earth will be
Pure -land -Paradise
Where a small candle is enough
To awake 'sleepy consciousness'.

A MODERN phase of life
With open secrets
Will connote
The end of all questionings
against Human temptations and bondage
Where the multiple-rays of sunrise
Will never 'bade goodbye'.

The last luxury of the pure truth
Will
Never forget the language of ecstasy
That is the only resolution.

The tragic drama of human bondage
Would not be repeated itself.
Science and Religion-two petals
of the same rose
Will design a golden future
Where humanity will not
Excavate a valley
therefore, hooking up with mountains.

Nobody will lose anything
The truth: beyond mind,
beyond language,
Where
After the dark-sill
night is the dawn.

You will not be same again
………..will know the unknown life
of revered Devatma
Where life will be ecstatic melody,
a dance
an intertwined panorama
for
Truth lovers that
Will never be on death-bed.

Life will be eternal,
The great secret,
The new man will not be
The very salt of the earth
Where the Archer would be perfect
The great challenge
…………no monopoly,
………..A complete holiday for your life

The earth will be more than a Paradise
The Values would be Truth in every respect
i.e. the veiled Harmony.
The sun will be 'up to the minute'
At each day
Where
Life's aim is life itself……..

Nobody will miss anything,
Each relation will be a mirror
Sublime life would only be a turnstile
Where truth would not be covered
REPEATEDLY
A rose is a rose
Though we call it by any name
ROSE WILL FLOURISH
THE SAME INCENSE………………….

Not for a single moment
But forever
Showering invisible flowers
People will come to their own festivals
In modern prospects
Where
An era of Crisis,
The roots of violence,
Will not be dominating over heart
The great pearl will realize the five-barred gate,
The dewdrop and the ocean,
The invitation of the last milestone,
Where words will forget to speak
In the search of a 'lost treasure'
The hidden splendour……………

This moment is more than enough

What more do you aspire?
Can a circle be more circular?
This would be last Dance
A dance untouched by time
An experience of immense thrill
A house where nobody lives.

Listen carefully
Can we celebrate
Here and now: the only time,
only place
The Master and his philosophy
The thought: from slavery to liberation
Discovery of your innermost Nature
Lost and found again...............

Nothing is higher than complete love of
Truth, Goodness and Beauty,
Where
Only centre and the circumference avowed
That is
complete and full in 'each and every aspect'
Where altruism ends
Love of Truth begins..........
This is the initiation of fresh communion.............

Choose the flute or perish
The tremendous statement
Remember: Sublime life is here for us
The sublime life's Roar accepts:
"The Goodness is for you
Die to the Future
The suffering transmutes you as
A 'gifted personality'
Where complete love of Truth

is 'clearing out the hallway'
to bless its warmth."

Truth is enough unto itself
for
Living spontaneously and embracing life
Where ignorance becomes luminous for
Our longings for the stars........

Wherever the cost is certain
And cheap,
A grand approach to reality....
The truth is what works
Still, it is not too late to search A NEW ISLAND
The bird of time has flown
Towards a new direction,
...towards ....
The seed of liberation,
The master of Masters,
The science of soul and sublimity,
Cultivating right attitude,
Beginning a new path
Of poets,
Scholars,
Philosophers of new species,
Opening
The hidden road of sublime ecstasy
Where the bird unfurls its feathers
Spreading the message,—

Our responsibility is tremendous
Now it is our turn
The day has been Hilarious
join the farthest Star
The muse-beyond-and-beyond

Where no Signatures on Water.
Hence,
A philosophy Whose COMPASSIONATE
MOMENTS TOUCH THE SOIL OF HEARTS..........

The First science grounded Religion
in the History of the World
unlatches the Doors of Light and Beyond,
The Dimension of the Mysterious,
The Language of the Golden Future,
The Highest Phenomenon on the Earth,
The VOYAGE Starts but Never Ends.......

This is the reflection of a sublime beauty,
The Fragrance of sublime life,
No more tears no more cry,
No one will pronounce:
"They Gave Him Crucifixion every moment",
Where
No one Unknown to Yourself
Truth Knows No Fifty-Fifty
It is STEADFAST
....
The Book of Secrets
Will
Liberate Yourself from Yourself..........

Recognize
How to live the 'highest meaning of Life'
With Nothing to Lose
Let It Be LIKEWISE
You Are the Source
A Little Taste of sublime life
THEREBY
Beyond Happiness Is Bliss

A-Magic- beyond- magic.........
Running with Your Whole Heart......

The Ultimate Freedom is
Free of All the Chains................
A RUBBER-STAMP to Your Freedom............

Thence,
Substantially,
The Choice Is Always Yours
Exposing Your Way from Ignorance to
Innocence...............
presenting
Flowers of Feelings at His Feet,
The Only Holy Approach
For the Sake of Harmony,
An Experience of Immense delight,
The Silent Gratitude,
Reverence, faith and love
Is the Only Prayer
To the Spiritual Master.................

For the Birth of a new species
And the verse of 'extreme chanting of beads',
Master is Enough Alone like a
A SOLITARY REAPER IN A DARK FOREST
What a Blissful Milieu!
Sublime Journey without LAST BREATH,
UNQUESTIONABLY,
Truth, Goodness, Beauty: VENTILATORS TO THE SUBLIMITY.

A Sunrise That Never Sets

What an ivory cave of imagination this is!
What an effigy of a brainwave!
An ocean of flames!
An inferno within an inferno!
When the most degenerating
ripple of low pleasure-affording loves
was at its height in the human world.
Naught! Naught!

When different clutches of low-hates
created by these low-loves
also ruled the hearts of people,
when on account of their degenerating
soul-diseases,
people had become lovers of various sorts
of sins
and exercises,.
While hardened by their soul-diseases,
the hearts of people were
wrapped in dark silk.

Thence, they had no consciousness,
as to what is life force,
what its diseases are,

or the horrible repercussions
of those soul-diseases.

Similarly, by what method,
through whom and from where,
can a man find true freedom or salvation
from these soul-diseases,
in accordance with the
immutable laws of nature.

When people considered such
things as Dharma,
as if they had no concern for them;
when people believed in false creeds
and inappropriate
worshipful beings; and

when people performed various exercises
in the name of religion
in order to obtain one or another
pleasure and happiness,
as if they were 'injurious' to their souls.

There was a vicious circle
of pauper –discernments,
When people tread the route
of soul-degeneration
by committing various stamps
of acts based on falsehood and sin,
When people throttled goodness
by miser-outlook,
through ignorance, accepting
happiness as the
object of their lives;
and thus inflicted harm,

not only to their soul-life but
also to their anatomy.

When people emphasized the
currency of different categories
of false stories in the name of religion
creating various false beliefs in credulous
minds by imparting
teachings against the immutable
laws of Nature,
that they could rise miracles
or do impossible acts or karamats,
could grant various kinds
of their wishes
.....could harm to them by curses,
imprecations, sharps or baddua &c;
and
hitherto,
being slaves to their lower feelings,
they committed heart-piercing acts
in relation to every kingdom of Nature.

When people, besides killing
their own souls,
proved inimical to the
souls of others,
by their darkest influences and
false teachings,
and
by being unconscious
or indifferent to the welfare of the soul,
they ruined their soul-life inch to inch.

Is it not a campfire of low feeling?
An imaginary camp of temptations?
When humanity was in such a deplorable state,
Thence,
Tables turned in an aesthetic direction
during the course of millions
of years of evolution in Nature,
appeared Devatma,
endowed with the love of truth and goodness,
and a desire to transform
humanity,
from every inch,
The messiah of humanity set his feet on this land.

The Secrets of the Evolutionary Process

In order to bring about a transformation
of the highly pitiable
and most degraded state of humanity,
it was urgent requirement
according to the immutable law of
evolution in Nature
that
evolutes should appear
on this earth to fulfill the following conditions:

• In accordance with the immutable
law of Nature,
he (that evolutes) may be in human
form for the expression
and evolution of his soul and its various forces;
yet, he would be above the
soul-degrading Nature of man.

In other words, he would be
truly angelic (dev) or superhuman in nature
which would be quite opposite to the most degrading
Nature of man such as:

a) Being cognizant of various CREEDS
of pleasures,
man becomes lover thereof
and does not recognize
or possess any higher idol for his soul
or other brands of low or higher pleasures.

b) Even on professing or believing in
any so-called religion,
man still desires the attainment of pleasures,

c) Alone as the prime object of his life
and on becoming lover of
or slave to various pleasures
and hater of various pains,
he naturally goes astray from
the path of truth
for the sake of attaining such
pleasures and of attaining freedom
from suffering; thus he
comes to believe in various kinds of false faiths.

d) Man seeks
to indulge in various act of hypocrisy
and deception based on falsehood,
and going contrary to the path of truth
and righteousness or goodness,
commits various kinds of injustice and
cruelties on the living
and non-living world of Nature.
In this town
man ruins his home.

e) Man hardens his soul
following the path of falsehood

and unrighteousness,
creates darkness and becomes
blind to the true existence of his soul
and its degeneration on
account of such darkness.

He remains satisfied or happy
even in the daily degenerating
state of his soul,
by indulging in different suites of worse and
unrighteous acts,
and does not feel
any remorse for such degrading actions.

f) Being blind and unconscious to the true welfare
of his soul and having
no love for such true welfare
within himself,
he feels no desire to renounce
his various pleasures and the relations
or objects affording such pleasures.

To sacrifice all his powers for such welfare,
is wasteland of low thoughts.
An array of 'feu de joie'
In other words,
such highest evolution should not be
the lover
of or slave to any kind of pleasures
and should not consider or have
the attainment of any kind of happiness
as his prime object; and, as
opposed to these pleasure affording loves,
whose soul should be possessed
of all-sided highest loves

of all kinds of truth and goodness;
And all-sided highest hatred
for all denominations of falsehood,
unrighteousness, evil, injustices, sins and crimes.

2. This evolution would be on account
of his being possessed of the unique highest loves
and highest hates,
be the true and all-round benefactor
of every department of nature,
and be the complete lover
and promoter of every kind of
goodness that is possible.

He would be able to carry out the true and
unique holy war with the followers of falsehood
and unrighteousness for their eradication
from the human world,
and the establishment of the highest kingdom
of truth and goodness.
During this unique war,
he would suffer all kinds of suffering
and bear all sorts of oppressions from his opponents.

He would be willing to sacrifice
his physical health and become diseased,
be ready to undergo all kinds of sufferings
as a result of diseases,
be prepared to cut off his connection
with his family and all other relations,
friends and other acquaintances,
or fraternity (biradri) samaj or society.

Whenever necessary,
he would be able to endure

all brands of calamity
or abuse for the protection of true Dharma
or his own realized self.

He would be able
to always fight with the lovers of falsehood
and evil
and would not back down from
such a fight under any circumstances.

He would always be prepared
to face the arrows of attacks and
be wounded during such fights.

However, he would never despise them
or wish ill-omens of them,
but would always remain ready
to do auspicious for them.

He would be able to surrender all his physical,
mental, and educational powers
as also all his money and property,
for the triumph of truth and goodness.

He would be able
to evolve in his soul
these supreme hates
which emanate the highest psychic
light and highest
psychic power, and by the evolution
of which he would become
the true worshipful being whose
spiritual worship could
prove truly beneficial for all capable persons.

3. He would, after the evolution of his highest psychic light
and highest psychic power to the sufficient degree,
become the seer or discoverer of the secret
and subtle truths about soul and its life,
and be able to teach true knowledge
of Dharma and thus be the mentor
of the only Nature-based or
science-grounded religion
for all mankind.

4. He would, by his highest psychic light
and highest psychic power,
be capable of bringing higher changes
in the souls of fit persons of every country,
nation, colour, or creed.

He would create in them
Nature-based true realization
and true faith about soul and religion.

He would further be able to
offer true freedom
from various kinds of false faiths.

5. He would be capable of giving true salvation
to all eligible persons, according
to their individual capacities from their
soul-degrading thoughts
and harmful acts.

And further than that to cleanse
their hearts from impurities as far
as possible,
He would also
be capable of nurturing and

evolving supreme wisdom in
capable souls,
according to their individual
capacities those higher or altruistic
feelings
which transmute the soul more
elevated and noble.

And he would,
on account of being the provider
of all these true benefits,
Be the all-sided spiritual benefactor
of all eligible persons.

In order to fulfill this very object,
Nature has, in the course,
of the gradual evolution of human domain,
brought into being
the approach of proper time,
the highest fountain of evolution,
a balm for wretched individuals.

Devatma, certainly was
Endowed with all the aforesaid
unique Dev Shakties (highest psychic powers).
Really,
An avant-garde of soul life,
A beatific 'envoy of truth and goodness'.

A Great Longing for the Master

SIR (Professor) JULIAN HUXLEY was right when he wrote:

I am sure that the world will see the birth of new religion...just how it will develop and flower, no one knows, but some of its underlying beliefs are beginning to emerge—its beliefs are not based on revelation in the supernatural sense but on the revelation of science and learning have given us about man and the universe. It believes with full assurance that man is not alien to Nature, but part of Nature, albeit a unique one. He is made of the same matter and works by the same energy as the rest of the universe. He is not only product of the universal process of evolution, but capable of affecting the process which has produced him and of affecting it for good or ill. His true destiny is to guide the future course of evolution on earth towards greater fulfillment, so as to realize more and higher potentialities.

I believe that an equally drastic reorganization of our pattern of religious thought is now becoming necessary —a humanistic evolution centered religion too needs divinity but divinity without God...

From the specifically religious points of view, the desirable direction of evolution might be defined as the divinization of existence........ But for this to have operative significance, we must frame a new definition of the divine, free from all connotations of supernatural beings.

India's mammoth poet and thinker Dr. Rabindranath Tagore has written the following:

It was the time
Whence
I have to contemplate
That
Fountain hood of civilization
Will be germinated from West
Therefore,
Whence,
At present,
Today,
I was on the death bed
On the stage
Too bade goodbye to world

Oh!
In this tormenting threshold
My that presupposition
Has left the home
Vague! Vain!
Today,
my final aspiration is wet with the axiom
That
World's deliverer will
Put his feet
In our pauper country
And
From the channel of Eastern sky
His sublime message will be heard
By all the world
And
humanity will heartily
welcome this enormous/elephantine aspiration

Who knows
That
Time/day had not appear only
Heretofore,
that sublime sun
has not only took root
in Asia's forlorn darkish sky
invariably,
Unquestionably,
this will
illuminate the world also

Master Born Before His Time

Alas! Alas!
Boundless people in this world
'Foot the bill'
On selfishness, low feelings,
low hatred,
Curses and myths
It is a
'Tragedy of views'
A mouse trap scene
Dilemma! Dilemma!

For this reason
Whatever milieu is all around the world
In this ambience
If anyone
Punches the clock
With
Abundance/plenty of perceptions
Or
little bit
Shining aestheticism
Or

Positive nature
Taking the inheritance of religious life

Thence
Few years of his (a person) life of inheritance
Have been ruined
By his surroundings
The wicked people have drowned
in the deep ocean of vulgarity
And
They don't know
How their life
Has been transforming
as the chaser of evil influences
With the horrible environs of vulgarity
They
Draw themselves
Nearer
To the followers of ruination
Heretofore,
They,
raise this horrible milieu
for themselves

Pushing
themselves along this path
Their near relatives
Leave no place vague
To spread filth and cure
Repeatedly
They condemn them

This world has become
a living pandemonium.
With the management of nature

The blessed event
The auspicious birth
of such a religious deity

Who has the capacity to transmute
this condition of humanity
With his pious birth

Opening the Doors of Light and Beyond

After getting feet wet
There has been phlegmatic like proficiency
In man
In the sphere of his highbrow, brainpower, reasoning
And other powers
Gradually,
he moved towards the bond of 'nuptial knots'
gazing at
the 'piquancy' of the relation of married life
Thence
Evolved infatuation
And several other relations between men and women
'opened their eyes'
Through mental power
The birth of
Their offspring
Was certain
It was the era of negligence
Man was deprived of the sense of sophisticated etiquettes
Like
Clothing, eating, reading, writing
henceforth

the craving for low pleasure
Savagery, looting, tortures, burning
Was still the 'tale of almost every house'
Dry! Vanity!
Hush! Hush! To dirty ears!
What a fierce sketch of mankind.
Woman was not considered as a 'companion/partner/soul mate'
She was noticed as the channel of lust,
hunger and temptation
Like a
Frailty within a frailty
Inferior and subordinate
Gradually,
Men enhanced into the street line of family,
pleasures and physical attractions
He learned the mechanism of fire
The Sati Pratha -tradition, where a woman dies with her dead husband,
was in full swing
During this inhuman stage
The killing of innocent animals was considered
A matter of 'valour'
In this flurry
This whirlwind of swirl
People 'set in motion of robbery'
And
Ruled over inferior ones
What a hedge!
What a network of confused paths!
Enormous mental burden.
A migraine of high depression.
There was slavery all around
Not a rainbow of liberation
O parching lips
O shrivelled individual
You are as dry as dust/scorched

What a windbreak
In this 'la-la land'
This soil of
'Bygone ages of individuals'
There is evidence of a dark history
And
abundance of low physical insights,
Anatomical attractions,
Low hatreds,
These low pleasures
Turned mankind into 'dwindling transmutation'
After this fierce stage
He was somewhat transformed
Which was 'out and out'
Magnificent
Certainly,
Nature alone
Has been the director, a producer of 'several sorts of comforts'
Genuine understanding of nature
Is veiled/hidden in scientific methods
With the assistance of mathematics
A new/untouched knowledge came into existence
The era of technology produced various pleasures
No doubt,
There has been a huge variety of 'progress
in art and industries'

Man began to realize 'accepting the right of others'
And quiet conduct in relations
Through the 'momentum build-up
of evolutionary process of nature'
Mankind,
Gradually
Evolved to be civilized

Tables turned
Man took out of mothballs of 'fake love,
slavery towards money,
Property, children, food, clothes
And superiority of name and fame over others
He was in the grip of conspiracy and politics
This implies:
'A harsh condition of 'lotus eaters'
Lethargy of unstable views
A stage of deterioration and frustration!'
Superior position and other enjoyments
Their sources of satisfaction
Turned the way of humanity
It was really
An intolerable condition of drowsiness
and infertility
Henceforth,
With the progression of civilization
Elephantine vulgarities 'come into light'
Which
Previously were hidden
When man was in his innocent stage
Of 'naïve life'
Of eating, drinking and merry making
Capitalists had their own 'majesty'
They did not understand the 'pauper condition
of housekeepers
And their helpers'
They did not realize 'mutual relation towards them'
What a murder of harmony and humanity
The relation between man and woman
Was based on sex, and physical pleasures
Before marriage
Physical relations were not considered
against pure rules

What a transient way of life.
FOR MOMENTARY COMFORT
THE GEM OF LIFE IS DESTROYED
The pious law of purity corrupted
Into the eddy billow of 'lust'
Because of the practice of unjust ruling of government
Among ruling classes of various countries
The emotion of amalgamation, integration
DISAPPEARED
What a vague consciousness of maladjustment!
Correlation and concord vanished
Disloyalty opened its fierce jaws
Conflicts, quarrels, revolutions
Suspicions,
Feeling of vanity in relations and
Mutual beliefs,
In the filth of hypocritical policies
Increased
In political matters
There was hyper filth
Men-women bond turned into divorce
With the huge yearning towards the flavours of
eatable things
Men started hunting
Killing of various sorts of innocent, weak
Serviceable animals were continuous
Many countries
That
Considered themselves
as the panacea of harmony
And tranquility
Turned into mutual disloyalty and
Suspicion
Begin to chase
The vague shadow fire of lust and desires

The desire of reverence
Turned them into the direction of vanity
These countries lost their strength of maintaining harmony
They were antagonists of reality
They lost their insight of seeing the finer side of others
They lived a life of hypocrisy, falsehood
And low pleasures of various sorts
Souls of boundless persons touched the poisonous ripples
Of
Boulder like hardness
Dark sill and garbage!
With the genuine consciousness of scientific understanding
Slavery of Inappropriate low pleasures
And
fake beliefs disappeared
On the name of religion
Who were slaves to their low pleasures
Changed
Lovey-dovey or warmheartedly
Positive energies evolved
In true sun shine of authentic ideas
Who were blind to reality
And its essence
Now transmuted
People compelled to leave the path of falsehood
Who were ignorant of the most significant thing
of their existence,
Namely their soul
Become conscious
With a fully-fledged mind
In this flowery-incense of truth and goodness
One will behold impetus____
An advancement of evolutionary process,
An embarkation of dawn
Which is a-light-within-a-light

Evergreen aestheticism of sublime light
Repercussion connotes:
Prior to Devatma
Mankind was in the crowd of darks ill
And spiritual dark sill
There was the dominance of degeneration,
Deterioration,
And dissolution
With the voyage of the pious feet of Devatma
Evolution of higher life has been noticed
With the blessings of Devatma
True knowledge about religion
Enhanced
Sublime light of Devatma 'selected a route of truth'
Devatma's sublime light is a shelter
"His home is our home
And his arms are always open for us"
Before the birth of Devatma
People were leading a life in harmful faiths
And
Love of low pleasure was elevated
People were thirsty of praise/appreciation
They were feeling glorified in name and fame
Acquiring reverence or position,
Gaining political positions
For satisfying various feelings of jealousy and sex
They were getting pleasures and comforts
in mutual relations
Before Pious Soul Devatma
People were in the circle of carcinogenic
Faiths
They were worshipping their false deities
Who were devoid of genuine sublime force
And true wisdom of religion
Their deities were not embodiments of certain powers

Not fit to be regarded as true worshipful beings
Too filthy!
They were
Devoid of true sublime forces.
About their sins,
they were ignorant
What absent-mindedness!
They adopted false faiths
Based on inappropriate seers and hermits
About salvation of sins
They adopted false thoughts
In the name of religion
They
Kept on knocking at the doors of useless spiritual practices
and ceremonies
Sacrifices,
Fasts and pilgrimages
They were lovers of
Low attractions and pleasures
They were enslaved
Chasing low hatreds
They
Indulged in unjust thoughts
Committed crimes in the 'gyre of falsehood'
In various sections of Nature
On the area of unsuitability
Their one or other low pleasure was on the top
Considering these comforts as the breathing of life
They
Destroyed their life veins
True knowledge of the soul was out of order
What ignorance
What callousness
A bale of tears
A tale of mercy

People kept on chanting the beads of unjust thoughts and actions
O! O! What a dilemma of vain views!
O slaves of wrong deities!
Come hither!
Towards the ambrosia of truth and goodness!
What a spiritual degeneration!
What ruination!
Infertility of perception!
No genuine awareness
No desire for liberation and salvation from the grip
of these pathetic conditions
Lack of true consciousness
Or spiritual goodness!

In this blind era
Dawn appeared
In this lurid, dingy, pitch-black
Dusky, sombre milieu
For the truth
For the goodness
For evergreen, blissful and new age

The pious voyage of Devatma was necessary
Who was the storehouse of true
and unique sublime forces
His birth brought a
New age
New refined enlightenment and illumination for mankind
Unquestionably,
As a matter of fact,
Verily,
His birth
Was inevitable on this earth
With the process of evolution in Nature

Fountain Head of a Sublime Lighthouse

Aye! Devatma alone is the Genuine Worshipful Being
Sun and solid fountain head of a Sublime Lighthouse
He is the only 'undeniable' supervisor of religion
He is 'unquestionably' the superior Godmother for all mankind
According to their strengths.

Ecstatic melody of vision
Pot of multi-coloured buds
Is only Devatma,
He 'set feet' from human species of this earth
of this solid nature,
after million years of the 'circuit' of the 'actual evolution'
in one of its branches decorated with unique powers
and has attained 'unfeigned -de facto' sublime conduct
attributed by his incredible Dev Shakties.

He is ornamented with all love for truth
and goodness,
and hatred for untruth and evil
which are the vigorous expressions of his rainbow of sublime behaviour

It is his supreme ideal of life to bring about
The reign of all sorts of truth and goodness
Absolutely to banish all categories of untruth and evil in the world,
to bring about supreme changes,
in accordance with the certain laws of nature,
in the capable souls of mankind to the limit of their strength,
to perform betterment to sub-human domains of nature and
heretofore, to be perfectly serviceable
to the evolutionary process of nature
through his nature given Dev Shakties

What a cosmopolitan service it is
In accordance with the laws of Nature,
he has dedicated every one of his strengths
in the service of his ideal life

In accordance with the laws of Nature,
he has 'buttoned up' all required sacrifices
in the service of this marvellous glory of his life

Apart from his first ranked ideal of truth and goodness,
he does not brook any epicurean/greedy ideal
He is, therefore, out and out,
free from all brands of low-loves and low-hates

He has along with the evolution of the glorious Dev Shakties,
Established in accordance with the laws of Nature,
Heart touching Dev Jyoti and extraordinary Dev Tej

What memorable heart ripple
Astonishing
Through this incredible Dev-jyoti of his,
he has been able to behold

and understand truths regarding the human soul,
its spiritual life, its deterioration, and liberation
from that ruination and its evolution
Is this not the everlasting footprint of a pious hermit?

It is he alone who has for the first time
'brought to light' the authentic realization of religion,
He is only one star, a discoverer and supervisor
of this genuine wisdom of religion on this earth,
He is alone the almoner,
worshipful being in virtue of his incomparable Dev Rup.

Perennial honey-cane
A rhythm within a rhythm
He is the Sun for the Divine World
by decorum of his unique Dev Jyoti and mind-blowing Dev Tej
By virtue of these irrefutable, blessed, sublime attributes
he is the 'unaffected garlanding being'
for all eligible souls of every country
as he is their spiritual guardian.

A Blissful Milieu-The Unknown Life of Master

It is a legend within a legend
These are the pearls of unbiased triumph
In the pious cottage of a sublime life
An individual is blessed by 'internal bliss'
Yes
It is through understanding the illumination
of Dev Jyoti, the light of truth in the divine field of the revered Devatma
that an eligible life force becomes
conscious of the absolute bliss of its soul,
the truths about its diseases and degradation
the horrible repercussions thereof,
and the highway of liberation
from them and the evolution of higher life in it
It is by the 'perfect enlightenment' of Dev Jyoti of Devatma
that a capable life force, on obtaining internal/boulder knowledge about soul
life can and absolutely does get wisdom of veritable religion and never without it.
without this grandeur
life goes in garbage –bin

A sack of filthy potatoes
Before the advent of Devatma,
no one had wisdom of what constitutes religion.

All suites of the so-called Gods,
named Ishwar, Khuda, Allah, Brahman,
Waheguru, Zirdust, among others
and their avatars and their so-called Rishies,
Munis, Acharyas, Hadi, Prophets, Pir, Vali, among others
Solid significance of religion was not everybody's cup of tea

Under the influence of the enlightenment of Dev Jyoti
and the dynamism of Dev Tej of Dev Atma,
innumerable men and women have
noticed the authentic character
of their inappropriate beliefs and demonic actions,
They have obtained liberation from them through framing hatred for
them
They had not been able to attain this real liberation
From their so-called deities
Gods/goddesses, their avatars or Devta or guru,
Acharya, or Rishi, Muni or Nabi, Pir or Saint etc. etc.
Prior to Devatma
This 'true and almsgiving knowledge' of religion
Was not everybody's cup of tea

It was the framework of the finest knitting of truth
Under the refuge of Devatma and the influence of his Dev Prabhavas,
every capable soul achieves a certain wisdom about religion
which they could not obtain from any of the so-called deities, gods/
goddesses,
or their avatar, avant-garde, or guide.
He also attains freedom
to the limit of his capacity,
from the various aspects of his vulgarity or irreligious nature

and evolves multi-colored aspects of his first ranked grace
or religious life,
He could not have obtained this 'absolute moksha' and 'vikas'
from any other source or place.

Devatma is the only lighthouse of truth
Who can show a 'corporeal route' to wretched souls

The Great Secret with a Question Mark

To understand truth and to love it, are not identical.
The love of truth leads to the discovery of truth,
Therefore,
possession of true knowledge does not ipso facto,
develop into a love of truth.
Apart from
some insane persons,
there are no human beings anywhere in the world
who are not
possessed with
some elementary knowledge-imparting sense organs
and
do not acquire/yearn for some knowledge
through these sense organs.
Besides mankind,
animals also possess
some elementary sensory knowledge
but they have no love of truth.
Just as millions of animals have some instinctive
and sensory knowledge
but
lack of progressive critical

and intellectual strengths,

in the same way,

millions among mankind have one or another sort of true knowledge
but they are deprived of love of truth.

The kind of psychology in which a love of truth can sprout
and progress is absent in millions of
men.

Just as in the course of evolution of the animal world,

millions of chimpanzees (who are

similar to man) did not and could not get the inheritance
to develop into human beings,

in the

same way,

in the evolution of human species,

there are millions

who

did not inherit the intelligence or desire which could sprout
into the love of truth.

In the course of human evolution of thousands of years

only in such an

extraordinary soul

and in him alone,

and nobody else,

could all-sided love of truth evolve

who:

(1) is free from the dominance of all evil dispositions which lead to
untruth;

(2) is awakened to the reality of his soul-life and is concerned about its
evolution

and devolution;

(3) has developed perfect longing for the evolution of his soul

and is contend that this as his destiny

and is possessed of altruistic feelings of one

or another kind for the fulfillment of this destiny;

and

(4) realizes, this truth in all clarity, that it is only through
more and more true knowledge and
true knowledge alone
about every kingdom of Nature
and it is only through
more and more
observance and practice
of what is truth-based goodness
that his soul can continuously
evolve
and show him the path of truth.
Millions and billions of men can acquire various kinds of knowledge
but love of all-sided truth
can be evolved
only in a soul which is characterized by the psychological equipment
mentioned above
and in none else.
Is it
no wonder that millions of people are enveloped in absolute darkness
about soul life
and though they are sinking in
soul-life,
yet they are not conscious of it,
a soul be born
who on being conscious of terrible
soul darkness refuses to remain content with it
and who makes it a slogan of his soul-life
that whatever is not true,
is not beneficial for soul life;
who values the light of truth for the
preservation of his soul life as much as he values air for the breath of
his life;
who loves truth
in every aspect of life;

who finds his greatest welfare
and satisfaction in the possession of
the light of truth that blesses soul-life?
Is it true?
What an achievement it is for
mankind to have a soul,
who does not merely praise truth in words,
but who loves
truth; who wants to live in the light of truth;
who devotes himself to searching for a greater truth
to guide his life; who considers it his highest destiny to share it with
others,
who
sacrifices his wealth, relatives, name, fame,
children and society in the pursuit of it.
What a jewel he is for humanity.
How great, how invaluable, how beautiful,
and how useful are all
such constituents of love of truth
whose evolution gives a soul the destiny of
being a lover of truth!
There is no gainsaying the fact that evolution of man in Nature
is a great event.
But man's condition remains deplorable so long as he
lacks those constituents of
the love of truth that have the strength in them to deliver him
from the path of untruth and puts
him on the path of truth.
He remains in this pitiable condition even though he be an emperor,
king/monarch, a capitalist, a man of genius, a poet,
an industrialist, a man of education
or position or name and fame.
As it is impossible for a man to breathe without air, even though
he possesses lungs,
henceforth,

it is impossible for a man without the constituents of the love of truth
to acquire the light of truth
and follow the path of truth in spite of his other accompaniments.
Just as light is necessary to dispel darkness,
the love of truth
is necessary to dispel
darkness in the soul.
'It is a wake-up call'
Unmistakably,
intellectual power is a beneficial thing.
But just as this intellectual
power is incapable to free a man from the life of sins and crimes,
Similarly,
a man obsessed by
one or another low passion,
leads a life of evil;
it is difficult for others to
motivate this man to a
life of truth.
Controlled by his superstitious beliefs,
evil feelings and passions,
he is driven to
the path of untruth,
The track of filth,
And garbage.
He
Even
deliberately accepts
untruths,
champions them,
supports them,
propagates them
consequently,
deepens,
day by day,

the darkness of his soul
It degenerates him
into extinction.
In this context,
how magnificent is the grandeur of the love of truth
Invariably,
for a soul
who has inhaled the whiff of truth,
and
all the constituents of the love of truth!
He is
Undoubtedly,
illumined by that light
which dispels untruth and shows the path of truth!
Truth is inevitable,
Certainly, truth needs no evidence.

Structural Principles of Truth and Goodness

Psychology of Goodness

- Duty
- Gratitude
- Helpfulness of others
- Attraction for the altruistic virtues of others
- Inviolate regard for sacred vows
- Doing things to finish
- Feelings to establish good producing harmony and peace.
- Respect and reverence for elders
- Compassion
- Cleanliness
- Feeling to prolong the life and utility of things (Feeling of Preservation for things)
- Feeling of attraction for flower
- Feelings of attraction for birds —pigeons, nightingales, parrots, doves——cats, dogs-
- Self-help
- Self-respect
- Sense of justice and discipline &c.

The love of goodness is a new foundation to the gamut of altruistic virtues.

To have the above virtues is not to have a love of goodness; however, with the love of goodness, all the virtues are part of it. From childhood, there is growth in the gamut of higher feelings rooted in a love of goodness of Devatma. Each one of them appeared to Devatma to be great, beautiful and sublime in comparison to elementary feelings.

The psychology of Devatma is not favourable for the absence of higher feelings and presence of antagonistic feelings.

Therefore, He can never give up what he considers good out of the opposition of others or out of fear or temptation of others. The absence of higher feelings and presence of antagonistic feelings cannot form the love of goodness.

(1)

Devatma posits that the ideal life begins with deepening the sense of relation to the four kingdoms – human beings, animals, plants and inanimate world – on the basis of feelings of appreciation, gratitude, love and service for the four kingdoms.

(2)

To feel related is to feel concerned, and to feel concerned is to discriminate good from bad environments – whether physical, biological, social or cultural – and to serve to preserve and cultivate the good elements and to reduce or remove the evil elements in them.

(3)

Good life begins with respect for whatever lives. Devatma makes it one of the principles of his ideal life to show respect for the life of beings of all the four kingdoms. For him, to be good is to respect all existences, and respect not only constitutes avoiding injury or damage to the form or qualities of both living and non-living things, but also in protecting and satisfying their rights to full life in 'length and width'.

(4)

To show respect is not the same thing as to feel respect. To feel respect is to see the good qualities of the elders or superiors, and to feel them superior in some respects or to accept fellow human beings as of co-essence with oneself.

Every human being is to be treated as a person without all forms of exploitation; that is, economic, social, sexual, political, moral or spiritual.

Each human being should also be entitled to unconditional respect. Under no circumstances are we to treat our fellow human beings, no matter how depraved, as an object to be discarded. To accept someone is to understand and respect the other's point of view in our conduct with them.

(5)

Wishing well happens in two ways:

- I may offer wishing well for the redress of suffering of others with the feeling of compassion or Karuna.
- I may offer wishing well for others to realize their greater potential with the feeling of Mudita.

Let us relieve them of all unnecessary suffering and to experience all innocent pleasures.

Let us wish everyone to get the optimum condition for growth, development and achievement of creative life in intellectual, artistic and moral and spiritual spheres.

As a final note, wishing well cultivates in us the twin feeling of Karuna and Mudita, which are the two wings of the human soul that allow us to fly freely in the world of holiness.

(6)

Devatma holds affection to be an essential factor in different relations. This is a basic principal of all interpersonal relationships and the first sadhana of affection is to greet others with a smile.

The second sadhana to cultivate affection is to be able to have a dialogue with others.

The third sadhana is to involve ourselves in our professional service.

An altruistic person gets his worst shocks from those whom he serves, but he continues to serve them with greater and greater enthusiasm.

Affection, when genuine, is unconditional in its disposability to others because, for the man of affection, others are a part of his own life.

(7)

Gratitude opens a unique window to the world, ushers in illumination and understanding in the dark chambers of mind, leads to development and enrichment of the embryonic moral life and brings joy, truth and beauty to 'life's unquiet dream'.

Gratitude is the conscious appreciation of the service which is being received and conscious longing to make some return to the benefactor.

It is the higher feelings that open us up to the world of truth, goodness, beauty and joy for the human soul. Without them, the soul has no life, growth, development, enrichment or joy.

The sense of gratitude opens reveals the truth that, in our origin – growth and development – we are dependent on the services rendered by others. For example our parents give us unconditional love whether we are ill or well, bright or dull or good or evil, and regardless of our successes or failures in life. The marvel of their love is that they feel more for us when we are ill, dull, evil or unsuccessful. In the whole world, they alone own us dearly when everybody else disowns us. When everyone else loses hope about us, it is they who do not cease to hope for us.

Are we able to see the beauty of the love and service of our parents and feel moved by it? Is there any part of the day when we remember them to offer our homage of heart to them? When we fail to remember our parents' efforts to raise and protect us, we lack truth in our life and this is because we lack the sense of gratitude.

Had we the feeling of gratitude, we would feel as much appreciation to our subordinates and colleagues at the success of the day as we feel annoyed with them when they fail us. We have a duty to feel appreciative and thankful when they do not fail us. If we fail to appreciate and thank our subordinates for their good service, we have no right to feel annoyed with them when they fail us.

The sense of gratitude makes us perceptive not only of the service done to us by our immediate benefactors, but it also reveals the thousands and millions of those remote benefactors who contribute to our life. Our intellectual, aesthetic, and moral culture links past to our current personality. Do we feel grateful to the past in which we are saturated? If not, how much truth we miss in our lives!

The sense of gratitude perceives that the world of benefactors is as wide as the world itself. Our activities are oriented to the satisfaction of our character forces. When gratitude is our character, we cannot help but remember our benefactors many times a day, with the feeling of appreciation and affection for them, and look forward for any opportunity to be serviceable to them.

The feeling of gratitude, when it is our character, seeks and finds ways to do something for the benefactors. A man of gratitude is never satisfied with what he has done. We cannot pay all our debts to our parents by serving them until eternity, for gratitude is a return, and therefore, a conditional act. In the same way, our parents' service is an unconditional act of pure delight in the service of what is loved. We can also pay our debt of favours completely, but only if we love them as they loved us, which is an impossible act for the human mind. How can I love my parents with the same love that they gave to me! If I serve them, how much of their love overflows to me, and in comparison, how small a thing is the service rendered by me!

Apart from cases when we receive service without any consideration of self-interest and out of sheer love, one receives benefits from society in the form of knowledge, skills, principles of conduct and ideals of life.

This truth spurs a man of gratitude to devote himself unsparingly to the service of others. In doing this, he would exert himself to his optimum to reduce his debt of gratitude and develop into an altruist of gratitude. A man with altruism of gratitude for his mother will not only serve his mother but will feel an urge to serve womankind. He may work for their education and their rights.

In whatever stage of development feeling of gratitude exists, either as act of gratitude, sentiment of gratitude or altruism of gratitude, it is characterized by making the other the direct object of service. It is not a case of dynamic gratitude, if my motivation in return of service for the service received is to promote the good of my soul. Such cases of gratitude do not reduce the centrality of self in one's welfare. In pure or unconditional feeling of gratitude, the welfare of the benefactor is the direct object of concern and tends to reduce one's centrality on the stage of life.

Thus, the feeling of gratitude has both a narrow and a wide range. When I make a return for a service received and forget about it, it is a case of spasmodic feeling of gratitude. When I regularly serve my mother out of gratitude, for example, gratitude is my character. If I serve womankind, besides serving my mother, I become an altruist of gratitude. However, whatever be the duration and depth of the feeling of gratitude in a human heart, the feeling gives out sparks of truth that light the path of service in interpersonal relationships.

The feeling of goodness creates a feeling that there is a lot of good in the world. Feelings of gratitude conjurs the belief that we can be a force of good to others; for instance, when one perfects the qualities required for his or her profession and provides dedicated professional service to others. In appreciating the service of others, and in rendering service to others, I live a life rich in truth and goodness.

The Psychology of Love of Truth

Love of Truth cuddles complete harmony
and unity with the most beautiful
and 'eye-opening' process of evolution.
This is an unparalleled love of Truth,
which matured the love of Goodness
culminated in becoming Devatma.

Love of truth should not be confused with
identity of thought and will......
There is a gap between
what we consider as auspicious
and actually doing good.........
We decide to perform some good work every day
and we have a history of failures
as our record.........
we will fail to carry through
our resolutions..................
There is no identity of will and thought.........

Great men of will always demonstrate
this personality trait – they carry
the routine perfectly
and are true to the great causes
they have decided to uphold,

passing through fire and brimstone unflinchingly.........
Their lives are inspiration to us................

Socrates sums up the psychology of the best
and highest minds of the world when he pronounces:
"I am not only now, but always a man who
follows nothing but reasoning,
which on consideration appears to me best".

However, this identity of thought
and will does not encompass a love of truth,
even though the love of truth is one of its aspects,
for this identity of thought and will is
found in bad men as often as it is found in altruistic men.

Identity of thought and will
means to do what we think to be right.........
However, our thinking may be vicious
and we remain evil characters in spite of the identity
of thought and will...........
Napoleon and Hitler, for example,
both displayed this identity,
therefore, we understand how they stand censured......
When thinking is in the interest of social and moral good,
such identity develops an altruistic character.
However, since this true perspective is also limited
and partial, as the altruistic person is
a mixture of both good and bad life.

Thus, identity of thought and will is also
found in bad characters,
while it is also found in altruistic persons
who have blind spots in many aspects of their character.
Therefore, a love of truth cannot be
defined as merely identifier of thought and will.

Love of truth cannot be identified
with love of knowledge,
though love of knowledge is a part of the love of truth.
Love of knowledge is developed from
the curiosity to know what attracts our attention.
Knowledge must not be unrelated
to the good of the human and sub-human
kingdom of the universe.

A philosopher is a synthetic genius –
he integrates his knowledge of the sciences
with his discoveries in the moral field and
presents a worldview...................
It is the task of philosophy and philosophers
to bless a 'synoptic view of reality' to
present the universe in an intellectual pattern
in which the physical, social, mental, moral
and spiritual aspects of the universe are presented as integrated...............

These two philosophers, Descartes and Leibnitz,
had a wonderful philosophic aptitude and great intellects,
but they were devoid of the moral courage to fight popular
false beliefs when they came to know that Galileo was persecuted.........
This proves that philosophic activity
does not cover the whole personality............
No wonder a great scientist or a great
philosopher is also a great person,
for it illumines his whole life.

However, love of truth is not a
particular aptitude,
whether practical, scientific or philosophic,
though all these aptitudes encompass it......
It stands for a new basis of personality itself.
Love of truth stands in contrast

to a love of pleasure.....................
We have different biological
and psychological urges.
These urges contain no
principles of control in themselves...
Each of these urges clamours
for unending satisfaction, even at
its own cost and the cost of others.
We lie, cheat and exploit in the
pursuit of our urges.
This happens because the principle
under which our urges work is in that
of the pleasure principle..........
Every satisfaction of an urge intensifies
that urge and it becomes more vehement,
seeking further, longer and if possible,
continuous satisfaction............
The ideal of urges is
the conception of the heaven
of sense, as drawn in sensuous details
in History of Religion...................
The principle of pleasure,
which is the determinant of the
urges in the way of weakening or strengthening
them, is not the principle of truth..........

An urge, under the pleasure principle,
seeks its satisfaction irrespective of truth
and goodness..................
Since we are under the principle
of pleasure in our urges,
we walk the way of untruth and evil.........

Love of truth is the new
basis of urges................

The urges are under the command
of the truth principle,
and therefore,
they do not know disposition to untruth and evil.

It is not the case that love of truth
is free from error in judgment and
conduct................

Error is inescapable from our finite existence.
We have a limited understanding and limited
knowledge of facts...................

However, when there is a love of truth, there
is no disposition to error in judgment or conduct.
The whole personality repulses untruth.
It insists on scrupulous regard for truth in every
bit of life......................
Such a personality is free from all propensities
of evil and untruth.
Such was the personality of Devatma,
the founder of Dev Dharma.

Devatma found in himself
love of truth,
and declared its evolution in him
as a unique manifestation in the human
world................
To understand him is to understand the love of truth.

In the context of human situation, how
great is the glory the love of Truth
and of the soul who has evolved
all the constituents of the love of Truth
and who is illumined by the light which
dispels untruth and shows the path of Truth.

The various constituents of the love of truth that evolved in Devatma comprise the following:

- Love of speaking truth;
- Love for unambiguous expression of truth;
- Love for acquiring true knowledge;
- Love for assimilating truth;
- Love to carry out right commitments or promises;
- Love for the dissemination of truth;
- Love to espouse truth; and
- Love for research in the field of religion.

The different feelings of 'vairagya', or aversion or repulsion for untruth as under:

- Complete repulsion for all forms of speaking untruth.
- Complete repulsion for false promises.
- Complete repulsion for accepting or assimilating any untruth.
- Complete repulsion for supporting any untruth.
- Complete repulsion for hypocrisy or insincerity.
- Complete repulsion for darkness born of untruth.
- Complete repulsion for all forms of pleasures obtainable by untruth.
- Complete repulsion for all forms of gains derivable from untruth.

Psychology of Beauty

Everyone has a soft corner
For the beauty,
the beautiful things according
to their level recite something
special; for example, a Beautiful and fragrant flower
attracts us
or
a beautiful house, or a bridge, a dawn,
a sunset or a beautiful landscape steals our
insights,
the list is endless................
Every beautiful object is so called
because it serves some rational end,
whether for security or for the gratification of man.

However, beauty is not limited to
physical things..............
It extends to music, dance and drama............
It goes further.........It characterizes some
systems of reasoning,

such as the Euclidean geometry or Spinoza's Ethics..............
Thus, beauty can be sensuous,
intellectual, emotional and spiritual.

Socrates appears to have attached
little importance to the immediate
gratification a beautiful object affords
to perception and contemplation,
but rather emphasized its power of
furthering the more necessary elements
of life,
The really valuable point in
his doctrine is the relativity of beauty.

The question is – when is a thing beautiful?
What blesses
beauty to a thing?
Beauty is not a thing – whether material or psychical,
as it characterizes the arrangement,
structure or form of something.............
Therefore, beauty does not refer to the
parts of a thing
but rather the arrangement
that pervades the whole............
As such, it is a formal character of the whole.

Moreover, colours do not knit
a thing beautiful – a colourful thing
can be ugly too. What makes a colourful
thing beautiful is the arrangement
of the colours or the form in which
colours harmonize with each other...............
It is how the elements intertwine that
determines the beauty or ugliness of things.........
If the mixture is proportionate,

the thing is beautiful; otherwise, it is not.

What makes a body beautiful is that
it has a complete number of organs
in complete growth that exist
in proportionate relationship
to one another..........
In addition,
what makes music beautiful is not sound –
songs sung can be disharmonious,
meaning that the sounds
are not related to each other in the right way.
There is a mathematical relationship
between sounds in music.
A dance is not just movements of a body – it comprises
the movements of a body in the right proportion
and in the right relation to each other and to the whole.

We speak of a beautiful play.
If what appeals to us in a drama is that
it has a moral lesson,
we have missed the play.
If what we like in a song is
its spiritual quality,
we have missed the music of it.
Most of the religious hymns,
in spite of their high international
quality, are as poor as poetry.
Classical music is pure music, for it is an exclusive
enjoyment of the relation of sounds
to each other, where no element
of meaning enters to distract the attention.

To a scientist,
the beauty of nature lies in the orderliness

of the events that happen within it.
The scientist's task is to discover such an orderliness
of events and call them the laws of nature.

We can understand that beauty
is not specific to a particular subject
matter
but it is the principle of the organization
of the parts of any subject or matter.............

Since beauty is the principle of the structure
or organization of things or thoughts,
it can exist in the humblest of materials
and absent in the best of materials..........

To illustrate, a hut may be beautiful whereas
a palace may be ugly,
even though it is made of the best of marbles.
A poem may be beautiful even though it
only describes sublime divinity.................

Thus, beauty is something other than
subject matter...................
Beauty is the principle of
structure of things and thoughts.

Devatma's soul is a complete union
of count, depth and detail,
and it is illuminated by the lights of beauty.........
This amalgamation of all ways makes
it complete,
filling it with sublime behaviour.
Devatma recites of truth,
goodness and beauty as his ideal,
all of which constitute love of truth

and goodness with a beautiful and proportional
structure that has the proper intensity,
depth, width and
relationship to other altruistic feelings.

His life is to be viewed as the
finest achievement of the highest beauty,
for the constituents of truth and goodness
are of the highest excellence
and he could evolve them in perfect harmony.

Thus, harmony within the sublime forces
of his sublime life and harmony with
the cosmos were in the service of his love of the aestheticism.

Psychology of Altruism

Altruism is limited in its vision.
An altruist who recognizes a compelling
obligation to serve the sick,
the idiot, the immoral and the unfortunate,
does not feel the same moral compulsion
to serve the immature in body,
intellect and spirit, neither the accomplished
in science, fine arts and morality...............

An altruist who realizes morally
drawn to the service of the accomplished
confesses his insensitiveness to the
moral obligation to serve the immature
or the unfit.....................

Each piece of value needs a separate
sense of its discrimination, appreciation,
acceptance and accomplishment.........
We would need thousands of eyes to have
a 'fair view' of the field of values that
await actualization through human appreciation and action.

The sense of altruism in some
altruists is appreciative of its moral
obligation to serve the evolutionary process.

It spurts and develops under a certain philosophic
vision and attitude of the universe.
There are different world views—Idealistic,
Theistic, Naturalistic and Evolutionistic.
The object of service is possible through
the Evolutionistic world view.

The discovery of the idea
of evolution as a universal principle
for interpretation and understanding of the
universe is a blessing,
but it is not sufficient; thus,
it requires a ripe and richer interpretation.

This is possible for a new ethical genius,
whose life fulfills the aims of
evolution i.e. a life dominated by a trinity
of values: truth, goodness and beauty..........
Such an evolved life is Deva Jiwan/sublime life
and he who lives it is Devatma...........

Devatma developed sublime life
in himself; as a repercussion,
in reflecting on the comprehensive drama
of evolution extending to millions and billions
of years, he saw his sublime light,
in that evolution was not merely a
biological process
but also a value process,
and the values it aims at are truth,
goodness and beauty..............

He further saw that he is under
an unconditional command to serve them.

The process of evolution
could be the object of altruism only
when two conditions were satisfied: the process
of evolution emerged to the knowledge of man.

A moral genius measured up to the stature to
properly interpret the process of evolution
and noticed a complete and unconditional obligation
to serve it..........................
Devatma, therefore, realized
.... this unique manifestation of his altruism
had a different object for its service than what others served.

An object transforms and transvalues a feeling.
When one fears to do wrong
or violates a moral principle,
it is a case of moral discipline,
and the man is called a god-fearing man.

When one embraces a great cause,
it is a case of altruism...........

When one loves truth, goodness and beauty,
It is certainly
a maze that stretches far beyond altruism...............

It is because of this that Devatma
called his altruism unique,
means: its object being different could not
be categorized as altruism................

He affirms: "There is no one who
Having
possessed and evolved
in himself

life of truth,
goodness and beauty,
has declared them as his
'ideal' to engage
himself in the service of
different domains
of nature, as I, having matured
the sublime forces,
declared this ideal................

The ideal avowed reads thus".

"May beautiful, truth and goodness
My foremost aim represent,
And in the service of the world
My life be fully spent."

The second part i.e. "In the service of the world, my life be fully spent"
was not so distinctive of his life
as the first............
There are an abundance of instances
of dynamic altruism.............
None of these cases of altruism
made service of evolution
as its object or service..............
The spirit of evolution is to
bring about a reign of truth, goodness and beauty...............

This is possible if there is superimposition
of the principle of truth
over the principle of pleasure
as the supervisor and examiner
of all human urges—biological, psychological
and social..................... This is made
possible to Devatma whose life is

the embodiment of this
ideal – the trinity of values.........

In framing the evolutionary
process as
the object of his altruism,
he was introducing a new
dimension to altruism,
a fresh eye and a new vision
is bestowed to mankind............

What is peculiarity about him
is not altruism,
but the object of altruism,
which could be his object,
because he evolved a magnificent life.

The altruism for the process of evolution is
different from the altruism for the unfit,
the immature or the accomplished.

In altruism for the unfit,
the immature or the accomplished,
what
the altruist strives for is
to serve something concrete...........
A sick child or an idiot is present
in flesh and blood to awaken the compassion
of an altruist...............

In the service of the immature,
the immaturity is present in the individual
one serves............
In the service of the accomplished,
the excellence of the object of service

stimulates the altruist to the
appreciation and service of it...........

The process of evolution is a process,
not a thing..............
Its apprehension lays far greater
demands on the intellectual and emotional
equipment of a person.

Invariably, altruism for the ineligible,
the immature or the accomplished,
an altruist develops attachment and partiality
for ones which he serves.........

Even an altruist who aims to remove their
social, political, educational barriers nourishes
partiality for them...................
He exaggerates their grievances.
He makes demands for them
which are neither just nor ultimately
to their interest.................
Partiality for the accomplished is
too clear a fact..............
An altruist enhances blind faith in the
Accomplished,
serves and inflates his virtues and
undervalues or fails to examine his shortcomings.

Partiality is not possible when the
object of altruism is the process
of evolution..............
One cannot be partial to truth,
goodness and beauty as a trinity...........

The process of evolution repulses it.......

Third, this form of altruism had to
wait for special and unique conditions
for it to rise in the moral consciousness........

Finally, even today, an altruist cannot directly notice
the process of evolution an object of service,
for he is psychologically unfit for it..........
Human urges are under the sway of the pleasure
principle..............
This often puts man in opposition to
the conduct that the process of
evolution dictates..............

Hence, according to the given
human psychology,
man cannot unfailingly drive
the process of evolution as his
direct object of service.

He can do aforesaid
if and so far as he is
under the psychic influence
of the life dominated by the trinity of values
of truth, goodness and beauty...........

Devatma evolved a life of the trinity
of these values, and his life has psychological influences
which show that truth, not pleasure, ought to be
the principle of conduct........

Moreover, these influences infuse that
strength, which notices person's capability
to walk the path of truth in his conduct...........

His light reveals this new object

of altruistic service to which we certify an unconditional moral
obligation to serve it,

'out and out' with his power,

we carry this unconditional moral obligation

to the extent our vision, capacity and will power.

Psychology of love

(Intrinsic Vs. Extrinsic)

Objects and human beings
have not only utility for us;
but their own intrinsic value also...............
When we are motivated by the benefit
of things, we fail to see their aspect
of intrinsic beauty.......................

As we pass from the level of things
to the living world of plants, animals
and human beings, the intrinsic worth
shoots up to the climax..............

Though things have inner worth, they do not
have equal intrinsic worth.................
Love, as a basis of relationship,
rises in glory as its object of love moves from
inanimate things to man.................
So great is the intrinsic worth of self-consciousness
in men that poets and philosophers,
in their love of the universe, interpret
it to consist of centres of consciousness,
or that the whole universe is

one universal-consciousness.

Love of mankind is a supreme
example of
the altruism of love......
However, love for mankind is not a pity
for mankind.
More precisely, love is not pity.
Pity is a very inferior basis of a relationship to love.

A parents' attitude towards his own child
is one of love; to others in distress,
that of pity.........
Pity is a desire to remove the suffering
of another without acceptance of it as an
object of absolute worth...........
Love is also a desire to serve another,
however, the other is accepted as superior to all
our devotion to it.

The mother accepts the child as
of absolute intrinsic worth,
not in terms of how he is going
to be useful for her.........
This advantage aspect is most repugnant to the
mother's love, and this poison is introduced
by the social conventions.........

It is the purity of love that makes
a mother to cuddle the service of her child,
even when he has been suffering from
incurable diseases
of body, mind and morals.......
What is of absolute worth
Lies not in child's helplessness weaknesses and wickedness– what

is of absolute worth is the child.

A mother believes, like a doctor, that weakness or
disease is not essential to her child's body
but rather, accidental to his/her body........
The essential thing about her child's body
is its health, not its diseases.........
It is the health of the body which is of intrinsic worth,
which a mother loves in the child.

It is pathetic to see a mother's affection towards her
child, who suffers from an incurable
physical diseases,
still prays and hopes for the cure
....
Only ignorance of the medical
profession stands between her faith and the
cure of the child..........
Again, a mother believes, having criminal child, like
a psychologist, that these are not the definitions
of the boy's psyche; rather, these are removable aspects
of the boy's psyche.

Sometimes the psychologist gives up
the case of her boy as hopeless.
However, for the mother, the helplessness
of the psychologist is not the hopelessness of the boy.
In the face of the brutal realities
of the situation,
she continues her simple faith in
the intrinsic worth of her child.

A mother's services are humble, but purity of her love
challenges the best services of the highest men.......
Her love is unconditional, her service is unsparing

and her faith in her child's worth is also unshakeable and eternal; hence,
nothing can remove her love, not
even the ungrateful and cruel conduct of her
child, the uncharitable opinion of the worldly-wise or
the cynicism of world philosophies.

Love is the unconditional acceptance
of the other as of intrinsic worth, as an
end in itself and service of it
as the whole meaning of one's life..........

Love does not appreciate the other for its utility
to it..............
It appreciates its intrinsic worth,
for which it feels an unconditional
obligation of devotion.
It is a fundamental character of altruism of love
that devotion and service are not conditioned
by-what others can mean to us
but what they are in their essential nature.

Therefore, things and persons
have both extrinsic and intrinsic worth.
When we are appreciative of the utility of others,
we develop gratitude in relation to them,
and when we are appreciative of their intrinsic worth,
we plant the seeds of love for them.
Just as a utility relationship can degenerate into
exploitation, with hatred, a love relationship
can degenerate into attachment and partiality.

This happens when utility and love are
based on the pleasure principle.
But when utility is based on the truth principle,
it becomes gratitude; when love is based

on truth, it rises above attachment
and partiality and becomes pure altruism.

There is a distinction between
the sentiment of love and altruism
of love...............
Sentiment of love may be for the virtues of
one's father and mother,
or one's teacher or Spiritual Master........

The altruism of love includes these
Heretofore goes beyond to the anonymous humanity,
to the world of animals and plants
and the infinite world of space and time.

The artist represents altruism
of love through the beauty of things..........

The philosopher and the scientist represent altruism of
love through the truth of things.........
The moral genius represents the altruism of love
through the goodness of things..........
No wonder, an artist thinks of the Universe as an
order of beauty, a philosopher as an
order of truth, and a moral genius as a moral order.

Though the artist, the philosopher and the moral genius
represent the altruism of love,
altruism controlled by truth rises to the highest glory.......
It is when beauty is truth,
and goodness is truth, that truth, goodness and beauty
become one............
Hence, it is when the artist awakens from the worship
of sensuous beauty to the worship of truth in life
and universe that he attains to the highest

achievement and
becomes the philosopher poet or a moral genius poet.

When love of truth is
the pillar of the relationship
between things and persons,
we realize that the whole meaning and significance
of our life lies in unconditional service,
which constitutes utter devotion
and building the ultimate sacrifice for them.

Unless we appreciate the inner and intrinsic worth
of what we serve, service is contemptible patronage,
hence, no service, naught
…….. Patronage is motivated by pity
not inspired by love.
It degrades the provider and the receiver of the service.
The receiver feels humiliated and the giver feels arrogant;
consequently, both notice as maladjusted-ones to
the truth of the inter-personal relationship.

There is no significance in the service of mankind
unless mankind is appreciated as of intrinsic worth.
Imagine a state of affairs in which the
whole of humanity
is destroyed by natural disaster except
one young couple……
This pair may be of very mediocre
abilities and character.
Yet, in their lives, they
have the power to create
a new humanity when all other existences
of the three orders
of existence stand helpless to give birth
to a human being – a being

who has the capacity to discover
or understand truth,
to create and appreciate beauty or
to behold some good
and live it..........

What is of intrinsic worth in a man
is his strength to move under certain
conditions, some untruths and evils
in him and contemplate and live
some truth and goodness in his life.

It is the characteristic of the lover-beloved
relationship that determines whether love is
divine or human.
It sheds, ego-cent the beloved
takes the place of the lover's ego.......
The lover's thoughts regard his beloved,
and his or her desires and actions are directed on and geared
to the other............
A young woman, when she becomes
a mother, undergoes a complete transformation of her psychology.
Her thoughts are for her tiny child,
her desires and dreams are for him and
her activities are centred on him/her.
The altruist's love widens and deepens as
his ego shrinks towards zero.
At this point, he enjoys
the freedom from ego-centrality
in the service of the four orders' existences.
He realizes his destiny of static or altruistic life.

Psychology of virtue

Why do virtues go wrong,
what makes them virtues,
when are they virtues?

Humans generally experiment with
the virtues of satisfaction and deprivation,
which are based on love and avoidance,
respectively............
For instance, patriotism is our love for our country.
Charming scenery, rivers and forests, and growing vegetables
and fruits, coupled with its literary firmament, art, literature,
science, philosophy and religion, etc.,
make us feel pride in our achievements.

These also urge us to take pleasure
in furthering such development and faculties.
Likewise, altruism finds pleasure in serving humanity to
relieve it from its physical pain.
It may add awakening about the universe
and to raise its moral tone.
Gratitude, in turn, seeks pleasure in sharing
knowledge, thence, generosity nurtures us
to share our auspicious fortune with others.

The other set of virtues
pertains to control, denial or deprivation.
Austerity minimizes our aspirations,
thereby pleasing us with denial of certain accesses
to ourselves.......
Humility contrasts with pride by
concentrating on what we are deprived of......
Surrendering certain things is the subject of discipline,
resignation, and submission,
whereas leadership asserts itself for
the positive satisfactions of
the enforcement of one's will.

Nivritti, or religious ethics,
places a special premium
on the virtues of self-deprivation.
It veils the simplicity, humility,
resignation, austerity, celibacy,
seriousness and self-devaluation........
Hence, these are monk-like virtues
that find their origin in myths and monasteries.

Pravritti is the secular ethics which emerges
due weight to self-satisfaction
in conjugal love, loyalty, and in living well
with all the attributes of leadership and
revolt alike...........

Therefore, both self-denial and self-satisfaction
are necessary to spiritual growth.........
However, these attributes lack something,
as by themselves they are blind.
Simplicity itself is denial,
but it can also lead to absurd asceticism.
In turn, submission is good
but it can degenerate into slavishness.

Humility is good but it leads to self-condemnation.
Celibacy is just acceptable under certain conditions
but it can degenerate into slavishness.
The same fate is shared by secular virtues – pride degenerates
into vanity; patriotism into national arrogance; married love
into moha; faith into blind faith; gratitude into partiality
for the benefactors; leadership into aggressive self-assertion and so on.

Why do virtues go wrong, what makes
the virtues and when are they virtues?

A virtue is a mean between two
extremes of excess and deficit,
as courage is something in-between rashness and cowardice,
which are two extremes of a single situation.
Likewise, temperance is a mean between
gluttony and asceticism, which are
also two extremes of a single necessity……..
Both excess and deficit must thus be avoided.
Non–observance of this norm is
devilish in nature………..
Truth happens to be the basis
of virtue in order to keep it a virtue,
and to rescue its degeneration into
evil by the worldly circumstances………
Truth has the capacity to develop a self-illuminating soul.

However, this is not so, as much
of the time they are based on partial truths
that show partiality in conduct.
Hence, it is clear to see
how a supposedly simple person
can become ascetic,
and how a person who is supposed to
live well becomes profligate.
Moreover, achievements develop vanity,

and shortcomings, which are supposed to be addressed,
grow an inferiority complex.
Further, obeisance urges slavery – thus, teach man any
virtue and he slips into vulgarity.
Virtues show this tragic character
because of the pleasure principle,
which is not the truth
principle in itself.
Hence, virtues bear the mark of untruth.

Of course, humility is better than vanity,
and submission is better than aggressive self-assertion.
Resignation is better than revolution.
Simplicity is better than the excessive show
of things.
Since vanity, arrogance, revolt and presentation of wealth
are common among humankind; therefore, such aforementioned
monkish virtues are cultivated
with an emphasis to counter the corrupt.
Historically, this emphasis has depicted
them as the true and topmost virtues; however, this is false.

We have seen that
these monkish virtues have blind spots,
and they are in no way superior to the other
set of secular virtues.
There is no doubt that simplicity
is better than the excessive show of things,
but it is not superior to decent living.
Humility is better than vanity
but not superior to pride.
Resignation is better than
revolution but not better than
protest, submission is better than
aggressive self-assertion, but not superior

to leadership.........
They are superior or inferior to the extent
that they walk or do not walk on the truth
and the sharp edge of truth – false humility
is as worse as false protest,
and false submission as bad as false leadership.

However, on the other hand,
there are dependent virtues.
Honesty has meaning if the money
has value...........
Money and things have satisfaction value
because our biological needs
come first...........
Thus, without the craving
of food, shelter and other
things of bodily satisfaction,
honesty has no meaning.
Without sex, chastity, love and
fidelity have no possibility
of existence, and without social assertion,
there cannot be rightful pride in an excellence.
Without social life, there cannot be justice, or
altruistic life. ....

Therefore, these are not possible
without the animal instincts.

We can appreciate the virtue if
we recognize the truth:

- True foundation of virtue is the truth.
- Virtues of deprivation are not superior
  to the virtues of fulfilling.
- Virtues intensify themselves
  with their foundation in truth.

Psychology of Man

Devatma's universal philosophy is the
application of a scientific method to
the discovery of the moral
and spiritual constitution of the human soul.
Certainly, the philosophical perspective knits
a complete departure from all other religious
studies of the human soul.

The human soul is an evolved and
organized living force that comprises several forces.
As its organism is not complete in all aspects,
like the human body,
we can define the soul
as thus: "The organized life force,
which comprises different powers, which
inhabit the human living body, is called the human soul."

Not only human beings
but also plants and animals have
Life-forces.
Man is a soul-body unit – both
the soul and body are products of the evolution.

The soul has evolved out of inanimate energy
as the body has evolved of inanimate matter.
The life/soul primarily appeared in
unicellular bodies, thence, in multi-cellular bodies
in plants and animals.
Therefore, the human soul is a highly evolved form of life.

The basic foundation of modern scientific study
of human soul is that
the human soul is a part of Nature.
It has a biological origin.
It is the product of the evolutionary process.
It is the product of changes
in the Natural world,
therefore, is in ceaseless
transformation for better and worse.

It can stay alive under certain
physical and psychological conditions.
It can 'breathe last' under certain
physical and psychological conditions.

It has a dependent origination.
The biological origin of the human soul
has the stamina of construction in it
to build, sustain, repair and
re-produce its own kind.

Fundamental characteristics common
to all organized life forces are:

To build one or other kind of body.
To maintain or nurture that living body.
To keeping the body alive.
To multiply itself.

However, the human soul, in addition
to the above, also has other functions
i.e. mental powers
in the form of sense, perception, recognition,
recall, imagination, spatial and
ego consciousnesses,
desires, emotions and conduct.
Furthermore, the human
soul is biological,
cognitive, emotive and
originative in its functions.

This constructive power of evolution,
which
is inherited from the process of evolution,
is the circuit of bringing into
being ever-evolving
species, thus resulting in man.

The emergence of man reveals the character
of the evolutionary process. ....
Human beings have the capacity to discover
some truths, to actualize
some elements
of justice and compassion in their
social life, similarly,
to appreciate and create beauty.

Truth and goodness are the
conditions for the preservation
and strengthening
of the constitution of the soul.

If the human souls indulges
in falsehoods and evil conduct,

they harm the constructive
power of the soul,
which sustains his or her being,
and if he persists
in falsehoods and black conduct,
the constructive power of his
soul is completely lost,
since there is no power of the soul
left to sustain the body,
both the soul and the body
come to be 'water under the bridge'.

Psychology of Sublime Life

Devatma is a soul,
which literally means 'above
and beyond worldly malaise',
which otherwise intervenes in the life
of a common man right from the
birth itself...........

Normally, a person inherits the values and vices
and lives with them
throughout his or her life.
However, it is near impossible to overcome
these bonds of carnal love and attachment to curses,
such as greed, etc.
Thus, it is necessary for society to
seek out souls who can be weighed
like this; an example of such an
individual is Sri Satyanad Agnihotri.

He successfully crossed the limits of lower loves
.... was able to develop his potential
by loving truth, hating untruth and inheriting
characters, as described by the evolutionary process.
This can be measured in such a way in that only
ethics should be the outcome so that
the society could be led in a truly social way.

Love of truth and goodness in Devatma
stands for a new dimension of psychology.
This advocates that all thoughts and conducts
are determined by the principle of truth and goodness.
This is in contrast to human nature,
which gravitates towards a love of pleasures
for the determination of thoughts translating into actions.

Throughout religious books,
historical accounts, there is a fact
that even the best
of altruistic men can fall victim to a weakness
of flesh or ego.
For example, many saints and sages have been
trapped by satanic forces due to a lack of such virtues,
as advocated by Devatma.
Therefore, sages could not break from the
hedonistic psychology that led them into
untruth and evil.
In fact, they could not practice
what they preached because their love
for truth was not 'completely' developed,
and the inheritance of satan
dawned heavily upon them,
thereby nurturing in them
a bent of mind for these temptations.

On the other hand, Devatma developed his inherited
virtues of character and could successfully
water not only a love for truth
but also a hate for the
lower temptations........
Such is his philosophy,
as enshrined in his autobiography
in such a 'rainbow'
that his followers are proud of.

Psychic forces of love of truth

When a soul evolves all-round psychic forces of love for truth, it:

•

Develops a concern to explore and assimilate
truth by establishing its contact
with a different kingdom of Nature,
which is an inexhaustible source
of useful knowledge.
It illuminates his soul,
equipping it with a greater ability to evolve truth.

•

Illuminates others in the light of truth
with which he rejoices himself,
proving prestige and dignity
of truth to the soul in touch.

Psychic forces of complete hatred for untruth

When a soul evolves complete hatred for falsehood:

•

It strengthens itself to give up
all that appears mythical,
which hinders discovery of truth
in different forms of Nature.
He will not entertain or support
whatever he recognizes to be mythical
that betrays the soul-illuminating
light and the high ideal of life;

•

It exerts according to his capacity
to set free the myth-ridden souls

with the true light emanating from his personality.

Psychic forces of a complete love of goodness

When a soul evolves a complete love for goodness:

-

It develops a complete concern and strength
to understand whatever is auspicious
and upholds it; and

-

It tries to actualize the part of Nature.

Psychic forces of a complete hatred for evil

A soul that has evolved complete hatred for evil:

-

It is beyond the access of any
vulgar activity,
and does not damage the
peaceful existence of Nature;

-

It impresses upon others with
his understanding of the things in the
right perspective to abstain from dark activities,
and harming nature to any existence.

According to the philosophy of Devatma,
only he can impart the scientific wisdom
of the soul-life,
who himself passes through
these tests.

To bear witness to higher truths
about the soul,
a sublime life is imperative,
in addition to a keen intellect.........
Without the sublime life,
there can be no light to notice higher truths
about the soul..........
This invaluable and supreme light enhanced
In Devatma day by day.
Hitherto,

1. This sublime life (of love of truth and goodness and hatred of untruth and evil).
2. The invaluable light produced by the sublime life.
3. The complete love for scientific method.
4. The most essential knowledge of the processes of evolution and devolution
were my total equipment for
study and research of soul-life.

Thus, Devatma is a competent authority to
study the origin, nature and destiny
of the human soul
while utilizing scientific methodology.

The House Where Nobody Lives

It is necessary
Not a 'call of time'
to caution the readers
that it is not the life-sketch
of a great man,
a noble soul, a high-minded saint,
an idealistic mahatma, a glorious mystic,
in one word of a perfect human being.

It is the 'life-sketch' of a religious genius
He founded a naturalism religion,
divergent in species from the theistic,
absolutistic or spiritualistic religions of the world.

The world of religion up to
his time has been
polytheistic, theistic, atheistic, spiritualistic,
and humanistic in its system
of thought, and humanistic in its
system of practice.

He offers a 'new spurt' in religious evolution,
build with complete commitment
to scientific temper and method

in untiring efforts to discover human nature
and its destiny.
His findings of evolutionary naturalism
offer no loopholes for easy deliverance
from human slavery
to passions and freedom into life
of light and salvation.
It was the pious bath of life.
His scriptures can be taken as books in science.
Philosophy and life are the concave and
convex of a person.
Such unique religion of absolute
excellence is reflection
of his unique life of absolute excellence.

It invites utmost curiosity to read it,
to rejoice being dazzled by it,
to realize in it most valuable fulfillment
of one's destiny.
It was a rational contemplation over imagination.

Life and philosophy of Devatma completely
broke away from
all classical religions
and established naturalistic
religions of Dev Dharma through study of the
value aspect of the human soul,
in the context of biological study and
the conditions of its life and death through
empirical methods.

If the reader is free from bondage to ancient scriptures
and is committed to scientific truth,
he will magnificently relish with abundant delight,
noticing the new horizons

of truth regarding the soul presented by him.

The literature of Devatma depicts
most graphically
the inner evolution of life and truth in the life
of the narrator,
it offers treasure house of truths in Nature,
human soul and human destiny discovered by Devatma.
Every great religious founder claims
some excellence for himself which distinguishes him
from mankind.
There is nothing wrong
about it for the founder
claims by his excellence the allegiance
of mankind for their destiny.

He attributed his special excellences
to natural conditions and creative renewal
of the process of evolution.

He came to reconstruct religion without
a supernatural God, heaven, and hell.
It was an aspect of the perfection of life.

He accepted the natural world as
studied by science
as the only reality
and his birth and excellence as much
explicable by natural conditions
as other events.

Since,
He has described his superior genius without
reference to Almighty,
the reader might mistake him as another

human being,
however exalted, talking too much about himself.

It is not taken as egotism when
Jesus Christ says: "I and Father are one" or "I am God."
Or when he says: "I am the way, the truth, and the life."

Therefore,
we must not commit the sin to think
of Devatma as egotistic when he says,
"I am alone the founder and teacher of true
religion and the
one true light and power for soul welfare."
What is that distinguishes the psychology
of Devatma
from the rest of mankind,
including the founders
of major religions?

The development of the gestalt of eight constituents
of the feeling of love of truth
and the eight constituents of 'Vairagya'
for untruth unknown to mankind.
Devatma has encountered the highest excellences
of spirit.
His altruistic (moral virtues) sprouted/opened
its feathers
from love of goodness,
whereas the human altruistic feelings
are motivated
by love of pleasure.

Human altruistic feelings are deprived of purity,
Comprehensiveness and depth
and are disposed to deviate into

untruth and evil.
Devatma's altruistic feelings were
free from all these defects
for they had their perennial motivation
in love of goodness and love of truth.

Human altruism is hedonistic
whereas Devatma's altruism is
philosophic in character,
to put it in the language of Plato.
The psychology of love of truth and goodness
And hatred
for untruth and evil
developed a life of light and power
called Dev Jiwan
which enabled him to 'seek truth'
about his own life and about the nature
and destiny of the human soul.

His light and power have
the potency to deliver mankind
from bondage of untruth
and evil,
and cultivate in him the
life of altruistic excellence.

The life and teachings of Devatma
open the gates
for the reader.
It is a new legend of spiritual life,
in the history of the earth.

Let us consider Devatma's description of the growth
and development
of inner spiritual genius
in a positive way for religious enjoyment and edification.

Aristotle rightly points out that "the
highest object of contemplation for the Master
is to recognize that the highest reality
and the supreme truth of the universe exists within him".

Devatma's presentation of himself in literature
as the highest unveiling of the process of evolution
offers understanding
of the process of evolution
which lights up the whole universe.

It was inevitable for Devatma
As a lover of the highest truth
to contemplate on his life,
for it was the supreme truth of the universe.

We feel blessed in reading his life
and teaching for we become
witness to the highest glory of the universe.

As the sun supremely favours us
with light to behold its splendour,
Devatma's literature also blesses us
with light and strength to bear witness
to the highest life which has emerged
in the world through evolution.

It is an evolution –within- an -evolution.

For the Sake of Evolution
and Harmony

The Mission of Devatma
Betokens
More than
A zealous social reformer,
a great political leader
and
a devoted scientist.

It is a 'life vow'
....
put up with
'Solitary reaper grandeur'
from rest of the human ideals.

It is a 'refined walk of life'
that liquefied
with the purpose of
evolution in nature
and
promises the highest evolution
of man's soul
that is

the greatest realization
of the goodness of nature.

Newton, Galileo, Darwin, Freud
in the world of science;
Lincoln, Shri Vidyasager,
Raja Ram Mohan Roy
in the social field;
Mazzini, Lenin, Gandhi
in the political field-
these are the great names,
Who connote
A boundless dignity
and solace to humanity_____
a 'movement of reformation' wet with
a benign goal of life.

Their contributions are
monuments in the sphere of greatness
and humanity,
they twinkled the 'hat of glory'
therefore,
We bow to their great sacrifices,
gigantic courage
and Master Intellects.

They have fought against
unripe beliefs, social tyrannies
and political injustices.

Henceforth, each one of them has fought
against some particular falsehoods,
some particular social evils
or some particular political injustices,
Even when these particular falsehoods

125

and evils are removed,
mankind's root problems remain as unsolved as before.
When one falsehood or social evil is removed
Another 'inappropriate fierceness enters'
As long as the human disposition/frame of mind
or nature
which produces falsehood and evils
is not handled and tackled
It is not easy to solve problems
Humanity's goal will not be achieved
in this 'wasteland of vanity'
What is to be improved
is man's nature which is tending towards falsehood
and evil.
To know human nature,
to discover its ideal and to provide the means for the realization
of the ideal is the highest service of Devatma.

The mission of Devatma is to produce religious life in human beings
and to leave living seeds of it in the spiritual world.
At the time of taking his life-vow,
Devatma said: Evil-loving souls have made a terrible hell of this world
by their falsehoods and various evils.
They are dangerous and have given a high place to irreligiousness
which has produced various kinds of injustices.
It is necessary for me to make all the required sacrifices of my wealth,
reputation, superiority, respect, comforts, health, and power.
For this most difficult task of changing these souls from their evil state
and to produce religious life in them.

The religion which Devatma wishes to bring includes
pearls of wisdom.
It removes all kinds of sins and crimes,
Makes individuals sweet, true, reliable,
and worthy in various relations so that their mutual dealings

could produce goodness in all aspects of their lives
Creates such a state of knowledge and higher life in human beings,
the possession of which makes any human being capable of doing the
greatest good
not only to human beings but also to the animal, vegetable and the
material world.
What a blessed mission!
The very thought of it staggers and stuns us.
It makes one drop the ball to think of what is implied in this statement.

Each word and term is pregnant with such wealth of meaning
and treasures of highest truths that at the present stage of human soul,
it is not even possible to put in words what the most beneficial results
and what kinds of highest good will be realized with the fulfillment of
this mission.
How uphill a task it is to remove a false belief in a person?
How tremendously difficult it is to free a man from a particular sin
which has directed his physically evil consequences.
Man loves his beliefs and habits of action more dearly than his children
and himself.
To touch them is to touch the tender spot in a wound.
It takes the combined energy of thousands to remove a particular false
belief
or a particular evil custom.
What sacrifice of wealth, reputation, comfort
and even life has been made by scientists, social reformers,
and political emancipators for the removal of a particular false belief,
an evil practice and a political injustice!
Why was all this terrible sacrifice needed?
Because the human soul is a slave to the pleasure
it derives from its particular beliefs and habits.
Man is not prepared to sacrifice the pleasure without putting
in the stoutest/strongest opposition.
Man's governing principle of life is pleasure and not truth.
This tale does not end here.

The masses of mankind have considered pleasure of low-loves of self
and body as their ideal.
Their pleasures are not even altruistic. We can almost count on fingers
those great men who loved
and lived for one or another kind of altruistic pleasures.

Had human nature made truth and goodness
as its governing and guiding principle,
we would not have needed all these sacrifices of scientists, social
reformers
and political emancipators.
All these sacrifices are a price to evil and falsehood-loving nature.

If the great minds have felt that it is easier to lift a mountain
on a fingertip than to remove a particular false belief
or particular social or political evil,
what must be the nature of the assignment
which is to transmute human nature from its love of evil and falsehood
and to make it love altruism and true knowledge!

And if it is noble to fight against particular beliefs
and particular evils,
Thence
It is noblest and highest mission to fight with evil
and falsehood-loving disposition of man
and that is the greatest and highest walk of life related to Devatma
This 'pious bath of life'
This handicraft of Devatma is one with the purpose of evolution.

Nature is striving to realize the highest virtues
Through higher forms of life and by producing higher harmony
based on truth and goodness.
Therefore,

When Devatma knitted his slot/day gig/ province
to fight
with evil and falsehood in human soul,
He was at that moment,
realizing nature's immutable evolutionary purpose.

The Message: A Matter of Life and Death

'The message of Devatma'
is the recent chapter of revolutionary truths
in the domain of the soul,
an absolutely new ideal for human beings
Invariably
a call to a fresh way of life.
This intrinsically bound, unparalleled mission,
yearning for the highest sort of
revolutionary message

Unquestionably
It is unique
Yes
It is the garden house of pious incense.
It includes a variety of perceptions
about the life force of the soul:

1. The soul is the most fundamental reality in human personality.

The soul is not only an origin for the body
in the sense that it caters, constructs,
contains,

and keeps it alive but also in the sense
That
it is singularly responsible
for the sublime experiences in the world
of truth, aesthetics and morality.

2. The soul is subject to its eternal and immutable laws being a part of nature.

The human soul,
like other versions of the nature is subject
of transformation
i.e., the first is evolutionary,
and the second is devolutionary.
The latter manifests itself in harming itself
and Others and is linked with
the evolution of nature.

This changing by the way of degenerating,
thus devolutionary change gradually diseases itself
by losing its constructive power,
by proceeding itself simultaneously towards
its extinction.

3. The human soul is pushed back by low-loves when it seeks its gratification in low- hates.

Low-loves such as SELF which are associated
with power, face, lust,
and undue attachment,
then blind faith creates in unison such a negativity
for the soul which leads
towards the lowest levels of existence.
Had the human soul not made
such pleasure as his ultimate?

Had it not been a slave to them?
It would not have followed evil and falsehood
while leaning towards spiritual darkness
and to become incapable of seeing truths of the spiritual.
This is irrespective of the worldly riches of a person,
intelligence, literary achievements, and political powers.
This equally covers saints and sages
or let us include the God incarnation himself.

4. If a human soul wants to progress and evolve it
must get rid of the disease, and must aver for the supreme goal of its life.

True knowledge and consciousness
about the organism of the soul discriminates diseases,
their true causes from the way of salvation therefore
Mere evolution of altruistic feelings cannot ensure
complete evolution of human soul
because no mass of altruistic feelings can take
the place of soul-consciousness.
It is also not free from all low-loves and low-hates
because the light of altruistic feelings cannot make us
soul-consciousness.
Therefore,
Undoubtedly,
It is the highest blessing as well as highest privilege
to have soul-consciousness
and to obtain living contact
with Devatma on the basis of unshakeable faith,
reverence, gratitude, and attraction
for Devatma's sublime influences.
Henceforth,
His grand message cannot be accustomed
in my language
but his memorable sayings get the measure of:

I. O man! You are not only body but soul also.
This body of your will be dispersed in dust one day.
In fact, soul is the most fundamental and primary thing,
in the being of man,
and there is greater good for man than to safeguard
and evolve his soul.

II. How pitiable and sad in the condition
of that person
who is absolutely unaware, ignorant
and in darkness about the being of his soul,
its organism, its degrading disease
and about the
law of its devolution and evolution
and who is lost in one or another false belief
in the name of religion
and being ignorant
of the various causes of soul degradation,
he himself becomes
the source of his soul-degradation
and death.

III. No kind of pleasure can be a human ideal.
When love of pleasure –whatever kind it may be –
enslaves a human being,
or to put it in another way,
when a human being becomes slave to it,
then it becomes inevitable for him to go
the way of various kinds of
harms or evils
and to love various kinds of falsehoods
and various kinds of other harmful acts.

IV. The various low-loves and their consequent low hates
in human soul,
based on man's craving for pleasure,
result in evil thoughts and actions.
True salvation consists in getting freedom
from all these evil thoughts
and actions.
True salvation consists in getting freedom
from all these evil thoughts and actions
and of the dirt and degradation of human soul
caused by these evil thoughts and actions.
If a human being cannot continuously serve some
living or non-living existence inspired
by some high altruistic feeling
and cannot come to love such service,
then no such characteristics develops
in his soul on which the constructive
force of his soul can feed for growth
and by which he can protect himself
from degradation.

You must know and realize the truth
that the safety and growth of your soul
depends on
disinterested service of others.

V. It is the highest privilege
and greatest good of man
to recognize the relation of his soul with
the divine life of Devatma
and to become capable of establishing
this spiritual relation with him.

It is only by getting sublime light of Devatma
that deserving persons can achieve true

knowledge about soul, its diseases and degradation,
and
Its most horrible consequences,
Related to salvation and higher evolution.
Devatma's sublime light is a universal light
that twinkles with truth and goodness.

Wonder of Wonders

Devatma's 'life-vow'
was only pregnant with the promises of the incredible
and extraordinary step
in the irresistible march of the inevitable process of evolution
Related to a new quality of life
where human beings need unshakable faith,
unconquerable determination,
ever-replenishing enthusiasm
and inexhaustible patience,
for the devotion and dedication to the service
of the process of evolution.

The false coins of miracles are most prevalent
in the religious world
That have driven out of view
the true miracles of nature and man.
These miracles have the following defects.
They are against the fundamental
and immutable laws of nature
Therefore, these are absolutely and complete false.

Even if,
for logic,
they are supposed to be true,

they do not frame
evergreen productive goodness
For example
Cursing a tree into a fruitless one,
Yet
Metamorphoses of a woman into a stone,
Transmuting a stick into a snake,
Transforming water into wine,
are out and out miracles
from which evils set feet.

These extraordinary changes are taking place
into physical world only which has lowest value
rather than ethical
or spiritual world.
Even if they claim,
for logic,
to produce goodness,
therefore,
this goodness is good for nothing
it is the lowest aura in the route of values,
such as physical values, mental values,
and moral values.

These religious leaders can never be better
'avant-garde'
to bring about anything
from these miracles
which are not being performed
at better level
by other mortals.

With the warm assistance from doctors,
in hospitals,
how many people are cured of their blindness,

Similarly,
who are apparently dead
are being brought back to consciousness
they are
unmistakably
cured into healthy individuals.
Again,
the sweet
which is supposed to be fallen from tree
is not better than the sweet-sellers
so and so on.

These miracles are non-repeatable incidents
and not performed regularly.
They support to blur the vision
that spirituality consists in freedom
from consciousness,
love of altruism,
and above all
love of truth and goodness.

'Miracles are those new evolutionary facts
which come into existence
under special conditions
With special methods and special powers.'

A true miracle is not a single isolated event
which comes into existence only once
then disappears into nothingness

Man who is one of nature's greatest miracles,
has helped the evolution
of nature in various directions.

Through the agency of great scientists,
philosophers, master artists
and moral geniuses,
true wonders took place.

In the physical world there are beautiful rivers, forests,
and great architectural buildings
such as the Taj Mahal.

In the plant world, new fruits, beautiful flowers
and vegetables come into existence
which are so attractive to look at
and so sweet to taste.

In the animal world, the beautiful horse,
the innocent looking cows overflowing with milk,
the faithful dog with wonderful
new qualities also come into being

In the human world, ambitious personalities, philosophers,
poets, master artists, great scientists, philanthropic, altruistic
and moral geniuses
took place after plenty years of evolutions.
The ever-growing sweet aroma of evolution is continuous
and continual conviction
Devatma has brought unique wondrous transitions
That
Certainly
inspires awe and wonder.

They constitute
the greatest manna from heaven in nature.
He has so miraculously changed some human beings
In a 'refined way'
that

they have become standing surprising events/miracles
for all who knew them before.

What a prodigy!
What a stroke of luck!

Debauchees have been
distorted into protectors of women's honour,
Dishonest dealers have been changed into trusted guardians
of the helpless widows' property.
Men who delighted in killing animal life
just for sport
and lust of taste,
have grown to be so morally courageous
as to forbid hunting within their own estates
and to refuse meat to the highest official authority.

For further knowledge
they have not only stopped being disloyal
to their wives by violating other women's honour,
but instead
they have developed true respect for women's personality.
It is not only that persons have given up dishonesty
Henceforth,
They have developed a hatred for it.

O for this rarity!
For this warm windfall!
We are overwhelmed!

What a marvel! What an aestheticism!
to transform love
for gross evils into hate for them!

What a good future!
What a revelation!
Amazing! Stunning!

Further transformation of human nature
has been brought about
how to be an ideal in different relations?

Does an average son behold the true relation in which
he stands to his parents?
Or does a son see parents in their true aspect in relation to him?
Not at all! Those rare children
who have seen parents as parents
have become idols of mankind.

In Indian history, there is only one Sharavan kumar-
an ideal son
who saw his duty of life to take his blind parents
from place to place
and spend his life in discharge
of this duty.

What a grace!
What a glory!
While dying, he had one wish and will to his murderer,
i.e. to fulfil his duty to his parents.

Devatma has produced hundreds of sons
like Shravans.
He has turned ungrateful children,
callous to the ills and ailments of their parents
into the greatest solace for their parents.

How many brothers are able to 'feast eyes on'
their true relation to their brothers?

Instead of relation of mutual respect,
mutual harmony, mutual service,
and mutual adjustment and accommodation,

We have enmity,
ill-will, fights, murders, jealousy
among mutual relations.
Words are 'speechless'
In this sketch
Linked to the 'plethora of maladjustment'

Devatma has converted
Aurangzeb sort of brothers
into Lakshamans
in such a degree
so that
property decisions,
instead of being dragged to courts,
have been solved by postcards.

Therefore,
miracle is not the word for such 'rolling punches'
Devatma has diversified
intensely
selfish persons into altruistic souls
who live for the good of others.
What a metamorphoses!
What a blessing!
It is more than a miracle.

Higher to these never-ceasing miracles
is the creation of soul-consciousness in human souls.

The whole humanity was in absolute darkness
about soul-consciousness.

The human soul
'wept and made sad sounds'
for salvation from the pains
of soul-diseases
produced
by man's inordinate and dominating
love of his own pleasure.

Therefore,
they found no satisfactory way.
Some deserving/fit souls have been provided
soul consciousness through Devatma.
We have some persons who think,
feel and act in terms of the soul well-being.

These highest modulations
in the human soul
are beyond the grasp of understanding
and therefore, beyond appreciation.

Therefore,
the autobiographical sketches
of these persons with soul-consciousness
have been read
like romances from religious world.
Devatma's miracles are the true
and the greatest achievement of nature
Because
They do not contradict the law of nature of human soul.
The miraculous 'readjustments'
brought about
by Devatma
definitely and invariably
direct the individual soul better than before
These miracles are not isolated events

once performed and never repeated.
These are knitting frames of continuous voyage
These true miracles are the repercussions
of true insight into the nature,
and organism of human soul,
its diseases and laws of its health and diseases.
Invariably
A perfect salvation.

Schedule of a New Species
with New Vision

(Schedule of Master)

While establishing a bond
with world, an incredible relation
of me, living in the condition of awareness and 'consciousness'
I have been deeply dipped in whatever works
These are:
For my life-vow, Dev Samaj and 'parlokvasi' (dead souls)
Relatives
I perform morning many prayers
Excited by one or another higher feeling
In relation of world's one or another
Department 'kept on thinking' and viewing

The numerous perceptions
And I fulfill works in an order in a systematic way
and catch other's hands to write it
Create/write any book, etc.
Work in the relation of creating 'Dev-Shastra'

I use the requisite proof of any book or suitable book necessary in
my any essay that is in press

I take care of my written book and to publish it again according to
suitable time
Editing monthly magazine
Occasionally, for one weekly letter, I hand over some writings
To edit society person's various essays
For the revolution of near and dear one's (as their deliverer) any of low
activity
I develop in them
Any of high feeling or force
To create councils related to education life-vow and 'sangat' (good
company)
And to raise his light and potential to everyone present with his sermons
While enlightening them with his knowledge and wisdom
An effort of their true salvation
Of the heart
'a freedom' from illiteracy and disloyalty

To show them their heart's low force
and showing them any curse, salvage them
and in relation to higher life, keep on noticing any glimpses of
aestheticism
have struggle to raise in them high love
To meet family member and local outsider assistants
And communicate with them about the 'welfare/benevolent conversation'

To study welfare books and newspapers

For the protection of his serviceable body, toilet, bathing, food rest and
medicine exercise

A contemplation while going outside for exercise
For 'various animals and numerous brands of trees'
And plants' protection
(noticing and thinking on their subject
and by conversation) to create his relation with physical

and other world to fulfill any service with hand
Have a prayer for Dev Samaj's main Life-workers
Have a 'view point' and contemplation in various works of Dev Samaj
To order letters related to the topic of DEVSHASTRA'S various performances

To organize Dev Samaj's council or in their relation handing over requisite subject
Amalgamation with employees to inform them various sorts of suitable works
Take a route outside working areas
Time to time, have a look and care of theirs' work
Building a council of sermons, etc.

To make enquiry of society's finance
A look at requisite Dev Samaj Parishad and officer's papers
and getting sign on essential papers
To excavate schemes of large social festivals _____and propagations_____
preparing 'a system of works'
And maintain requisite arrangements

According to the experience of every year, in relation of social structure and source –system,
Keep on maintaining essential things

To write and modernize them
While seeing any of diseased one
Have an eye of 'take care' of him

To make for him requisite and auspicious system
Cleanliness of home and places related to Dev-Ashram
Renovation, decoration and plants (take care of) protection
Time to time schemes of any new home's creation and its transmutation

Having a thought to fulfill its arrangement
With entire devotion

To make prayer for any wretched or diseased one in obstacles in family
clan
or other short or small bodily related sorrow at day night
Repeatedly remembering
The letter (reached through post or any sort) in abundance
to read them and writing an 'answer' in their area in suitable way
Appropriate (proper looking after) shelter in relation of any mishap_____
its remedy and essential discernment

To take care of his houses' finance
In living room of his family clans
A drive of cleanliness, renovation, decoration of things and protection
of home plants
Having knowledge of family members' various needs
Fulfilling them and take assistance to fulfill them
Knowledge of dependent animals' condition
for the removing of tiredness and heart's activeness
having in the group of shelter of any amusing talk of any type
Or occasionally
suitable singing and listening to instrument whilst body's harsh tiredness
Standing or walking, a brain wind_____
any benevolent activity
for whose auspiciousness and wellbeing
I have adopted my prime welfare and unique but harsh difficult life-vow
out of them while suffering from anyone's unsuitable behaviour or curse
Torture and affliction
I am pierced and pierced

With the tempest of heart attack
Invariably, such a super terrible and unbearable tortures
That cannot be described in words, for its solution 'catching the thread
of struggle' etc. etc

As a repercussion, as long as I have not been in condition of complete
sleep
or unconscious stage
by any physical disease or sorrow
at that level my soul has been continuous in aforesaid 'one or another
work' equally.

The Fire Test of Piousness

Actions
have an internal and external side.
The internal side of actions is
influenced by his man's passions.
Certainly,
Every action is executed by some feelings.
One aesthetic action can be undertaken with different feelings.
Some assistants
work to please their boss
or
to attain a promotion.
However,
there are some
who consider it to be their duty
or they have an interest in their work.
The external aspect of an action is the same
Even then
it is executed by different internal feelings.

This is like a witchcraft of various things,
A magnetism,
Hocus pocus of feelings,
Where one should have to select 'a pendant of piousness'
Feeling which guides

the action is the basis of evaluation of the action.
The same behaviour can show whether the person
is of high moral values
or ordinary values or low values of money.
If we accept the fact that feelings
evaluate a person's life,
then,
it is important to understand the nature and working of feelings.
The nature of feelings is
that a person wishes to satisfy them.
These are sovereign
and a person yearns for them
to be satisfied directly or indirectly.
The psychology
Also
Provides evidence
that a person satisfies his feelings
consciously or unconsciously.
Besides, different feelings
are found in the sub-conscious mind
of a person and he endeavours to gratify them
with his behaviour and actions.
The interplay of dreamland,
And wakeful moments,
Cherishes boundless desires.
One noble act gratifies many feelings.
When we serve others
the feeling of serving others is satisfied.
While serving others,
one tries to save money,
thus, the feeling of miserliness is satisfied.
When we help a girl
Then
Not the feeling of serving others is fulfilled

Henceforth,
the pleasure of the company of the opposite sex is also fulfilled.

It is physical thirst among low pleasures,
The very seed of lust.
In administration, the feeling of discipline
as well as the feeling of ruling others
is gratified.
If we scold children,
Through and through,
the feeling of welfare and the feeling of cruelty are satisfied.
If we realize
that our various categories of feelings influence
each other
and can be gratified by one action,
we can understand the difference
in the internal aspect of behavior of an ordinary man
and
the noble behaviour of DEVATMA.
We,
the human beings
have both virtues and vices.

Men have virtues like gratitude, respect, and service for others.
They also love justice,
are logical, dutiful, and disciplined.
Besides
these virtues,
they have vices which incite them
to indulge in activities harmful to other human beings or animals.
It is a callous and deteriorating portrait of mankind.
Some accept bribes out of greed,
some steal
and some indulge in adultery and cheat customers.
Some men are unfaithful to their life-partner

and outrage the modesty of other women or young girls.
There are others
who attempt to justify unsuitable actions towards their families
and indulge in undesirable social behaviour.
We attempt to gratify our low feelings of ego, selfishness, false pride,
hatred, jealousy, false beliefs.
These vulgar traits are low-hates
and low-loves
and do not allow a person to adopt the path of Truth and Aestheticism.
The route of moral values
Has been set aside
In the maze of low, destructible pleasures.
It is a woeful tale of wasteland.
Therefore,
Human beings
have not only good feelings
out and out,
but low-hates and low-loves also.
These low-hates and low-loves
adversely affect the good feelings.
The feeling of ego is stronger
than
other feelings of low-loves and low-hates.
Ego vanishes the tender petals of love and reverence.

DEAVATMA is free from low-loves and low-hates.
He has been absolutely free of evil feelings of jealousy,
Cruelty, and ego.
Besides,
his personality was such that these evils could not take birth in him.
In a pious plant
No vulgarity
Can frame its existence,
Never, never.
Thus,

there is a psychological difference in the feelings of Devatma and mankind.

The external aspect of the behaviour of Devatma and mankind may be the same on some level but,

there is a basic difference.

Man's good behaviour may be guided by low-loves and low-hates.

In contrast,

Devatma's smallest activity is also absolutely full of pious feelings.

He is the garden house of goodness and piousness.

The Only Holy Approach:
Completeness

Assume,

that individuals are free from all vulgar feelings
Will there be a disparity between humans' and the internal difference
of good behaviour of Devatma?
There are many incompleteness in the feeling of humans, the altruistic
feelings of a human:

- Incomplete in the sight of calculation or incomplete in the
  evaluation.
- Very brief in comprehensiveness or limited in expansion
- Lack of appropriate depth
- Lack of direction and balance in the structure of pure feeling
  towards the respective good qualities.

Devatma's sublime feelings
are liberal from these four scarcities.
Therefore,
Comprehensiveness of his sublime feelings is complete.
The depth of his sublime feelings is complete.
There
is wholeness of structure in his sublime feelings.
Therefore,

there is an 'attribute of wholeness' in his sublime behaviour
where our positive behaviour hold
the finger of the curse of incompleteness.
He is perfection within perfection!
Man's good behaviour is imperfect
as a nominee of pure feelings.
In contrast,
Devatma's pure feelings are complete
and free from such abnormalities,
they have comprehensive quality of depth and evaluation.
In brief, there is not only difference in human soul,
Unmistakably.
Devatma is blessed with
The purity of feelings
And
There is
A difference of comprehensiveness
regarding the internal feelings also.

If man's good behaviour is motivated
by only positive feelings
then
they will be lower to Devatma's sublime behaviour.
In the structure of man's positive emotions,
there are vulgarities of calculations,
comprehensiveness,
depth and structure
from which Devatma's sublime feelings
are completely liberal.
It was not possible 'for his love of goodness'
that he might neglect any of the goodness.
His love of goodness
with his positive structure
provided him with
attributes of calculation,

comprehensiveness, depth, and structure, making him whole.
In his good behaviour
There
Has been the attribute of completeness,
Something which
man's good behaviour is devoid of.
Certainly,
The land of patience and
Harmony
can produce the fruits of goodness and truth.

The Door to Bliss and Beauty

Assume,
the altruistic feelings of an individual are complete in numbers,
comprehensiveness, depth, and structure
even then
in the structure of altruistic feelings
there has been the tendency of untruth
though it does not take the shape of behaviour
but
it is present in the shape of thought
henceforth
in the structure of altruistic feelings
there is this minor ugliness.
The structural foundation of Devatma's sublime feelings
is love of truth and goodness,
that's why
there is not a 'room left in his positive emotional structure'
for filthy views of untruth and inauspiciousness.

There are no clouds of untruth and inauspiciousness in his positive
emotions.
In man's good behaviour's motivational altruistic feelings,
if there is less mixture of low
feelings
and the calculation

of altruistic feelings in great proposition, i.e.
comprehensiveness, depth and structure,
the continue to be aesthetic.
Low powers in less degree
in a person
implies
that
he can obtain the emotions of altruistic feelings.
But
Because
for man there is an ideal limitation
to get rid of lower emotions
and to obtain all altruistic feelings' complete structure,
so that
the positive behaviour of a person may be aesthetic in
a less or more proportion.
In his positive emotions,
there is no mixture of any shapeup
and invisible low-love
or the emotion of ego.
His sublime feelings are completely pure.
In spite of this,
in his structure,
there is no deprivation of altruistic feelings.
There is no negativity in the comprehensiveness, depth, and structure
of his altruistic feelings.
They are aesthetic.
His good behaviours are enlightening with the aesthetic structure of
altruistic feelings.
The proper match of his good behaviours and positive emotions makes
a supremely aesthetic structure.
The sublime behaviour of Devatma is replete with complete beauty.
This connotes:
"He is well-packed module of Altruism."
When any good action is

Performed
with any one altruistic feeling
thence,
it is less valuable to altruistic feeling
that might be done with two or three altruistic feelings.
The numbering of man's higher feeling is limited to one or two higher
feelings only;
Therefore, there is not the beauty in our good actions
such like a rainbow.

From the external side, there may be similarities
between human and Devatma's good actions
but
from the inside,
there is a huge difference, much like the divide between land and sky.
There is a complete aestheticism
like 'rainbow'
in the good actions of Devatma
and human is deprived of this feature of good action.
Therefore,
He is well-formed
properly
who's numbering of parts is complete,
the development of parts is complete
and
all parts are mutually balanced in proportion.
There is dearth in man's positive structure
In the area of
numbering of altruistic
Feelings.
There is incompleteness in men
and the mutual balance of these altruistic feelings does not reside
in man.
In addition to this,
along with man's altruistic feelings,

his low feelings are
also
mutually linked.
Completely,
the shape created in man's altruistic feelings and good behaviour
shows
that
its beauty is the amalgamation of the beauty of a common low class.
The numbering/calculation of Devatma's sublime structure,
comprehensiveness, depth and structure is complete;
through and through,
the balance of these feelings is complete.
Unquestionably
It is complete.
As a repercussion,
the structure
of his
sober/benign behaviour
and complete positive shape
is supremely beautiful and close to the heart
Yes,
Symmetrically magnificent.

The Pulse of the Foundation

The foundation of Devatma's sublime behaviour is the love of truth and goodness, and man's supreme level of action is based on altruistic love. Altruistic love does not form the whole of higher feelings.

Having one higher feeling means the absence of other higher feelings. For the love of goodness, the absence of any altruistic feeling is intolerable and immoral. Love of goodness is emotional to all spiritual goodness. Therefore, it develops all the sublime feelings in Devatma so that no goodness is left behind.

One altruistic feeling is not only devoid of other altruistic feelings but rather it accompanies other sorts of inauspiciousness. So, with altruistic feelings, low-love and low hatreds can live together. There are low feelings that can also accompany higher feelings; thus, there is a mixture of lower feelings in man's good behaviour.

However, with the love of goodness, there is no possibility of low-love and low hatreds. The reason is this love of goodness is not devoid of any goodness. Therefore, it cannot bear any inauspiciousness. The love of goodness is an attraction and love for all goodness, and with the love of goodness there cannot live any lower love and lower hatred.

The basis of love of goodness is the supreme goodness of soul. The lover of goodness displays the same behaviour that might be the source of the supremacy of his soul, and thus makes the supremacy of soul an ideal. He measures the various behaviours to the extent that is he helpful in performing services to others. This attribute is not present in altruistic feelings – the parameter of their decision is only the essential and limited goodness, not the supreme goodness of soul.

If the altruistic feelings of an individual are established in the love of goodness, then humans should have a complete love for the goodness of soul. Further, if humans hold love for the supremacy of his soul, then this must be the motivation towards the precaution of the doing untrue and inauspicious behaviour, because untruthfulness and inauspicious behaviour are harmful to the soul.

In man, there is no love for the supreme goodness of the soul, so for any man who is a lover of pleasure, he himself cannot establish his higher feeling in the love of supremacy of soul, nor can he enslave them.

There is no trait in man to understand the supreme goodness of soul in itself, so while having altruistic feelings, he does not have scientific knowledge of his altruistic feelings. Only the supremacy of the soul can appreciate the necessity of positive feelings, grandeur, and appreciation of the beauty, and can show it in the soul's supreme law. Along with this, it can show that how higher feelings that connect with Devatma can allow the soul to reach its supreme condition. This spiritual stage enables us to revere the sublime beauty (Dev roop), which is beyond the reach of ordinary altruistic feelings.

Hence, only the lover of goodness can understand such altruistic feelings in a scientific way. Instead of perceiving such feelings in the shape of law and understanding, humans see their altruistic feelings only in the contour of incidents and attempt to understand them. Only the lover of truth can write the scientific book of altruistic feelings and can publish it in the laws of the soul's supreme goodness. In addition to higher feelings, there is a sublime light in Devatma that is absent from the altruistic behaviour of human beings; as such, the light of understanding is absent from human behaviour. Devatma sees higher feeling in the light of the supremacy of the soul, so there is a sublime light in his positive behaviour, to which the positive behaviour of humans is zero.

The love of goodness taught Devatma that the life of a soul depends on having a relationship with the four worlds, and this relation should be linked to the highest values of the soul. Devatma, with his love of goodness, created a relationship with the four worlds on the basis of the supremacy of the soul. Only the basis of the supremacy of the soul made the behaviour of these worlds' existences possible.

- The life of the lover of truth, Devatma, and his behaviour due to the establishment on soul's supremacy, have become important subjects of worship and love. The lover of truth and goodness, Devatma, has the eligibility of all goodness, so his life is the source of motivation and enthusiasm for all persons who possess positive eligibility. Nobody with a positive lifestyle can be the fountain of goodness, which Devatma only achieved because he has no eligibility to enhance positive energy.
- Not an eligibility to see higher feelings in the supremacy of soul in the shape of a law.
- He has those orders and prohibitions to establish a relation with four worlds but he has no capacity to provide them knowledge and education.

Therefore, man's good behaviour can be motivated from altruistic feelings only. He cannot cross this boundary himself, and he cannot situate his altruistic feelings in the supreme soul's goodness and love. Devatma's sublime feelings are situated in the supreme love of the soul. Devatma's motivators of sublime behaviour derive from the supreme soul and comprise goodness-related altruistic feelings. Whereas man's good behaviour carries the colour of altruistic feelings, Devatma's sublime behaviour is coloured in supreme goodness of soul.

From the Wave to the Cosmic Ocean: Subjectivity

If we assume that a human can free him or herself from all low feelings and develops all altruistic feelings, there will be a clear difference between his or her behaviour and Devatma's good behaviour. The reason is that the love of goodness does not equate to the completeness of altruistic feelings; thus, this is the ambivalent attribute of a new life.

One altruistic feeling has many aspects; its difference is because every altruistic man lays emphasis to his decision in the light of his supremacy of his predominate subjectivity of altruistic feelings. There is no rule left for him other than the supremacy to which he could decide right or wrong.

Every altruistic feeling and every part of altruistic feeling has the capacity to see only its own value. In addition to this, every altruistic feeling assumes its demand as a whole, because in front of him there has not a plethora of higher feelings and no aim above the feelings that could help him to prove the opposition of higher feelings or select them. Due to this limitation of man's higher feelings, according to philosopher Hegel, human life is a tragedy.

The higher decisions of a man are based on the self, not subjectivity. These decisions are based on selflessness, as our tastes are selfless.

For example, some cherish salty delicacies, while others prefer sweet dishes. Also, some people like Rasgulla in sweets, whereas others prefer Gulabjamun. The basis of such preferences are not the attribute of the subject but the feature of the nature of the experienced person. This liking is not subjective, but rather, based on the self.

The sublime feelings of Devatma do not lack this structure. His sublime feelings are the production of the love of goodness and Truth. These are complete in calculation, intensity and depth, with a fully balanced structure. Above this, their love of goodness in them produces the aesthetic attribute of neutrality. No altruistic feeling considers itself complete, as it is completely emotional for the truth of other emotions. On top of this, when there is a disparity in the values of these higher feelings or oppositions, then Devatma's love of truth becomes the law of their decision. Hence, where there is a curse of selfless in the altruistic nature of humans, Devatma's sublime behaviour is replete with subjective completeness. Where we are in the grip of our feelings, and what is accurate from the point of view of the subject, we forget that Devatma feeds higher feelings with the subject of correctness. Because humans have no traits of love of truth, he has no basis for decision-making, except for subjectivity in the opposition of the values of higher feelings, and he is separate from the behaviour. We hear people saying that he is more compassionate, meaning that he is compassionate where he should not be compassionate, where he should not be from the insight of subjectivity. In the nature of Devatma, no feeling shows more than excessive difference because he is under the feeling of love of truth, and is, therefore, completely subjective.

Truth: The Ultimate Value

Let us see whether Devatma's love of truth makes a difference in his positive structure from man's positive structure.

There is a part of myth in the altruistic nature of humans. The reason for this is that man's higher feelings bear the curse of prejudice. Take, for instance, the altruistic feeling of seeing and appreciating the attributes of others. We see and feel any other attribute in our devotion from the insight of beauty. This attribute touches our heart, but the same attribute of other people does not touch our heart. We do not feel any motivation to appreciate him. There are many reasons for this, though it is mainly due to our disparity with other person that we have a lower hatred for that person. In the same way, it is common that people from a particular religious society do not feel appreciation for any attribute of any other mentor of a religious society.

Much of the time, due to the absence of lower hatred, we behave in such a way. The reason for this is the bias for our devotion. We do not feel an intensity to appreciate other personality traits through poor tongue and voice, and we do not feel power in our pens, though both have the same qualities. When I behold only one attribute of appreciation to others, in addition to not praising them similarly and do not feel motivation, then I experience a limitation of seeing truth in my higher feeling. I have an eye for spotting this attribute – I see it in one person clearly, while in others there is only a faint presence. Thus, my emotion of seeing positive attributes is mythical. From the insight of a truth, any positive attribute in oneself should be held in its own truthful contour. The insight of truth cannot accept individual, social and caste differences. Thus, the lover of truth, Devatma, this mythical difference is not possible in his sublime emotions; thus, he sees and appreciates any positive attribute, and there are no individual, social or caste prejudices between him and his positive attributes. This is not a nature of the individual's higher feelings and it is not above from bias, for its foundation is not the love of truth.

Let us look at the second mythical difference in the higher feelings of humans: there can be enormous positive attributes in our one devotion, and their contours are good and healthy. Moreover, the method of walking and speaking is good, as well as the way of living. Humans are scholars and hold compassion for others. This emotion, which enables us to see the qualities of others, is not able to see every positive attribute. Let us assume I have an eligibility to appreciate physical attributes. In this condition, I am attracted towards my devotion's physical attributes but do not feel enthusiasm by knowing his or her other attributes on an intellectual plane. This mythical difference is the partial contour of our positive emotions. To see the others' emotion shows one sort of attributes, which is not the only quality that makes us compelled to be by his side.

Because of this, their reverence does not show others' positive attributes to the same extent. Most people behold compassion, and in this manner, they do not give them a place in heart by knowing other attributes on an intellectual plane. The demand of the love of truth is that every virtue should be seen in the light of truth. For example, soul-related virtues hold a higher position than other positive attributes; however, this does not mean that other positive attributes should be disregarded. The basis of Devatma's sublime feelings is the love of truth. He does not disregard any of goodness out of all goodness. In himself, he evolved all positive emotions of physical, mental, social and spiritual and provided its teaching.

The third mythical difference of higher feelings is related to structure. All higher attributes are not equal in value, since mental attributes are more valuable than physical attributes. In spiritual attributes, the more valuable higher feelings are linked to Devatma, and the sublime qualities that bind us to Devatma are more important. Assume that the altruistic feeling of seeing others' attributes motivates us to appreciate many sorts of attributes, and to see the qualities of others motivates us to appreciate other qualities; however, this is not enough. From truthful insight, it is also important that this praise should be in accordance with quality. If our appreciation beholds less valuable attributes as greater than the more valuable attributes and feelings, then it is mythical.

In spite of the mythical differences, man's altruistic feelings also use myths. When our higher feeling sees any higher attribute, then there is the possibility of two sorts of curses in its appreciation. Take the common perception of freedom: to achieve freedom, revolution and sacrifice is the thing of appreciation. However, the songs that are sung for freedom are more in abundance than its genuine quality. Henceforth, when we describe our attributes of reverence we describe them in hyperbole.

There is no such attribute in our altruistic feeling of appreciation that does not separate truth from the description of the attributes of others that can bind us in truth. There should be no appreciation greater or less than truth, and this should not let him allow to appreciate no greater or less than truth. In our altruistic feelings, there is tendency to separate the truth. Most of us become superstitious in our relationships, and most of the persons who do not trust others do suspicion only. Most of us are blindly devotional and few people lack these attributes. Further, many of us are blindly grateful, and many do not admit others' benevolence. In our altruistic nature, there is a tendency to voyage from one or second extreme, and so our behaviour becomes untruthful.

Due to these four mythical parts in man's higher feelings, he has a lack of a love for truth. The basis of Devatma's sublime feelings is a love of truth, and henceforth, his sublime feelings, which are motivated by good behaviour, are liberal from positive attributes. He sees where and in whom any positive attribute cannot help without praising it. He was not the follower of any attribute and cannot be bereft of any attribute. He has the eligibility to praise and evaluate the attributes according to the value. There is no question of saying in abundance and in minority in the appreciation of their positive attributes. His genuine insight, which is generated by measuring attributes, has evaluated it accurately.

Therefore, by nature, human beings have (I) lower hatred and frustration, (II) prejudices, (III) illiteracy and (IV) curses of mythical faiths, so their good thoughts have a mythical touch. Devatma has a love of truth and goodness, which liberates his soul from low feelings, prejudices, illiteracy and mythical tendencies, and does not let these myths control his sublime behaviour.

Wings for the Truthful Knowledge

We know how bias and untruth impact the positive behaviour of man. By appreciating others' attributes of positive feeling, a person with positive attributes can become a follower of his devotional attribute.

- He praises one attribute in his devotion, though he does not feel same appreciation for others who have the same attribute.
- How he becomes in favour of an attribute out of his devotional attributes.
- How he imputes the structure of attributes.
- How he appreciates one attribute in hyperbole or in minor.

Because of these four biases, man carries the part of untruth in his positive feelings. The lover of truth, Devatma's sublime emotion is liberal from this part of untruth. Hence, his truthful emotion is not only pure in terms of goodness, but pure from the outlook of truth. Devatma's love of truth in the book of positivity does this first transformation, which liberates him from mythical differences and angles.

In human truth, altruistic feelings, such as goodness, which are related to his higher feelings, can often be incomplete or underdeveloped. Every scientist wants to understand any of the truths he devotes his powers to, but does not feel any motivation to propagate that truth.

Further, any human who publishes his or her theoretical or scientific truth may not feel any motivation to propagate it. For instance, a common researcher with a positive love of truth-related incidents does not show supportive truthful motivations towards debate, perfect debate and truthful propaganda. In Devatma, he sees which behaviour is true, and that positive feeling related to truth are wholly complete. He has also seen which truth shows truthful debate, accurate declamation, truth absorption, truth propagation and motivations of support of truth.

Truth-related altruistic feelings remain incomplete in almost all humans. For example, consider a scientist who wishes to conduct truthful knowledge research and absorb higher feeling, and devotes his or her powers to connecting the two. Assume that the scientist has truthful debate, accurate debate, truth absorption, truth propagation and truth support, even when some or all of these skills are incomplete. Where he or she displays a proficiency for a particular field, they do not show motivation towards other fields; essential truth in one aspect does not motivate the others. If a scientist uses a scientific method in his field, he or she will probably not apply that method to his or her religious beliefs, and furthermore, the scientist does not enquire into the nature of his traditions and ceremony by applying or considering scientific methods.

When Descartes learned that the scientist Galileo had been sent to jail by the Roman church on the basis of his astronomical scientific theory, he chose not to publish his latest book that was due to be published. This book detailed his beliefs related to astronomy, which were equal to Galileo. Scottish philosopher David Hume wrote a book entitled Dialogues on Natural Religion, which argued against the existence of God. At that time in England, there were harsh punishments for those who protested against the faith of God, and he and his companions assumed that nobody would publish this book, and if it was, nobody would let him live. With this fear, this book could not be published in their lifetime. Today, this book is one of the most important books on the negation of God's existence. Darwin published his research on biology in a book, but there was such a huge protest that he did not participate in its support. However, Huxley was a prominent supporter of Darwin. For this reason, his life shows truthful behaviour in one or two angles, but in the rest of the angles of life, his behaviour shows an untruthful angle.

The love of the truth of Devatma is the law of his whole life, and is the law of his every thought and behaviour. This law dominates the whole corner of life. Therefore, his whole life is enlightened with truth. In contrast, positive human life related to truth does not have this right.

The ego love present in humans is the harsh difficulty of having the absorption of truth. The history of science presents strong evidence of the fact that human beings developed from the animal kingdom, and that common man is not ready to accept this for a number of reasons. One reason was that this truth goes against the religious beliefs of individuals around the world. The second reason was that this truth was the wound on his ego. Humans are proud beings, and many are devoted to the word of God, for he is the all-knowing, unique and supreme powerful God. When the scientific community retorted that man is the son of animals, many people took this as an insult of the highest order, and this feeling of inferiority was the difficulty of the human absorption of truth. Similarly, when the scientific community told that earth was not the centre of a universe, then it does not only hurt his faith but it is also an attack on his pride. Considering earth as the centre of universe is very important to humankind, so for them, hearing statements that go against this belief are difficult to bear. Henceforth, modern psychology has presented many of these aforementioned truths, whose acceptance has been limited because they are often considered as attacks on the beliefs of the common man.

The evolution of science is the evidence that ego love may be the obstacle in absorbing knowledge. Initially, the evolution of science was because of energy. The reason for this was that scientists could study freely in this field rather being more biased. We can accept these bitter truths in the scientific world much more than we can difficulties, for we do not bind in love in the sphere of field of energy – we love our ego more. Thus, relating the knowledge of truth and absorption of truth is not difficult, but in relation to oneself, the search of truth and absorption is more difficult. After many years of the evolution of energy science, there was a revolutionary evolution of life science. Darwin's search represented a wound in human pride, and considering the evolutionary life force as the creation of God, some satisfied their egos. When life science showed truths, individuals stepped into psychology. Hitherto there are not spent hundred years of psychology when it takes itself as laboratory science. The history of science shows that man has devoted a vast amount of time to search for the truth of his existence using scientific methods, all for the love of his ego. Devatma, being the lover of goodness, his love of truth made the knowledge of the soul the central point of his study.

The Value of Scientific Knowledge

- Incidents and existences have two sides: fact and value. To understand incidents and existences is to know their factual aspects. Every realistic science is the name to know the factual aspects of both evidence and existence. In order to gain this knowledge, it is necessary to employ these two essential methods. In the seventeenth century, the discovery of scientific methods opened the door of knowledge to the factual side of incidents and existences. Before these scientific methods, the methods in use were devoid of the factual aspect of incidents and existences. At the initial stage, humans analyzed the factual side of incidences on the basis of their ego. Our processes focus on our mind because of mind alone. Hence, we endeavour to harm others due to the anger and dispute in mind. We do this process to help others because of our mind's compassion and love. Human analyses natural incidents on the basis of the paradigm of their process.

An individual sees the incidents of nature through his spectacles. Science removed these glasses and tried to observe such incidents as incidents with their sight.

- Science did not only renounce the sight centred on mind but also discovered a new instrument for this insight. Neutrally, knowing the factual side of incidents through scientific methods is called science.

Science clearly tells the factual side of the incidents of knowledge, but incidents and existences do not only have a factual side but also a value side. The difference in the factual side of existence is not the evidence of what such things possess, nor the nature of aestheticism and/or ugliness.

Darwin did not analyze the incidents of evolution from the insight of goodness and evil, but only on the basis of the factual side. His theory is that there is always a possibility for the genes of a species to mutate, and there is a difference in the attributes of species. The species that possess useful and positive attributes precede those species that possess useless or disadvantageous attributes. The dawn of new attributes and the development of new species are not based on the ideals of value. The reasons behind this regard the dawn of the attributes of utilization and non-utilization, but this reason is neither ideal nor valuable. The comprehensive workplace of evolution does not have any relation to values. Darwin considered his evolution only as transformation. As energetic things link to certain conditions, and when some conditions separate at various conditions, so too does this happen in the field of life.

Complete knowledge is not only the factual side of the processes of the mind, but it also comprises those which describe mental processes in terms of values.

- If we leave the value side of the evolution of species then there is not a satisfactory description of this thing, which is why the development of species continues in a way that is helpful for the development of man. When the change of species is without any purpose then how can we describe various species in various times and their interest in one side?

- There are two parts of incidents and existences. For this knowledge, there should have been knowledge of mind and goodness. The possibility of the complete knowledge of incidents and existences is due to these two mental levels. To understand the feeling of facts that gained development in modern science is not suitable. It is also essential to understand the emotion of values. In any field, the altruistic feeling of knowing the true knowledge of facts is not suitable, therefore, it is necessary to understand the values related to knowledge.

It is not sufficient that there should be these two mental weapons; however, the depth should be same in them in the same proportion. If it is not possible, then there would be no balance in the fact- and value-related knowledge of existences and values. Our knowledge will bow either to factual side or value-related knowledge. These two leanings are problems in the complete knowledge of both incidents and existences.

There are two sorts of instruments in Devatma, since he has a love for truth in complete ratio. Thus, he adopted scientific neutrality and scientific methods in order to know the factual side of soul. Man's soul has derives from the animal world as a living – he has seen its factual contour and presented it. However, a love of truth is not possible without a love of goodness. In Devatma, there is a love of goodness in complete shape. He did not only present the factual side of incidents of evolution but also valuable insight. He declared that change in the soul is due to goodness and evil. The soul has an evolutionary side as well as a devolutionary side. The higher knowledge and higher consciousness of the soul is a track of its evolution. The selfishness of the soul- and ego-related pleasure is the path of its destruction.

Hence, by these loves related to truth and goodness, Devatma gave a complete description of the soul incidents of human beings, and this knowledge is not possible for any person devoid of these feelings. The goal of the human soul is to obtain altruistic feelings; however, we know that altruistic feeling does not concern the love of the supremacy of the soul. The scientific knowledge of the factual side of the soul is only possible when the researcher has the complete love of the supreme goodness of soul. The sublime feelings of Devatma are situated in the supreme love of soul. He has the complete ability to evolve and destroy the research law of the soul. He gained a prestigious award to research the truth as a good behaviour in soul. We, as individuals linking ourselves to him, in his light, know that truth by him can show good behaviour. As a researcher of the goodness of soul, Devatma's sublime behaviour is the good behaviour of a scientist, and our behaviour is the good behaviour of a disciple to absorb the truths discovered by him.

The Highest Phenomenon on the Earth: Devatma and Fools

As a result of Devatma's 'Dev Bodhs' (the sublime consciousness of truth and goodness) and 'Dev Anurag' (the sublime love of truth and goodness), there are a number of fundamental distinctions between him and all of the other human souls for all time to come:

- The highest sublime forces of complete love of truth and goodness and the necessary fruit of their evolution form the true unique ideal type of life which the Devatma has been able to evolve in his soul in virtue, and by means of his various kinds of all the requisite surrenders and sacrifices and other evolutionary cosmic forces.

- The highest progressive sublime light is known as Dev Jyoti, which the Devatma has been able to gradually generate in his soul in accordance with the law of the soul-world, together with the evolution of his highest forces of complete love of truth and goodness.

This sublime light can alone reveal those nature-based kinds of truths and principles about the organized being of that very subtle but real thing called soul, its organism, its diseases and degradation, as well as their most horrible consequences, its freedom and its evolution in higher life, of which truths alone constitute the knowledge of true religion.

- The highest sublime power, called Dev Tej, was developed in Devatma's soul in accordance with the laws of Nature governing the soul world, in virtue of the evolution of his highest psychic forces of complete love of truth and goodness, and by which sublime power creates higher hatred and higher pain for all pleasure-affording low loves and low hates, thus resulting in all kinds of falsehoods and evils.

- In his sublime light, Devatma has discovered various truths about the soul and has given the true philosophy of true religion based on the bedrock of the cosmic facts and laws of Nature.

- The unique and supreme objective of his manifestation, which the Devatma proclaimed as a result of the evolution in his soul of the unique psychic forces of complete love for truth and goodness, and being solely ruled and motivated by them.

- The unique example of life led purely and exclusively in relation to either human beings or the sub-human existences, on the basis of the highest psychic forces of the love of truth and goodness (and not on the basis of a love of pleasure and a hatred of pain), which the Devatma has set before the world by virtue of, and, as governed solely by his sublime love or 'Dev Anurags', and the highest and most beneficial ideal of life, which he has thereby presented in all these relations.

- The necessary and complete surrenders and sacrifices which the Devatma made in virtue of his highest psychic loves, for the accomplishment of the supreme objective of his life based on those loves.

- The most remarkable changes, which the Devatma, being the spiritual sun of this darkness-ridden soul-world, has been able, by means of his sublime light (Dev Jyoti) and sublime power (Dev Tej) to bring about in the world. These higher changes have been, and are being, brought about in fit souls through the alchemy of the rays of his unique psychic light and power by creating a true and higher repulsion, and moreover, a true and higher pain for one another's pleasure-affording. However, there are false beliefs and creeds about the soul-life in the name of religion and for pleasure-affording, but unjust or evil deeds in relation to the various existences in Nature.

- Unlike human souls, the Devatma, being possessed of the highest psychic loves for truth and goodness, could not, in accordance with the immutable law of Nature, develop a love of pleasure or make pleasure the goal of his life. Despite possessing multiple consciousnesses for pleasure and pain, he did not, like other human beings, fall in love with pleasure, and did not make it the goal of his life.

- Unlike the human souls, the Devatma, in virtue of his unique and highest psychic loves of truth and goodness, could not establish his relation with any human being, animal, plant, or inanimate object on the basis of any pleasure-seeking feeling, and hence, he did not form any such relation on that basis with any being.

- The Devatma, in virtue of his unique highest psychic forces of love of truth and goodness, did not form a relationship with any animate or inanimate existence of nature on the basis of pleasure, and hence, like other human beings did not form any bias or prejudice for any of them and so he did not do so.

- The Devatma, in virtue of his highest psychic loves of truth and goodness, as well as his absolute freedom from every form of pleasure-seeking love, could not become a slave to any kind of pleasure, and hence, unlike the men and women of this world, he never became such a slave. In short, just as in the evolutionary scale of Nature, the inorganic living objects possess superiority over non-living matter, the organic living plants and animals possess superiority over the inorganic living objects and the human beings are superior to all these existences; in the same way, in the human world, the Devatma possesses superiority over all the human souls.

Hence, as the Devatma, the virtue of his – these true and unique highest psychic forces – is in the scale of the human evolution in this world, the most noble, the all-sided benefactor and the highest emergence. Having attained to the true and unique highest psychic forces and all their unique characteristics, he possesses a fundamental distinction from or superiority over every being of the human world, just as the human beings, on account of several kinds of special powers, have a fundamental distinction from and superiority over every being of the animal world.

Therefore, belief in all the so-called gods, goddesses or worshipful beings – whether they belonged to human species or came from animal or vegetable or inanimate worlds, or were the creation of mere fancy –has been propagated throughout the world. These deities are devoid of the true highest sublime forces ('Dev Shaktian') that have appeared and evolved in the Devatma.

From the outset, these wholly imaginary gods and goddesses never truly existed, at least in the physical realm, yet, even the real beings of the human, animal, vegetable and inanimate kingdoms were called, accepted and propagated to be gods, goddesses or worshipful beings, in spite of their true existence and devoid of the real sublime forces of the Devatma. Then again, those from amongst the human beings who were called or believed to be gods, having human nature in them, were one and all lovers of pleasure alone, and were absolutely destitute of the real sublime forces which have emerged in the Devatma in the evolutionary course of Nature. Therefore, the Devatma has, and should be considered to have, the same distinction from all of them as he has from all other human souls.

Philosophy

The Secret Taste of Honey
on the Tongue

Human beings are so situated that they must deal with others than himself in order to simply be. The 'other' is inseparable from life and consciousness, in fact and value, in ontology and axiology; hence, our response to the 'other' is inescapable to it at the level of understanding, feeling or will, and can be scientific, aesthetic or moral.

In the aspect of morality, our dealings with others can be one of exploitation, cooperation or service. When we seek our own good at the cost of the good of others, it is exploitation; on the other hand, when we seek our good along with others, it is co-operation. When we seek the good of others, which is not a perfect duty, it is a case of altruism. In light of these points, it is worth considering the following question: Why should we do meritorious good to others or be altruist?

(1)

Philosophy and religion see 'eye to eye' when it comes to the challenge of the problem of egoism and altruism at different levels, which draw distinction between different types of good things. The material goods are at the base of the value pyramid, the intellectual goods constitute the middle and the spiritual goods come at the top in a hierarchy. The conflict goes on decreasing as we pass from lower goods to higher goods and reaches its highest intensity at the level of 'material goods'.

If spiritual goods are emotionally accepted as higher, they reduce the conflict of material goods. If spiritual goods are acquired and are considered the best, 'give and take' about material goods become easy.

Hence, the reply to the question as to why I should prefer to share my good with others is that it is to my own good to do so. We may call this reply the altruism of Self-consciousness, for it is motivated by the truth that the best form of 'goodness' is the good of one's own soul and it consists of altruistic non-competitive goods.

Self-consciousness in the form of service of others is not selfishness, for selfishness seeks the lowest goods at the cost of others.

For example, a selfish man seeks material goods and political power. Again, the goods he seeks make him to deny the same goods to others. On the other hand, a man of self-consciousness seeks to cultivate the virtues of purity, chastity, charity, love and understanding and service of others. By the nature of the goods he seeks, he not only safeguards the rights of others but he also proves benevolent to them too.

This is clear from the practical involvement of thousands of men and women of different religions who serve education, medicine and social welfare throughout the world and usher in good for millions of people in order to save their own souls. Whatever the pathway of dedication they follow, for them, the supreme good is the salvation of their own individual soul. However, the philosophical distinction between my good and the good of others remains irremovable, even though the pursuit of higher goods leads to altruistic conduct. If the good of my soul (i.e. its salvation is the highest good for me), then the good of others is not the highest good, as either of them cannot be the highest good, in the same way as two people cannot be the most beautiful person.

What the theory of Self-consciousness can establish is that when good is properly conceived as spiritual good, the same altruistic conduct can flow from a man of Self-consciousness as from a man of dynamic altruism.

(2)

If the distinction between motivation of self-awareness and pure or dynamic altruism is grasped, the qualitative differences between the two shine forth in all clearness. To illustrate, a man of self-awareness makes his soul's welfare his absolute concern, whereas a man of dynamic altruism makes society the direct object of his service. A man of self-awareness is a man of calculation, whereas a man of dynamic altruism knows no calculation. A man of self-awareness, consistent with his ideal, can never brook sacrifice of his soul, whereas a man of dynamic altruism would risk everything, including his soul, for the others in complete conformity with his ideal. A man of self-awareness cannot consistently accept an inferior spiritual state for the good of others, for he is absolutely attached to the good of his soul, whereas a man of dynamic altruism transcends the attachment even to his highest self.

Thus, the psychology of a man of dynamic altruism is in the spirit of an explosive, which, in order to remove a mountain of untruth and evil in the way of human progress, would not mind exploding itself to non-existence.

Dynamic altruism makes the service of others the direct object of realization as it is the first and last object of concern.

The qualitative difference of concern with others makes for different levels of motivation in the order of altruism of gratitude, altruism of justice, altruism of compassion, altruism of mudita and altruism of love.

The first level arises when one shows too much concern with the self's welfare as a direct object of realization, which comes through the feeling of gratitude, thus making the other the direct object of service, without any concern of what the benefactor may mean for the person. In the future, he or she will not serve the other because he will do something further for him in the future for example, by leaving a patrimony, his services will win approval, appreciation and applause for him either here or in heaven. However, the release from the umbilical cord is not complete – the other is still served because of his service to one's self – it is the utility aspect of the other that gains its recognition as the direct object of service for the individual.

The feeling of justice still further weakens the predominant place of self in relation to others. It places the other at par with oneself. The rights of others are of equal value with him. He is to count for one, and only one, among the millions. Discrimination is allowed on the basis of colour, creed, caste, status, position, power, community, nationality or species of man, animals and plants. The feeling of justice abhors privileges and perks based on the denial of basic common humanity.

To hold that all men are equal is to say that all men are ends in themselves and that no man is a means or thing employed to serve another person's purposes. Slavery is evil, for it treats certain people as objects to be purchased and sold. The sense of justice awakens us to the truth that since all humans have basic rights and all men are equal. Our self-assertions must end where others' freedom begins – the-sense of justice reduces egoistic partialities and prejudices.

The motivation of compassion goes a step further to move beyond respect for the rights of others – it feels an obligation to serve the sick, the hungry and the abandoned and shares a part of one's gifts of life in terms of one's talent, time and money with the lower-placed humanity.

Mudita still further reduces the place of self in one's count and regards feeling joy in the progress of others. Here, the ego love is further down-graded. To serve those who, through service, will rise to higher merit to the limit of over shadowing them is to realize greater liberation from ego-centric concern.

It is the feelings of justice, compassion and mudita that led to the altruism of love for others. In feeling love, the individual has abolished the distinction of the good of the self and the good of others – he or she is the other and the other is installed in place of him or herself.

The feeling of love makes the final deliverance from making one's self as the direct and final object of realization. The self is eclipsed and the other takes the sovereign place of service.

These motivations are not like separate switches on a switch board of mind, which operate separately or independently of each other – they exist in an organic unity, with several of them operating together in different hierarchies in different individuals under different sets of situations.

(3)

Altruistic motivations are distinguished on the grounds of the degree to which they release us from the centrality of ego-welfare in our altruistic service.

The motivations for the service of others operate individually and jointly, depending on their presence in an individual. Thus, a person of gratitude may have a feeling for justice at a minimum level and may not feel interested to fight for rights of women and children, for example. A person of justice may lack compassion for the oppressed and down-trodden in the world, and although they may fight against oppressive laws, they may not go out to share the suffering of the oppressed. However, there can be altruists with a strong sense of justice and love or gratitude and mudita, or self-consciousness and compassion or other motivations; these individuals may join hands for some social service.

189

The same motivation may work in one field of service or another. Those with self-awareness skills, for example, may serve the mentally retarded, gifted children or great men and may serve to preserve the past, reform the present, or create the future that give us the colourful crown of altruists.

We do not associate ourselves with those who do not share our level of excellence-

- Who are physical, mental or moral –are unfit in life
- Who are blind, deaf or lame, and those who suffer from infectious and incurable diseases.
- Who are insane, and criminals who can be educated to live in society.

This form of altruism for the unfit is psychologically challenging and goes against our general tendency to be with a group of our kind or with a better group.

However, altruism for the unfit calls upon us to associate with those who are at the bottom. One must have extraordinary love for the good of the unfortunate ones to overcome the psychological resistance to associate with and serve them. To serve those who suffer from infectious and incurable diseases or those who are idiots or insane or moral lepers calls for superhuman psychology. The greater the gifts and achievements of the altruistic person and the more unfortunate or condemned the unfit he serves are, the greater is his moral development in self-sacrifice.

The altruism for the unfit involves not only the sacrifice of a healthy psychic impulse to associate with one's kind but it also involves far greater sacrifice, as it endangers the good of the altruist. All evil is infectious. An atmosphere of evil has adverse effects, for instance, we know how Father Damien contracted leprosy while serving the lepers. In mental hospitals, the superintendents of the hospitals are found to go insane; thus, we cannot remain unaffected by the evils and weaknesses we deal with.

We have limited energy and time, so we just make a choice. When we are to choose between two goods, one is to be sacrificed, for to choose one of the alternatives is to sacrifice the other. When one is engaged in dealing with sinful humanity, there is a greater chance of being infected with evil or losing sensitiveness to evil.

Altruism for the unfit is different from the love of truth, goodness and beauty. To be a philosopher, a scientist or an artist is not ipso facto to be a messiah for mankind. These two ideals – service of truth and service of mankind.

Devatma, in his life vow, clearly distinguished the two ideals. If he had entirely devoted himself to the discover of a true philosophy of religion and soul, he would have been master philosopher but not master Guru.

It was the second part of his ideal, the service of mankind in the light of his philosophy that made him Spiritual Master for all mankind.

Altruism for the unfit calls for the ultimate psychological sacrifice. It claims a part of our highest good, which concerns devotion to study or research of truth, goodness and beauty. What makes this sacrifice and suffering bearable is the feeling of compassion for the condemned humanity, and finally, it is the hardest ethical service on two counts.

The unfit people consciously or unconsciously behave in a manner to hurt the altruist. As we pass from the physical to the mental and then moral unfits, we find that their misbehaviour mounts up. They misunderstand the service and mistake their benefactor for enemy.

Devatma's *vilaap* is a classical expression of what sufferings he had to experience in the service of men and women addicted to low-loves and low-hates. His Advitiya Tyag (unique sacrifice) is a record of the unbearable pains he received at the hands of such unfortunate souls.

Again, It is a ceaseless fight against the evils about which one does not know how to overcome them. To put it in the language of a Greek tragedy, such an altruistic person is a tragic hero who challenges the evil decree of fate without success to his death, for this altruistic service is so anfractuous that one must have the patience of a mother to remain engaged, due its negligible results against those of a service that benefits other groups of humanity.

An idealist view of life may be- if our ideal is to attain a truly efficient society, we must not tolerate the weak and diseased. This way of thinking appeals to the man of compassion who is devoted to the unfit. He is inspired by the thinking of a mother, for a mother no child is to be cast to the waste. For her, every child has a place in her love, which is not related to efficiency or utility. Should her child suffer from an incurable disease or mental issues, she will give the same amount of love – this mother-love finds extension in the altruists of the unfit. Compassion in such altruists cannot disown anyone of their fellow human beings, however condemned they are by heredity or environment. There is no question of casting out any brother human being, as all brother fellow beings are unconditionally accepted and respected, however unfit and inefficient they may be.

We need to be humane to the least gifted among us, in order to recognize their claim on us for their advancement and welfare. Without this core virtue, the inter-personal relationship will be without sweetness and light. To this altar of humanity, the altruist of the unfit sacrifices his psychological and ethical scruples to the point of extinction. A man of altruism of the unfit has dedicated his soul to the humanity in him. What it serves is of little value but his services have a quality unshakable by any other form of altruism. It is the altruism of the mother extended to the unfits in humanity.

(4).

Altruism for the immature in human species takes various forms, for human personality is a complex of many-sided immaturity, whether physical, mental, moral and spiritual.

- Altruism for the immature is based on an admiration for the developing capacities of the immature, and rejoices at the progress of others who may surpass the altruist himself.
- Altruism for the immature calls for self-development to the measure of service which the altruist is to render.

For example, a lecturer needs greater mental development than a school teacher, and a professor needs far greater intellectual illumination to be of service in education. Altruistic service provides intellectual stimulus to students under him – to which only a Newton or an Einstein is able to do.

Moral life can be imparted by moral life. If I wish to help others to develop honesty, I must be honest. If I want to help others to be chaste, I must be chaste myself. The host of virtues, such as honesty, purity, disinterested service, and a love for knowledge, among many others, needs their first development in the altruist before he can serve to develop them in others. Beyond these moral virtues are the spiritual virtues of faith, reverence, love and service for the holiest in mankind. These virtues are spiritual, for spiritual life is a life of association with the holiest in mankind. Religion is an attempt; however, it may have blundered and bungled to develop these spiritual virtues, which can put us in living contact with the living perennial sources of goodness. Bhakti, faith, reverence and service (i.e. devotion to the worshipful-being – the lover of Satyam, Shivam and Sundram) constitute the conditions for the fullest and finest satisfaction of human personality.

It is clear that altruism for the immature is higher than the altruism for the unfit, when it claims a higher development of us for the higher mental, moral, and spiritual services of others, As services grow superior, those who can engage in them decrease. Those who can guide research work are fewer than those who can lecture in colleges; likewise, those who can develop moral virtues are fewer than those who can develop good etiquette.

Devatma developed a love of truth, goodness and beauty. This is a love of spiritual development beyond the moral virtue of altruism. Hence, the service he could do to the immature stands in its own category and could not be done by a person who had not developed this level. Those who are truly under his blessed influence are, therefore, charged by them, and are able to render to fellow human beings the services that others outside these influences cannot render.

Altruism for the immature, even though ethically more difficult than altruism for the unfit, does not evoke as much admiration as altruism for the unfit. Altruism for the unfit consists of the removal of sickness, mental backwardness and anti-social behaviour. We all appreciate how evil bodily illness, idiocy, stealing, drinking or womanizing can be. These evils threaten the biological values of survival. Hence, we have appreciation for those who try to remove these evils. We do not appreciate the service of the research guide as much, for we have not yet developed that degree of appreciation for the values of research in truth as we have for biological values. We might appreciate a worker who helps to develop honesty, chastity, discipline and good neighbourliness than a worker who builds up devotion for the worshipful being who is Satyam, Shivam and Sundram in his life and character, for appreciation of such virtues for the highest is far less than that of social virtues. The altruist who works for the highest good stands neglected and ignored, for he deals with something foreign to the common appreciation. Devatma, who catered to the highest good, felt ignored, neglected and even hated by those around him.

(5).

Unfitness and immaturity are different in kind. Unfitness is a condition of limitation, while immaturity is a condition of progress. Unfitness is to be removed, whereas immaturity is to be developed. Unfitness stands in the way of the development of maturity, for maturity compensates for unfitness, while for the unfit, altruism is to engage. In the work of salvation, altruism for the immature is to work for evolution. Altruism for the unfit concentrates on the present evil, while altruism for the immature looks to the future good. Altruism for the unfit is grounded in sympathy ('karuna') for the condemned or the unfortunate aspect of the unfit. For the immature, altruism is grounded in joy (mudita) at the developing aspect of the immature. For the unfit, altruism regards preserving and serving those of the humblest and most intrinsic worth. For the immature, altruism concerns developing immature persons to high intrinsic worth. For the unfit, altruism is psychologically the hardest, while altruism for the immature is psychologically the most rewarding.

(6).

Altruism for the accomplished as a service inspired by the appreciation of the excellence of a class whose member or members highly excel in some desirable gifts, and feel worthwhile of serving it. Altruism for the accomplished arises when two conditions are satisfied in the lift of the altruist:

- The excellence of the accomplished person is highly appreciated, and
- The worthwhileness of the accomplished perceived to be superior to all other forms of service.

The altruist is to recognize is the superiority of this service of the accomplished. Are the lights on in the houses of mankind in the process of evolution? They encompass an evolution made concrete in flesh and blood to provide the conditions for the progress of the less-developed. Suppose that Galileo, Newton, Darwin, Karl Marx, Freud and Einstein, Ibsen, Hegel, Gandhi and Devatma had died in childhood, we would have been deprived of the rich heritage in physics, biology, psychology, literature, economics, politics and religion. Altruism for the accomplished rests on the perception that the accomplished are indispensable to evolution, and that their service has a peculiar claim and extraordinary value. This perception of the truth of the place of the accomplished in the economy of human evolution and the consciousness of moral duty to personally serve them gives these altruists a place next to the accomplished in the appreciation and gratitude of humankind.

Altruism for the Accomplished calls for four forms of humility.

- It involves a recognition of the superiority of those whom one serves, which thus requires a great humility in an altruist. Humility is a condition for appreciating the excellence in others. When one is full of oneself, one loses vision to see the beauty in the life of others. Therefore, one has to humble to appreciate the excellence of the accomplished.

- An altruist is to accept himself as inferior in excellence and allow him to be treated as subordinate. It involves a crucifixion of one's ego affirmations, to which even the best of altruists may fail to show this humility. In the case of the service for the unfit and the immature, one is accepted as superior and enjoys a superior position. Therefore, One has to humble to subordinate his judgement to the accomplished.

- The altruist has to develop a tolerance for the weaknesses of the accomplished. No accomplishment is achieved without limitations, angularities, idiosyncrasies, and weaknesses. The altruist must have an abundance of the spirit of tolerance to adjust to them in the service of the Accomplished. For this one needs an extraordinary humility and appreciation of the excellence of the accomplished.

- An altruist has to humble to do humble service to the excellence of the accomplished. One can serve the physical needs of the accomplished in health or illness or one can attend to his public calls on him or to the publication of his works.

Personal service of the accomplished requires a moral vigilance of an unusual order. Familiarity breeds intensiveness, blindness and even contempt for the person of the accomplished. A certain distance is essential for the average or even distinguished to appreciate the miracle of excellence in a great human. This distance is not possible for those who engage themselves in the personal service of the accomplished. Hence, only those can prove fit for such service through the possession of natural gifts or spiritual training, or both. By doing so, they can maintain or evolve the vision of the excellence as perceived in the first flash of discovery.

In summary, the moral equipment of the altruist in the service of the accomplished includes:

- a perception of the excellence of the accomplished;
- an extra-ordinary moral vigilance to keep intact or evolve his perception of the excellence;
- to value such service as the highest;
- to subordinate one's judgment to that of the accomplished;
- to have an abundance of tolerance for the angularities of the accomplished; and
- to the content to do humble work.

However, the altruist should feel rewarded in this personal services of the accomplished. He lives, breathes and has his being in the atmosphere of the best. He is most blessed in the service of the blessed in his accomplishments.

The Last Milestone:
Philosophy of Truth

Truth as a virtue is basic to psychological health, social good and spiritual deliverance. Mutual relationship is valued so high for it permits communication with others, sharing our puzzles and problems, our struggles and triumphs and our visions and ecstasies. It helps the emotional catharsis of the individual and society, for all this is truth-sharing.

- Truth builds credits on which social life revolves such as moral solidarity, social mobility and business efficiency.
- Truth rises to highest excellence in moral and spiritual fields for salvation. Generally, truth as a virtue takes the form of truth-speaking or veracity.
- Truth-speaking involves truth-finding. It requires the insistence on the correct knowledge of observing facts.
- Truth-speaking is a different virtue from sincerity as it involves truth finding and avoid carelessness, prejudice and ignorance.
- Our low-loves and low-hates feed on falsehood, and hence, we deliberately but unconsciously ignore facts which show how little we satisfy even first condition of truthful living.
- Truth-speaking is a virtue in those who can patiently and fairly ascertain facts according to logical principles and scientific procedures, and in those who can express the ascertained facts in a transparent language which mirrors truth.

- Truth speaking, which is the correct communication of facts, is a virtue only if it satisfies other conditions. A person who thinks and talks of real weakness of another may be a back-biter, which is not a virtue. Truth-reporting must be controlled by good. It is only virtuous to explore another's true faults when it is to the good of the speaker, as well as to the subject of criticism and to social good. Correct reporting in gossip is not a virtue for it serves no good purpose.

- Truth speaking never gives the moral right to be brutish, arrogant or sarcastic in one's expression. It is always wrong to express facts in a manner which unnecessarily hurts the others.

- In order to be a virtue, truth-speaking must be inspired by pure motive with a consideration for the good of the subject of the criticism and in language designed not to hurt.

- It is virtuous to indulge in imaginative satisfaction through the art activities of creation and appreciation because it is related to our aesthetic good.

- Truth-speaking is bound up with good. Truth-speaking is respected as a moral virtue because of its relation to spiritual good. Truth-speaking shows a regard for spiritual excellence over material, social and personal advantages. It is when truth-speaking indexes or affirms this regard that a person develops ethical excellence.

- Though truth-speaking is thus defined as a great excellence, it is not the sublime virtue that prophets have proclaimed and poets have sung about.

- Truth as a virtue rises in excellence in terms of the object of observation and discovery. The greater the excellence of the object of discovery, the greater is the mind that discovers or revels in it. A philosopher scientist discovers truths that are true for all fields. A philosopher is a scientist philosopher, as his function throughout the ages has been to see through the truth that transcends the truth of particular sciences and suggests corrections and reorientations of the studies.

- The greatest piece of literature must have a sublime object for its theme. The artist, like the scientist, sees beneath the superficial experiences of life and appreciates or discovers a great idea or conceives a great character, and whose powers of expression are matched to the gigantic structure of his idea or character.

- The spiritual principle is implicit in the universe and has become explicit through the evolution of higher and higher levels of existences. From single cell organisms to humans to Devatma is a story of the gradual explicitness of the spiritual principle. There is a greater appreciation of the spiritual principle of the universe than in the study of the single cell organism as it is wider and deeper understanding of the spiritual principle. In theology, God is also thought to be an object to itself, which thus constitutes the highest form of knowledge.

These are perceptions of the truth that the highest is the knowledge of a spiritual principle, even though the spiritual principle is not truly conceived here.

The spiritual principle is best manifested in the sublime life (Dev Jiwan) and Dev Roop of Devatma. Hence, his observation has the sublimest object for reporting (i.e. Himself). In knowing himself, he knows the spiritual principle in its full explicitness. His truth experience has a quality unto its own. Its knowledge by Devatma is His Own in the way in which it cannot belong to others. Hence, he is heir to a truth of highest sublimity unapproachable by human genius. Thus, it is this dimension to his knowledge which places truth as a virtue in him of highest importance.

When we can observe the spiritual principle in him and express it truly, we observe and speak that it is the noblest. Truth experience of Devatma is the ideal for all who wish to develop a virtue of truth in them. Through faith and love for Devatma, humans bask the light of the spiritual principle made explicit in him at its best.

PHILOSOPHY OF DEVATMA

Devatma as a philosopher has touched the four sphere of philosophy-

- Ontology
- Epistemology
- Ethics
- Religion

The Nature of The
Universe-Ontology

The Laws of Nature: Metaphysics

Naturalistic ontology deals with the nature of the universe. Devatma's philosophy demands concrete evidence about occurrences and happenings as per the demands of scientific research, and therefore, this conviction is in parallel with ontology. Plato's dichotomy between the world of ideas, the world of essences, the world of senses and the world of appearances has no place in it. Simultaneously, world-views based on conjunctures and surmises get annulled, since they shatter when questioned systematically at the pivot of rationality.

Like many other Indian thinkers, such as Raja Ram Mohan Roy and Keshab Chandra Sen, Devatma also revolts against traditional Hinduism, altogether rejecting the Brahamnvada of Samkara, the concept of incarnation of the Gita, the doctrine of karma and the transmigration of Indian philosophy, in general.

Devatma did not believe in the existence of the God as a creator or anything like the ways people admit his existence. It is not proved that God created nature and neither is nature an entity like an individual person; rather, God and Nature are mutually exclusive. Since scientific methodology cannot prove otherwise, the concept of God is out-rightly denied and thus rejected. He is not a creator of Nature. Nature is not a person, and God and nature are not equivalent. As God's existence cannot be established, Devatma ejects transcendentalism in metaphysics.

The philosophy holds that Nature is a reality and its events can be explained with conviction and authenticity. In such a structure, where concrete proof is required from every phenomenon for its occurrence, there cannot be stories about miracles or any agency that is supernatural in essence to convince us in the occurrence of these miracles.

The universe is one where its constituents function as a matter-force unit. Its ceaseless changes are not a series of 'chance-products' but there are laws governing these. Certain happenings may appear to us as good ones and others may be bad ones, but the laws governing these have inseparable dimensions of value and disvalue. Evolution and devolution are not exceptions to these laws. Devatma, an emergent evolutionist, holds that man plays a vital role in shaping this universe.

Since Nature is the totality of all its constituents, human personality happens to be an organism and thus a constituent of Nature, like many others. There cannot be a human origin outside the realm of Nature – neither can his destiny be outside this circle.

Devatma ejects Bradley's conception of the absolute as it is beyond change and relations. He holds that, 'To be is to be related', 'To be is to be casually connected', 'To be is to be change' and 'To be is to be different'.

The soul is a life-force in human beings similar to life-force in all fauna and flora. One who is born or grown cannot escape change. As the soul is a doer, it is not immortal and the souls are many. All creations exist in plurality, and continue to change all the time in adherence to the laws of nature.

'To be is to be embodied'. The soul does not exist apart from the body, and even after death, it can take a subtle body out of the finer particles at death from its own gross body, as believed in the philosophy of Devatma.

The modern era of science and technology weighs the concept of God differently. It raises questions to such an existence that cannot be proved, and in an elaborate experimentation on godliness, the modern era asks why we need it if it cannot be proved as a supernatural being, and thus wants it to be dethroned, since it does not explain the occurrence of events in nature. God has to vacate his chair immediately; otherwise, further awareness among humans will replace him with the scientific instruments it is going to invent. Thus, it is high time we review the old views, surmises and his being.

Nature exists for us with its multifarious magnificence. This is wrongly believed as the creation of God – Who is that God? Where does he live? How does he procreate? Given its magnificence, where does he derive the quantum of energy to regulate the nature? Certainly, this is a pious conception of a fear we are obsessed with! So far, there is no viable explanation of the entity we believe as God – only mere speculation, of course!

Nature was not created. It has neither a beginning nor end – it is eternal. Yes, of course, if we try to understand the matter, it is a process of evolution. In this process, Earth has attained fine stages beginning with the crude form.

Darwin's theory of evolution and subsequent studies in the sciences, such as psychology, physiology and biological science, etc. can explain how we have travelled so far and the journey continues today and will continue tomorrow.

This research will prove how much God is responsible for the creation of the universe and how much it happens to be a lie. And strangely enough, humans bluffed by the existence of God preach godliness, but his faith is found infirm when he commits crime. This means there is no God, since dailies are replete with reports about religion going wrong in civil matters. This proves contradictory in itself. If we still have faith in the scriptural doctrines, we are thus committing a crime and doing great injustice to the sciences.

Nevertheless, with the passage of time, the old beliefs would shatter, and society would believe in theories of science and not have blind faith. The philosophy of Devatma can reply to all our questions, and God can sit silent, whereas, in silence, this would mean falsehood. In its own accord, let us say, society will learn how to be inquisitive about things and God will be stripped to nothingness. Yes, change will come, but only with the passage of time.

Therefore, in contrast to the unfounded and baseless beliefs about God, which will soon be redundant, the naturalistic ontology of Devatma sees everything in terms of firmly-grounded scientific truth.

Devatma sings:

We all are part of Nature,
which is the only real Nature;
most spacious is this Nature,
wondrous and boundless is this Nature.

Ever changing is this Nature,
yet indestructible is this Nature;
everlasting and endless is this Nature,
self-existent and eternal is this Nature.

Always changes this Nature,
by its own laws this Nature,
which always prove true in Nature;
trustworthy is always Nature.

Every existence appears in Nature,
it has its being in Nature;
it grows better or worse in Nature,
it involves or devolves in Nature.

Nature Alone Is a Source
of All Knowledge

The reasons for Devatma's belief in the non-existence of God - we will consider what his philosophy of nature is.

"Universe is Nature——one unlimited, uncreated, self-existent, eternal whole of embodied existences, in ceaseless change for better or worse." The basic tenet of his conception of Nature is that all entities of Nature can be divided into matter and force. Further, matter and force are inseparable. He refutes the theory that there is only matter and no force. The presence of force cannot be denied, as all matter is subject to change, and change implies force. Even bodies at rest imply force, says Devatma, because they are "characterized by impenetrability and inertia" which can be understood in terms of force itself.

Devatma defines perception as the process to see objects in space and time. To him, knowledge of the external world is true only if it is scientific. All scientific knowledge is based on matter, force, space and time. All living bodies are governed by laws of physics and chemistry. However, they are also under the biological laws. Devatma is not reductionist and does not reduce biological laws to physics and chemical laws.

Devatma repeatedly asserts that while we can trace the evolution from the inanimate to the animate, there is absolute no evidence to prove the existence of disembodied beings. Hence, this leads to the conclusion that there is no God. He denies the existence of the disembodied soul. He holds that Nature is one. On the basis of this tenet he argues that since Nature is one, it is independent and there is no existence beyond it, either supernatural or transcendental. If Nature alone is real then it is a source of all knowledge, and all mystic experience are false. Since Devatma totally rejects the existence of God, there is no need for a dual approach to the study of ethics. the scientific approach that he follows denies Brahman and requires the study of Nature only.

1. NATURE. "Nature is self-sufficient and autonomous. Nature and nature alone is real... There can be no existence outside of Nature."

"The universe is natural. It acts in accordance with its own nature and is not influenced by anything outside it. The universe includes everything, so there can be nothing outside it to influence it. It is self-contained, self-sufficient, self-caused....."

2. RELATIONS. "To be is to be related". "Nothing exists without being related".

3. CAUSATION. "To be is to causally. The hypothesis that nothing happens without being caused to happen does not seem to be unreasonable as a continuingly reliable working hypothesis in metaphysics."

4. CAUSATION OF NOVELTY. "Causation...can...be emergent... The effect can be very different from its cause."

"There is some novelty and thus some creation in every cause-effect relation."

5. CHANGE. "To be is to change. To exist is to change and to change is to exist."

"We propose the thesis that to 'exist is to change' and of course, 'to change is to exist.'"

6. PERMANENCE. "There is no evidence of permanence in our experience."

We Share Devatma's antipathy toward "a nominal world of changeless being" but since "To remain the same is to be permanent." Devatma recognizes that "there is some experience of stability..."; that change itself "is characterized by regularity, immutability, and variability," and that "the same set of conditions produce the same effect."

7. DIFFERENCE. "To be is to be different. Every existing thing...is different from every other existing thing in at least one way."

8. SAMENESS.

We share Devatma's antipathy for the idea of "unchanging substance" which "is ceaseless change," if that implies that man cannot remain the same in any respect, then I must not disagree. Perhaps I misunderstand him here since he also says that man "has continued existence under certain conditions," and he is very much concerned about "value as a necessary condition for persistence in existence."

9. VALUE AND EXISTENCE. "Good and evil both exist."

"He holds to a casual relation between value and existence. Value is a necessary condition which further existence and disvalue is a necessary condition which reduces further existence. As new existents emerge, new goods emerge, but as new existents bring new conflicts, they also bring evils."

10. PERSONALITY.

Human nature "is an evolute from the biological life. As an evolute, it shares certain common characteristics with the lowest life forces." But also "it has capacity for language...ideals...abstraction and generalization. It can develop social life. It can plan and execute things. Human personality is from body and society."

"Biology, by giving us insight into heredity and evolution, reveals other questions about the nature of ourselves." "We are not born human, except as members of a biological species, but we become human after birth through the socializing influences of others upon us."

Human species, like other animals species, has biological origin. But human species has its own psychology different in some respects from animal psychology, e.g., we have the capacity for verbal language, abstraction, and generalization which are not possessed by animals. We are born human and humans develop through social intercourse.

11. AGENCY.

Is the human soul a doer?" Yes, of course.

"Not only do you function as an agent, but because you act in many different kinds."

12. INTELLIGENCE.

"Man's doing shows an operation of intelligence which extends the scope & quality of his doings."

In its broadest and deepest meaning, 'intelligent' is something all-pervasive and is essentially equivalent with ethical living in the broadest and deepest meaning of the term 'ethics.'

That nature was, is and will ever remain real; and it never was, nor can be an illusion. That man is evolved from and "lives, moves, and has his being" in Nature, and cannot know anything supposed to be above or beyond or outside Nature. That the fact and immutable laws of Nature are the only sure foundation of man's knowledge. That no knowledge about any objective existence can be called true, unless it is verified by scientific methods,

1. Accurate observation.
2. Accurate reasoning.
3. Accurate experiment or test, where possible.
4. Accurate reconciliation with other known facts and laws of Nature.

1. That Nature is one indivisible whole, consisting of all kinds of existences whether "inorganic" or "organic," which are all its inter-related parts.
2. That all existences in Nature are composed of two things only, namely one or other kind of matter and one or other kind of force: living or non-living.
3. Both matter and force that compose Nature are interconnected and are indestructible in their sum-total, hence Nature is eternal and self-existing.
4. That force in Nature by their own motion, change matter into different forms and themselves under change or transformation of various kind according to their own inherent properties or immutable laws.

Hence, infinite number of forms of non-living and living beings, composed of different kind of matter and force, appear and disappear in Nature.

1. That every living organism, lives and grows only under certain in Nature.
2. That every living organism is bound to decay and die, if necessary conditions of life are not fulfilled in Nature.

3. That every living organism in Nature changes by its own motions and by the influences of other beings surrounding it.

4. That the unceasing change going on in Nature, affects every living organism in two ways i.e., either it makes its organism better or higher, or it worse or lower than before, as regards,

    (a) its physical form.

    (b) its inner power or functions.

5. That the change for the worse or deterioration in living organism, if not checked in time, gradually leads or ends in the extinction, of that particular entity.

6. That the change for the better in a living organism leads towards completeness and perfection of its organism and its right adjustment in relation to other parts of Nature.

7. That the higher change in living organism depends upon:

    (a) its own capacity to resist the destructive influences of its unfavourable Environment on the one hand and to adapt itself to the constructive influences of its Favourable Environment on the other.

    (b) its getting an Environment of such forces as are favourable to its growth.

8. That a lower change in a living organism depends upon either:

    (a) its own incapacity to resist the destructive influences of adapt itself to the constructive influences of its favourable environment on the other, or

    (b) not being able to get an environment that is favourable to its growth.

    • Evolution—All reality is a single process of evolution. The two eyes for discovery in every field—factual or valuational— are evolution and scientific method.

    • There is no need or room for supernaturalism in understanding the universe and life

- Evolutionary man feels at home in the natural world in which he has his roots and destiny.
- Evolutionary perspective is futurist in point of knowledge and principles of conduct.
- Man of Evolution has global perspective
- The ideal for a man of evolution in within Nature and consists in realization life-potentialities as participant in evolutionary process.
- A man of evolution can visualize the religion of the future.

Truth Cannot Be Lost: Evolution

The basis of the entire structure of the universe is evolution. Its processes can be explained by the theories of science. The verification of the processes by these theories compels every modern thinker to accept the truth regarding evolution. His inquisitive mind finds out the what, how and why of evolution.

And where will the thinking of Devatma stand? It is naturalistic, dialectical (understanding things and events that are always in their interrelationship), scientific, evolutionary, developmental, optimistic, responsible and altruistic. Its goal is a life of service in which low-hates and low-loves are kept to a minimum, while the individual tries in high loves to remove evil in life wherever he may find it.

Accordingly, nature is constantly creating fresh and fragrant values pertaining to humanity. Moreover, the course of time means more sublimation of human values. Therefore, the evolutionary process means a persistent development of new and ever new values.

Evolution and devolution, utility and futility, life and death and creation and destruction are the various two aspects of this seeming enigma which interact within themselves to create a specific tension amongst them all, and when there is a strict adherence to the rules governing them, this can lead to creativity.

Those with a high capacity for progress and are proactive when they happen to be in a conducive environment rise higher in their personal capacity. On the other hand, millions of living and non-living beings do not find themselves in such proactive environments and gradually degenerate, which, if left unchecked, may cause their annihilation.

Devatma differs from Darwin's fundamentals concerning evolution, though he himself was prompted by his theories to work for the verification of the things in a systematic manner. While presenting the concept of 'natural selection', Darwin is generally understood to be stating that the survival, propagation and reproductive variations of the species is a purely random or an irrational process. However, for Devatma, there are the laws of evolution that determine the successive rise of dominant types.

Devatma's metaphysical position is that the universe is law-bound. Darwin proposes his fundamentals without reference to values. For Darwin, the emergence of destructive animals is as much a case of evolution as useful animals. However, Devatma gives value meaning to the concept of evolution. The emergence of a useful species is evolutionary. The emergence of a ferocious species is devolutionary. There are two opposing processes in Nature: one is to sustain, the other is to atrophy.

Secondly, other evolutionists, such as Herbert Spencer, maintain that since only the fittest survive as a result of natural selection, those who survive are perfect. Thus, he equates survival with perfection. However, Devatma does not equate mere survival with perfection. For him, it is not a contradiction to say 'XYZ has survived, but it is not perfect'. Therefore, Devatma says that, according to the ceaseless process of change, such existences in every department of Nature follow the degrading activities of harming others, and thus cannot sink to nothingness over the course of time. Similarly, such existences show higher conduct, progress in their utility to others and achieve better and better harmony with other existences, which, in turn, prolongs their life. Hence, a time must come when there will be existences in each kingdom whose intra-group and extra-group relationship will be one of pure service and absolute harmony.

The process of evolution has a direction, and hence, it is teleological. There is an emergence of species and individuals, which makes the realization of a world of values possible. The process of evolution is teleological both at the unconscious and conscious levels. On the other hand, the evolutionary process is both biological as well as cultural. When Devatma speaks of the process of evolution, it is not limited to biological evolution. With the appearance of man, a new technique of evolution has come into operation – the method of cumulation and communication: the cultural method.

Man is a tool-making animal. His tools preserve his manipulation of material for use in defence and production. He can think in symbols and his written language preserves his thinking. These socio-psychological processes of cumulation and communication of learned responses have replaced the biological process of mutation through genes. For example, a science student at university level may know more science than any great scientist did. Thus, the part played by genes in biological evolution is also played by culture in social evolution. This cultural process is as much a natural process as the biological process is.

Therefore, human evolution concerns the health, strength and growth of the human life-force. What constitutes the content of inner and outer conditions of evolution is determinable through the study of the human soul, just as what constitutes the health, strength and growth of a body is determinable through the study of the body.

All those personal feelings, thoughts, actions and social conditions of customs, conventions and laws, which contribute to the health, strength and growth of the soul, are the inner and outer conditions of evolution. Thus, human good consists of the conditions of evolution, and human evil consists of the conditions of human bondage.

Low-loves and low-hates are human evils, for they are destruction of the health and strength of the soul and other existents. Higher loves and higher hates are human good, for they make for the strength of the soul and contribute to the evolution of others.

Last but not least, what is the future should it not concern completing the course of evolution? Can human beings be Devatma or can they choose to be perfect? Man's moral perfection is possible only because of cultural evolution. The advances of humankind towards optimum moral perfection have developed through association and rapport with fellows, and moreover, through Devatma. However, he cannot become Devatma because a person who attains to the evolution of his altruistic feelings is sattvick jiwan Dhari (an altruistic person), not Devatma. A person can become Devatma if he develops sublime powers amounting to an absolute love for what is true and good, as well as having an equal intensity for hating evil and untruth. Altruistic feelings, such as compassion, justice, gratitude, reverence, honesty, etc., remain under the influence of pleasure principles and they dispose him to partiality and untruth. Devatma alone is the ideal soul, as he has no disposition towards evil and untruth.

Therefore, the sum of all the higher feelings is not Devatma. No doubt, as believed by Devatma, there is no end of evolution; thus, moral perfection is not possible. Of course! One can be the best altruist, but not Devatma, because altruism falls under the influence of pleasure principles rather than truth and Goodness.

Devatma's philosophy will through rapport with the Devatma alone, in that a human soul can understand the highest development of the process of evolution in the sublime life of Devatma and the beneficial evolution it will bring in all the orders of existences – human, animal, plant and the inanimate world.

Thanks to evolution for the emergence of Devatma, where mankind leaps forward in evolution under the light and power, which is the embodiment of truth and goodness.

Evolutionary Naturalism in Devatma

The naturalism of Devatma attempts to integrate the physical world and the self-consciousness world, keeping their distinctive features intact. This is obtained through its theory of evolution, which has the following characteristics:

- New qualities emerge themselves which exhibit new laws of behaviour. So evolution is not merely change but it incorporates in itself an overhauling pertaining to novel qualities and behaviour. There cannot be evolution in the process of home coming. Naturalism of the inanimate world is fundamental to all existences. The primary substances of the universe are matter and physical force. The existence of the higher levels lies in the existence of the matter-force.

- The evolved levels of consciousness carry with them the defining characteristics of its origin. This is to say that life has evolved certain chemical and physical conditions. Therefore, a living body is analyzable into chemical constituents. This shows the pattern of carrying defining characteristics that constitute the earlier levels of existence.

The direction of the evolution is a complicated embodied existence. The human being, which is a multi-cellular organism, is more embodied than amoebae, for instance. This fashioning of characters puts the human soul in no disembodied existence either in the present or in its future.

With these embodied entities, subject to evolution, we can define the knowledge spheres. Its simple implication is that if there is no knowledge about God, Brahma or disembodied souls, there cannot be existence in either the perceptible or imperceptible thought universe. However, knowledge-imparting cognitive powers are not exclusive, but rather inclusive for understanding of the universe. The highest cognitive powers thus need the lowest cognitive powers in order to arrive at theory and verification thereof.

The evolutionary ethics of Devatma does not reject the other-worldly ethics. It also rejects such forms of Naturalism which advocate satisfying our biological urges, such as animals. For this lower world of animals, the rule of survival of the fittest applies itself to eliminating the weak. An animal does not require any justification for its deeds given to the basic idea of being an animal only, and has not evolved itself as man. Man has, as per the law of evolution, accumulated its social character, and therefore, it cannot seek shelter by comparing himself with animals for its behavioural lowering to the extent of animals, for this would mean to ignore the laws of evolution.

The ethics of Devatma reject the idealist ethics materialisms of getting haphazard satisfaction from biological urges. All needs have a space in true ethics and religion. But these needs must be so evolved that they contribute to both the good of the individual and society.

A need is sinful only if it harms the independent existences of others. The ethics is the requirement of a religious life. The true religious genius is the sublimation of biological urges and interpersonal and infra-personal relationships on the basis of truth and goodness.

Devatma, the father of Dev Dharma, represents a type of religious genius. Aesthetics exhibits itself in his eating, neat living, pat wearing, and a beautiful married life. In doing this, Devatma develops virtues of purity and loyalty for the partner by recognizing the truth of the multiplicity of relationships and servicing humankind for their conduction of a religious life. Animals, plants and inanimate objects all fall in line for getting their due from Devatma. All business inspired by goodness for himself and for others. This life of comprehensive values is based upon the second characteristic of evolution, which Devatma offers as an ideal religious genius. This may be the 'the way, the truth and the life' for the whole of humankind.

- Evolution is not directed by a single value of survival. Darwin interprets the facts of evolution in purely biological terms (i.e. chance variations occur in species). Those variations in a species, which are helpful for adjustment with physical environments, persist in the course of time and give rise to new species. The new species is the fittest but not the best. There is one value which explains the rise and persistence of species (i.e. the capacity to meet the challenge of physical environments). This is too limited an interpretation of the facts of evolution and will not explain the evolution of man. It is true that man has the capacity of survival, but we find that man also has capacity to discover truth and appreciate beauty.

Man could have survived even if he had not evolved these higher capacities of cognition and conduct. Why should evolution give rise to a species that shows some capacity for truth, goodness and beauty? The evolutionary process shows direction towards bringing forth a species with an increasing capacity for understanding and learning, thus leading to man with capacities for values of truth, goodness and beauty, besides the value of survival. In fact, the generation sweep of evolution indicates that those species have a future which does not harm others. Such animal species have a greater chance of survival which do not harm to other species but help other species. Goodness is a condition for survival. There is no conflict between survival and goodness.

Therefore, the evolutionary process is the process of the survival of species or groups which contribute to goodness, truth and beauty. Evolutionary ethics circumscribes the satisfactions of human desires within the bounds of truth, goodness and beauty. Man is to bring beauty and grace in all his thought and behaviour. Truth, goodness, and beauty are conducive to the survival of the human person and human group.

- There is no single method as to evolution. Up until the rise of man, evolution has followed the biological method. For any new characteristic to rise, new species are to emerge. This was the process of the rise of new species.

The evolution in human species is socio-cultural. What was once possible through the rise of new species is now realizable through the rise of a new man of genius in human society who educates the rest of the species into a new mode of life. Through language and group life, treasures of knowledge, ethics, and aesthetics are accumulated and preserved for future generations. What mankind gained in knowledge and conduct in thousands of years has now been acquired by the younger generation of the last twenty years. The scientific mode of thinking is now socially inherited for every child in modern schools. Mankind is acquiring a new mode of scientific thinking, and turning new species apart from the superstitious mind of the primitive man of the forest and the cave. Every master genius helps mankind to rise to a new level of behaviour that we have defined to be evolution. These characteristics of the process of the evolution have a significant bearing on the future of mankind on earth. It is clear that evolution is not purely biological in character but also is multi-valuational. Further, evolution does not only involve genes but also through education.

Devatma holds that, just as the evolutionary process has thrown up men of genius to invent scientific methods and discover the truths in the fields of physics, chemistry, biology and social sciences; it has given rise to a unique religious genius in his person with a new psychology to further man's evolution in feelings and conduct. Man, at his best, is altruistic, and we find that different religious founders have been endowed with some altruistic virtues, such as non-violence, compassion, benevolence, justice, brotherhood and disinterested service, and through these virtues they have helped mankind to build the civilized life as we know it today.

However, altruistic virtues are limited in their vision and conduct. In light of this, they only carry the civilizing activity of man to a limited extent. An altruistic virtue does not cover the whole of the psychology of man because each virtue cannot see beyond its own value that it pursues. Secondly, each virtue makes us partial to its own good, and hence, a life of virtue may deviate us into untruth and evil.

To remove and reduce the reign of evil and untruth in social life, it was not sufficient to have a religious leader with altruistic virtues. Thus, the process of evolution has evolved a genius with a supra- altruistic character, whose virtues are not under the bewitchment of pleasure principle, and hence, are not vitiated by untruthful disposition but are rather under the principle of truth and goodness. Hence, such a genius is free from partiality and prejudice, and whose vision is wide awake to the total field of values. Such a religious genius can help mankind to see the ugliness of vice, create desire to abjure it and give strength to get rid of anyone who is a complete lover of truth and goodness as well as a complete hater of the untruth and evil, which evolved in Devatma.

Therefore, Devatma claims that he is the moral and religious genius thrown up by evolution to fashion a moral and spiritual culture, as scientific geniuses have established scientific culture.

The evolution of mankind into a new level of mentality and conduct, as manifested by the new geniuses, brings in the need of social institutions of education and religion. The function of social institutions is to further man's evolution. In this task, Dev Dharma is fashioning a new species of human beings.

Keep The Doors Open:
The Human Evolution

Human evolution means the health, strength and growth of the human soul. Soul-consciousness is the peak of evolution but it is not last step, the climax. If we evolve, grow and create a blissful state of soul, it is Human evolution.

Thus, human good and human evil are determinable by the study of the human soul. However, good and evil are not humanistic concepts, they are cosmic concepts.

Devatma holds the human soul is a life-force in that it is nutritive, reproductive, sensitive, intellectual, aesthetic and emotional. Moreover, it is born, grows and decays like any other living organism. Therefore, for Devatma, the good and bad carry the same meaning as health and growth, disease or decay carry for the medical scientist.

He extends the application of good and bad to non-living things. The conditions that preserve such an inanimate entity are good, and the conditions that injure or destroy it, are bad.

He takes a cosmic view of both good and bad values. The entities in the cosmos are in casual relationships – when a causal interrelation betters the figure, form and qualities in a relationship, it is good, and when it harms them, it is bad. There are changes in the entities that produce a pattern of mutual co-operation for better existence, those that are called evolutionary or good, and changes in the entities that produce a pattern of mutual destruction, with such changes considered devolutionary or bad.

Ethically, the value situation of our planet as a whole, there have been changes in the physical conditions that have made life possible, and these conditions continue to persist. These changes are good or evolutionary. Therefore, there have been changes in the growth of life under the stimuli of certain physical conditions that good of all existences: human, animal, plant and mineral – these are evolutionary changes. There are changes in the cosmos which threaten the extinction of life and delays in further improvements of species or qualities in the animal or plant world or in human communities—these are called devolutionary changes.

Devatma holds that good or evolution of man is not in conflict with the good or evolution of other entities, but is rather part of it. Whenever man participates in the process of evolution, he ensures the health, strength and the growth of his soul.

For example, when low-loves and low-hates injure and exploit others, they constitute the pathology of human soul and its bondage and tend to blind, pervert and weaken the soul, and ultimately, bring about its death.

Higher loves and higher hates make us fair, just and serviceable to others and they strengthen the human soul. They constitute human evolution.

Devatma employs two concepts in his philosophy: salvation and evolution. Salvation means deliverance from low-loves and low-hates, while evolution means the development of higher loves and higher hates. Just as health is not only freedom from diseases but the positive functioning of bodily organs for the strength of the body, the health of the soul not only regards freedom from low-loves and low-hates, but positive development of altruistic feelings-higher loves and higher hates.

226

Always on the Funeral Pyre— Human Altruistic personality

Human Altruistic personality, even at its best, is degraded with certain limitations which decrease against its full growth and satisfaction.

For example, I may have an altruistic feeling to appreciate the achievements of others, but my self-love is jealous of the free satisfaction this altruistic feeling brings.

Similarly, I may have an altruistic feeling of justice, but my partiality towards some issues may make its full operation impossible.

Likewise, I may have a feeling of service of others, but my partiality for my own group may make me cold to the service of other groups, or even make me hostile and harmful to them. Thus, my inter-group altruism may be accompanied by extra-group indifference and even enmity.

I may develop love for a good cause and may desire to part with my money for it, but my attachment to money or children may bar my way to this altruistic satisfaction. The cause of women's emancipation may touch me but my service may be soiled by my sexual weakness. I may feel attraction for a great personality and start serving him, but my vanity may make my adjustment to him difficult, and I may cease to be of service to him. Our altruistic personality grows with the weeds of low-loves and low-hates, sapping the full growth of altruistic feelings and leaving a stunted personality for us.

Even if low-loves and low-hates are not allowed to grow or are removed forever, there will still be certain difficulties standing in the way completing the altruistic personality of the human being.

- Human personality does not show the capacity to develop total configuration of all the altruistic feelings.

- The growth and development of all altruistic feelings in us is limited by our individual inherited capacities and social influences. Since human personality shows incapacity for love of good as such, it must continue to remain incomplete in its altruistic altruism organism for us to have an idea of the state of an incomplete altruistic organism.

- There are even further limitations to the human altruistic personality, with each altruistic feeling showing limited spread.

- Human altruism also shows limitation in relation to depth. The depth of an altruistic feeling should correspond to the extent and the quality of the values in a person or thing towards which the altruistic feeling is directed. It is directed toward specific values and is exclusive rather than inclusive of all the benefactors and benefits.

- Apart from this limitation in relation to love of goodness, human altruism in infected with an element of untruth. To live a truthful life is to have impartial appreciation of and adjustment to the true character of values of persons and things. When our altruism shows partiality for certain persons rather than others, there is an element of untruth in it. There is also an element of untruth in my feeling of the appreciation of good qualities, even if I am not able to the do so, in relation to a person who does not belong to my social group, community or country, or to whom feel hostile towards, even though he possesses the same qualities which I appreciate in others. There is an element of untruth when my gratitude is touched by some benefactors and where the depth of my reverence does not take note of the quality of excellences of the persons concerned. This is unjust and untrue to the constituents of the value world, and this element of untruth exposes the fact that human altruism is not founded on a love of truth.

If it is ideal for human evolution to develop adjustment with all the four kingdoms of Nature on truth and goodness, man's altruism is not sufficient unto him.

The Great Love Affair
with the Universe

1. The universe is one, everything is interconnected.

2. The universe consists of two elements: matter and force.

3. The weighted element is matter and its weightless counterpart is force. Each of these constituents has entirely different characteristics. Therefore, the two elements cannot be combined into one, and neither can they transform into each other.

4. There is an inseparable relationship between matter and force, meaning that they can never become dissociated from one another — they always stay together.

5. Matter exists in different forms, such as solids, liquids or gases. The most suitable form of matter is that which flows through the entire universe.

6. Material objects consist of atoms. It is through force that all of them are in a state of vibration. Vibration produces the long and short waves within them.

7. Force manifests itself in both attraction and repulsion. It assumes new forms through its own activities and it can also change matter to create new forms.

8. The universe is always in a state of change due to its ceaseless activity of force. Every aspect of the universe undergoes change. The fundamental law of change is universal and immutable in the universe.

{Note: Under the law of change, force and matter mutually change their forms, thus giving rise to innumerable worlds, including our solar system, which also contains our Earth. This Earth plays host to innumerable existences in the form of plants, animals and human beings. Under this law, just as numerous worlds and living beings keep appearing, so too do they lose their individual forms over the course of time}.

9. Under the law of change, whereas some parts of the universe take an upward course and assume higher forms, some other parts take a downward course and assume lower forms. According to these simultaneous courses of activity, when one part or individual undergoes constructive change, another part or individual undergoes destructive change. In this process, some develop positively while others experience decline; or in other words, some evolve while others devolve.

10. In the universe, when an existence takes an upward course in its development, it is considered to have evolved, whereas when an existence takes a downward course and becomes worse than before, it is said to have devolved or degenerated.

11. Although it is clear that matter and force change their forms, both of them are indestructible, and are, therefore, eternal.

{Note: The universe was not made or created or built by some Ishwar, or God – the common belief that the universe was made or created by God is entirely false}.

12. Matter and force are inseparably united. Their mutual action and reaction is the main cause of the appearance and disappearance of millions of beings in the inanimate, vegetable, animal, and human kingdoms.

13. The higher or lower changes in any non-living or living existence are dependent on the following conditions:

    (i)   the capacity to change;
    (ii) surrounding relationships;
    (iii) the medium that relates to its environing conditions; and
    (iv) the influence of mutual action and reaction between its surroundings.

14. If an existence is closely associated with its environing conditions to the extent that it becomes degraded, then its association is called degrading, and if it becomes better, this association is called upgrading.

15. If an existence takes a downward course through its association with its environing conditions, then these conditions are considered unfavourable or devolutionary. In contrast, if such environing conditions lead to an upward course, they are considered favourable or evolutionary.

16. In the universe, millions of different existences go on to assume higher and higher forms through their favourable association with the environing conditions, while others go on degrading from higher forms, thereby assuming evil forms through evil association and degrading environ conditions.

The Philosophy Whose
Time Has Come

1. The force that exists in the various kinds of embodied living beings, which also operates in all activities of life is called an (organized) life force.

2. The organized life force constructs its living body independently and maintains its life force by consuming food. Being an independent life force, it directs the course of its life by itself and reproduces with other living bodies similar to it. Therefore, the organized life force is known by the four characteristic activities of

(i) construction, (ii) maintenance, (iii) direction, and (iv) reproduction.

{Note: There is an elementary consciousness present in the life force in terms of its physical activities of assimilation of food and protection}.

3. Millions of years ago, Monera, the most elementary form of life, first appeared in water

{Note: Monera are so tiny that they can only be perceived with a microscope. The size of a monera ranges between a seven-thousandth of an inch to two-thousand-five hundredths of an inch. These bloodless and boneless cells are incomplete living organisms.}

Monera comprise two kinds of organisms: (i) Protophytes and (ii) Protozoa. Protophytes assimilate nourishment from inanimate substances, while protozoa survive by eating protophytes. It is the protophytes that give birth to protozoa.

The first type of monera (i.e. protophytes), which are like subtle balls, are entirely homogeneous in both their interior and exterior. Some of them can become complete cells when in favourable environments, (i.e. the interior of a monera is hard while the exterior is soft). This hard, point-like part on the interior is called the nucleus, while the soft exterior is called the shell or covering.

4. Under certain environmental conditions, the unitary cells (i.e. nucleus) combine to form multi-cellular organisms. They go on organizing their energies and external bodies, which have taken the form of large and small plants and animals over millions of years. During the course of evolution, man – both his soul and body – has emerged from the animal world.

{Note: Apart from life force, there is no creator or maker called God or any other imaginary divine being among the bodies of plants or animals or human beings.}

ORGANISM OF THE HUMAN SOUL

5. The human soul contains numerous powers. The various groups in which these powers can be classified are as follows:

(i)   Body building and protecting powers;
(ii) Powers that produce sensuous consciousness (i.e. consciousness of physical shape and size, sound, smell, taste, heat and cold, hunger, thirst, pain and comfort).
(iii) Powers of (vasna) desires, i.e., the desire to live, the desire to protect oneself from sorrow, pain and degeneration; the desire

for the pleasure of taste, smell, vocal and instrumental music, listening, sexual intercourse, possessions and praise, etc.

(iv) Power of (uttejna) or passions, i.e., the passion of anger, vindictiveness, violence, jealousy, etc.

(v) Mental powers i.e., the topographical sense, temporal sense, sense of beauty, sense of rhythm, imagination, memory, word formation, thinking or reasoning, etc.

(vi) Ego powers, i.e., feelings of arrogance, vanity etc.

These powers are not found in all men in the same number and with the same strength. They vary to a great degree among people. The organism of the soul does not become complete with these six kinds of powers. It remains very much incomplete. Besides these six kinds of powers, some altruistic powers have developed in some souls to a greater or lesser degree. Therefore, from the point of view of altruistic powers, there are several souls, who more or less possess the seventh kind of powers. There is another kind of power above the altruistic group of powers that are called Dev Kosha; the soul on the one hand attains its complete soul organism and on the other hand, develops the whole gamut of altruistic powers.

6. There is an inseparable relationship between a soul with a dynamic force (shakti- meiy atma) and its body. Both are essential for the total being of man. Neither of them can stay alive without the other. Just as body, when it is separated from soul does not stay alive, so also, when soul is deprived of its body and is not able to build a new (subtle) body, then, it, too, does not stay alive and loses its individual entity and turns into physical force.

{Note: It is as necessary for the life of the soul to remain united to body (gross or subtle) as it is necessary for the life of the body to remain united to soul.}

7. Under the grand, immutable and universal of law of change, the forces of the inner organism of the soul undergo as much change as its external body does.

8. According to the grand law of change, millions of existences of the vegetable, the animals and the human kingdoms have different forms from one another and are different form one another in virtue of their characteristics and qualities and are higher or lower in their state in terms of their value character. Millions of human souls are graded in millions of kinds in virtue of their high or low, noble or ignoble state of life.

{Note: It is false belief of Advaita Vedantists and Vedantists that one formless universal Brahman pervades millions of human bodies of which each human soul is an aspect. The truth is that millions of individual souls inhabiting millions of bodies stay as separate existences with different characteristics. Among these millions of souls, there is one who is complete in its organism and the rest of the millions of them are different in gradation of completeness – some are very incomplete and some less incomplete, some very degraded, some less degraded, some very bad and some less bad, some very noble, and some others less noble}.

9. According to the immutable and grand law of change, the extent to which a soul is born with ability to evolve higher powers and attain favourable conditions of associating with higher souls, to that extent it develops higher life in itself. A soul that develops higher powers of complete soul organism can also obtain the privilege of becoming immortal.

10. If a soul is incapable of developing life-conducive higher powers in itself, then in this state, it gradually gets debilitated and one day it becomes extinct.

{Note: On of the one hand, persons ignorant of the grand law of change and on the other hand motivated with strong urge for continued existence and enmeshed in false traditional beliefs, hold that every human soul is immortal. This belief of theirs is absolutely false.}

11. The life force in every living human being, i.e. its soul, is the most fundamental essence of it. In its preservation is his continued existence, and in its death is his extinction. If a soul continues to function according to the various kinds of consciousnesses, then on the one hand he can satisfy his true natural and strong urge for longevity and on the other hand, he becomes capable of enjoying certain pleasures according to its state of development. But if one's soul is extinct, then with this loss, his natural desire to get pleasurable satisfactions dies and he becomes incapable of enjoying pleasure of any kind.

12. It is the primary aim of man to preserve his soul by making it free from slavery to lower passions and their evil distortion and by evolving in it higher altruistic or Dharmic feelings.

GOOD AND EVIL ACTIVITIES & THEIR CONSCIOUSNESS

13. A person responds internally and externally in relation to experiences. His internal reaction is called thought and his external reaction is called overt activity or action or karma (and the two together are called conduct).

14. Various feelings are the chief motivation of good and bad thoughts and actions. If a person is devoid of a feeling, then he does not do any action corresponding to that feeling.

{Note: A person devoid of the feeling of compassion does think about alleviating the suffering of others. On the contrary, such a person does not feel remorse about inflicting pain and suffering on others. A person possessed of the feeling of violence puts to death various innocent living creatures for the satisfaction of his evil feelings. A greedy man steals, cheats, experiences jealousy when they hear someone being praised more than him even for some good quality and wishes him ill etc.}

15. A person undesirably motivated by appetites, passions, ego loves, and intellectual powers takes to various evil courses of action and thus greatly harms the existence of his soul by his evil thoughts and actions in relation to various orders of existents in Nature. For instance,

    (i)   Dominated by pleasure-affording appetites a person in satisfaction of them, indulges in various courses of evil conduct in relation to various orders of existence and besides harming others, he very much harms his own soul;

    (ii) Dominated by various passions, a person in his urge for satisfaction indulges in undesirable thoughts and overt activity in relation to various orders of existence and besides harming others, he very much harms his own soul-life;

    (iii) Dominated by ego-loves, a person in their satisfaction indulges in undesirable thoughts and actions in relation to various orders of existences and thus very much harms his own soul-life;

    (iv) Dominated by false beliefs and evil superstitions, a person in satisfaction of them, adopts evil courses of action and thus very much harms his own soul-life.

16. Though all good and bad urges have their origin in the psychology of a person, yet they may sometimes be reinforced by other men of this world and of 'parloka'.

{Note: God or Satan do not exist and therefore cannot cause urges in man. Therefore, the belief in the 'voice of God' through 'conscience' is pure myth.}

17. Without the awakening of genuine consciousness of the relatively superior importance and value of his soul in comparison to his body, and other things of the world, a person remains completely unconcerned to know what is good and evil for his soul. He spends his life in the gratification of his pleasure or pain producing appetites and passions which are dominant in him. He does not experience

any genuine concern to evolve religious feelings of altruism and to get rid of evil feelings in him.

18. A person who does not possess to a sufficient degree higher consciousness about what is good or bad for him or others cannot in the nature of things have direct knowledge about good or bad. In such a state of ignorance he cannot but rest his beliefs about what is good or bad, right or wrong. What is virtuous or vicious, noble or ignorable, sacred or sinful, on his imagination or speculation or received tradition.

19. The belief about right and wrong, good and bad, virtues and vice, sacred or sinful, which a person entertains, on the basis of his imagination or speculation, traditional faith or belief may be true or may not be true. No wonder different religions on this earth have different views on what is right or wrong, sacred or sinful; in several cases, contradictory beliefs are prevalent. That is, what is sin in one religion is not a sin in another religion or even more it is believed to be right or sacred.

{Note: The believers in one, all-good God hold different things or even self-contradicting things to be sacred or sinful as the word of God. Since belief in God is pure myth, it is no wonder that religious founders, being at different levels of moral consciousness, have propagated different and even self-contradictory beliefs about what is right or wrong.}

20. Apart from a complete embodiment of religious life or a true Devatma who in the course of evolution has evolved all-sided consciousness of what is right or wrong, good or bad in relation to all living and non-living orders of existences, no human being or so-called god – including 'God', can give true consciousness or knowledge of what is true or false, virtue or vice, noble or ignoble, sacred or sinful life.

HIGHER AND LOWER INFLUENCES THROUGH ASSOCIATION

21. Like other living and non-living existences, man also emanates every moment of his being, some type of subtle particles. These subtle particles resemble smoke and have good or bad character according to the good or bad character of the person from whom they emanate.

22. The good or bad subtle particles emanating from the being of man spread themselves all round. They pervade all living and non-living things, (such as) surrounding air, the walls of a house, clothes and other fellow human beings, animals, and trees to the extent of their attractiveness for them.

23. The material particles of things of good or bad odour are not sighted by the eyes of man but on striking the olfactory nerve give evidence of their good or bad odor and though a person who lacks the sense of smell does not sense the good or bad odours, yet they cast their good or bad influence on him. In the same way, though ordinary persons are not conscious of high or low influences of the subtle particles through their sight, but higher souls are able to have conscious experience of them. Those who lack conscious experience of them yet assimilate them according to their good or bad nature and thus become better or worse persons.

24. Just as the residence and objects therein assimilate the higher influences of noble souls through association with them, the same is true for living plants, animals and men. In the same way the various inanimate things like house and clothes, no less living things like plants, animals and men become degraded through association with evil souls.

25. A person benefits himself or does good to himself to the extent he dissociates himself from such men, animals and plants, house, clothes,

places, and air that contain evil influences, and associates himself with men, animals, places, and clothes, that exercise higher influences.

26. The sprouting and development of a higher feeling which leads a man to higher activity not only elevates his soul-life to greater and smaller extent but also improves the quality of the cells of his body. In the same way every evil appetite, passion and ego-love and false belief degrades not only the soul of a person but degrades the cells of his body also.

27. Both thought or feeling waves which emanates out of a man spread every moment and thus the whole atmosphere is charged with good or bad influences of different people. The people of different character and life attract such of the influences suited to their nature and capacity. Thus, knowingly or unknowingly they are moulded by them in good or bad natures and feel pleasure or pain according to them.

28. A person here on earth, all of sudden and without any apparent cause feels sorrow and depressed by receiving without his knowledge the ethereal current of thought or feeling of some relation of his living at a great distance from him or one who has departed to 'Parloka' on account of the latter being stricken with some special sorrow, pain or misfortune. Some persons possessing and acute sense directly see that a particular relation of theirs is in trouble. Some persons are able to see by inner visual sense in day time or in dream state or hear sentences by auditory sense that a particular relation is in trouble.

{Note: Those special men and women who possess inner sight or inner auditory sense can serve as mediums and if they so desire, they can prove helpful to others by arranging interviews with their departed relations who are living in the Parloka.}

29. It is the soul alone which is the architect of its own body. It pervades in every part of its body. It is united with every part of it. Thus, just

as it influences the body with its good or bad state so also the body influences the soul with its good or bad state.

30. The various feelings of the soul exhibit themselves on the face of a person. One can judge by seeing the facial expression of a man whether he is sad, sorrowful, happy or unhappy, lustful, angry, vindictiveness, hypocrite, wicked, sincere, modest, gentle etc. Nobility of a soul casts a beautiful reflection on the face of a person and its attractiveness is felt by noble souls. An evil, low and wicked soul casts an ugly and dreadful reflection on the face of a person and is felt as bad and dreadful by noble souls. To the extent a soul is free from distortion of evil-producing feelings, to that extent the purity of the soul is reflected on the face of a person. To the extent a soul is decked with beautiful feelings and love of higher activities to that extent the inner beauty of life casts a beautiful and attractive glow on the face of the person. Evil life makes a soul ugly and repulsive and noble life makes a soul beautiful and attractive.

THE CONSEQUENCES OF HIGHER & LOWER COURSES OF LIFE

31. According to the immutable law of change, just as the body suffers immediately the consequences of its violation of the laws of health, i.e., in getting diseased or ill, in the same way the soul of man too reaps immediately the consequences of its evil doing by its distortion (i.e., in getting diseased).

32. A man who takes poison experiences its consequences in his body and there is no need of an outside punishing authority. In the same way, there is no punishing authority needed for a soul to suffer the consequences of its evil conduct. The same principle applies to good conduct. Therefore, the belief of being punished or rewarded for conduct by 'Ishwar,' 'Khuda,' 'God,' or 'Yama-raja' at some specific time is absolutely mythical and false.

33. The laws relating to punishment of crime which human society has gradually set up and developed for maintaining external peace is altogether different from the model of punishment based on the universal and inevitable laws of Nature. The former punishments are different in different countries. The latter system of punishment is the same for all countries. The former system change but the latter never changes. The former is different for different people but the latter system is the same for the whole of humanity. Under the former system hundreds of persons escape punishment for one or another of their crimes but under the latter system no man or animal or tree or any other object, can ever and under any conditions escape from the operation of its laws.

34. Just as a human life force builds in the womb of the mother, a human body similar to that of its parents and not the body of an animal like elephant, horse, donkey, cat, rat, pigeon, partridge, crow, etc. or that of any tree, or plant like mango, jambu, mulberry, marigold, gulmehdi, jasmine, radish, coriander, spinach, fenugreek etc. in the same way the soul after leaving the gross body builds from its subtle particles a subtle human body and not the body of an animal or plant nor assumes the body of an animal or plant. Such transformation is against the laws of Nature. Those who believe that a human soul after the death of its gross body assumes the body of some animal or tree, according to its deeds, cherish false beliefs.

PLEASURE AND EVOLUTION

35. Pleasure and evolution are not identical. Evolution inevitably leads to pleasure but pleasure does not in all cases lead to evolution; rather, more often than not, it produces evil and unhappiness.

36. A person given entirely to love of pleasure can never evolve to a higher life; by following the evolutionary course of life, he not only gets ordinary pleasure but is heir to higher pleasures also.

A Journey From Fiction to Reality

1. Every big or small organized living being of the vegetable world:
   (a) wants to live; and
   (b) does not want to become extinct.

So, it struggles every moment to save itself from extinction and to stay alive. Above the vegetable world every member of the animal and the human kingdoms has, besides the desire to live, developed consciousness of pleasure. It

   (a) wants to live;
   (b) does not want to become extinct;
   (c) wants to live in a pleasurable state; and
   (d) does not want to suffer pain.

It strives to save itself from death and suffering and to stay alive and happy. Despite moments of suffering, it strives to stay alive. It is the principal instinct of animals and men to stay alive and stay happy, on the one hand, and to avoid death and suffering on the other hand.

Further, between the two strivings, the striving to stay alive is far more dominant in them than the striving for pleasurable satisfactions. Hence except in the case of morbidity, no man, or animal ever tries to destroy itself. On the contrary, it always struggles to live.

The teaching of true religion is based on the knowledge of universal and immutable laws, and the fulfilment or failure of these basic urges for life and pleasure.

2. It depends on the strength of the life force of a man or an animal or a plant for it to stay alive, i.e., life can exist only so long as the life force remains intact. If a life force becomes extinct under certain conditions or loses the capacity to keep its body alive, then, it too does not remain alive. When it loses its organic character, it gets converted to physical force. And then its individuality as a man, an animal or a plant is totally destroyed. So long a man does not, on the one hand, possess knowledge about his life force, i.e., the organism of his soul, the fundamental and immutable laws of its evolution and preservation for the longest duration and its degradation and gradual decay and death, and on the other hand does not develop various higher consciousnesses which protect him from destruction and evolve capacity for more and more life, he cannot fulfil his dominant urge to stay alive and resist extinction.

3. Those higher forces, which help to germinate and develop altruistic feelings conducive to prolonging life in a soul, giving it the character of complete organism, constitute religion. A person develops religious life in his soul to the extent he grows these religious (higher) forces in himself and is entitled to be called a religious soul. Apart from these religious forces, whatever beliefs, dress, rituals or other actions are current in different countries under the name of religion, are not religious at all.

4. Every such appetite, passion, egoism or any false faith or belief or action which induces a human soul to develop pro-attitude to evil and produces in it distorted or deteriorated life, in violation of the religious feelings or force, is irreligious or 'adharma.'

5. Just as in a human body, the various organs for its protection and preservation are the same in all human beings, in the same way

in a human soul, the various religious forces for its protection and evolution are the same for all men, that is, there is the same identical complete religious life or ideal for all mankind.

6. Just as there are the same scientific truths about the human body for all mankind, in the same way, there are the same scientific truths for all mankind about the organism of human souls, its degradation and evolution, or what is 'dharmic' (religious) and 'adharmic' (irreligious).

Altruistic and Sublime or Complete Religious life

7. The higher forces, which germinate and develop real religious life and which in course of time show capacity to mature to complete the soul organism, can be divided into two categories, one of which is sattvic kosha or altruistic forces and the other Devkosha or Sublime forces.

8. By the germination and development of sattvic (altruistic) and Dev (sublime) forces, there is sprouting and development of higher conduct and higher life in a soul. This is what constitutes its evolution. Contrary to it, dominance of the forces of egoism, appetites, passions, and superstitious beliefs give rise to and develop evil conduct and evil life in soul. The evil conduct produces harmful suffering and the soul gradually decays and dies in course of time as an organized entity. This is its devolution.

9. In the course of the evolution from among the altruistic souls, when a soul appears which develops in itself all the altruistic forces which complete its organism in all respects, and which on attaining this complete organism, is on the one hand, blissfully free from undesirable conduct of untruth and evil in relation to all the kingdoms of Nature and on the other hand is in love with conduct based on truth and goodness and is thus capable to establish complete harmony with higher evolution, then, it rises superior to

all altruistic souls to become the most worshipful embodiment of Devrupa; such a Devatma (or embodiment of Devrupa of truth and goodness) on being equipped to establish his relation with all the kingdoms of Nature on higher conduct and on being free from all evil attachments in relation to them, becomes capable to evolve his soul higher every day and becomes the most exalted and indispensable part of higher evolution.

10. When a feeling germinates in a soul which urges it to do some disinterested service in relation to some kingdom of Nature, there is addition in the soul of a new part of beneficial conduct and through it, there is beginning of higher conduct. These higher-conduct-producing feelings are of various kinds and they are called altruistic feelings.

11. In the course of evolution of mankind, under the law of variation, several souls are born who came in the world with inheritance of one or more altruistic feelings which they have grown or can grow in their heart in a greater or less degree according to their capacity and conditions. A soul is better in comparison to other souls to the extent and depth of the altruistic feelings which he develops and proves beneficial in relation to one or other kingdom of Nature.

12. When some altruistic feeling is absent in a soul, that person is capable of harming others. (For example, just as it is natural for a man of mercy to feel anxious or desirous to do an altruistic service, in the same way it is natural for a man with a passion for cruelty to feel anxious or desirous to inflict injury on someone.)

13. Though altruistic souls motivated by one or more altruistic feelings prove useful to the existences in the universe in one or another respect, yet being bereft of complete love for truth and goodness and complete hatred for untruth and evil, which characterize the complete soul organism of Devatma, they remain disposed to untruth and evil in many respects; as a consequence, they cannot

attain a life of complete freedom from evil conduct and complete development in higher conduct.

14. An altruistic soul is privileged, according to the excellence of his altruistic life, to enjoy longer life (on earth) unless some untoward accident overtakes him and to live in higher regions of Parloka (after death); and experience higher satisfaction or happiness in comparison to other souls inferior to him.

15. Crores of human souls lack the capacity to develop a higher life; on the contrary they are disposed to become more evil each day. Some souls have the capacity to develop higher life for a limited extent but not reach beyond it. There are others who have capacity to continuously grow into a higher life.

16. Under the law of variation operative in mankind, there are souls who not only lack any altruistic feeling, but their souls do not have the capacity at all of germinating any altruistic feeling. It is an absolute false belief of theists that each soul is born with a spark of divinity with the capacity to progress (in spiritual life) till eternity.

Knowledge: POSSIBLE AND IMPOSSIBLE

17. It is only through some of his knowledge-imparting consciousness that man does and can gain direct knowledge about any subject.

18. When a man lacks a particular knowledge-imparting consciousness, he can never obtain direct knowledge open to that consciousness.

19. Due to difference in the number and acuity of knowledge-imparting consciousnesses, men do not attain to the same degree of knowledge.

20. Man cannot obtain knowledge apart from all kinds of his knowledge-imparting consciousnesses.

TRUE AND FALSE

21. That proposition which man's knowledge-imparting consciousness finds absolutely necessary to accept and impossible to disbelieve is self-evident or direct knowledge.

22. All knowledge, other that self-evident or direct knowledge, is indirect knowledge.

23. Indirect knowledge is of three kinds:

    (i)   Traditional;
    (ii) Faith; and
    (iii) Inference.

24. Indirect beliefs can either be true or false.

25. A belief which is consonant with,
    (a) a direct-knowledge-imparting consciousness;
    (b) right test;
    (c) logical reasoning; and
    (d) previous knowledge, is true. A belief which is against any one of these criteria is false.

26. The power of imagination or speculation in man can be helpful in gaining knowledge but by itself it cannot always yield knowledge.

27. Knowledge is always desirable for man and therefore worthy to be assimilated.

28. False belief is always undesirable for man and therefore needs to be rejected.

29. For man, knowledge about the soul is of the highest value and therefore primary knowledge, for it is by getting this knowledge

only that man is able to protect and evolve his soul as far as it is possible according to his competence.

30. Apart from all-sided knowledge of the soul, no other knowledge is primary; rather it is secondary.

31. In order to gain complete knowledge of the soul, it is essential and therefore desirable for man to obtain knowledge of the fundamental truths of the universe.

32. In comparison with knowledge of other kinds, the propagation of all-sided knowledge of soul is more essential and more desirable than any other form of knowledge.

FAITH

33. To rely on or trust the word or conduct of another person in some field is called faith.

34. Just as it is essential so also it is natural for man to trust or to rely on the word and the conduct or some person.

35. There are two kinds of faith: true and false. When a belief is based on truth, it is true faith, and when a belief is based on falsehood it is blind faith.

36. The greater our faith in the word or conduct of any person, the greater our trust in him.

37. It is only trough knowledge, and not through false belief, that man can have real and superior welfare in life. It is therefore essential for him to test his belief against the criteria of knowledge and immediately give up all such beliefs that do not meet the criteria.

38. It is only through knowledge and not through false belief that man can gain real and superior welfare of life. Therefore, it is imperative

for every man anxious for his soul-welfare that he remains loyal with rock-like determination to the beliefs which satisfy the criteria of truth and should never give them up, despite the opinions of others.

39. It is essential for a fit soul (adhikari atma), anxious to develop religious life and gain true salvation to have full faith in his guru, who is the supreme well-wisher, supreme good-doer, imparter of religious life and salvation.

40. To the extent a person, desirous of obtaining true religion and salvation, gives up self-centeredness, that is, the dominance of appetites, passions or ego loves of his and the understanding and thinking motivated by them, and comes to believe his life-imparting guru as superior and superb to him and through habitual spiritual exercises grows faith in him, day-by-day, to that extent he becomes more reverential to him and establishes deep communion with him and gains capacity to get his higher light and higher consciousness.

ADORATION AND WORSHIP

41. When a person becomes desirous to attain freedom from certain evil conduct and to evolve to a higher state of being and live a more altruistic life, he establishes communion with Him so He may illuminate his soul. This enables him to:

(i)   see in His higher light one or another of his evil conduct in its true ugliness and develop aversion for it;

(ii) to see in His higher light one or another defilement of his soul and become purified through reparation; and

(iii) to see the beauty of one or another sublime religious feeling in Him; feels attraction for it and strives to develop it as far as possible.

This process of spiritual exercises is called true worship.

42. All such religious exercises of a person constitute false and harmful worship which do not help to obtain that light and that awakening which reveal evil conduct as evil and produce an urge to get rid of it; on the contrary, they render his soul less illuminated, insensible, sinful, defiled, and evil.

(Note – Just as there are various kinds of mythical worshipful beings in different communities and religions, there are also various kinds of exercises of false worship in relation to them.)

43. So long there is no awakening in a person about the organism of his soul and its evolution and degradation, he remains ill-equipped to accept a true worshipful being and the true method of worshipping him.

44. A person can develop awakening about the real nature of the organism of his soul, its evolution and degradation through the benevolence and true association of such souls who have this awakening or consciousness in them.

WORSHIPFUL BEING & WORSHIPPER

45. When a person considers someone as his malefactor or benefactor or presents him adoration, concentration, prayer, and offerings, then the latter is called his worshipful being. A worshipful being is also called god or goddess in ordinary language, and he who worships him is called worshipper or 'bhakta' or 'sevak.'

46. There are various kinds of gods and goddesses which people worship; while some are true most are mythical.

47. The various real beings that have been worshiped are as follows:

    (i) Worship of one's own ancestors or ancestors of others: This worship is called ancestor worship, guru worship, sadhu worship, avatar worship, prophet worship, peer worship, saint worship, hero worship, etc.

(ii) Worship of some beneficent or harmful animals: There is the worship of cow, bull, horse, snake etc.

(iii) Worship of trees: peepal (Ficus religiosa or sacred fig) tree, banyan etc.

(iv) Worship of some inanimate objects: worship of sky, earth, sun, moon, fire, lightening, air, water, etc.

48. The various mythical beings who are worshipped on this earth are as follows:

(i) The various imaginary creators of this universe such as 'Brahma', 'Ishwar', 'Vishnu', 'Allaha', 'Khuda', 'God', etc.

(ii) Wish-fulfilling gods and goddesses, for example Durga, Saraswati, Kali, Shitla, Ganesh, etc.

49. The various kinds of worshippers in the world are as follows:

(i) Some go in for worship in order to seek satisfaction of some worldly gain such as wealth, land, property, or a cure from some disease, etc.

(ii) Some worship in order to get, after death, some pleasure-affording place called 'Swarag', 'Baikuntha', 'Goloka', 'Shivloka', 'Bahishat', or 'Heaven', etc.

(iii) Some worship to get their daily livelihood.

(iv) Some worship to get satisfaction of some saatvic or altruistic feeling or bliss.

50. For a person

(i) who has received truth-revealing light of true guru about religion; and

(ii) who has in him desire to get true deliverance from irreligious ('adharmic') or evil conduct and to evolve true religious (or altruistic feelings), it is imperative:

(a) to completely reject (belief in) gods and goddesses who are purely mythical; and

(b) also to dissociate from worshipful beings, who had or have at present real being but who have not manifested in their lives all-sided religious forces of love of truth and goodness and hatred of untruth and evil.

51. It is absolutely imperative for a person with some capacity to obtain freedom from a destructive life and to evolve to a higher or altruistic life. Those who have the desire to work for the above desirable change and to establish communion with Devatma who has manifested all religious forces (complete love of truth and goodness and complete hatred for untruth and evil) will develop complete soul organism.

52. It is only in communion with the soul which has attained to all-sided sublime life (Deva Jiwan), that a fit soul gets light and power that reveal sublime, wonderful and invaluable world of knowledge and feeling. They germinate and grow in the fit soul various consciousness in relation to his evil thoughts and actions which deliver him of them, and develop other various evolutionary consciousness which evolve in him the evolutionary altruistic feelings. Devatma possessed of complete soul-organism and complete Deva Jiwan is the one true worshipful being among mankind for all those desirous of true deliverance and true religious or altruistic life. It is the primary obligation of every fit soul who is desirous of true religion to offer true worship of this one true worshipful being (Satya Deva).

ATTAINMENT OF TRUE MOKSHA AND TRUE RELIGIOUS LIFE

53. So long as a man does not develop various kinds of consciousness of repulsion for those forces in him whose improper operation leads him to evil courses of conduct and thus makes him entangled in the devolutionary process, he cannot be free from their undesirable operation or slavery (especially if they happen to be pleasure-affording). In most cases, he does not even feel an urge to obtain such freedom, so much so that if some soul superior to him tries to deliver him from such evil courses of life, he frustrates his efforts through his opposition to him, and wants and persists in his pleasure-affording, though evil course of life.

(Note: One can imagine how difficult and uphill a task it is to develop some higher or religious feeling in such a soul even if he has the capacity for developing that higher or religious feeling!)

54. So long as a person is not desirous to gain true knowledge about religious life, till then he does not put in any effort or take to any means or any exercise which can develop some religious virtue which is absent in him. On the contrary if some higher soul, with the object of doing good to him, persuasively suggests to him such religious exercise, he feels offended and wishes to stay and does stay satisfied with one or another religious short coming.

(Note: The task of reclaiming millions of human beings who are in this terrible state of recalcitrance is an uphill battle.)

55. To obtain true salvation and reach a higher life (Dharmic Jiwan), it is necessary, for man according to the universal and immutable law of change in the universe,

   (i)   to have the capacity or potency to awaken various consciousnesses relating to one or both of these objectives; and

(ii) to obtain suitable associates for awakening such consciousness.

56. Those souls who

(i)   do not possess the capacity to develop consciousness in relation to true salvation and a true higher life (Dharmic Jiwan); or

(ii) even if they do possess the capacity for those consciousness but fail to get suitable associates to develop them, they cannot meet either of the objectives.

57. In the higher evolution of mankind Devatma is the only one true complete ideal of all-sided true salvation and higher life (Dharmic Jiwan). He is the one complete discoverer and knowledge-imparter of the truths of true salvation and true higher life.

58. To develop urge for true salvation and true higher life (Dharmic Jiwan) in a man it is necessary that true understanding should arise in him about the separate and distinct existence of the body and the soul and their inter-relation.

59. Of all the desires in man, the desire to live is naturally the most powerful. So if a man gets true understanding about the separate and distinct existence of his body and soul and their inter-relation, he will necessarily develop the desire to get true salvation and true higher life (Dharmic Jiwan).

60. The four different powers through whose exercise, a man can take to the spiritual exercises to get true salvation and true higher life (Dharma Jiwan) are as follows:

(i)   The exercise of meditation includes the spiritual exercises of reading, singing, repeated recitation (Jap) and concentration;

(ii) The exercise of concern of wishing well for oneself and others;

(iii) The exercise of linguistic power of speech; and

(iv) The exercise of physical organs.

(The first two powers are mental and the other two are physical.)

61. Man is a part of the composite universe. It is, therefore, necessary
    for him to get rid of his evil intent toward all aspects of the universe
    (human, animal, plant).

Man is a part of the composite universe. So in order to develop higher
life. it is imperative for him to take to all the necessary exercises to
develop various kinds of higher or 'dharmic' feelings in relation to every
aspect of the universe.

(Note: All those spiritual exercises that a man undertakes in relation
to every aspect of the universe for his true salvation and higher life are
called spiritual exercises or Brat or yajna in relation to that department.
A statement of the method and commandments concerning all such
spiritual exercises in relation to the various departments are given in
Dev Shastra IV.)

62. The aim of all spiritual exercises concerning true salvation and
    Dharma Jiwan is to give real self-realizations, that is:

    (i)   to be rid of evil intent for the universe and to purify his soul.

          A man (sadhak) must develop:

          (a) complete awakening (of various low conducts);
          (b) complete repulsion or hatred for them;
          (c) complete repentance; and
          (d) reparation and purification.

    (ii) on getting light about higher-life-producing consciousness a
          man must develop in relation to them:

          (a) complete awakening;
          (b) complete attraction or love;

(c) higher bliss or happiness; and

(d) higher power.

63. Due to ignorance of the nature of true salvation, the various religious founders have given false teachings about salvation which are most harmful and deserve to be rejected.

Skies beyond Skies

The fundamental principles of One Universal, Scientific True Religion

I. The universe and man's relation to it

(1) The universe is the name of the totality of all matter and all force, and it is one.
(2) Matter and force are indestructible and therefore are eternal. They always change in one or another form. No one has created or produced them.
(3) Force produces movement and movement brings about change. It is due to the operation of the immutable law of change that various entities come into existence or disappear.
(4) The universe has four divisions which are closely inter-related; (a) the inanimate world; (b) the plant world; (c) the animal world; and (d) the human world. The inanimate world is the basic world. It is from the inanimate force that life force evolved and has manifested itself in all the existences of the other three kingdoms.

II. The life force in man, its evolution and dissolution

(5) Man's life force alone is the builder, preserver, and operator of his body. It is therefore the most fundamental essence in him. Man's life force is his soul.

(6) Man's soul, like his body, is an organized existence, i.e., its organism consists of intelligence, appetites, passions and several other feelings.

(7) The soul of man, being a part of this universe, is under the operation of the immutable law of change, in the same way as other existences.

(8) Being under the operation of the immutable law of change, the soul of man either evolves when it changes for good or degrades when it changes for evil. It gradually becomes extinct through continuous degradation.

(9) When a human soul has the capacity to become good and gets evolutionary associates, then it evolves or rises higher in life.

(10) When a human soul has no capacity to become good or does not get evolutionary associates, it becomes degraded or devolves. Eventually, it devolves to a point where the human entity is extinct.

(11) Man's soul stays alive after the death of its gross body by constructing a subtle body similar to its earlier body, when it fulfils certain necessary laws.

III. True and Complete Religious Life in Man

(12) True religious life begins for a human soul when:

(a) it puts in effort to awaken consciousness in relation to one or another evil disposition in it in some cosmic relation and makes effort to get rid of all kinds of unfavourable or evil influences; and

(b) is in earnest to develop some unselfish good desire or urge in some cosmic relation.

The developments of higher dispositions whose evolution gives a human soul complete religious life are as follows:

(a) The development of the disposition of complete repulsion for what is untruthful and evil, which disposition protects it from degradation and devolution; and

(b) The development of the disposition of the complete attraction for what is true and good, which on the one hand brings about his evolution and on the other hand, establishes its harmony and unity with the evolutionary entities.

True religion is another name for higher life and complete true life is complete true religion.

It is only when a person achieves complete higher life that he can hope to protect himself from every form of degradation or devolution.

(13) It is the one and only one true and highest ideal or sublime ideal for man to completely protect himself from any deterioration and devolution on the one hand and to develop complete higher life and thus establish absolute harmony and unity with all evolutionary entities.

(14) In order to attain to knowledge of higher life and have complete development of dispositions or forces of repulsion and love (as stated and defined above), it is imperative for a human soul to establish rapport with one who is fully equipped with them.

(15) Devatma has achieved complete soul-organism by developing all the true and all-sided religious or higher forces or dispositions and, therefore, He is the relation who is the true and all-sided evolver for human souls.

IV. The Unique Manifestation of Dev Dharma

(16) Dev Dharma is another name for the manifestation of complete soul life in Devatma; the Dev Jyoti in him is the soul-life which reveals the truth about higher life. The metaphysical teaching of this religion is according to the immutable and true laws of Nature.

Therefore:

(a) Dev Dharma is the highest and noblest gift of Nature to man.

(b) Dev Dharma is alone scientific and therefore a true, universal and complete religion for humanity.

Apart from Dev Dharma, all other religions of the world and their ideals which are not based on science are:

(a) Fictitious and harmful in various ways; and

(b) They not only keep man away from knowledge of higher life and from achieving complete religious or higher life but they are also harmful to him and various other existences of the universe.

A Journey Without End

(PRINCIPLES OF TRUE SCIENTIFIC PHILOSOPHY OF LIFE AFTER LIFE)

1. On our gross solar system assuming organized form, each of its parts has been emitting subtle particles, according to the ceaseless law of change, and they have, under the law of gravitation formed themselves into a subtle solar system, similar in form to the gross solar system. The subtle earth of this subtle solar system is called Paraloka.

2. This subtle earth is divided into more and more graded regions. Each region is called a 'Loka' in Hindi (each higher region is higher in value content). The second is more beauteous and superior than the first, the third is more beauteous and superior than second etc. Below the first region there are comparatively speaking lower regions called 'Pradesha' in which persons and creatures of very low nature reside.

3. If the soul of a deceased person is able to obtain in sufficient amount, subtle particles from its gross body and has in it sufficient form-giving creative power to give them a form, then it can in a short time have a new subtle body, similar to its earlier gross body and lives as before as a living organism. On assuming subtle but similar bodily existence, the soul goes to reside in one or another lower or higher region of 'Parloka' or 'Pradesha' according to its higher or lower character. However, if it is not qualified to enter 'Parloka' or

'Pradesha', it stays on this earth or in an area surrounding it. Such unqualified souls are called Adhamatmas (evil souls) and their place of residence is called Adham-loka (evil region).

4. As a soul rises higher in character, it correspondingly produces a higher quality of subtle particles and on its death uses this to construct its new and finer body. It becomes qualified to enter and reside in a higher subtle region to the measure of its noble and higher character.

5. To the extent a soul is low in character, to that extent it produces subtle particles of lower quality and at the time of death of its body, it forms a subtle body of poor quality (if it has the constructive power to do so), and qualifies to stay either on earth or in one or another region of Paraloka according to the quality of its life.

6. To the extent a soul has capacity for higher and higher life and becomes noble, it correspondingly can live longer and is privileged to ascend to higher and higher regions of Parloka.

7. A soul, in whatever region it may be, which lacks the capacity to rise in higher life, gradually goes on deteriorating in its constructive power, and one day it is completely extinct in that or some other region.

8. A soul given to evil activity loses its capacity to produce subtle particles of that organ of the body (say, hands, feet, mouth, eye, ear, sex-organs etc.) to the extent it uses it to harm existences of some kingdom of Nature and therefore on the death of the gross body, it does not make that subtle organ for which it does not get the necessary amount of subtle particles or forms and incomplete organ if it receives inadequate subtle particles.

9. The subtle body which a sin-ridden soul forms on the death of its gross body either does not possess one or more of organs or possesses incomplete and useless organs. Due to the absence of some organs or having incomplete and useless organs, it suffers heart-rending pain besides the pain it experiences due to its degraded state of life.

10. These degraded souls subsist on the subtle particles that emanate from the food prepared in the houses of their relatives or other persons or which are found on shops for sale or on the edible fruits

of trees. They quench their thirst by subtle particles of water. The degraded souls given to meat diet go to slaughter houses or meat shops and take the subtle particles of the blood and flesh of the slaughtered animals. Besides, they kill and eat the subtle-bodied animals which on death do not qualify to enter Parloka and are condemned to stay in 'degraded region. Sometimes they kill and eat children who on death are able to form subtle bodies for themselves but cannot defend themselves in the absence of their guardians or protectors in degraded region or higher regions.

11. Millions of beings of the animal kingdom which are exclusively carnivorous or otherwise harmful become extinct on their death. Apart from them, there are several kinds of animals which go to Parloka. They go to the higher regions of Parloka according to the degree of their usefulness in cosmic relations. Millions of sin-ridden human souls, (which include thousands of believers of one God) are condemned to stay in 'Adham loka' or cannot go beyond the first or the second loka, while useful animals like cow and bull etc., qualify to comparatively higher regions on their death. The same law is operative in the case of beings of the vegetable kingdom. However, no plant or tree, big or small, builds its subtle body after its death near the place where it stood. On being capable of going to Parloka, it goes there with subtle particles, finds roots in that ground and then assumes a subtle body similar to its gross body on earth.

12. Men, animals and plants staying in different regions of Parloka go through similar routine of daily activities which they did on earth with their gross bodies. The only difference is that unlike the villages and cities of this earth, men and animals of low and higher character do not stay mixed together but persons and animals of more or less same character stay together in a region to which they are qualified.

13. The higher the regions of Parloka, the better are its physical geography and nobler are its men, animals and plants which inhabit it. There is comparatively greater harmony and happiness amongst them, i.e., their mutual relations is sweeter, happier, more peaceful, and life-promoting. As opposed to this, the lower the region, the

lower are the men, animals etc., which inhabit it. Their mutual relations are comparatively less sweet, less peaceful and less happy. The condition of the inhabitants of very low regions is comparatively worse and the condition of the inhabitants of adham loka is most wretched and painful.

14. Hundreds of the inhabitants of Parloka on finding someone of their relations on earth in a state of trouble come to his rescue by their suggestion or prayers. If anyone among the relations is dying, then besides helping him to assume new subtle body, they take him along to Parloka if he is qualified for it and help him in one or another way.

15. So long as a person does not develop an altruistic feeling in him by which he does unselfish service in relation to some department of Nature, he cannot rise to a region higher that the second. Though a soul rises to higher and higher regions as it develops various altruistic feelings, yet so long it does not develop complete Deva Jiwan, he cannot establish complete harmony with the higher evolutionary process and make for endless progress in higher life.

16. The souls devoid of altruistic feelings and given to pleasures do not progress. Those who work for social good gain more pleasure in life in comparison to those souls who do no social good.

The Whole World

1. The universe is real and eternal.
2. The universe is composed of matter and force.
3. There is ceaseless change in the universe due to interaction of matter and force.
4. This ceaseless change in the universe proves evolutionary or devolutionary for different existences.
5. The evolutionary and devolutionary changes in the existences of the universe are due to their higher or lower activities. Every existence in the universe gets degraded by low activities and get up-graded by higher activities.
6. The human soul gets degraded by evil activities. If it cannot get freedom from evil activities, it goes on getting degraded and one day it becomes completely extinct.
7. The presence of evolutionary forces in a human soul alone constitutes religious forces. The life which is manifested by these religious forces is called religious life.
8. Apart from true religious life and its true teaching, whatever else is prevalent in the name of religion on this earth is pure imagination. Through the acceptance of any fictitious religion or faith or spiritual exercise, one gains nothing but greatly harms himself and others.
9. In the evolution of human species Devatma alone gained complete soul-organism. There is complete manifestation of religious life in him. Through his influence of higher forces, fit (deserving) souls get deliverance from low activities and get evolution in religious life.

10. Human soul by itself on fulfilling certain laws, builds a gross body by itself. On the death of its gross body, it also keeps alive by constructing a subtle body from its gross body similar to its gross body on fulfilling certain laws. However, this subtle body has superior or inferior form, according to higher or lower character of a soul.

11. The universe consists of gross regions and subtle regions. Persons in the higher subtle regions show a degree of harmony in all respects to the extent of their superior life.

12. Extremely degraded souls after building their subtle bodies cannot reach any of the subtle regions in Parloka. But other souls higher to these extremely degraded souls, reach one or another subtle region of Parloka according to their character.

To the extent a soul obtains deliverance from low activities and attains evolution through higher activities, and reaches a higher region of Parloka, to that extent it is recipient of higher and satisfying influences and rises higher in evolution on being capable of it.

When a soul reaches such a region of Parloka where there is perfect harmony between the different kingdoms of Nature, it obtains perfectly good well-wishers as his companions and enjoys perfect peace and bliss and becomes capable to higher and higher evolution. Without evolving complete religious life, a soul cannot become an inhabitant of this region

Human Soul: Unknown to Yourself

The human soul is a part of Nature. The human personality is a soul-body organism and its soul is as much a part of Nature as its body is.

- The human soul has its origins in the biological history of Earth. It is neither uncreated nor created but evolved.
- A human soul is born as a result of the coalescence of the sperm and the ovum. It is a unique, emergent entity, unknown to the previous history of excellence. There is no transmigration.
- The constructive power of the human soul can construct a body peculiar to its own species. It cannot, therefore, take the form of a goat or a cow in any future life. Transmigration further violates the truth that each life-force can construct a body peculiar to it and not any other.
- The human soul, like any other life-force, is functionally related to its body as its builder, maintainer, sustainer and repairer. If the human soul is so functionally related to its body, it cannot leave it by any yogic exercise and return to it.
- The highest powers of the human soul, its power to discover and understand truth, to appreciate and create beauty and to build institutions of justice and welfare are as much evolved as the motor and sensory functions of the animal soul have evolved from the nutritive, motor and sensory functions. They are necessary to the functioning of these higher powers and are integral to any achievement of the higher powers. The entire soul of man is an evolute from biological life.

The Book of Secrets: Embodied Soul

All evolved species are embodied species. The soul, as one of the evolved life-forces, is an embodied entity. Scientific psychology studies man as an embodied existence, as a psycho-physical organism. There is no support for the theory of the disembodied soul in the scientific study of human personality.

The soul is a part of Nature, not only in its biological history, but also in its origin and in its ethical and spiritual destiny.

No activity of human life falls outside the study of biology, psychology, sociology and other sciences; therefore, the disembodied soul is functionless and consequently non-existent.

Transmigration is not required for the ethical problem as to how man is rewarded or punished for his good or evil Karmas or deeds.

The physical conditions must, invariably and unconditionally, give effect to other physical conditions and not to utility or beauty.

In the same way, in the valuational field, an action must produce its appropriate value effects invariably and unconditionally, which happens frequently. If I grasp some new truths, I must be illumined; if I serve others, I must and do become an altruist; if I create or appreciate works of arts, I must and do become an artist or aesthete. To be illumined or to be altruistic or an aesthete are inner experiences which give us satisfactions of truth, goodness and beauty. These are the direct consequences of my valuational actions and there are no effects of the laws of Karma. Further, there is no moral ground for believing in transmigration, for the reward of good action is immediate and incomparable in the form of inner excellence of mind, even if this mental state or mind does not last beyond the moments of its realisation. The punishment for immoral actions is immediate and immense in the form of the disfigurement and ugliness of inner life, even if it is not followed by loss of money, wealth or social face – the evil action sets rot at the core of life.

If we develop consciousness about the health and disease of our soul, we will think it proper to observe moral laws and feel satisfied that the reward of good life is health of the soul. We will seek and desire no reward beyond it. Therefore, the moral ground for transmigration is dispensed with it. The moral laws of the health of the human soul and their violation as leading to the disease of the human soul therefore reject transmigration as an uncalled for hypothesis for a pseudo-moral problem.

Thus, neither the natural and social sciences of biology, sociology, economics and psychology, nor the normal sciences, such as ethics, need the hypothesis of the disembodied soul for the explanation of human activities. So, the hypothesis of the disembodied soul is redundant and thus stands condemned.

In Search of a Lost Treasure

Each one of us feels in himself a separate centre of experiencing individuality. My experience is mine in the sense in which experiencing others is not mine, even though the object of experience and enjoyment may happen to be the same.

I experience my body in a way in which I do not experience the body of another, even though it happens to be my child. Its date of birth is different and its death may be different – the fact of sympathy does not obliterate the demarcation between the sympathiser and the sympathised, but rather focuses it. If separate centres of experiencing of individuals are denied, sympathy turns into self-pity, which is a contemptible state of mind in comparison to the glory of sympathy. My satisfaction or happiness at the prosperity or progress of another is divine virtue and not a case of psychological self-glutting. In the same way, my love for another is not a case of self-love.

The experiencing of the glow of illumination in me is exclusively and entirely mine. What can be shared is the common object of experiencing, but not the experiencing of it.

There is a difference in the organs and sense organs of different individuals. Also, there is a difference in the qualities of different individuals. Some are altruistic or sattvic, such as sages, some are tamasic or evil, with others are rajasic or ambitious. Therefore, all souls are not one.

Soul is a part of the natural order (i.e. empirical in origin, character and content). Hence, the human soul is born and the human species has evolved from the mammalian branch of the animal world and human souls are born every day through the sperm's impregnation of the ovum. The science of biology establishes the truth that each human soul is a unique product of separate conditions, and hence, the factual evidence for plurality of the souls is irrefutable.

You cannot Escape Change

To exist is to change. Whatever exists is a matter-force unit. The modern discovery of the convertibility of matter into force and force into matter affirms the fundamental thesis of Devatma, in that no unit of existence stays unchanged.

Devatma places the soul in the vortex of change, for he places it in Nature and cuts all its association with some transcendental reality for either its origin or destiny. The soul is no foreigner in Nature, which has lost its way. In every inch of its being, it bears the indelible marks of its origin and growth in Nature. It is one with all other existents in Nature in its being under the law of ceaseless change, thereby running the risk of extinction.

Change in soul has a value dimension. Every change helps or hinders the integrity, vitality and quality of the soul. Changes that help to preserve, evolve and strengthen the human soul are good, whereas changes that hinder the preservation, progress and constructive power of the soul are bad. Value is an inseparable dimension of changes in human consciousness. For the human soul, to be is to be change and to change is to evolve or decay, to be good or evil.

A Small Candle is Enough

There are no disembodied individuals and the human soul is an evolute. The human soul has originated from an animal species. The higher life-force is inclusive of the functions of the lower-forces from which it has evolved. Since the lowest nutritive function is inseparable from the human soul, the human soul is embodied. The individual transforms his environment, and in transforming the environment, transforms itself. Man's life force shows the maximum capacity for transforming his environment in comparison to plants and animals.

Man has transformed himself from a savage soul to a civilized soul in knowledge, feeling and conduct. Thus, to be a doer is to effect change, and in effecting change, be changed in turn.

Therefore, the human soul is neither substance nor pure cognition – it is a nutritive organism, with motor, sensory, affective, conative and cognitive functions. As such, it is the doer, as it effects change and gets changed. It is under the law of change, subject to growth, decay and death under certain conditions.

You are not immortal

The human soul is similar to the life-forces in plants and animals and is under the laws of change in Nature. Hence, it is not immortal. A human personality is a psycho-physical organism, here and hereafter. Hence, its continued existence depends on physical as well as psychic conditions.

The psychic conditions for the persistence of a human personality are two-fold:

- Its soul must remain free from the diseases of evil dispositions and actions;
- It must maintain and evolve altruistic or beneficial dispositions and actions.

A human soul is diseased when it follows the guidance of pleasure in the exclusive determination of its course of thoughts and actions. The freedom from low-loves and low-hates and the evolution of altruistic forces are essential for soul preservation.

If a human soul does not possess some altruistic feelings, the existent body building power will continue to gradually decrease in the absence of any thought or action which could create such power, and that soul will become weaker by the day. Again, it has some altruistic feelings through which it is able to produce some strength in itself by doing altruistic activities. Even if some hindrance occurs in their working of any account, or if there is any decrease in or a complete cessation of their functioning, the soul's power will stop increasing and will go on decreasing. At some point in time, when its power is completely lost, it will die in the same way in which its own or another person's living body dies on the complete loss of its strength.

The soul of man is most intimately connected with its body (i.e. as the body of man cannot remain alive when the soul departs from it and consequently it dies). In the same way, the soul cannot live and it dies if it is not able to build a body for itself to live in.

The human soul is not able to function at all without a living body possessing a brain and nervous system. Without such a living body, it can never grow conscious of anything and can never get any knowledge without this medium. Furthermore, it cannot feel any pain or pleasure, nor feel love or hate for a person or an object, nor manifest any other activity. Consequently, if the soul is not able to build its body and is not able to live in it, then not only does it die, but even its living body dies. Thus, the entire being of the man becomes extinct.

Hence, if at the time of the death of its gross body the soul of man is not able to build a subtle body for itself, in which it can live as it did in respect of the gross body, then the entire being of the man is extinct.

But if, at the time of the death of its gross body, the soul is able to draw the finer living cells or particles that are stored within its gross body – from the feet to the head – and build out of them, by means of its constructive power, a body almost identical in form and features with its gross body, though finer in its essence, can continue the pilgrimage of life.

Thus, the subtle body, though finer in texture, is still the same human body and can be easily identified. This living but subtle body, like the gross body, feels hunger, thirst, the need for recuperation or rest, the heat and cold of seasons, the pleasant and unpleasant sensations, etc.

Also, it retains its sex and possesses the self-same organs barring those which the deceased has, by its misuse, destroyed. He or she has to fulfil the same laws of Nature in order to exist, as he or she fulfilled them here on Earth. The soul also possesses the same mental powers, the same feelings, etc.

The finer cells of the subtle body are built by the soul of man. This capacity to build finer cells is acquired by the soul of the human child several weeks after its birth on this Earth if the work of its preservation and maintenance continues uninterrupted thereafter. It is at this point that its constructive power grows sufficiently strong and it is able to build finer cells and store them in the body.

But even after it has required the capacity to build the finer cells out of its gross body, it does not, in all cases, at the time of its physical death, build a new subtle body and continue its existence. If under certain unfavourable circumstances it is not able, at the time of death, to draw the finer cells from its gross body and collect them in one place for the construction of its subtle body, it cannot build such a body for itself and become extinct.

A Little Taste of Human Life-force

An evolutionary view of the human soul:

- Human soul is an organized life-force.
- It has its origin in the animal kingdom. It has evolved from mammals and shows the characteristics of the life-force in them.
- It builds the peculiar human body, as the life-force in a cow constructs the peculiar body of a cow.
- It is essentially a doer.
- It not only constructs the human body, but also maintains, sustains and repairs itself, and reproduces new individuals of its species with the procreative powers integral to it.
- If the soul loses the constructive power to preserve its body, however gross or subtle, it meets death. The soul has no life apart from the human body, so its biological powers are intrinsic to it.
- The constructive power of the human soul is central to its existence. If it is destroyed, the soul is destroyed.
- Good is what preserves and strengths the constructive power of the soul; bad is what weakens and damages it.
- Besides the constructive power, the soul has a large number of drives, motives or desires.
- The attraction to pleasure and aversion to pain deviates the drive behaviour to augment pleasure and reduce pain irrespective of the health of the body.

- When a human soul develops ego consciousness, he or she experiences certain needs connected with it, such as praise, honour, name and fame, selfishness, vanity, etc. These deviations are untruthful and evil in character.
- The motivation of gregariousness, sociability, self-assertion, acquisition and the possession of wealth and property, children and family life, aggressiveness and social beliefs and practices brings untruth and evil in interpersonal relationships because of love for pleasure.
- There are some human beings in whom the altruistic feelings of justice, reverence, gratitude and responsiveness to the needs of others, etc., are present.
- Aesthetic feelings, such as a sense of beauty, a linguistic sense, a sense of music, a sense of order and a sense of cleanliness, are also present in some human souls.

Education for Life before Permanent Death

(Theory of knowledge-what we can know or what we know)

The human soul acquires a knowledge of such forms and qualities of embodied existences as his various consciousnesses lay open to him. Devatma takes an evolutionary view of the various sources of knowledge and the form of knowledge.

The structure of human consciousness has been classified into eight groups. Man can get direct knowledge about the different matters concerning Nature by means of these eight types of consciousnesses. They are:

- Direct-knowledge-giving elementary consciousnesses (sense organs)

Nature has given man various sense organs in order to get direct true knowledge about the forms, sounds, smiles, and tastes, etc. of different existences. It is only through these sense organs and through no other means that humans acquire direct knowledge about perceptual objects.

- Direct-knowledge-giving intellectual powers

The following are the cognitive powers by the evolution of which man can or does get direct knowledge about the different aspects of Nature:

(1) Power of retention; (2) Power of memory; (3) Power of imagination; (4) Power of concentration; (5) Power of Reasoning.

- Direct-knowledge-giving consciousnesses connected with the conception of Ego or "I"

The human child has no consciousness of own, particularly during the time of its babyhood and even for some time thereafter. In the course of time, it becomes conscious of its individuality of the 'self' or 'I', which was previously absent, and begins using the terms 'I', 'me', 'mine' and 'my' in connection with one or other activity or feeling. Thus, the child uses language such as: 'I am feeling hungry', 'where is my cap?' etc.

- Direct-knowledge-giving lower kind of consciousnesses of sensual feeling

Direct knowledge about the the reality of certain aspects of Nature that can be obtained through some particular feeling can only be acquired by that feeling alone, such as:

(1) Passion or love for money, (2) passion or love for children and (3) passion or love for lust, etc.

- Direct-knowledge-giving aesthetic senses or consciousnesses, which are:

(1)   Sense of Beauty
(2)   Linguistic Sense
(3)   Sense of Music
(4)   Sense of Order
(5)   Sense of Cleanliness, etc.

- Direct-Knowledge-giving higher feelings based on justice

- Direct-Knowledge-giving higher feelings of Reverence and Service of others

(1) Feeling of altruistic reverence
(2) The altruistic feeling of gratitude
(3) The altruistic feeling of sympathy or the realization of the pain of others
(4) The altruistic feeling of responsiveness to the needs of others; etc.

- Direct-Knowledge-giving several kinds of Dev shaktis or Higher psychic Forces

(1) Complete Love for true and only true knowledge in respect of every department of Nature;
(2) Complete hatred for all Kinds of False beliefs pertaining to every department of Nature;
(3) Complete love for all that is good or beneficial in respect of every department of Nature;
(4) Complete hatred for all kinds of wrongs or evils in relation to every department of Nature;

- Necessity of sufficient or love for every truth relating to the subject about which true knowledge is sought.
- Necessity of sufficient attraction or love for the scientific method of investigation for the acquisition of true knowledge in any field of Nature.
- The necessity of sufficient love for the method of logical reasoning in order to master a true knowledge of any subject.
- The necessity of various life-forms to perceive the truths in nature.

The Devatma accepts the evolutionary theory of knowledge. A child learns what its parents and teachers in school teach it, passively accepting all that it is taught. This is why millions of people acquire false beliefs, and once acquired, they stick to them. Since they are people, they lack the complete love for truth and goodness and complete hatred for falsehood and evil, and fail to question them. Moreover, low loves for sensual pleasures, wealth, prestige, fame, idleness etc., and low hates lead people to accept and fabricate all sorts of falsehoods and evil deeds. Thus, "all kinds of falsehoods, evil deeds, crimes and sins, which are rampant across the globe, are the direct and inevitable outcome of the various kinds of low loves and low hates which dominate the human heart."

It is not possible for anyone to learn all the truths about Nature all by oneself directly from childhood, so it is necessary to have faith in a teacher, for without such a belief, life would be impossible. Moreover, one may not have the particular faculty by which one can acquire direct and true knowledge in any specific sphere of Nature. In such cases, if one desires knowledge in that field, one has to put faith in the words and teachings of another person, who is believed to possess the direct knowledge in that sphere. "In short", says Devatma, "it is impossible for any man, related as he is to other men, not to put some kind of faith in any other man in the world."

In a case in which a person accepts certain beliefs on the authority of some other person, it is necessary to check or find out whether the beliefs or statements accepted by him on the authority of some other person are true or false.

The Devatma holds that there are four Nature-based criteria for testing such belief. They are:

1. Only beliefs about existents in Nature can be true and all beliefs in supernatural objects are false.
2. Any belief which goes against the direct knowledge obtained through any of the eight kinds of direct-knowledge-giving consciousnesses is false.
3. Any belief inconsistent with the principles of validity in logic cannot be true.
4. Any belief inconsistent with or which violates any immutable laws of Nature, i.e. those which can never be or are not proved by any experience cannot be true. After giving these four criteria, the

Devatma adds, "If any of the teachings of the Devatma also fail to prove true on being tested by any one of these four criteria, it, too, does not deserve to be accepted as true."

Nature (Reality) is conceived to be the infinite fountain source of all and every aspect of true knowledge. It is pre-supposed that there is an intimate relationship between knowledge and Nature. The structure of truth involves the corresponding structure of Nature, devoid of which truth stands obstructed from reality, and thus, become a contentless, barren concept that would fail to yield true knowledge:

(1)   Existence of corresponding sphere of reality (Nature); and
(2)   Presence of direct knowledge-giving consciousness.

* The necessity of true knowledge for man
* Eight consciousnesses giving direct knowledge
* Four loves
* Motivation for the origin of falsehood
* Necessity for faith in another human
* The nature–based criteria for testing beliefs

Naturally, we cannot expect Devatma to discuss these problems using the language of an epistemologist.

An empiricist in epistemology need not be a materialist, but he must be a naturalist. Devatma is a Naturalist philosophy. It would be futile to ask whether Devatma's ontology determines his epistemology or vice-versa. The truth seems to be that a philosophical commitment, which is simultaneously expressed through metaphysics, epistemology, logic, ethics, aesthetic, religion, and other aspects of life.

According to Devatma, 'It is the highest and noblest privilege of man to have the capacity to acquire greater and greater true knowledge about Nature in general and in particular about his own soul, which is the most essential part of his being and to get more and more freedom from all false beliefs, superstitions, fictions and false religion, and to be able to not only to get rid of every kind of falsehood but also to accept truth and truth alone'. Devatma is able to clearly demarcate the boundary between the sphere of (true) knowledge and the sphere of false beliefs, superstitions, etc.

All aspects of existences have been classified into four spheres of Nature. The following list comprises the spheres of Nature in respect of which man can acquire true knowledge.

- The reality of the various kind of existences in Nature composed of matter and force.
- The physical forms and qualities of various kind of real existences in Nature.
- The inanimate and animate forces of the various kinds of real existences in Nature and their attributes.
- The immutable processes of Nature, also called its immutable laws, which act under the operation of the changes take occur in Nature and the facts concerning such changes.

'Excepting these four true spheres of real Nature, the teachings of all other prevalent matters in the human world are but vain gossip or false'.

The Light-The Gateway of Devatma

(Sublime Light)

Dev Jyoti is a light in the field of values.

- It helps a person to see what is good or bad and right or wrong in one's conduct and character.
- In this light, one is able to see what is harmful and thus hateful in certain habits, such as smoking, drinking, and excessive indulgence in food, sex, rest, gossip, etc.
- It enables one to see how evil it is to see what causes harm to others, such as unnecessary injury to the form and/or qualities of things, cruelty to animals, meat-eating, stealing, and cheating, etc. This light also shows the ugliness of character.
- In this light, one is able to see the ugliness and hatefulness of greed for money, which leads one to exploit labour and the customer in business.
- It exposes the hatefulness of lust for power, which leads one to deprive others of their rights and treat them as things.
- It makes one beholder to the evils of over attachments and under-attachments.
- It provides a condition for seeing the beauty of what is good and right in both conduct and character.
- It opens the world of altruistic feelings in all its beauty and grandeur.

- One perceives one's unconditional love and service in beautiful colours and sees one's obligation to do something for them in return, thereby expanding intrinsic worth from the human world to the animal, plant and inanimate world.
- One awakens in this sublime light to the exalted excellences of great souls and one dances in appreciation of their great virtues and also reshapes one's life in the service of one or another excellence.
- One sees the beauty of the service of the unfortunate, the diseased and the poor with the feeling of compassion.
- One sees the urgency to change socio-economic conditions which perpetuate the misery of the masses with the feeling of justice.
- In the sublime light, one sees conflict between good and evil, but also conflict between good and good, such as justice and compassion, reverence and compassion, etc.
- One sees how to resolve conflict between altruistic feelings and determine what is the right thing to do when these conflicts arise, because each altruistic feeling is partial to its good and is blind to the good of other altruistic feelings.
- One sees the best law and best principles, which are framed with a complete love of truth and goodness. In the sublime light, one can see the extrinsic and intrinsic beauty of the species that is fully evolved in Nature, which is Devatma.

Ethics and Laws of the Soul

Devatma's ethics are within the reach of all men, regardless of whether one is an intellectual, a philosopher or a layman. The core of Devatma's ethics is the human-soul and the aim of his philosophy is the advancement of the human soul. Soul consciousness can only be acquired by one who considers his soul as the highest good and who tries to gain freedom from low-loves and low-hates while cultivating higher-loves and higher-hates. Devatma's ethics is unique, meaning that, while a total empiricist, he employs the empirical method to study the laws of the soul, for to study of the soul is religion and morality.

Devatma re-examines the maps of the geography of the universe and the human soul as drawn by speculation, human desire and aspirations, and rejects all such elements that do not satisfy the demands of scientific method, logic and the direct evidence of the eight-fold consciousnesses. He draws his own blueprint in accordance with the demands of the scientific method.

When Devatma comes to deal with Ethics, he employs the same scientific spirit and the same scientific method to understand it. Values do not constitute a world apart, a world of essences, just as he rejects it in Ethics. There is nothing outside Nature – value, like facts, are part of Nature.

289

For Devatma, Ethics is a science that aims to discover the laws of the soul and its conditions of health and ill-health, just as medicine aims to discover the laws of the body, as well as its condition of health and ill-health. Just as no reference to the super-naturalism is required for the science of medicine, no reference to it is necessary for the science of Ethics.

The whole empirical life is thus worth discarding as valueless, for it appears to be infested with unavoidable pains and impermanent pleasures. It is the aesthete's hatred of pain that makes the philosopher, in general, theorize a way out of body involvement.

Devatma rejects this ideal of freedom from pain or of a permanent state of uninterrupted pleasure as bad ethics. For him, neither empirical Hedonism nor transcendental Hedonism is the human ideal. He saw clearly that the pursuit of pleasure – whether empirical or transcendental – is not the pursuit of good. More than any other philosopher, he has brought out the moral and spiritual evils or diseases that attend to the exclusive pursuit of the pleasure, regardless of whether the pleasure pursued is empirical or transcendental. His moral perceptions on the invidious influences of the pleasure principle on the health of the human soul are classic in the philosophic literature.

Ethics with a difference

Different methods have been employed in the study of the problems of conduct in human thought.

Devatma denies the existence of God, and naturally rejects the method of revelation. He rejects that commandments in the scriptures are right because they are the word of god or revealed. He exposes the evil character of many of the commandments given in different scriptures. For him, moral laws are as verifiable as the laws of health.

Devatma also rejects the apriority approach to the problems of conduct. Reason is most competent to deal with the world of the possible or essences where the relations between entities are necessary. It cannot, by itself, know the laws of the existents. Just as we cannot do research in medicine through the apriority method, we cannot have an apriority method for ethical research. Medicine discovers the laws of the health of the body. Ethics, for Devatma, discovers the law of the health of the soul. Medicine uses empirical methods in its study and Devatma urges the use of the empirical method in the study of Ethics.

Devatma holds that good essentially centres around the soul. The principles of goodness are the law of the health of soul. Any moral principle can be verified to be true, in the same manner as any principle of health can be verified to be the true verification of the principles of goodness in the manner of a medical scientist.

Though Devatma employs an empirical method, he avoids the error of some of the empiricists. He would not accept Mill's identification of the desirable or good with what is desired, for what is desired may be bad. He does not reduce Ethics to Psychology nor to Biology or any other natural science and considers Ethics as analogous to bodily hygiene. The laws of physical health, which are purely descriptive, are not like the laws of gravity, which are partly descriptive and partly prescriptive. We find in them at once the elements of description and prescription. In the same way, the moral laws are both descriptive and prescriptive and the prescriptive element is amenable to the empirical method. The statements of metal hygiene are empirical prescriptive statements. Devatma employs the empirical method parallel to the way a mental hygiene scientist uses this method to develop and verifying their conclusions.

Devatma, however, thinks that special equipment is required for the discovery of moral laws, in contrast to the equipment required for the discovery of physical laws. This is a valuation consciousness that is essential for a worker in this field. One requires a sense of justice to discover the conditions that violate justice or those which can promote justice. In the absence of the sense of justice, no investigator can set out to discover just laws to regulate human relations. An investigator with a sense of compassion can discover the laws for the amelioration of the conditions of the down-trodden.

The moral equipment is not to be identified with conscience. Devatma rejects conscience as a single power, which unerringly tells us what is right or wrong in interpersonal relationships. Each vale needs a specific sense for its perception and practice. An individual equipped with a sense of justice can perceive what is just in certain situations, but not what is generous. Again, this sense of justice is not a single power. In the same way, a man with a sense of justice in the economic field may lack a sense of justice in certain familial relationships.

Devatma calls these senses of value altruistic feelings. Each altruistic feeling is a condition for the cognition of value corresponding to its specific sensitivity. The altruistic feeling of justice is a condition for the discovery of one or another right of man as or of man in certain social or occupational contexts. The altruistic feeling of compassion is a condition for the perception of the needs of a helpless and unfortunate group.

Devatma holds that, whereas each altruistic feeling can help to discover certain laws for the regulation of the relationship between man and the sub-human kingdoms, none of them can singly and collectively know the nature of soul, its laws of health and disease, its freedom from disease and the evolution of its health. It is a person endowed with a love of all-sided goodness and all-sided truth who is mentally equipped to undertake this task. This love of goodness is not the sum total of all altruistic feelings about goodness, though a person with love of goodness will have the whole gamut of altruistic feelings. Nor is the love of truth the sum total of altruistic feelings for the understanding and discovery of truths in different fields. Man is crippled in this slavery to the principle of pleasure. Devatma claims himself as the only soul equipped for this task.

However, even the deliverance of one possessed of love of goodness and truth need not be accepted as true. Since no human understanding is immune from error. Our beliefs, whether concerning facts or values, or both, are on eternal probation to be re-checked every time new facts, values or both come to light.

Devatma is a true empiricist in both method and spirit. Though a man of religion, a religion and a religious leader who challenged all religions, he never put his deliverance outside the possibility of error and insisted that, from his philosophy, whatever does not satisfy the scientific criteria of truth must be rejected. He writes, "If any of the teachings of the Devatma also fail to satisfy any one of these four criteria, it too does not deserve to be accepted as true".

However, his empirical Ethics is an Ethics with a difference. Though it employs the empirical method, what it studies are the laws of the health of the soul, which, for him, are the laws of morality and religion. The modern empiricists in Ethics are not sensitive to the relation of soul and values, and are found to mainly concern systematizing the values discovered by certain altruistic feelings. There is all the difference between a codified common-sense and a science about the subject, which is the difference between other Empirical Ethics and the Empirical Ethics of Devatma.

The Root Problems of All Problems

The feeling of pleasure inevitably accompanies the satisfaction of all desires, whether biological or social, evil or altruistic.

The satisfaction of desire cannot escape the feeling of pleasure. A man may find that pleasure will prompt him to repeat the acts of cruelty and he would, through a repetition of cruel acts, develop the character of cruelty. For example, when someone finds and cares for an injured bird, he or she finds pleasure in the satisfaction of this desire. This pleasure prompts him to do acts of kindness towards animals, and thus, he becomes a man of compassion. The difference between the man of cruelty and the man of compassion is not that one experiences pleasure and the other does not do so – both experience pleasure. The difference is 'in their desires' – cruelty and compassion – and not in the presence or absence of pleasure.

Dark Slavery of Human bondage

The human tragedy is the human tendency to deviate into evil and untruth. This is man's bondage. The problem for philosophy is to pinpoint this tendency and to find out how this tendency can be checkmated or hedged round to safeguard human personality from its devastating influences.

The human will is subject to deviations into untruth and evil because it is often under the dominant or exclusive sway of the pleasure principle. The pursuit of pleasure is not the pursuit of the true. If a will is determined in its choice by the principle of truth and goodness, it can only give consent to the beliefs to which logic and facts would warrant and approve conduct and to which the situation and values would recommend. However, if a will is determined by the pleasure principle alone, it may believe what is contrary to logic and fact, and act contrary to what situations and values demand.

It is not the human vices that are under the sway of the pleasure principle but rather our moral virtues too. So long as the influence of the pleasure principle is present in human thought and actions, humans will not be able to deviate into untruth and evil. There are vast dark corners in the human soul, which, due to the dominance of the pleasure principle, stay in bondage to untruth and evil. And there is not a single corner in the human soul that completely shines with truth and goodness. However, there are shades of the pleasure principle which dim the brightness of the best of the moral and intellectual virtues in man – this is the human limitation and sets the limit to human ethics.

Fallen a Prey to Bondage

There are drives, motives, desires or forms of will that admit of dominance through their feeling of satisfaction. More specifically, this is true for such volitions as they concern themselves with bodily and ego-centric urges. These are the special areas of human bondage.

Devatma takes the major biological, psychological and social human drives and holds a mirror to humankind to see how many low-loves and corresponding low-hates he has developed, and thus falls a prey to bondage.

Devatma divides the urges into these main groups:

- There are urges for food, drink, sex and bodily comforts. These urges are connected with the body. If there were no body, these urges would be absent in the human soul.
- There are urges connected with the consciousness of ego. If there were no consciousness of ego or 'I', there would be no urge for praise, name and fame, superiority, or self-seeking.
- There are urges for affection of offspring or children.
- There are urges for acquisition of money and property.
- There are urges for traditional beliefs, social connections and various habits.
- There is an urge for violence or destructiveness.
- There are urges for false beliefs.

- There are urges for sympathy, benevolence, compassion, disinterested service, etc.

The Roots of several bodily pleasures

There is a bondage of low love of taste in a person who, in spite of his knowledge, finds himself compelled to eat and drink.

- What is not edible for the human organism;
- what is injurious to his body;
- what involves cruelty and injustice to others;

There is bondage to the low-love of sex in a person when, in spite of himself, he knowingly indulges in

- excessive sexual satisfaction;
- is tyrannical to his partner in marriage in insisting on sexual satisfaction when she or he is diseased or unwell or unwilling;
- transgresses the social sex ethics by seeking pre- and extra-marital sexual intercourse or prostitution.

There is satisfaction in bodily rest or in other effortless satisfactions. One develops a low-love for effortless life or laziness when he lives:

- as a parasite on his patrimony;
- takes to cheating or borrowing for his living when patrimony or other means are not open to him;
- shirks work assigned to his job;
- neglects his duties or obligations of service to others;
- takes to the life of a beggar or conventional 'sadhu' or 'fakir' and becomes a parasite on others;
- takes to a do-nothing life when he retires from work after earning enough for his livelihood;
- wastes time in sexual gossip or talking or hearing ill of others; or

- becomes incapable of observing the principle of self-help in the satisfactions of his needs, or in protection of things under his care.

The Roots of Ego

The growth of the consciousness of self – the consciousness of 'I', 'mine'. This consciousness of one's self extends beyond one's body, thought and actions, to other things and persons. We identify ourselves with things and persons until their loss becomes our total loss. As a result, we lose our bearings or commit suicide.

When we develop the consciousness of self, we find satisfaction in the approval and appreciation of others about our person and thoughts and about such things and persons with which we have identified ourselves. This urge for acceptance, approval and appreciation by others is innocent. It is part of our mental health to accept ourselves and gain the acceptance of others. However, when pleasure, which comes from the satisfaction of this urge, gets the better of the urge and deviates it into paths of untruth and evil, it becomes a bondage.

Devatma distinguishes four deviations that this urge undergoes, and thus leads to the four kinds of low-loves into which it degenerates.

We enjoy receiving praise from others. When the praise is truthful about us, its enjoyment or satisfaction or pleasure is right, but when such pleasure gets the better of some persons, it becomes a low-love of praise, which leads them to:

- enjoy undeserved praise;
- render even unprincipled help to their flatterers;
- profess faith in what they do not believe out of fear of loss of the approval of the social group;
- observe ceremonies in which they have no faith in order to avoid disapproval;

- keep external symbols of a faith, even when they consider them unnecessary or harmful and thus turn hypocrites; or
- develop low-hate for a man who truly exposes even their undeserved praise. They sometimes go to the extent of harming him or getting him harmed.

The second deviation of this urge is to seek social respect, name and fame. It is a healthful urge to seek recognition. There is a moral justification if a great soul feels sad or laments the neglect of his greatness or contribution or merit by his society. He has a moral claim that his service be given recognition and respect.

However, when a person seeks positions of respect and power without reference to the excellence of his character, calibre or achievements, he is in bondage to the love-love of name and fame. A person is under bondage if he seeks political, social or religious distinctions by either:

1. squandering money;
2. using the wrong means of flattering or doing unprincipled service towards those who can confer such distinctions on him or her; or
3. propagating his or her own false image to impress his merit on them. Such an enslaved person:
4. feels pained and hurt if someone points out the wrong, evil, undesirability and vulgarity in such of his actions;
5. harbours hatred for such a person;
6. stops helping him if he was giving him help;
7. in case his hatred is intense, he devises ways and means to harm him.

The third form of deviation of this urge is the desire for superiority. We want to be superior to others in body strength, ability and achievement. This natural urge to excel each other is innocent and helpful to social progress. However, we do suffer from a false sense of superiority. When this happens, we have a low-love for superiority.

We have a low-love for superiority when we:

- falsely believe, declare or show ourselves to be superior to another in skill, knowledge and character when the other person is, in fact, superior to us in these respects;
- falsely claim to possess some excellence which we do not infect, possess or exaggerate some excellence which we do possess;
- take to bragging about our vices;
- unnecessarily challenge those of superior strength or ability;
- squander money to be accepted as superior;
- feel small to take help or advice from persons who know better about matters in which we know nothing or little;
- criticise or disrespectfully say something to a person who is superior or elder to us in the family or generation, or is otherwise worthy of our respect;
- fail to acknowledge some of our real faults or wrongdoings;
- grow vain, and thus fail to see the beauty or superiority of others;
- become cruel to others who have different beliefs and ways of life; or
- feel pained when someone else is even truly praised and to feel pleasure even when someone falsely praises us. This low-love, like other low-loves, hates the light of truth and hence develops a low-hatred for such a person who evens our false beliefs about our superiority.

The fourth urge is to seek one's own pleasure. It becomes a low-love of selfishness in us only when we seek our pleasure without consideration or at the cost of the good of others.

We are entirely selfish when:

- we do not utilize our time, energy, skill, education or money for a social good;
- make no return for the services received from others;

- fail to prove serviceable to the animal, the plant and the mineral world from which we receive so many benefits; or
- become self-willed and insist on going our own way, however harmful it is to us and others, and disrespect the discipline of our group.

The Roots of the Affection of Children

The affection, love and service of parents for children is an enormous good. One has only to visualize the social problem of the orphans to realize how great the service rendered by the parents is. Only if parents were to remain true parents, they cannot, exceptions apart, render a greater social good than to rear healthy and noble children. When the pleasure in the service of children comes to dominate parents it deviates their love and service into untruthful and evil pathways and becomes their bondage.

This love of children degenerates into bondage to children when:

- we concede to such of the wishes of our children, which are harmful to them and arise from a fear of displeasing or losing them;
- become partial to them and conceal their faults, vices or wrong actions or crimes and tell lies about them;
- come to hate persons who complain against them to us;
- develop partiality for some children against others, and thus, be unjust to them;
- give away or will away our self-acquired property to our children.

    1. who are adults, self-earning and able to meet the needs of their family;
    2. even to children who have already squandered our earnings by their evil life; or

3. who neglect us in our serious illness and wish for our death so as to possess our property and go to the extent of being hostile to us. Such are the limits of this bondage.

The Roots of possession of money and property

Economic activity is basic to living a good life for the individual and society. Not to earn the goods of life when adult and fit is to be a parasite and what a contemptible life it is!

Through successful economic activity, we gain satisfaction, which is healthy. However, then we become slaves to this satisfaction to the extent that it becomes the be-all and end-all of life. Therefore, for many of us, our lives are geared to earning, possessing or hoarding money as a means to an end. We earn for the sake of earning and we employ the methods of exploitation to increase our piles.

Devatma lists as many as forty practices and professions in which the bondage for money or property manifests itself. All these may be divided into three groups.

- There are certain criminal methods by which some earn their livelihood, such as stealing, robbery, hired killing, the forcible confiscation of others' land and property, child kidnapping, taking away women by force or seduction for prostitution, the forging of documents or making of counterfeit notes or coins, gambling, the suppression of debts, misappropriation of the property of one's brother or sister and cheating others by pretending to be an alchemist or miracle worker, etc.
- The second group consists of professions that may be legally permissible but which involve harm or injustice to others. These include trade in wine, tobacco and other intoxicants; meat, animal skin, silk and prostitution in some countries; and

fortune-telling, speculation, and putting one's daughter or wife to prostitution.

- The third group consists of economic activities that are otherwise unobjectionable but in which a slave of money brings in evil practices. A man in business or private practice may take to false advertisement and the exploitation of customers and workers. For example, a medical practitioner may issue false certificates; an official may take to bridge-taking or misappropriation of the funds of his office, firm or institution; a man in a business partnership may unnecessarily risk the money of the investors or cheat other partners out of their partnership; a money-lender may suppress pawned possessions; a social or national worker may misappropriate the funds collected for some good cause or divert them to some purpose other than for which they are collected; and a ruler may take to empire building or the forcible occupation of land beyond his border, etc.

However, a slave of money need not take to these or any other undesirable professions or practices; yet, he does not cease to be a slave unless he turns into a miser and refuses to spend for his needs or progress or for the needs or progress of his dependants, or if he does not contribute some share of his money to the good causes which call for help from everyone able to afford in lesser or greater measure.

In short, we are slaves or in bondage to love for money or property. If we acquire it through evil trades or indulge in evil practices in otherwise socially useful professions, or if we fail to spend it for our needs or for the needs of our dependents, or for contributing to some good cause.

The Roots of wrong impressions, associations and habits

There are low-loves concerned with the attachment to group ethos, place of residence and sociability. For instance, a child is born into a family with its own ethos, beliefs about God, the soul and the universe and its beliefs about what is right or wrong in its conduct and etiquette and in its own habits and profession. The child assimilates all this, and as he grows into an adolescent, he is influenced by the social ethos in his beliefs, practices and lifestyle.

This assimilation of familial and social ethos is helpful to the growth of the human personality. This is mental food for the maturity of the mind. There is satisfaction in this process of assimilation and identification. However, repeated satisfactions make us partial to the ethos and put us in bondage. The bound man does not take to the critical evolution of the beliefs and practices of his ethos. On the contrary, he utilizes his intellectual and emotional gifts to defend even the false beliefs and evil practices – he rationalizes them even when he finds beliefs false or a practice evil and is unable to give it up. No wonder a reformer has such a hard time to make his group see the evil character of a practice or to make them give it up. The conservatism, when it is attachment to the ethos for the sake of it, rather than for the truth or goodness of it, is bondage.

Similarly, we develop the inertia to move out of our place of residence where we have stayed for long, even when our professional need or physical health or cultural advancement requires it. A man may starve in his village but he may not move out to a place where better opportunities await him. A man may not go to an outside place or change his residence, even when medically advised as desirable for his health. A man may tour other places and countries when he has time, money and health. Such a conduct is symptomatic of a low-love for one's place or residence.

Sociability is another urge in human beings. We feel drawn to those who share our temper, character, habits, interests, ideology, or pursuit of some good cause. Even when such friendship or association is innocent or socially useful, its repeated satisfaction leads to partiality for the associated. We come to help or defend our friends even when it is unjust, and we come to believe what our friend or group tells us against others, even when it is false. Finally, this low-love involves some persons in so great a mental suffering at the separation from a dear one, whether it be a wife, husband, child or friend, that this shatters their nervous system, and when this suffering becomes unbearable, they commit suicide or pine away into premature death.

The Roots of Violence

The low-loves of the fourth group concern the urge to inflict suffering on others. This may be compared in some respects to the death instinct in Freudian psychology. It can be traced to the hunting stage in man when he survived by shooting animals for food. With the invention of agriculture, hunting gradually came to be a sport. This urge has extended to inflicting pain on fellow human beings and becomes a low-love when:

- we shoot animals for sport or food;
- we delight in cruel sports, such as bullfighting;
- we tease or torture animals or human beings;
- we give mental pain to someone by giving them false news of the death of a loved one; or
- become destructive of things or the properties of others.

The Roots of False Beliefs

Low-loves concern the human weakness to accept or use untruth and evil if it appeals to or satisfies someone of his desires or provides safeguards or escape from some feared consequences. The parents give false fears to children to silence them from crying or to force them into obedience. In doing so, they teach their children evil practices of their professions. In knowing this, low-love can be traced the origin of false religions. This weakness in man accepts or uses falsehood to evade the difficulties or obstacles of life and is exploited by departed spirits and the priestly class to foster false beliefs about supernatural powers and actual persons to serve their own ends.

The epidemic of untruths or falsehoods in speech and evils in conduct in the day-to-day commerce of life is due to the fact that they help satisfactions for our low-loves and low-hates. We use falsehoods to make a better bargain in a deal, to win in an argument or election or to seduce a person into agreement to our advantage or passion, to escape unpleasant consequences of wrongdoing or to harm a person who has antagonized us. We indulge in evil practices of cheating or forcible possession or intimidation to satisfy the ends of low-loves and low-hates.

Devatma devotes in tracing out the various deviations, which urge otherwise innocent and useful flow due to the exclusive domination by the pleasure of the satisfactions for which the agent develops attachment, and thus, his urge into bondage.

Therefore, It reveals as to at how many points the human personality is threatened with bondage. Each one of us can verify for him how many boring low-loves and low-hates he has made in his personality.

The Roots of Altruistic Pleasures in Human Beings

There are many individuals who, apart from the members of their own family and with those whom they are attached by the tie of some pleasure do not perceive some pain, trouble or want of another person (with whom they are not attached by the tie of some pleasure) and do not possess any feeling to remove it by some legitimate means; therefore, these persons do not bestow on their own to do any such thing for any such person.

However, if there are those whose soul feels the need to remove physical pain or disease or physical or mental want, or to help in the improvement of mental knowledge or to eradicate a false belief, evil custom or ritual of any such person or persons, and if that feeling of his is also pure (i.e.

in doing some good through this feeling, the individual feels no longing to receive a praise, title, position or reward from somebody in this world or of obtaining the pleasures of an imaginary heaven or afterlife in the next world. Motivated by this pure feeling, this individual makes the sacrifice of some of his or her wealth, property, physical energy or intellectual learning and knowledge, etc. for the above-mentioned object, then such a sacrifice will be pure altruism. If this kind of feeling becomes so strong in a person that it overpowers his or her love of other pleasures, and actuated by this feeling, he or she regularly or faithfully dedicates themselves to their work and feels satisfied with a higher kind of pleasure or happiness, which, in accordance with the laws of Nature, he experiences in doing such action, then his love of pleasure would be a love of altruistic pleasure.

The Inferno of Low-Hates

Whenever the satisfaction of any of our low-loves is hindered, it gives rise to hatred for the object of interference and pulls into the dark slavery of low-hates.

Developed low-love of self-esteem, makes us unhappy with the seniors and the superiors who point out some of our shortcomings or mistakes and we develop low-hate for them, start harbouring ill feelings against them.

Therefore, I have the feeling of low-hate for someone if I:

- find satisfaction in thinking, wishing, and talking ill of him;
- inflate his shortcomings and devalue his virtues;
- find satisfaction when some harm comes to him; or
- actively go about to cause him harm either directly or indirectly.

1

One way to know why low-hate is bondage is to understand how we come to hate. The psychological causes will reveal the untruthfulness of them.

One of the chief causes of low-hate is difference of thought, feeling, and behaviour. We find customs, conventions, and etiquette of a group to be different from our customs, conventions, and etiquette. We regard the dress of another as 'shameless' or 'grotesque' or 'ugly' or 'unbecoming.' We dislike a person for his manner of eating which is different from ours and we call it 'uncivilized.' Hatred between social groups rests in part on differences of language, mode of dress, diet, customs, religious beliefs, etc.

We hate when we differ in physiognomy from others. Each hates the other because of their differences. We hate a particular voice, handicap, gait, some particular dimensions of a body, or a particular deportment of a person.

We hate a person who holds opposite opinions to us. We hate another who presents things differently from us.

When this is one of the psychological causes of hatred, we see how untruth lies at the root of it. We make our customs, etiquette, modes of dress, speech, gait, physical constitution, beliefs, interpretations, likes, and dislike the standards of truth, beauty, and goodness. True is what I believe, good is what I do, and beautiful is what pleases me. So what differs from my point of view is neither true, nor good, nor beautiful. This is the lie in the soul which feeds fat our passion for hatred. What is ugly about low-hatred is that it rests on untruth. A belief different from mine is not necessarily false. A life different from mine is not necessarily evil. Both beliefs, both lives, both interpretations may have an equal degree of truth in them or different degrees of truth in them, or what I believe, live, or paint may untrue, evil, and ugly. Two modes of writing may be equally effective, even if each presentation is diametrically different. Two different bodies can be beautiful, though no two bodies are alike. Different music can be aesthetically satisfactory. Different customs, conventions, etiquettes can be morally unobjectionable.

During certain periods the virtues of 'honour,' 'courage,' and 'sacrifice in war' were considered exclusively good. In the medieval religious period, devotion, humility, control of appetite, non-attachment, etc., were regarded exclusively good. Today 'social good,' 'democratic living,' and 'freedom' are regarded as exclusively good. The past emphasized the ethics of duty. The present emphasizes the ethics of rights. The standard of good admits both rights and duties, humility and pride, control of appetite and satisfaction of appetite, etc. Again, the scientists admit different interpretations of, for example matter-as particle or wave - as acceptable in the study of phenomena in different contexts.

No standard is identical with one of the things that fall under it. Hence it can admit different from of behaviour, thought and feeling as good, true and beautiful.

Thus, one untruth that feeds low-hate is ego-love, i.e., making oneself the standard of what is true, good, and beautiful. Instead of utilizing the facts of differences to care oneself of one's ego-centric outlook, belief, and practices, one exploit them untruth is made, by low-hate, to strangulate us.

II

Another psychological cause of hatred is the unfulfilled expectations and unsatisfied demands made on others. I claim certain respect, praise, and service of another and he fails to do any one of these things. I lay claim of my desires on others and when they do not comply with my desires, I develop low-hatred for them.

Not only this, I have needs which I expect others to meet, which they are not even aware of. All frustrations of expectations rest on this. Most of the low-hates in family and social relations rise from this source.

This psychological cause of hatred shows another foundation of untruth on which low-hate is based. I assume that my desire is good which may be false. I may desire respect from others which I don't deserve. I build expectations of my children which go against the facts of their hereditary capacities. I ask for support in an appointment which others deserve better. My low-hate takes for granted that my claim is just. Again, I assume that I have a rightful claim on the others to get satisfaction of my request.

III

When to hate a person is to hate the whole of him, the glaring degree of untruth stands exposed. Where is the justification in extending my hate to the whole area of his life, which is the case, when I hate him! To hate a person is to hate the whole of him. It is clear from the fact that I am no more enthusiastic or touched by his virtues as I was before the different arose. The virtues of my object of hate receive an unbecoming gloss over them by my hate. Nay, I even see his virtues in perverted light. I try to reduce them to evil.

Nothing can exist for a moment whose every activity is geared to evil and destruction. A man whose body is damaged in every part and each part refuses to co-operate with others, cannot just exist. What is bad on the whole is not bad in every part of it. Nothing is known to exist which is pure evil or ugly. Since nothing is pure evil, nothing deserves to be hated completely.

So, when I hate, I am through and through with untruth. Since obligation to truth is unconditional, low-hate is unconditionally evil.

IV

Low hate is not only evil under all conditions; it is the worst of evils. Its direct object is to harm another. In this state of low-hate, every time they would think of the critic, they would think ill of him, wishing him harm. A man who has love of money directly aims at accumulating wealth. He may resort to dishonest ways. Here he harms another. But he does not grow vindictive and hate him.

Again, there is a lot of good which comes through low-loves, though evil over-weighs the good. The low-love of sex leads to family life. There may be low attachment between the partners. There may be low attachment to children. But we know what good has come to society through the low-love for children. One has to imagine the lot of orphans to realize what good comes from the institution of family life. The low-love for wealth is a factor for the magnificent evolution of world industry. Not only this but low-hatreds directly aim at destruction and spread destruction. They are the most loathsome diseases of the human soul, for unmitigated evil flows from them, Involving destruction of others as well as of one's own self.

V

In jealousy one hates the points of superiority in the other. He wishes to harm or damage his superiority and even destroy him.

Vindictiveness is the worst form of low-hate. It is a passion of destruction, pure and simple. It is cruelty conceived in cold blood. It scorches every tender feeling of the soul. It is the limit of human bondage.

There are four ways which lead to the production of low-hates:

(i)   When one does not obtain from another the satisfaction of one's desired pleasure.

(ii)   When one is attached to himself or some other person or society by some low-love.

(iii)   When one's self-love develops extra-ordinarily.

(iv)   When a person becomes a lover of his false traditions or false beliefs and therefore becomes partial to them, then:

   (1)   he hates a person or society who have different religious beliefs from his own;

   (2)   he hates a person on finding him not akin to himself in dress, manners, or the way of living or language etc.;

   (3)   he hates a person on finding him inferior to himself in some respects;

(4) he hates a person on account of difference in profession, colour or community, etc.

The psychological make-up of a person given to hate is as follows:

1. Human longing for wish - however evil and undesirable it may be in relation to someone else— should be necessary satisfied by each one.
2. No one should have a belief or opinion against any of his religious beliefs-even when it is absolutely false in the eyes of others. And no one should ever express or propagate any opinion or view which is against his views and wishes.
3. No one should be considered or accepted, or declared to be superior to or better than he and no one should be praised more highly than he, in any respect.
4. He should not be considered or called, or accepted or believed to have a defect or, to be lower or inferior by any one even when he has really got some defect or inferiority.

It is this untruthfulness of low-hates that makes them unconditionally evil and it is their expression in the form of wishing evil, jealousy, and vindictiveness that condemns them as the worst evils. They complete the bondage of the soul.

The Range of Human Bondage

There are a range of dimensions of low-loves and low-hates. Each low-love and low-hate shows the dimension of extension. A person may falsely think too much of themselves in education or scholarship, but may show no vanity in relation to matters spiritual or vice-versa.

A low-love shows specificity of area. Either chillies or sweets are low-loves of palate. This blurs the question of the extent of human bondage. For in every low-love we can trace its extent.

The more limited the extent of the low-love, the lesser the extent of the harm it can do to the welfare of the individual. Extension is one of the dimensions in which the influence of low-loves and low-hates should be considered.

Low-hates are also correlated to low-loves. As I extend the area of my hatred, my thoughts and conduct grow increasingly untruthful and the harm I do becomes wider in extent. My bondage becomes worse as the area of my low-loves and their consequent low-hates gets extended.

Intensity is another dimension in which low-loves and low-hates may be considered. As my low loves and low-hates gain in intensity, my bondage grows ever deeper and darker in character.

The next dimension concerns the number of low-loves and low-hates. The greater the number of low-loves and low-hates, the greater is the bondage. Only exceptional persons show freedom from certain low-loves and only if man were conscious of the net spread around his personality by low-loves and low-hates, he would realize that he was everywhere in chains.

The next dimension concerns the quality of low-loves. There is no low-love that does not involve harm to others, yet we can see that some do greater harm to the individual than to the society.

Low-hates are worse than low-loves, for low-hates directly aim at injury to others. Nothing is more vicious than low-hates — they set the soul to destroy the object of hatred. The worst consequence of low-loves are low-hates.

Vanity, selfishness, self-wildness and low-hates are the most evil and degraded low-feelings of man.

The final measure of human bondage is the absence of altruistic feelings. If a person has some altruistic feelings, they can checkmate the untruth and evil operations of low-loves and low-hates.

Therefore, the presence of some altruistic feelings can reduce the untruthful and evil operations of low-loves and low-hates and reduce bondage.

If man has no capacity for altruistic feelings, or if he has not cultivated altruistic feelings, he lives a life of pure low-loves and low-hates. They constitute a life of unrelieved evil and untruth and complete bondage — such souls are destined for degradation and death.

The Crucial Symptoms
of Human Bondage

The life of human bondage, is a life of blindness, perversions, sufferings and ultimately 'a garbage of extinction.' Let us examine these tragic symptoms of human bondage.

• Spiritual Blindness

A human being who, becoming conscious of some of his low pleasures grows as a lover of and a slave to them, considers the getting of these pleasures as his ideal and engages himself in the task of achieving them, spends his various energies in their pursuit, violates the Nature's law of evolution (which can be fulfilled in the life of a soul by following the route of truth and goodness) by causing various brands of falsehood and several sorts of crimes through various suits of his activities.

By the violation of this grand law of Nature, the organism of the human soul gradually loses his way—if he had inherited any such stamina from his birth to examine the truth in connection with his soul-life, and when he misplaces it, altogether he becomes completely blind. This state of blindness of human soul is called his state of insensitiveness or hardness.

The exclusive dominance of the pleasure determinant in our choices blinds us to the goodness which could be realized through that desire for the entire personality.

What is right and what is wrong are not identical with what is pleasant and what is unpleasant. The comprehensive net of human bondage does not only fructify moral blindness about what is appropriate or inappropriate in various relations, thus compels us to trample other existences under our feet and enhance our own life one of bumps and injury, it does for us something more tragic.

The love of pleasure—the secret subtle foe of the soul, would not let the soul to 'open its eyes' in the lighthouse of truth to gaze at where lies the goodness or health of the soul. Every perception of the goodness of the soul presents the bondage in its ugliness and no wonders the low-loves must blind us to the truths about the goodness of our soul. To fail to see the truths about the goodness of the soul is spiritual blindness and this is practically universal in mankind.

• Spiritual Perversions

It is the distorted vision in a human soul by which he beholds the various things in Nature in a perverted aspect i.e., whatever is authentic, he believes it to be false, whatever is false, he believes it to be true, and whatever is auspicious, he believes to be bad. Similarly, whatever is bad, he believes it to be auspicious.

The spiritual perversion caused by low-loves and low-hates is much worse than being spiritual blind.

Every low-love erects itself into true ideal of life and rejects the true goodness of life as foolishness, inappropriateness and falsehood. This low-love of pleasure in general, leads the man attainment of maximum pleasure or ecstasy as the ideal. A pervert takes offence if some benefactor endeavours to help him to the right of highway of life.

Spiritual perversion lessens the circumstances of moral blindness being reduced or cured at all. It throws a man into greater dungeon of darkness, transmutes him as an 'eyeless one' to his blindness and enemy of the friends of his goodness.

- Avoidable Sufferings

Having low-loves and low hates, people bring about avoidable suffering. If one is neutral from bondage, he is free from all the suffering that come from intemperance.

Devatma holds that low-loves and low-hates, the mate of the exclusive pursuit of pleasures, are as much the diseases of a human soul as typhoid, bronchitis, T.B. and cancer are diseases of the body, torture an individual with pain. Jealousy strangulates us with pain as stomach ache injures us. Again, since we are psycho-physical organisms, the diseases of the soul cause physical pain, too. The low-loves of sex and drink ruin an individual's health and transform him heir to painful diseases besides giving him the pain of frustrated hopes or denied satisfactions. The suffering which various low-loves and low-hates inflict on an individual into the following groups:

(1) Various categories of the most harmful bodily troubles and pains which bring about man's premature death. Man can obtain salvation from such suffering if he attains salvation from these low-loves of taste, drinks, sex, and laziness.

(2) Various suites of the most harmful pains for the soul, produced by bonds of undue attachments.

    There is intense and persistent suffering caused by loss or separation. A man experiences persistent pain through loss or separation from a dear one.

(3) Various sorts of the most harmful pains produced by frustrated hopes. Life is all suffering we do not mean to refer only to sufferings which come to consequences on specific occasions but also to the sickening films of frustrations which cover the whole space and span of life. Sometimes the sufferings from frustration are so intense that a man commits suicide.

(4) Various harmful pains produced by superstitions. Sometimes sufferings emerge from the low-love of false believes in traditions or hearsay. What a toll of suffering!

Heretofore, it can be removed in human society if we rise above the low-love of traditional beliefs and practices and cultivate impartial evaluation of them in the light of new knowledge.

(5) Most harmful pains produced by jealousy.

Jealousy is a breeding ground of suffering. A person in robust health and in possession of favourable conditions in day-to-day life, may suffer from the crucifying pain of jealousy. Nothing can extinguish this hell-fire of suffering in us unless we get salvation from the low-feeling of jealousy.

(6) Most harmful pains produced by revenge.

When someone refuses to comply with what we desire most, we may develop hatred for him; and this hatred may take the form of revenge. The feeling of revenge robs a man of revenge, of his peace of mind. He is restless and in the hell-fire of suffering.

(7) Most harmful pains produced by vanity.

Vanity is another fertile source of acute suffering.

(8) Various sorts of harmful pains produced by crime.

Suffering may come through the use of illegal practices such as stealing, robbery, cheating, forgery, bribes-taking, murder, scandals etc.

They are not only pains but evils in themselves. Moksha is deliverance from these diseases and their sufferings.

- The Loss of the Strength of the Soul and its Complete Extinction

The low-loves and the low-hates sap the spiritual strength of a soul, and if they remain unchecked and unaddressed, they can cause the death of the soul.

The symptoms are as follows:

(a) A soul suffers a loss of strength when its higher hatred for some evil conduct is lessened or disappears.

(b) When the higher feeling of hatred for some evil is lost in an individual, indulgence in that evil no more gives him pain. When we are sensitive to the evils of a wrong conduct, we experience pain.

When this pain at the loss of some higher sense of feeling or at the pain or injury done to others decreases or disappears, or when the urge or the capacity to make amends to another for the harm done to him his decreased or lost, the soul experiences death in some part of its being.

(c) The decreased vitality of the soul is its the soul of satisfaction in rapport with noble souls all service of one's benefactors or of some good cause.

(d) The decreased vitality of the soul is its reduced capability to get rid of low-loves and low-hates and to evolve altruistic loves.

When a soul loses its sensitiveness, attraction, and serviceableness for things good, true, and beautiful, it fails to reinforce vitality. It is on its way to death.

From Human Bondage to Freedom

Salvation must carry together different connotations for the philosophy of Devatma. Salvation refers to freedom from low-loves and low-hates and the untruthful and evil thoughts, actions and disposition produced by them.

Low-loves and low-hates are dispositions to seek the pleasures of body and ego which lead to untruths and actions which thus degrade and disease the soul, thereby constituting human bondage. Every low-love and low-hate goes the way of untruth and thereby diseases the soul and brings about its death if moksha is not attained from it.

According to Devatma true moksha consists in getting rid of

- Low-love and their consequent low-hates;
- the untruthful and evil thoughts practices produced by them; and
- to remove the spiritual impurities accumulated by the past activities of low-loves and low-hates".

The problem posed by Devatma in interpreting the state of moksha is not how to eliminate pain in life but how to eliminate untruth and evil in life. For him, pain is not evil in all cases. There are pains and frustrations involved in scientific research, in espousing great causes for human good, in adventures for discovery and in the conquest of new worlds. There are also pains involved in moral and spiritual ascent.

Second, it is impossible to avoid pain altogether, for human personality – both body and soul – is part of Nature and cannot avoid contacts which prove painful.

Third, the problem of moksha is not the attainment of pleasure as the goal of life, regardless of whether the pleasure is empirical or transcendental. The exclusive pursuit of pleasure is pathological in all cases, whether the pursuit is for either empirical or transcendental pleasure.

The problem of moksha is neither the elimination of pain nor the attainment of pleasure, whether empirical or transcendental. It is to eliminate low-loves and low-hates; that is, to eliminate dispositions to untruthful and evil thoughts and actions, which disease, disintegrate and destroy the soul.

Let us concentrate on Devatma's interpretation of moksha. One obtains moksha from a low-love or a low-hate when he satisfies the following conditions:

1. He must awaken to the repulsive character of a low-love and the untruthful and evil thoughts and actions produced by it as symptomatic of the diseased state of his soul.
2. He must cognise the repulsive character of the low-loves and the untruthful and evil thoughts and evil practices in the same way as a man cognises certain physical symptoms as symptomatic of cancer in his body.

Moksha admits of degrees. To fain moksha from one low-love or one low-hate is not ipso facto to get moksha from other low-loves and low-hates. One may obtain freedom from the low-love of greed, but may also fail to get rid of the low-love of sex. He may hate dishonest ways of earning money and may hate to hoard money. He may also be fair in his dealings with his labour and customers but may also be blind to the harm involved in attaining excessive sexual satisfaction, or behave tyrannically toward his wife in his sexual demands, or in seeking sexual satisfaction outside marital relationships through untruthful and evil means. He may get moksha from some biological low-loves but remain a slave to the low-love of self. He may adhere to sexual and business ethics, but indulge in false self-praise and waste money on ostentations. Since low-loves and low-hates are many, moksha remains a matter of degrees. Some can attain moksha from a greater number of low-loves than others.

It is not only true that there are different low-loves, with each one to be separately tackled and conquered for the health and safety of the soul; however, each low-love is many-sided in character. I may give up the low love for meat diet but fail to give up my low-love for sweet things. I may develop enough hatred for a meat-based diet as it involves cruelty to the animal world, but I may also fail to develop hatred for the harm involved when eating sweet things as a diabetic patient.

In order to get moksha from a low-love, I need to see the repulsive character of the untruthful and evil thoughts and actions produced by that low-love and the strength to root out the disposition. Also, I need education from a moral inspirer who is free from that low-love. Devatma provides the psychological climate in which my eyes can open in the light to see the ugly and repulsive character of that low-love and get inspiration to root it out. This is possible if I am not given to too much self-love or vanity, which does not let me recognize the moral inspirer as my superior and saviour. If my self-loves are intense, I block my way to moksha.

Health, Strength and Growth of Soul

Human evolution means the health, strength and growth of the whole personality, and this not possible in aloneness but only in natural and social worlds. All such forms of relationships with others help to build up the health, strength and growth of a personality that constitutes the spheres of human evolution.

Out of the three spheres of powers – mental, aesthetic, and altruistic – that define our evolution, altruistic feelings are pivotal in the philosophy of Devatma. Intellectual and aesthetic powers can be employed in the service of low-loves and low-hates. When they are so employed, they do great harm all around. We know how intellectual gifts can be used for destructive purposes. Such employment of intellectual powers, which involve the injury and ruin of others, is a prostitution of these powers. We know how intellectual powers are exploited in daily life in inventing ways of lying and cheating others. Further, intellectual powers are misused in the religious world to support or rationalize the myths, false-beliefs and dogmas of the super-natural. In the same way, artistic gifts can be harnessed for the satisfaction of the low-love of sex. Such misuse is a perversion of these powers, whether intellectual or aesthetic, and it is not in the hands of low-loves and low-hates but work for higher values, meaning that their activities are conducive to the health, strength and growth of the soul.

However, intellectual and aesthetic powers have their own specific good to achieve for human personality. Intellectual powers, when they take to the scientific method, illumine the events of the universe and no other power can discharge this function. Aesthetic sensibilities yield us an ineffable joy of appreciation and creation of beauty. Nothing else can play their role in the appreciation and creation of beauty. However, their intellectual and aesthetic powers can play a benign role when they remain untouched by low-loves and low-hates and remain within the bounds of altruistic feelings.

Devatma, therefore, emphasizes the value of altruism in his philosophy, for it helps the healthy and blessed functioning of intellectual and aesthetic powers and contributes to their vital role in knowledge and conduct in relation to other existences, and thus, in strengthening the soul.

He defines the basic altruistic feeling is gratitude, while the second major altruistic feeling is compassion or mercy, as it is sensitive to the pain of others and desires to remove it, and the third major altruistic feeling is responsiveness to the needs of others. The fourth major altruistic feeling is reverence, which is a form of sincere appreciation.

Where there is an appreciation of certain skills or knowledge of some persons, it is a case of admiration, not of reverence. Reverence is the appreciation of altruistic feelings in others.

Devatma recognizes a fifth group of altruistic feelings which concern the man of religion in relation to his Master.

Devatma recognizes a separate group of altruistic feelings of justice. These feelings are concerned to establish the rights of others.

Thus, the trinity of the feelings of scientific discovery, appreciation and creation of beauty and service of others, as inspired by reverence, gratitude, sympathy, justice and the love of the good of the other, constitutes human evolution in the sphere of the good.

Higher Hates are Dynamic Motives

Higher hates constitute the repulsion for specific untruths and evils in thought and conduct. Salvation from any low-love involves strengthening of a higher hatred for the untruth and vulgarity indulging in the satisfaction of that low-love.

1. Each higher hate is specific in its aspect. The higher hate concerned with salvation from the slavery of wealth is a hatred for the negative practices of disloyalty and cheating in earning wealth or exclusive selfish use of it; however, it is not hatred for other forms of untruthful and wicked practices. My salvation from the low-love of self-esteem demands me to hate any untruthful and false appreciation of myself and others. I must hate all the devastating, harmful and unprincipled sources that I adopted to get appreciation.

2. Different low-loves involve different sorts of untruthful and vulgar practices and salvation from them requires a higher hate for these different suits of untruthful and calamitous practices, since higher hates are as specific as low-loves. Just as deliverance from one's low-loves, the nourishment of higher hates for one of the forms of untruthful and evil practices is not ipso facto hatred for all forms of untruthful and evil practices. Further, a person may hate dishonesty but 'on the other edge' may not hate the dereliction of duty in his office work.

3. There are as many higher hates as there are untruths and evils connected with different loves. All higher hates are not tied to salvation from low-loves. There are higher hates not tied to salvation from low-loves. There are higher hates consequent to higher loves. A person of compassion is directly concerned with removing the suffering of others, thence, he too hates suffering. A person of gratitude is directly concerned with proving the quality of service to his or her benefactors hence hates ingratitude wherever he perceives it. A man of reverence is directly appreciative of the superior virtues of his object of reverence and hatred acts of fault-finding and superior backbiting of others, and finds selfishness in themselves, similarly in others as a deplorable feature.

4. There are specific hates which concern with the specific areas of higher love. Suffering is the specific object of higher hate in a man of compassion, ingratitude in a man of gratitude, irreverence in a man of reverence, and selfishness in a man of selflessness. A selfless man may be devoid of gratitude or reverence, on the other hand may not hate ingratitude or irreverence in himself or in others.

5. There are also higher feelings, which dominantly and directly constitute higher hatreds too. Feelings of justice are such feelings, and the feeling of justice is a hatred for the cruelty or exploitation and denial of other's rights.

6. A feeling of higher hate is to have a hatred for some specific sort of untruth and evil in some sphere of thought and conduct. According to Devatma, the human soul is not capable of developing a higher hate for untruth or evil, as such. It is not eligible to nourish a disposition to hate every form of untruth and every form of wickedness in his behaviour. This is so, because he cannot 'open eyes in full swing' above the influence of the pleasure principle in his choices of beliefs and conduct.

Henceforth, he washes hand in the 'bloody-water' filled with untruth or immoral dilemma in some spheres of life. It is beyond his brain—wind to abjure all inappropriate beliefs and all 'no good' practices in all the relationships. In spite of this limitation, every higher hate is an achievement and a blessing for the individual and society. While catching the reins of higher hate (e.g. for untruthful business practices and the exclusive use of wealth for selfish needs) an individual safeguards his soul from tremendous degradation and the society achieves a 'dauntless' life. By developing a higher hate for untruth, mean and cruel practices in one's sexual life, an individual rescues themselves from deterioration and degradation, heretofore avoids wrecking the chastity, loyalty, tranquility and love found in domestic life. Every higher hate cleanses some stables of untruth and heinous life for the individual and the society.

7. Higher-hates are the antithesis of low-hates. Low-hates are hates for the individual and things. When he obtains salvation from vanity, one chases the tracks of higher hate for untruthful self-esteem and accepts genuine criticism with gratitude. He does not hate other persons as other 'no-win' persons do. However, he hates their barrenness and feels sympathy for them as if they are sick persons. He thinks well of them and wishes that they were helped out of their untruthfulness in life. A man with compassion dislikes the suffering but not the sufferer. Likewise, a man of justice hates the tyranny but not the tyrant.

8. Higher hates help to remove the evil of human society and establish loyal and rapport that allows mutual harmony and evolution in interpersonal and infra-personal relationships.

For a final outlook, higher loves are dynamic motives to achieve some specific goodness in others and oneself. Higher hates are dynamic motives to remove some specific obscene in others and in oneself. The two together define the evolution of man.

Universal agreement remains untouched

Man is gifted with the capacity to reflect, which helps him to change himself and his environments for his ideals. When reflection is directed towards refining our life and conduct, it is called meditation. Meditation is a human method to pass from a purely biological life of appetites and passions to a cultural life of understanding, beauty and goodness in interpersonal relations. It is to pass from the darkness to ignorance to the light of knowledge, from insensitivity to beauty to its appreciation and from the bondage of passions to the freedom of altruistic loves.

Although there are many books on meditation, none of them can be used by men of all climes and cultures, faiths and traditions. Applied Ethics of Devatma is tied to particular systems of beliefs and traditions, history and culture. We offer meditations that are universal in appeal, as His applied ethical thought does not require the reader to have any specific faith in order to benefit from them and omit any of the speculative beliefs about God and the soul. Whether the reader believes in God or does not do so, he can concentrate over these meditations on different relations without feeling that he has been put in the strait jacket of a particular faith.

No one questions that there is a human society and how we relate to our parents, brothers and sisters, partner in life, community, country, humankind and the natural world for our needs and enjoyments. This universal agreement remains untouched whether one believes or does not believe in a changeless soul both besides and beyond the empirical consciousness of thoughts, feelings and emotions connected with our nervous system and social world. Further, there is a universal agreement that good conduct in social relations is indispensable in the quest for the highest spiritual life or moksha or salvation; however, moksha may be conceived as either a disembodied existence in the transcendental world or as an embodied existence in the natural world.

These meditations are based on these universal agreements. They aim to cultivate a refined relationship with fellow human beings, the animal world, the plant world and the inanimate world. They are meditations to foster an appreciation of our relatedness to others and with the methods to sublimate those relationships by feelings of gratitude, affection, service and reparation. This moral culture is categorical in its claim on every one of us, to whatever clime, culture, faith and tradition one may belong. One may believe that this moral culture is inferior to spiritual culture, which is to establish relation with God. Even so, one cannot doubt that moral culture is an indispensable stage to the spiritual culture of a relation with God. One may believe that relationship with fellow human beings in the form of parents, brothers and sisters, partner in life, community, country and mankind is bondage. However, one cannot deny that this bondage can be removed by developing altruistic feelings for them.

There is no escape from moral culture or altruistic life. Hence, the present meditations have universal significance and appeal.

Applied Ethics: Each Relationship is a Mirror

(Meditations for Moral Cultures)

We are altruistic when we have experience feelings of appreciation, gratitude, affection, respect, reverence, justice, disinterested service, and harmony in various relations.

Let us discuss the practical and concrete delineation of the altruistic feelings as they should manifest themselves in interpersonal and social relationships.

Social relations are a complex of relations. One is son/daughter, a brother/sister, husband/wife, a father/mother, employee/employer, a member of community, and of mankind. Man is related to the animal world, plant world and the inanimate world. Each of these twelve relations can enrich moral life if one brings altruistic feelings in his conduct towards them.

The Relation Between Parents and Children

The family is the primary unit of society. It involves multiple relationships.

It is imperative for every child to:

- Live the truth that his parents are the birth-givers, nurturers, protectors and educators and he should feel his most sacred and intimate relation with them.
- He must free from all kinds of evil thoughts and evil actions and develop every higher-conduct-inspiring noble feeling in relation to them.
- He must feel and properly express genuine respect to them.
- He must repeatedly recall the love and service he is received from them and thus develop the feeling of gratitude for them.
- He must serve them with all his heart in the state of disease, pain, trouble or helplessness. He should fulfill the physical needs, and other necessities of his parents, with his body, mind and money as far as it is in his power and he should do proper service to a dependent human being, animal or plant of theirs also. He should, on being capable, be helpful, as far as possible, in the mental and moral evolution of his parents.
- He should preserve and evolve whatever good qualities he has inherited from his parents or from other genealogical ancestors to their maximum capacity.
- He should, as far as possible, properly preserve or increase every property received from his parents or inherited from his ancestors and that he should utilize it properly.
- He should, as far as possible, protect and develop any work of social welfare established by his parents, during or after their lifetime.
- He should make amends for any wrong done to his parents or if parents have received improper pain and trouble or some harm, he should purify his relation with them by proper and sufficient reparation.
- He should offer best wishes (mangal kamna) for them, in a proper form every day even after their death.

As a parent:

- One should know his/her responsibility about inheritance that one may pass on to one's children; one should aim at giving birth to excellent children by having excellent physical health and spiritual evolution.
- One should free oneself from every evil thought and action and evolve higher-conduct-inspiring feeling in relation to their children
- One should give love and affection to them remaining free from low attachment and without any improper discrimination.
- One should bestow proper care on their health and bringing up well-protected from physical diseases, to the limit of their capacity, make all efforts to, develop in excellent form, the physical organism of every child of theirs.
- One should give as good an education and training in various languages and in general knowledge and science etc. to them as possible so as to develop their abilities and aptitudes.
- One should give them moral education which illumines and inspire them to lead an altruistic life.
- One should instill self-discipline in them.
- One should make amends for any improper conduct in relation to them.
- One should offer best wishes (mangal kamna) for every one of their children in proper form even after their death.

The Relation Between Brothers and Sisters

I. Consciousness of Relation

One should realize his very intimate relation with him or her and keep oneself free from every evil thought and action and of awakening and developing every higher-conduct-inspiring feeling in relation to every brother and every sister of his.

II. Feeling of Respect

One should show proper respect towards every brother and every sister of his, in his behaviour, actions, social intercourse, manners, conversation and correspondence etc.

III. Feeling of Affection

One should develop love and affection for them by joining them innocent play, entertainment, social ceremonies, and by giving them presents.

IV. Feeling of Gratitude

One should endeavour to awaken and develop the feeling of gratitude in his heart towards every brother or sister of his, by repeatedly recalling the favours received from them and to express it through his various actions.

V. Safeguarding of Rights

One should be liberal when parental property is to be distributed between all the brothers and sisters with fully respect the law of the land.

VI. Help and Service

One should be helpful them in their bringing up and education, illness, trouble, helplessness. One should give proper protection to the helpless wife of a brother of his and helpless children of a brother or sister of his and should be helpful in proper degree in every good of theirs.

VII. Reparation

One should make amends for any wrong or sin committed or improper conduct in relation to any brother or sister.

VIII. Good Wishes

One should offer good wishes (mangal kamna) for the good of every brother and every sister of his.

The Relation Between Husband and Wife

For the husband:

I. Consciousness of Relation

He should feel with his wife, the good relation of a true friend and fully realize the necessity of making and keeping himself free from every evil thought and action and of awakening or developing every higher-conduct-inspiring feeling in relation to his wife.

II. Feeling of Respect

He should show proper respect to his wife and her relatives in his daily conduct. He should remember her with respect and in the presence of others also, speak of her with respect even after the death of his wife.

III. Feeling of Affection

He should awaken or develop the feeling of affection and love to his wife by reflecting over her good qualities through innocent means and always make efforts to secure the proper happiness; joining her in innocent eating and drinking, playing, exercises, walking or in some good act, by opening his heart to her.

IV. Acceptance of Responsibility

He should meet all kinds of necessary expenses of food, clothes, ornaments etc., of his wife in accordance with his means and status, unless there is a special reason for his not during so.

V. Help and Service

He should take her advice on familial or any other matter; he should give her encouragement and help in getting some higher training and education. He should make efforts to save his wife from every vulgar, criminal and sinful activity and inspire her towards good life. He should help or nurse his wife at the time of her disease, grief or suffering, in accordance with his capacity.

VI. Reparation

He should purify his relation with her by doing proper reparations for any improper conduct done.

VII. Good Wishes

He should offer good wishes (mangal kamna) for her.

For the wife:

Similarly, instructions are also offered for the wife for her proper ethical evolution. There is no double standards for a husband and wife; there is no strict code for a wife a soft one for a husband. Nor is there a code of obedience and service for a wife and one of dominance and privilege for a husband. Both are under the same moral obligation to develop altruistic feelings of love, respect, and understanding for each other, to avoid injury to each other, to protect each other from evil courses of life, to inspire each other to higher altruistic life, to make proper recompense for the harm and hurt done to each other, and to offer good wishes for each other during meditation.

The Relation to the Dear Departed

I. Consciousness of Relation

It is part of the altruistic life for one to fully realize his relations with all his close departed relatives and to keep himself free from evil thoughts and actions.

II. Fundamental Knowledge

He should fully know the truth that every soul fashions its form according to its thoughts or actions actuated by good or bad feelings. He should gather as much scientific knowledge as possible life-after death.

III. Social Intercourse

He should acquire knowledge of one's deceased relatives through various scientific media.

IV. Feeling of Reverence & Respect

He should grow or develop in his heart feelings of respect and reverence for them.

V. Feeling of gratitude

He should recall the services rendered by them and develop gratitude for them.

VI. Reparation

He should purify his relations with them by making proper reparations for wrongs done.

VII. Happiness and Satisfaction

He should satisfy good wishes of theirs by fulfilling them to the limit of his capacity, and please them.

VIII. Good Wishes

By recalling his very intimate departed relatives, he should offer good wishes (mangal kamna) for them.

The Relation to Lineage

Our moral evolution requires:

I. Consciousness of Relation

1. One should feel our intimate relation to our lineage to which we belong.

II. Knowledge

One should, gain true information, as far as possible, about the education and training; tradition and customs; manners and morals; and character and conduct of his lineage, besides broad facts about it and its members.

III. Feeling of Respect

One should know about such of the members of his lineage as have given proof of the possession of some special virtues in their souls or who have raised the prestige of their lineage through some altruistic work and should feel respect towards them.

IV. Feeling of Gratitude

One should feel gratitude in his heart for such members of his lineage through whom he has been specially benefitted.

V. Preservation of Memory

One should write and publish the biography of some distinguished member of his lineage famous for some great quality or start or contribute to some institution of social welfare in their name.

VI. Ordinary Help, Service, and Donation

One should give shelter and proper protection and nurture to some orphaned boy or girl of his own lineage.

He should open an institution for the good of such members of his own lineage who for one reason or another are incapable of earning their livelihood, or should render whatever service he can for some such good work.

He should, as far as possible, make efforts to remove some degrading or evil custom in his own lineage.

He should open some hostel or give some scholarships, prizes and medals etc. for the cause of mental evolution of the members of his own lineage or be helpful in it.

He should give away at least half out of the property he has received from some member of his lineage, other than his parents, for the work of freedom and evolution of souls.

VII. Improvement in Souls

He should educate members of one's lineage to give up some evil customs and inspire altruistic life in them with the influences of Devatma.

VIII. Good Wishes

16. He should offer good wishes for their all-round evolution by receiving the influences of Devatma in one's meditations.

The Relation to One's Community

Consciousness of Relation

One should realize one's relation with his community and the members of his community. One should free from every evil thought and action and grow and develop every higher-conduct-inspiring feeling in relation to the members of his own community.

II. Information

One should gain information about all kinds of good and bad traits of the members of his own community. One should study appreciatively and critically its philosophy, ethics, literature, tradition, customs and ceremonies, as well as its manners and morals.

III. Feeling of Respect and Pride

One should show proper respect and gratitude towards such women and men of one's community who have achieved distinction for the community in various fields of art, literature, science, social reformation, education, welfare institutions. One should show proper respect and feeling of pride towards all such places and symbols, literature, arts and crafts which are marks of the honour of one's community.

IV. Help and Service

One should contribute one's share to the development of one's community in higher character and altruistic life in art and literature, in knowledge and skill, in education and science, in industry and business, in welfare institutions and in preserving the memory of the great men of the community. One should help the orphans, widows, physical disabled or ailments, illiterate, jobless, financial support for reformers, scientists, scholars if needed for one's community.

V. Reparation

One should, by making proper reparation, endeavour to purify his heart from its defilement for harm done to community.

VI. Good Wishes

One should offer good wishes (mangal kamna) for one's community during meditation.

The Relation to One's Countrymen

I. Consciousness of Relation

One should realize his close relation with his country and his country-men and to keep oneself free from every evil thought and action and develop altruistic conduct in relation to it.

II. Knowledge of One's Own Country

One should develop intimate relation with one's country by acquiring knowledge about its history and present condition. He should study its history, science, art, and literature, as well as visit its beautiful natural and historical places.

III. Expression of Respect

One should show proper respect for the government, its officers, and proper administrative laws of his country.

IV. Help and Service

A person shows altruism towards his country when he helps in the service of his country; when he pays all his taxes; creates good will among the various communities, gives preference to goods made in his country; sides with forces for peace; shares in the work of social welfare; and advances his country in knowledge and skill.

V. Perpetuation of Memory

He should put in effort and render help to perpetuate the memory of such men and women of his country, who have made special contribution to the progress of democratic policy of good government or praiseworthy administration and achieved extraordinary accomplishments.

VI. Administrative Duties

One should discharge his official duties, if he happens to be in the service of his government, with care and concern, safeguard the rights of citizens and is just in his conduct to his subordinates and citizens according to the laws of the land and justice.

VII. Reparation

He should become conscious of some evil-conduct or sin of his, in relation to his country, he should purify his relation with it by making proper reparations for wrong actions.

VIII. Good Wishes

He should offer good wishes (mangal kamna) for the removal of the ordinary evils and for the growth or development of the good of his country.

The Relation to Mankind

I. Consciousness of Relation

Each one of us must realize that he bears relation with mankind irrespective of difference of family, clan, community, nationality. Each person must be aware of the need to free himself from perverse conduct and evolve altruistic conduct in relation to it.

II. Social Intercourse

One should observe etiquette, i.e. one should be clean, well-dressed, before presenting himself before others; one should meet others punctually at the appointed time and stay as long as need or propriety may demand.

III. Expression of Respect

One should show proper respect towards a person for his age, attainments, position, lineal superiority in government, society, or religion and to show genuine concern in his illness.

IV. Conversation

In conversation with others, one should be brief, clear, precise and sincere, useful, agreeable and sweet. One should converse with another person when it is proper time, occasion to talk or talk on things according to the occasion and mood of the other person. One should keep secret from another person such things which it is proper and necessary to do so.

V. Hospitality

One should accept hospitality in the house of a person only when it is absolutely necessary and as a guest one should not burden the host or make as few demands for service or attendance as possible. As host, one should look to the conveniences of the guest as much as it is proper to do according to his status in life and in accordance with his wishes and daily habits.

VI. Business or Service

If one makes a promise with someone in connection with his business, he should fully keep it. One should fulfill terms of contracts, written or verbal, i.e., one should do work on time, complete as much work as promised, devote as much time as and attention to the work contracted, and do good work for the wages.

VII. Confidence

One should response confidence in another person having fully tested the person himself or on getting a testimony of some trustworthy person on him. And always prove true to the nature and amount of confidence rightly placed in him by someone in some matter.

VIII. Association

One should, as far as possible, associate with persons with higher life or noble character and read highly inspiring books and articles.

IX. Loan or Pawn

In taking a loan from another person or keeping something of another person as pawn one should return it in time.

X. Undertaking

One should discharge, whenever and whatever proper and enjoined responsibility he undertakes for a person.

XI. Fulfillment of Responsibility

One should, apart from very special reasons, do the work for which he accepts responsibility or is considered responsible, before or in time and do it very well.

XII. Education

One should pay necessary attention to the instruction or education that he receives from some person and use it to some good end. In turn, he should impart education to other persons lovingly.

XIII. Assimilation and Imitation

One should learn to advantage an excellence in some person or community and one should assimilate such virtues in another person or community which are useful and suitable to him.

XIV. Sacrifice

One should cut off his relation from all such persons, however dear they may be, who try to deviate him from the pursuit of higher life.

One should sacrifice or give up his rightful gain or comfort for the sake of the rightful gain or comfort of a greater number of persons.

One should live to promote the good causes of one's community, one's nation, and mankind.

XV. Discipline

One should develop the discipline to observe the procedure rules of meeting on attending it, to show respect to the proper political laws of his country, to reply to his correspondence, to convey message or instructions in time, to carry out the instructions of the teacher from whom one is learning, of the doctor who is treating him, on all occasions which rightfully demand it.

XVI. Peace

One should wish and work for peace in the world by helping to create an atmosphere which reduces or eliminates quarrels, controversies, civil strife, and wars.

One should keep himself away from useless discussions and quarrels among men.

XVII. Forgiveness

One should forgive to a proper extent, the wrong or sin of any person, in his relation.

XVIII. Gratitude

One should develop gratitude for everyone from whom one has been benefitted.

XIX. Removal of Misunderstanding

One should try to remove lack of understanding or misunderstanding with him speedily and properly when one creates some kind of disharmony or ill feeling with some person.

XX. Impartiality

One should always be unbiased in forming his views about or criticizing another person. One should explain or support without bias what is good and true in the teaching of other person, association or religion.

XXI. Presents

One should give morally unobjectionable present and one which is to the liking of the recipient.

XXII. Donation

While giving charity, one should be sure that the recipient deserves it. The form of charity may be in cash or kind, or in the form of advantages or concessions and should be according to the needs and necessity of the recipient. One should give charity without pride and with good and humble feelings.

XXIII. Help and Service

One should render, whenever the occasion demands it, help or service to the limit of his capacity, to some person who is penniless, unprotected, orphaned, caught in a fire, buried under a weight, drowning, or wrongfully in trouble.

XXIV. Reparation

When one comes to know of some wrong or evil done by him in relation to some person, he should, make an effort to purify his heart by making proper reparations to the wronged person.

XXV. Good Wishes

One should offer good wishes to victims of natural calamities, such as an epidemic or earthquake, or a fire in one's country or in a foreign country.

The Relation Between the Employer and Employee

For the Employer

I. Consciousness of Relation

One should feel and realize that his employee is beneficial and spiritually based and concern himself to be get rid of perverse feelings and develop altruistic feelings in his relation.

II. Respect and Obedience

One should show proper respect to their employer. One should listen and carry out instructions which relate to the contracted work, and does justice to the payment made for his work.

III. Duty

One should develop an attitude of carrying out his duties faithfully and punctually.

IV. Confession of Fault and Prayer for Forgiveness

One should admit his lapses in work and express regrets for it and properly pray for his forgiveness that on becoming aware of having done some wrong action due to ignorance or misunderstanding.

V. Reparation

One should do proper reparation making amends to the limit of one's capacity for spoilt work or for causing unnecessary pain to his employer.

VI. Leave and Resignation

One should not be absent without giving proper notice of resignation according to the rules of service.

VII. Protection

One should inform the latter in regard to any kind of hindrance in the discharge of his duties in relation to his employer. Also, one should protect the character of the employer when it is falsely sullied by others.

VIII. Trustworthiness

One should prove trustworthy to his employer.

IX. Development of Good Feelings

One should develop appreciation for his good traits.

X. Gratitude

On receiving any kind of special help, nursing, or service from his employer, he should be grateful.

XI. Help and Service

One should do more work for his employer or his dependents in times of difficulty, than the settled regular work.

One should help to protect his employer and his dependents from evil curses and help cultivate in them good conduct.

XII. Good Wishes

One should offer good wishes (mangal kamna) for his employer and some special dependents of his.

This account of altruistic conduct between employer and employee saves the relationship from becoming impersonal, mechanical, and inhuman.

An employer is altruistic towards his employee if he:

- Realizes that his employee is an indispensable help to him and develops deep relation with him; and he makes efforts to free himself from perverse conduct and develops altruistic relation with him.
- Shows proper respect and regard in his dealings with him, shares in his happiness, appreciates and rewards his services.
- Keeps the trust of the employee in him and trusts him too on the basis of his experience.
- Shows concern to give clear and precise instructions about work to be done, to ask of him to do that work for which he is contracted, and lays claim only to contracted work at the appointed time.
- Gives proper wages in a prompt manner.
- Gives weekly off day for leisure and earned for prolonged rest and personal work.
- Gives proper and adequate assistance when he is ill and in trouble and shows concern to help his moral growth.
- Is forgiving to him on his making mistakes in work, gives warning in some cases and punishes only in exceptional cases
- Makes reparation to him for any improper conduct.
- Offers good wishes for him in his meditation.

Therefore, both the employer and employee, are to develop altruistic relations for mutual good, mutual respect and regard, as well as mutual trust.

Our Relation to the Animal World

1. Consciousness of Relation

One should stand in intimate relationship with the animal world and free himself from evil conduct and evolve noble conduct in relation to it.

II. Acquisition of Knowledge

One should develop inquisitiveness to acquire useful knowledge about the various kinds of living beings of the animal kingdom.

III. Feeling of Affection or Love

One should develop feeling of affection of their beautiful forms and the good qualities which have evolved in animals.

IV. Growth & Development of Good and Altruistic Feelings

One should contemplate the wonderful qualities found in the animal kingdom.

(1) Innocent play – e.g., in various kinds of fish, birds and dogs, etc.
(2) Agility – e.g., monkeys and deer
(3) Courage – e.g., tiger
(4) Spontaneous joy – e.g., in various kinds of birds
(5) Diligence —e.g., in ants and bees
(6) Organization – e.g., in ants and bees
(7) Group unity – e.g., in ants and bees
(8) Insight – e.g., in ants and bees
(9) Monogamy – e.g., in pigeons and peacocks
(10) Concentration – e.g., in storks

V. Germination & Development of Altruistic Feelings

One should develop the altruistic feelings, which have evolved in various species of the animal kingdom such as passionless parental love, feeling of Discipline and feeling of mercy etc.

VI. Protection and Bringing up

One is moral in relation to the animal kingdom when he realizes as a token of his feelings of appreciation and gratitude for them, he spares a part of his meals for them, and wishes them well. He provides water in clean utensils for the birds and animals at some suitable place. He provides ponds at such places where water is scarce. He opens an animal hospitals or contribute to such a hospital. He opens an animal home or contribute to such a home. He helps the efforts of experts to evolve better species of animals.

VII. Treatment and Attendance

One should provide proper medication and nursing of wounded or diseased animals under his care.

VIII. Work

One should take work from any of his useful animals to the extent to which it is fit in terms of health and capacity and give them sufficient rest.

IX. Respect, Affection and Service

One should show respect and affection in some proper way, towards all kinds of animals under his care.

X. Proper Rights

One should fight for animal rights with the vision —a world without animal suffering and support to create laws or animal welfare acts to protect useful species.

Also, one has the right to destroy various kinds of dangerous, pain and disease-producing germs in the human body or useful animals, and to help in the work of their destruction.

XI. Reparation

One should proper amends to the animals whom one has harmed and make efforts to purify his heart by making proper reparations.

XII. Good Wishes

One should offer good wishes in his daily routine for the animals that have been serviceable to him.

Our Relation to the Vegetable World

I. Consciousness of Relation

One should fully realize his extremely intimate relation with the vegetable kingdom and try to free one's from low conduct and cultivate noble conduct to it.

II. Consciousness of Beauty

One should develop feelings of appreciation for the beauty of this kingdom such as beautiful flowers and leaves of various plants and creepers of the vegetable kingdom.

III. Consciousness of Sweetness, Juiciness, and Fruitfulness

One should develop sweetness, tenderness and fruitful life by reflecting over the sweet, juicy and fruit-bearing character of trees.

IV. Acquisition of Knowledge

One should acquire adequate knowledge about the vegetable kingdom.

V. Proper Behaviour

One should make proper use of the various products of the vegetable kingdom for his good, another human being or animal and for removing some physical disease or deformity of his and others. One should make use, with good feelings, of some fragrant flowers and fragrance produced from the vegetable kingdom.

VI. Feeling of Affection

One should show affection for the serviceable aspect and beautiful aspect.

VII. Feeling of Gratitude

One should cultivate gratitude for the services received from it.

VIII. Protection and Service

One should prove serviceable to plants under his charge by taking proper care of them in respect of manure, water, sunshine, and protect them from being diseased or mutilated.

One should support the laws and acts in favour of the vegetable kingdom.

IX. Good Wishes

One should offer good wishes (mangal kamna) for plants.

Our Relation to the Inanimate World

I. Consciousness of Relation

One should deepen consciousness of his close relation with the inanimate world and keep himself free from perverse conduct and cultivate higher-conduct-inspiring feelings in relation to it.

II. Acquisition of Knowledge

One should get knowledge of the various gross and subtle existences of the kingdom.

III. Place of Residence

One should live in a place and house which satisfy the principles of hygiene.

One should keep his home clean.

IV. Use

One should make proper use of light, heat, water, and air, and show respect and restraint in exploiting natural resources.

V. Use of Things

One should place things in proper order, in clean and beautiful manner.

One should decorate his house in a tasteful way.

On should properly protect everything of his things.

VI. Construction Work

One should build some house, temple, ashrams, hospital, office, tank, well or road etc. according to its natural purpose and in beautiful and dignified form.

VII. Safeguard against Low Attachment

One should always safeguard his heart from any harmful or low-attachment with them esp. house, property, money.

VIII. Feeling of Gratitude & Service

22. One should have a feeling of gratitude for the earth, air, sun, moon, and other similar inanimate entities that are beneficial.

IX. Good Wishes

By feeling himself indebted by invaluable benefits from the mineral kingdom, one should offer them good wishes.

X. Reparation

One should make efforts to purify his heart by making proper reparations for wrong conduct with the mineral world.

New Frontier- From the Limitations to Limitless

Human psychology bounds the frontiers of human salvation and evolution. It fosters low-loves and low-hates in the satisfaction of its biological, social and spiritual requirements.

It develops the low-loves of

- palate, sex, intoxicants and laziness in relation to body;
- vanity, praise, selfishness and self-will in relation to self;
- attachment to children, property and association in social context;
- blind reverence, false worship and false sadhanas in relation to spiritual needs
- the low-hates of jealousy, ill-will and revenge or vindictiveness, etc.

These low-loves and low-hates deviate a human soul into the pathways of evils and untruths and lead it into blind alleys of no return. They set up its bondage and create the frontiers on their head to crush it out of existence. Can we reduce our low-loves and low-hates and thus push back our frontiers to have a living space for our life?

The human psychology has the capacity for altruistic life. However, it is severely limited in extent and depth and has blind spots in relation to certain evil means and untruths.

Can we extend and deepen our altruistic life and keep it clean from untruths?

The ideal limit for the new frontiers of human freedom and evolution is the optimum soul-consciousness which repulses low-loves and low-hates as fatal diseases for the soul and feels attraction and love for different altruistic feelings in their comprehension and depth as essential to health, thus leading to rightful and truthful adjustments and service of the four kingdoms of Nature. The soul enjoys the widest life-space to grow into the image of the Ekta Vadi with the evolutionary process of Nature.

A person can free themselves from bondage to a low-love if:

- He can gather enough light to see his low-love in all its repulsive ugliness;
- He can build enough moral strength to throw off the bondage; and he can develop an altruistic feeling to its full maturity if:
- He is able to see and appreciate its charming beauty, and
- he gains the moral strength to live it.

Further, such freedom from low-loves and the evolution of altruistic feeling does not push the frontiers far enough, this the individual must develop a soul consciousness, which consists of:

- Emotionally appreciating and accepting the good of soul as a thing of utmost concern.
- Having a knowledge of the psychology of the soul, its conditions of ill-health in the form of low-loves and low-hates and how to get rid of them, as well as its conditions of health in the form of altruistic loves and higher hates and how to evolve them.

The question is how these conditions can be satisfied as we find that some low-loves are reduced or removed through some shock experience. We can also systematically help ourselves to this evolution if we develop rapport with a character who has evolved all the altruistic feelings in their comprehensiveness and depth, and who has the devotion to help others to see the beauty of altruistic feelings and to gain strength in developing them.

Further, we have seen that hatred for low-loves and low-hates and attraction and love for altruistic feelings must be founded on soul-consciousness. Unless this happens, the work of elimination of low-loves and low-hates and the evolution of altruistic feelings must remain haphazard. It is only when the soul consciousness is developed that the systematic elimination of low-loves and evolution of altruistic feelings can work out to the extent of an individual's capacity.

We can acquire soul consciousness through association with a character who:

- Values his soul life as the highest good in the world;
- is awakened to the concern to evolve his soul life;
- has love of goodness to evolve all his Altruistic feelings and hatred of evil to repel the growth of low-loves and low-hates; and
- has a love of truth to develop it in the all-sidedness and hatred of untruth to repel any trace or form of it.

A soul with such characteristics may be labeled Devatma.

Devatma evolved a life of all-sided hatred for untruth and all-sided love of goodness and all-sided hatred of evil in himself and called upon man to 'participate in this life of his' to advance to the new frontiers of moksha and vikas.

Freedom: The Source of Truth and Goodness

- Altruists of freedom are inspired by having uncompromising respect for the individual as such. An individual is, for them, the ultimate value in human-society.

- Their insight is that an individual is sacred, and hence, his freedom is inviolable.

- Since authority shows an irresistible tendency to encroach on the freedom of individual. Covered by it, the altruists suspect authority as 'inherently evil, and to be vigilant of it twenty-four hours of the day'. As Mill, one of the Prophets among the altruists of freedom, stated, 'Vigilance is the price of freedom'.

- The freedom to the individual is not a concession to the passion of self-assertion in him. Freedom is founded on the truth that an individual alone can be the source of truth and goodness. It is history that no belief, even scientific belief, which is based on factual verification, is insulated from revision or rejection. Newton's grand discovery – the laws of gravitation – was soon modified by Einstein, whose Theory of Relativity was developed within the short span of a hundred years.

Apart from history, there are limitations to an individual's understanding, however gifted he may be. It is in the interest of truth that independent and different thoughts should be encouraged. It is better that 99 errors be allowed expression so that some new truths may be allowed to bear fruit. Again, truth is served by refuting errors. The refutation of error itself leads to a strengthening of truth by disclosing new and better foundations for it. In the same way, freedom makes for a variety of character types and expressions of human nature in innumerable and conflicting directions. Here, the range of character types and direction of expression may be evil, but it is in the interest of the evolution that we should allow the freedom to develop. Truth and development of variegated types of personalities of a higher order have a future in the freedom of the individual. Freedom is the most important condition for any experiment in truth and better life.

- This vigilance for freedom has taken the form of building up systems of rights for the individual and separating the executive from the judiciary. For the protection of the right against their violation by the executive, rights are safety valves against the evil passion of authority for power others. Altruists, therefore, draw up charters of rights of the common man, the rights of women and the rights of children, etc.

- As the inner significance of the individual's life expands, the system of rights also grow. The achievement took the shape of enactments granting freedom to slaves, the right to vote, and hence, the voice to the suppressed and change of legal, social and educational systems, thereby removing barriers in the way of free choice by women, children and outcasts.

- What the altruists seek through rights is the affirmation of the dignity of humans as they are, rather than the mere advantages they give. Altruists work for truth in human relationships more than for benefits. A federal court judgment on segregation is an apt illustration of this point – the Negro school may be equal to schools for Americans in building, equipment and staff, and hence, there may be no material disadvantage to them through segregation. Yet, segregation is unjust, for the foundation of such racial discrimination is false! Since the foundation of the distinction is untruthful, it is unjust. Any relationship between human beings is untruthful, which compromises the dignity of man as man.

- The moral sensitivity of the altruists for freedom is the perception that the distinction on which discrimination is made is false in relation to the specific situation. 'For example, in relation to marriage, the gender distinction is irrelevant – a woman has the same needs as a man has in entering a second marriage after the death of the first partner in life. The distinction of colours and race is irrelevant in relation to civic and legal rights. Authority or power is a false foundation in relation to the truth of a belief, and hence, the criterion of truth is not any authority but facts and principles of logic. Finally, adulthood is irrelevant to the methods of a child's education. The adult has no right to force his method of learning and his ambitions on the child. The fact that the child is in a position of helplessness gives no ground for the claim to impose ourselves on the child.

To perceive that certain distinction as false and hence, that discrimination based on it is evil, thus forms the characteristic of altruists of freedom. Their contribution is to revise the laws, institutions and social structure of the society by eliminating the false or arbitrary foundation of discrimination in the form of colours race, sex, country, power, position and social connections.

- The altruists of freedom work for the dignity of human being. This is because man condemns the regimentation of thoughts, feelings and actions, thereby acting as a steamroller crushing out all individual differences to produce robots. Dictatorship is evil, even benevolent dictatorship, for it treats other men as they treat animals under their charge. It is evil in all fields – political, religious, educational, familial and personal. Altruists of freedom champion democracy in all areas of life, since they recognize the dignity of humans as they are, and shows faith in diversity and differences as essential to truth and creativity.

An altruist who perceives injustice in one specific situation may oppose an altruist in another specific situation. Further, revolutionaries of one segment of social life may be reactionaries for another segment.

The vision of the altruists of freedom is focal in relation to securing the autonomy of the individual and marginal in relation to the fulfillment of his destiny. The education system, which is set up by the leaders of the freedom for the child movement, is found deficient in providing a positive environment for the development of the child's uniqueness. Therefore, the contribution of such altruists is negative as it consists of removing some barriers that stand in the way of individual autonomy.

However, the proper exercise of autonomy requires not only the removal of the barriers in its way, but also positive environment. The sense of justice shows further development when it realizes this truth and works to provide positive conditions for the fulfillment of the autonomy of the individual.

Humanism: A New Direction

Modern Humanism takes Nature as perennial and holds that Nature has always been, is and will be in existence. It is a reality which does not exceed its limits to go beyond the same entity and was not the creation of a superpower. Therefore, no disembodied souls, or no disembodied God finds its existence in Nature. Things occur as per self-governing universal laws without any outside governance, excluding miracles from their purview. Yes, law and only law is functional in a system of things.

Nature, as per its established laws, takes man as a product of evolution only descending from the animal world ignoring the concept of the creation of God. With such a realistic concept, nature happens to be the first and last home of the human race. Humans have strong intrinsic characters, which may worsen due to unfavourable conditions.

Humanism further explains that the basis of good conduct is the human being itself. Exploitation means to treat a human being as a thing of mechanical 'utilization'. However, ethics demands the recognition of fellow human beings as complete beings, different from material objects and not to vehement exploitation. Humanism entails human rights rendering an action as a right one if it brings respect for the rights of others, in addition to respect for others' rights to live in a civil society, and the purpose of all kinds of learning. Humanity has fought wars for ensuring this perspective of life and have reached up to voluminous statutes to say that a right action cannot ignore the rights of others.

This means man's ideal is also within nature and is not supernatural. It remains within the society and seeks his highest evolution through creative adjustment within nature. This ends with the love and service of mankind and cannot be God-centred. It advocates the love and service of humanity, and not the worship of God, discovering truth in a systematic way under the laws of Nature, having verification rather than to be merely a matter of faith. This finds a solution for the social and moral problems of humanity.

Historically, humanism took the shape of a challenge to theistic religion with Marxism. Marx assumes the role of a prophet of the secular age by giving a new vision to man to live and work for the ideal of a classless society. However, being too mechanical and hoping for the betterment of society may be as bad as inequality in the division of resources. More than once, things shaped themselves and reshaped themselves for the establishment of a better society but for a want of altruism in the deep layers of the minds of the kings, and emperors distorted their visions to greed, which ultimately found themselves in the trap of exploitation.

Yes, human life can be civilized if the economic relations are civilized. It is the profit motive in economic relations that poisons human relations. Marx thought that if a new species can appear under changed economic conditions, a new humanity can be evolved if we changed the economic structure of the society. He thought of the future classless society on the pattern of an undivided extended family, where all members own the means of production and each contributes according to his abilities and needs.

Marx says, "Religion is the sigh of the oppressed creature, the heart of the heartless world and the soul of the soulless world. It is the opium of the people". Humans devote themselves to religion like lizards because it provides the illusion of God and heaven to make bearable the unending tale of tortures on Earth. Marx thought religion would disappear when the classless society comes into being, in which there will be no oppressor and no oppressed.

Dev Dharma holds religion is not just the sigh of the oppressed creatures, but rather, it is also the demand of the altruistic human. Man wants to love, to be at peace with others as well as to be grateful to his benefactors. He also wants to rejoice in the happiness of others instead of harming them, but sometimes his selfishness takes the form of greed, which intercepts his unconditional love for others. His ego-love stands in the way of his understanding of others and to be at peace with them. This results into his intention to exploit his fellow-human beings. And then, his passions make him cruel.

Humanism, when inculcated in the lovely souls of fellow beings, saves them from the trap of meanness. In this way, the ideal of humanism stretches itself to altruism. Its maturity requires institutional changes as well as individual psychological changes to complement each other. Since humanism is primarily concerned with work for institutional changes, it does not take up the function of the religion of Dev Dharma, which specializes in the development of altruism in individuals.

Marx felt intensely for the misery of the labour class and devoted his life to their cause, but he did not hesitate to say that all means are right to liberate the labour class from the bondage of the capitalists. Violence and falsehood are permissible if they can help in the realization of a classless society. It is clear that altruism drives us away from untruth and evil. Hence, altruistic loves are not sufficient for the health of both the individual and society in general. It is the task of religion to checkmate the tendency towards untruth and evil. Now, humanism can provide no way to discharge this function of religion. We need a religion which can provide a spiritual culture in which this tendency to untruth and evil can be held in check. Dev Dharma calls such a cultural climate Dev Prabhavas (sublime influences). Humanism has no super human soul to provide the culture of truth and goodness.

Marx's dream of a classless society is as distant today as when it was conceived. However, let us take it for granted that a society is established in which means of production are in the hands of society. Will there still be a need for religion under such ideal economic conditions?

Marx and humanist researchers have not studied true human nature in depth. Human nature shows a tendency to degrade itself under all conditions, particularly in both poverty and riches. Man's virtues gradually develop blind spots. They lack the vision of truth and goodness and hence they deviate into weaknesses. Teach a person to be self-dependent and he develops pride, teach him to take counsel and he fails to develop judgement, teach him to be just and he becomes blind to the claims of compassion.

We can perceive this truth to human psychology in the Shakespearian tragedies. Take Shakespeare's Othello, for example. General Othello was the leader of his men and showed virtue of faith in his lieutenants. He loved his wife Desdemona dearly. His faith in the statements of his lieutenant Iago, and his intense love for his wife Desdemona, blinded him to the extent to smother her in her bed.

Therefore, the Shakespearian theory of tragedy is that the strongest characteristic in the hero becomes his weakest point, which inevitably draws him into tragedy.

Humanism is limited to altruistic feelings and cannot cure partiality and blind spots of altruism. It needs Devatma, and therefore, humanism complements Dev Dharma for it finds that both aver for building an ideal society.

Humanism has played a noble part in changing the institutions of society. Likewise, Dev Dharma specializes in changing the hearts of men for altruism. Together, the two are working for the same clientele of truth and goodness. Humanism fulfills itself with the Dev Dharma of Devatma. Therefore, modernism aspires to be more human. This mechanism welcomes any institution of the world not exclusive of any religion, which could grind itself as per the laws of Nature, studying theories of evolution, and seeking verification of every kind through scientific method. Therefore, modern humanism will welcome a religion which is grounded in nature, evolution, scientific methods and Devatma.

Discover Your Face-

(The Blessed Ones)

If we wish to know whether we are altruists in some social field, we can check up against the following questions. The positive answer shows the presence of that element of altruistic life.

1. Do we feel the pain or suffering or want of another as our own, as we feel our pain, suffering or want as our own or as we feel the pain, suffering or want of our dear one, say of our child or parent, as our own?

Further, do we feel some pain for the evil in another or in the social group as we feel pained at some evil in our child or dear one?

2. Do we feel an urge to remove the pain, suffering, want or weakness of another as we feel an urge to remove the pain or suffering, want or weakness of our dear one?

We have altruistic feeling when we do not only feel the pain of others but possess other senses which give an urge to remove the pain in others. The pain in others should appear an evil worthy of being removed.

3. Is the urge to remove pain or suffering of another enough in us to make us act for the betterment of another? Does the urge in us issue in action?

If we feel the pain of another, we sometimes feel an urge to remove it but stop short at action or persistence in action, as we are not altruists. To be an altruist is to also act habitually and altruistically. A mere altruistic feeling does not ipso facto make for altruistic life.

4. Do we look for the satisfaction of the urge within the object of the urge?

Sometimes we do altruistic work as a means to some advantage in social recognition, better prospectus here and hereafter. In that case, the object or the end of the urge is not to remove the suffering of another, and therefore, it is not the expression of altruistic feeling.

5. Does our inspiration or enthusiasm for social service keep its brilliance or intensity when we meet social opposition or condemnation or other difficulties?

An altruistic work is to be carried through the gloom of social hostility, both external and eternal, and ignorance of how to find a solution to the social situation at hand. Does our inspiration and enthusiasm maintain its steady flame throughout the evolving social and intellectual gloom? If an altruistic feeling is built into our life, and if we have the non-moral gifts (i.e., the capacity to take blows cheerfully, to accept adversity, to persist in our course of action, courage, intellectual grit, etc.), our inspiration and enthusiasm may continue to shine brightly.

6. Does our social work remain uninfluenced as a result of the hostility of the social world, or failure or frustration?

Actual social work is the measure of the strength of our altruistic feeling. If we continue to devote the same time and energy to our altruistic work, we are altruistic.

- Do we feel no disillusionment or disgust for altruistic work in spite of poor or bitter returns?

- Does such ingratitude or failure at results produce disgust for those served or the cause?
- Do we throw in the towel when failure gets in the way? If we do, we have not built altruism in our life.
- Does our altruistic urge gather in strength with the passage of time?

The law of urge or desire is that it gathers in strength with its satisfaction. If altruistic feelings get satisfaction in altruistic work they should get strengthened.

However, no urge in us works in isolation. There are many urges in us that try to get the better of each other. Now, we feel the urge to be socially accepted, as well as achieving social recognition and social appreciation. These urges do get some satisfaction in altruistic work. If these urges seek and find more satisfaction, they may swamp the urge to serve. The urge to serve may be weakened, rather than strengthened by such altruistic work if we seek and find satisfaction of social appreciations.

Again, certain urges, for example, for money, home, body appetites and comforts, may gather strength and overcome our altruistic urge. In the absence of the influence of these two groups of urges: the urges of social approbation and the urges for bodily appetites and accumulations, the urge to serve should grow in intensity with every satisfaction into an irresistible passion.

If our altruistic urge does not grow with time, it is infested with urges of social approbation or bodily appetites and accumulations, and becomes crippled and devitalized through disfigurement and death.

A Synthesis of Truth, Goodness and Beauty

Devatma declares his sublime life as unique in the evolution process. To understand the uniqueness of sublime life, we have to understand the uniqueness of the evolutionary process. Uniqueness means 'not comparable', and from this insight of meaning, every existence is unique because any two existences are not same – the only difference being the law of Nature.

Not even one tree's two leaves are same, so every leaf is unique. In nature, there is a law of change, as not any existence can live even for a moment in the same stage. Thus, every existence has uniqueness in every moment. In this view, the initiation of the caste of the lion is as unique as the birth of a man is unique.

It is clear that when we use the word unique, we are not only pinpointing its difference from other existences, and along with that difference, the meaning of value is also linked. When we say that this painting is unique, then it does not mean that this painting is different from other paintings, but rather that any other painting is not so beautiful. From the outlook of value, this painting is supreme. Uniqueness is invaluable, in that the uniqueness of any existence lies in its attributable value absent from others.

Uniqueness related to values has two angles: the theoretical and the evolutionary. From the traditional theoretical view, the uniqueness of any existence lies in that it should be liberated lower and degraded level. From this perspective, the uniqueness of a person lies in liberating him or her from their animal life and to live for their intellectual and soul eligibility. There are universal motivations in the animal world: for instance, they eat and copulate and take care of their children until they become independent. Also, higher class animals have the motivation of lower class social company. These are all animal motivations. From this traditional point of view, the uniqueness of a person lies in the fact that he may separate himself from animal motivations. Our religions have an ideal that man should increasingly renounce his eating and clothing. Moreover, if possible, he should live on a bit of rice and avoid lust and sex. Also, he should not marry and should refrain from social gatherings or going to jungles. He has to live the life of soul being seated in a stable place. In other words, he has to renounce every motivation of the animal world, as well as eligibility and attributes, and gain only his soul satisfaction.

This traditional outlook is due to the view of God or Brahma, or in other words, it has ascertained the attributes of God or Brahma. There is no body of God or Brahma because humans and animals also have a body. Thus, it can be insulting to believe in the body of God or Brahma, because God or Brahma has no body, and has no bodily activities, such as eating, sex and lust's motivations and activities. God has a separate existence, so he has no motivation of societal company. He is a bodiless consciousness that is devoid of change entirely, because change is the attribute of social things. This imaginary figure of the uniqueness of God or Brahma has been created and humans have tried their best to merge themselves in it. In turn, they have suffered and insulted his body with meditational fasts and other challenging exercises. A Paramhans is an individual who has decreased his bodily life and merged lifeless things in the appreciation of God. Because of this traditional outlook, the common man cannot appreciate the uniqueness of Devatma. The appreciation of the uniqueness of the sublime life of Devatma is possible only if a person moves away from the traditional outlook to develop evolutionary insight.

From the outlook of evolution, the uniqueness of any existence could lie in a number of aspects. There was a time when animals did not exist on this earth. There was a time when the evolution of the attributes of life began. At that time, animal existences were unique existences of nature.

Now, in which aspect does the uniqueness of the animal lie? The existence of an animal does not lie in the fact that he might be devoid of non-living energy forces. The life devoid of forces of energy is not possible. The uniqueness of an animal is that he might plough energy forces in a new structure and new work. There are two attributes in animals that are not in lifeless energetic existences. One animal makes organic elements out of inorganic elements and uses it for fertilizer, while the other, either alone or with another person joins others in producing other animals.

It is clear from the evolutionary outlook that the uniqueness of any existence is not to throw the lower world, but rather to provide it with a new structure and work. This truth is verified through the animal world. What is the uniqueness of the animal world from the natural world? Can the classed animals traverse from one place to another place? They have the capacity of walking, running or flying, and they have senses through which they can gain the initial knowledge of atmosphere for them; but it does not mean that they might be different from the animal world in every aspect. Animals, like nature existences, maintain their body with edible things, thus producing their race. In animals, there are attributes of the natural world, and in the bodies of animals, there is an energy force, like plants. The animal world assumes the attributes of the energy world and the natural world and makes it the foundation for its new qualities from which to develop or link it in the activity of its new quality. If the animal world renounces the special attributes of energy world and nature world as a minor, then it will be ruined itself. Uniqueness does not mean the negation of the attributes of its lower worlds but rather to accompany it. Uniqueness means to use an ever greater number of attributes together.

By seeing the uniqueness of humans over animals, one can more feel the knowledge of the meaning of uniqueness and grandeur. In one's life, one accompanies the attributes of lower life. The human being evolutes their body and progresses their creed through the attribute of living a natural life and edible things, which humans develop in new outlooks. Man eats food by decorating it on a plate (a utensil thali), which is absent in the natural and animal world. To eat food decoratively does not mean to complete the needs of the body but to satisfy and develop the feeling of beauty. Thus, humans eat food with others and develop a social feeling, and while satisfying one's sexual feelings, humans also create various ethics. Humans have developed the highest aesthetic institution of marriage and, along with it, linked the feelings of loyalty of wife-husband, purity, friendship and mutual service. In doing so, humans did not renounce the senses of animals, as to renounce it is his death. If they did not use the senses, then they would not be able to recognise edible and non-edible things, and would thus not be able to live. However, the human being evolved to link their senses with new powers and duly gained scientific knowledge.

Therefore, the uniqueness of any existence is not that he throws out the attributes of lower existences, which is impossible and a mythical ideal. In addition, this uniqueness is less valuable because it is not multi-coloured. Evolutionary uniqueness is multi-coloured.

The uniqueness of Devatma's sublime life is evolutionary – he did not renounce the attributes of the lower worlds, but instead chose to accompany each and every attribute of the lower worlds in his life and decorate it, which shows his uniqueness.

One greatest attribute of nature is the evolution of the individual. Devatma did not renounce his living body; his needs comforts did not condemn it. To oppose this, he completely accepted the living body's emotionality, declaring that in the separation of the living body, there is no separate existence of a soul. He also accompanied the fulfillment of the body's needs in his sublime life, and never questioned that the body could live on a minimal diet. Moreover, he did not ruin the investigation of his taste as enunciators do, and did not take it as opposition to take healthy food.

So, he got married and became a father to his children, thus incorporating his married life as a part of his sublime life. He decorated this relation in higher attributes, and above this, he developed a feeling of friendship with his wife that was based on the highest sublime life. He did not accompany this with a view that wife might be transformed as a mother, for this transformation is mythical and inappropriate from the insight of evolution.

The second attribute of nature is the evolution of animals who can develop sensual awareness of their surroundings. Devatma, in his sublime life, accepted these two attributes and used them. He never accepted sitting in one place having no movement and thus worked to flourish and enhance his sublime mission in traversing various places. He did not assume his senses as a flaw for truth knowledge, but rather as being helpful. In reality, by accepting the scientific method, he placed the senses in an esteemed position for the investigation of knowledge.

The third supreme attribute of nature was the evolution of a man. The attribute of a man lies in his progressive intellectual powers and its supreme knowledge and higher feelings. Devatma adopted the evolution of intellectual powers as a part of his sublime life. With these, intellectual powers and logic methods accompanied them in part of his truthful knowledge. As he did not assume truth knowledge as supreme to logic methods, Devatma developed the knowledge of beauty, structure, cleanliness, duty, rule, punctuality, loyalty, self-respect, self-confidence and self-help. He made their evolution as a part of sublime life, and developed the higher feelings of gratitude, altruism, compassion, justice and obeisance, etc. He did not only adopt these intellectual developments, higher knowledge and positive feelings but also lead them to the highest level. He made their basis a truth and love of goodness, thereby liberating human attributes from its curses. The description of the limitations of human positive nature and curses and their salvation in sublime life. It is clear that the uniqueness of Devatma is evolutionary. It is the law of evolution that every supreme class uniqueness lays in that fact that he might accompany the attributes of existences of lower life in his attribute and with his attribute provides lower worlds with new value and work. Devatma, with his sublime life, provided animals with edible foods, the qualities of caste production and the ability to walk and sense knowledge, while he provided humans with intellectual powers, the pathway to supreme knowledge and higher feelings, beauty and the ability to plan into the future.

The Door From Impulsive
Level to Freedom

When life plays its tune, we dance. However, we live at different levels, and hence, we are in tune with the different levels of life and thus exhibit different kinds of behaviour.

- Impulsiveness.

There is the impulsive level of the child life. He does not think out the consequences of his action in his future life – he just acts. The animal life is lived at impulsive level.

- Consideration of consequences

People are inspired by self-interest, though they have different ideas about the ideal version of the self they wish to acquire. This life of self-interest is far superior to a life of impulse, since the consideration of advantage and disadvantage and good and bad ideals characterise this level.

- The higher level of life (The life of altruism)

Benevolence is different from piety as piety is an impulse. When this impulse of piety institutionalizes itself, it becomes benevolence, though both may lead to the same action.

- The level of life inspired by 'Right' (The love of Truth and Goodness).

There is a distinction between ends and means. Those great men who live at this level can be true guides for humankind, and as such, humans with that spiritual sensibility are the highest and noblest. These men cannot be corrupted to compromise in the sphere of means. So long as man does not rise to this level of life, he cannot be corrupted by good ideals any less than he can by the low ideals of life.

The Purpose of Life

Devatma opens with a statement of the fundamental insight that the unexamined life of the cave is not worth living and nothing surpasses in terms of the knowledge and cultivation of the good of the soul. The sublime utterances of Devatma concerning the need of Soul-consciousness and Soul-knowledge.

- Who could be more pitiable than a man, born a human soul, who feels no concern to get true knowledge about his own personality.

- There is no greater privilege for a man as man to feel concerned to get knowledge about his own person-especially his soul-for no animal lower to him has the privilege to get such knowledge about its being.

- It is an extremely pitiable condition for man, as human soul, to feel concern to get true knowledge about his soul but be incapable to gain such knowledge or be bereft of such concern to get knowledge and thus live a life of complete ignorance and blindness about his soul.

- It is the highest privilege for a man as a human soul, to be capable and to get opportunity to develop soul-consciousness and gain soul-knowledge.

Devatma's diagnosis is that man's soul has a weakness for the life of pleasure and that the dominance of the love of pleasure would not let him attend to the understanding and cultivation of the life of the soul.

The dominance of the love for pleasures not only usurps the time and energy of millions of people, thus leaving no time and attention for the study of the good of the soul, but it also produces an aversion to gaining such knowledge. The dominance of the love of pleasures produces spiritual darkness and blindness, which would not let one be sensitive and perceptive to truths about the good of the soul. And the love of these pleasures goes further – it produces spiritual perversion.

One who lives in a dark cave of sensuous and ego pleasure loses sight of what is good in the soul, and comes to hate the good within it. They develop so much hatred for what is good about the soul that they would rather hate and kill the philosopher who would bring them the light of what is good and true about it.

The law of pleasure is not the law of good. Pleasure and good are not identical, nor is pleasure the only good. Neither are they antagonistic as independent principles of conduct. Pleasure is as good as subordinate to good, but not as an autonomous principle of conduct.

The knowledge of the soul or soul consciousness will open the eyes to the truth that the dominance of the pleasure principle on our psychology is pathological; it breeds diseases of the soul that produce the epidemic of evil and untruth in society and threaten its very existence as an entity.

Thus, the dominance of the pleasure principle is the main hurdle to the human concern about their highest good. Humans do not sit down to examine how they lead their life, what values they pursue in their activities or what goals they put before themselves. However, such an unexamined life is not worth living.

Why is soul-consciousness and soul knowledge is the most important? Devatma believes that the soul is the source of all human activities. If we wish to produce refinement in our activities, it is essential to know the nature of the soul. The evolution of higher activities needs soul-knowledge. Again, since certain activities are felt to do harm to us and to others, it is essential to know the cause of them to be able to eliminate them, which requires the study of soul. Our present and further existence depends on the present and the further existence of the soul. The soul's further existence depends on what our activities do to it. Some of our activities contribute to the health and strength of the soul, some of our activities weaken and disease the soul. As all our good depends on the continued existence of our soul, we must know what the activities are which contribute to our soul-health and what activities dissipate soul-health. That is, we must know the laws of the health of the soul and how to observe them; further, we must know the causes of the diseases to which our soul is liable, and how to get rid of the diseases when we get them.

All our concerns are concerns so long as our soul lives. How unwise it is to neglect to get knowledge of our soul on which everything depends and busy ourselves with activities that may lead to extinction of our life, here and hereafter.

Devatma is never more eloquent than in arousing human beings to shame in their pursuit of wealth, reputation, honour or power, at the cost of the good of the soul. This was the mission he felt was the object of his scientific investigations. His light showed him that the highest task for man is to discover what constitutes the greatest good of his life-force (soul). But he was more than a pure scientist —he carried his torch of knowledge of the good of the life of slumber in which they may die if they do not wake up to the truths about their life-force (soul) life.

In the Service of the Past

The memories of those who have loved or served us are compelling in their call on us to offer our mite of service towards them. The world's population is overwhelmed by the marvellous personalities of bygone ages. Memory enshrines the bond with the past in the flower-garden of service, with the moral obligation entwined to recognize the buds of refinement. We store the tender emotion of our ancestors' assets. The footsteps of unmatched valuations of Renaissance are the prints of altruistic past.

In such periods, some great altruists devote their entire lives to the work of deciphering the treasurers of art, literature, religion and philosophy that have suffered eclipse due to the neglect of generations. They serve the past by making the achievements to recreate in the thoughts and feelings of the present generation.

In recent years, the U.N.O. has struggled enormously to rescue the treasure of literary translations in the English language. Such an altruistic feeling is in the lap of all countries, and overall, the panorama of the past has been restored. These feelings also link us to the psychological level. We chase the soil of our ancestral brain-wind. Psychology presents ageless modules while we inhale the ancestral whiff, and the wire of the future is recharged with the transmutations (i.e. contemplation of past triumphs).

Einstein's theory was built on Newton's theory, though Newton's theory has been fundamentally modified.

Modernism plays several games in the lap of past.

Thus, those who are inspired by the altruism of the past help the society to:

1. Forge links of the present generation with the ancestors and thus enriching the psychological life.
2. Preserve the capital achievements of one's ancestors.
3. Provide the medium for the development of new thought.
4. Conserve the social order from disintegration.

However, this form of altruism has blind spots, like every other form of altruism. At its worst, it is orthodoxy. It cannot see and tolerate the greatness of new achievements. It puts intellectual constructions in the past in terms of the present thoughts, which the ancient thought would not bear. It feels an undue attachment to everything in the past and sees beauty in it which exists nowhere. It imposes the past on the present, which it cannot accept without injury to itself. It is partial to the past from the point of view of truth and goodness. In spite of all their deviations, the service of the altruists of the past to society is indispensable.

In the past, altruism was the form of the preservation of values. To preserve values is to preserve our customs and conventions, our etiquette and traditions, our festivals and pilgrimages, our literature and art, our religion and philosophy, our methods of acquiring knowledge and of framing laws. They are the capital equipment of society in knowledge and practices. The altruist perceives them as capital and strives to preserve them with his own life. He uses his intellectual and emotional gifts to bring out the truth and beauty in them. He gifts away huge sums of money for acquisition and research into old documents and excavations of buried civilizations. He is jealous that nothing of value in the past is to be lost.

Again, in fighting for the rejuvenation of the old and the conservation of the past, he serves to maintain the integrity of the group. A social group cannot maintain its identity as a social group if its customs, conventions, culture and traditions are allowed to be questioned lightly and disregarded indiscriminately by the individual members.

Selflessness in the Service
of the Present

If renaissance spotlighted the altruism for the past, reformations blazed the altruism for the present; therefore, our consciousness is time bound. Though time is continuous, it lends itself to division into past, present and future. Time has its own language, and there is always a past for us whose consciousness differs from our consciousness of the present and the consciousness of the future. We show partiality for one section of time over others, and there are persons whose consciousness is dominated by the past, there are others whose consciousness is swayed by the present and there are still others whose visions are lifted to the future.

This bias or peculiarity is a matter of individual differences in terms of the time dimension and affects our interests, attitudes, activities and approaches to life and knowledge. Persons who are dominated by the past are known as traditionalists, who are sensitive to the values of tried practices in art, culture and business, industry, politics and social life and stick to them in all their aspects of life. The past weighs on them so much that they cannot see that the present is different from the past and calls for modification of the past practices. On the other hand, those persons whose consciousness is swayed by the present are called realists or practical men. They are sensitive to the relevant differences of the present from the past, and are anxious to take to new ways to meet the challenges of the time away entirely by the present. Their vision is narrow and though they achieve success, the success may be of small consequence. Those who have a vision of the future are called idealists or visionaries. They are so caught up with future possibilities that they are not sensitive to the actual conditions that defy their dreams. They lack realism, and hence, fail to handle the environment to work out their plans. Their thinking may be original and intrinsically valuable but they cannot realize them in their life. They may also be failures in their activities concerned with art, culture, business, industry, politics and social life. This is a broad division of persons into traditionalists, realists and idealists, as they are influenced and determined by the past, the present or the future.

These three aspects of time bear relation to the three-fold aims of evolution, which are to conserve, correct and create values. Conservation is what has been achieved in the way of higher species, or of truth in a society's and an individual's thoughts, feelings and habits in art, science and philosophy. Correction is of what is defective in our present-day culture, business, social, moral and religious life. Creation brings into being new thoughts or new methods in all walks of life, whether practical, intellectual, social or religious. When we say that our consciousness is partial either to the immediate present or the hoary past or the distant future, we do not mean that a man is influenced, for example, by the present, and does not take note of the past or the future.

We are conscious of all the three sections of time and also perceive the values of the past, the present and the future. What is being brought out is that, in spite of the presence of all three sections, their attraction is different for different persons. Knowing my past and knowing the future consequence of my present actions, I may yet be carried away by the immediate present. For instance, one's present job may not have paid well in the past, so the individual knows that it is not going to pay him in the future. Yet, he may not choose to resign and try for a new opening but is overwhelmed by the present. Another person in similar conditions, albeit dominated by the future, resigns from the job and tries for a new job. The two differ in their partiality of time. The first is obsessed by the advantages of the present while the second is charmed by the adventures of the future.

Altruists are also under this time-consciousness-peculiarity as common men. We know how altruists, whose consciousness is sensitive to the past, have been leaders of the renaissance in many different countries of the world. They surrender their entire personality in protecting and preserving the treasures of the past and serve evolution by serving its conservative function.

Let us discuss altruists whose consciousness weighs heavily by the present. Their service is to correct what is defective in the present.

They are the reformers. A reformer is conscious of and sensitive to the imperfections. A reformer in social life is sensitive to the evils of the prevalent practices in society.

We must answer two questions to understand the framework of altruism:

- What is the characteristic of the thinking of a reformer?
- What motives inspire his or her work?

The reformer accepts the fundamental structure of the social and cultural life of his country. He or she only corrects its abnormalities or adds valuable modifications to it. The writings of the reformers invariably show how they plead with their generation on the basis of ancient thought.

In art, religion and philosophy, contemporary movements are merely the variations of an ancient framework. This is the logic of the thinking of a reformer. He takes help from the past literature to rid society of its present evil customs.

The moral values of a reformer are different from the moral values of a man of renaissance. A reformer is intensely sensitive to injustices.

He realizes, for example, how it is unjust to women to force them to burn themselves alive or remain widows throughout life, to deny them education and vocation or to draw distinctions on basis of birth, or to deny a section of society the rights of citizenship. A man of renaissance is motivated by appreciation, reverence and love for past achievements. He prizes the old works of art, literature, sculpture, religion and philosophy, and feels reverence for the authors of those achievements. Therefore, he works to preserve them.

Again, a reformer is inspired by having sympathy for the sufferings of those who are the victims of the unjust social customs. The piercing cries of the burning widows, the helplessness of the uneducated women, the degradation of the untouchables or slaves smote the hearts of the great reformers of the world and made them restless and sleepless.

It is these two feelings of justice and sympathy that the reformer appeals to in changing the outlook and conduct of the masses of his society.

Let us sum up the contrast between two different kinds of altruists. The altruists of these two types have obvious differences. Altruists for the past are judged by history. Altruists for the present are judged by immediacy or regency. Altruists for the past are keenly sensitive and appreciative of what is of value in our ancestral achievements.

In the Service of the Future

If altruism for the past can be called conservative altruism and the altruism for the present corrective altruism, the altruism for the future may be called creative altruism. Altruism for the past comprises conserving what is of value in the achievements of our ancestors. In today's world, to be altruistic is to correct the evils that bear down upon traditional social practices and religious beliefs, or in modifying the moral or occupational life within the traditional pattern of society. Altruists for the past and for the present both accept the ancestral framework of thought and life, with the two serving the conservative and corrective processes of evolution.

Altruism for the future is altruism for the creative process of evolution. It envisages the vision of a new method of truth discovery.

He breaks with the past. He works with new visions, new possibilities, new freedoms and new opportunities for thought and action for the human spirit. By nature, humans are both selfish and altruistic, and they realize repentance in loss. Physical conditions are integral to the spirit, which is the meaning and message of evolution. Certain physical conditions also plant new conditions in the animal world. For example, human advances in science will give rise to a new sphere of evolution. Many evolutionists and reformers see the changes that Marx predicted, which will thus give a materialistic interpretation to the history of human culture. However, the truth is that new modes of production may themselves result from the cultural matrix. Cultural and economic motives are inseparable interactions in man's march toward an ideal society.

The Sweet Taste of Altruism: The Future

Understanding the relationship between altruism and the past will contribute to our understanding of altruism for the future if we explain what we really mean when we say that a creative act involves both a break with and an assimilation of the past. Let us take the creative act of the emergence of life. Life consists of elements of phosphorus, fats, salts, iron, calcium, water, etc. – this is the chemistry of living bodies. The living matter has unique properties and laws of behaviour in comparison to the inanimate matter. The living matter has unique laws, because the process of life is not additive but transformative and assimilative in character.

Two kinds of errors have arisen in the history of thought in the interpretation of the creative act of life. Science analyses life into chemical elements. The materialists jumped to the conclusion that since life could be shown to be made of these chemical elements, there is nothing unique about life and attempted to reduce biology to chemistry and chemistry to physics, and thus explain away the novelty and uniqueness of life. "Life is just matter arranged in a certain way".

Life and matter have a similarity of chemical elements, but the chemical elements as part of a living body behave differently from the same chemical elements in an inanimate body. The differences between matter and life are unique and fundamental in spite of the points of similarity between them. The 'old' survives in the 'new', but the 'old' does not 'survive' as it did in the 'old'.

The 'new' assimilates and transmutes that it is no longer 'old' as it exists by itself. In addition, matter survives in life but matter does not survive in life as it is apart from life. What is unique in life is the process and principle of life and not the materials of life. The laws and properties of water are different from those of oxygen and hydrogen. Thus, we bend the truth by saying that water is nothing but oxygen and hydrogen, and it is wrong to state $H20$ = water, as = is a misinterpretation. In truth, $H20$—water.

Life is unique and cannot be explained by chemistry. Ideas about life vary from person to person and the elements can change from the same old ways. There is no end to our refined consciousness. If we accept what is said, we are illumined by two truths. A creative leap in evolution or civilization is unique and fundamentally distinct in its differences from the element from which it emerges; that is, its uniqueness or fundamental difference is not exclusive of similarity. The newness of the creative leap is its unique unity of old and new, and in this unique unity, the old is transformed or digested. The creative leap in evolutionary process carries the old in its sweep. A married love combines the old and the new into a unique unity. What is defective should have been rejected. The literary field takes help from the understanding of creative altruism.

Shakespeare's specialization exists in understanding human nature and the delineation. The great truth of uniqueness lies in a literary composition is its 'form'. Take the greatest scientific methods and achievements of the last three centuries.

The elements of the scientific method are found in the old methods (i.e. 'old wine in new glasses'). Through reasoning, we can understand how the continuity of creative altruism is different from the continuity involved in conservative and correlative altruism, which is repetitive in character. There is no new vision or process to lift up the past into new and unique unity. Hence, their continuity is inferior to the continuity involved in creative altruism.

Future: Crucifixion and Deliverance

We have carried out an objective study of creative altruism in which we have shown how a creative act involves both a break with and an assimilation of the past.

We propose to analyze the reflex of the creative act in the experience of the creative altruist. The 'break' with and assimilation of the past is felt by him as at once his 'crucifixion' and 'deliverance'.

- What do these psychological processes mean?
- How do they differ from the same processes in corrective and conservative altruists?

A corrective altruist questions the present social practices by quoting past authorities. Raja Ram Mohun Roy's opposition to suttee is a case in point.

When the greatest law-givers give no countenance to suttee, the lesser lights, such as Ungira's views, must be considered inadmissible, but the reformer is not in a position of authority. The social isolation is not psychological crucifixion of the altruist. A conservative or corrective altruist carries the social cross in his psychological make-up. However, the social cross in the case of the creative altruist is complete. He is isolated and unwanted, not only by the present but also by the past – what his vision denies is both the past and the present.

Thus, disbelief crept over me at a very slow rate, but was at last complete. Devatma inherited the radical belief in the existence of God. He dedicated his life to the love and service of God. As he says, 'The conflict arises between my truth-loving mind and my blind faith', whereas Truth says, 'I cannot renounce my prop of life. I feel death in the very attempt'. My developed mind awoke with the cry of my cherished and nurtured blind faith: 'Oh heart, be not sentimental! Thy faith is not based on truth. It is mistaken and false'.

This appeal of the love of truth combined with its cogent reasoning gradually began to change my heart.

This crucifixion is compensated by deliverance, and nothing can deliver except truth. A conservative or reformative altruist re-establishes and rehabilitates an old truth or value, while a creative altruist discovers a new truth and a new way of life.

Devatma gave up his belief in God and discovered the following truths:

- To realize oneself and all existences as real.
- To realize the bonds of relationship which the creator has established among all existences.
- To regret the desire to make oneself able to fulfill all duties and obligations in every one of these relations.
- In order to realize this true desire to mould one's life.

There, the twelve main relationships with which a disciple is required to establish a higher harmony based on higher life, parents and children, brothers and sisters, the vegetable kingdom, husband and wife, great men and saints of the world, masters and servants, neighbours, the departed ones, the animal kingdom, the mineral world, one's own nation or country, the Dev Guru and the Dev Samaj.

As Devatma argued, "I felt my true and real relation of all kinds with the true and real Nature".

This was indeed a most blessed moment and he wishes to be united with Nature in a harmonious way with Devat, as all visible scenery and animals are dipped in nature, whose flame nourishes all. Devatma is whole-heartedly blessed. Who can realize this glory? When did the glory and sublimity of the evolution dawn on me?

Law is not Enough

The first and elementary expression of the altruists of justice is to bring about the regeneration of civic life through law. Is law a check against arbitrariness or unrestrained despotism? Moreover, against the sense of justice, law prevents anarchic behaviour, and hence, it is sought after by altruists of justice. In the Magna Carta of 1215, we can examine the historical records of arbitrariness in the political field. The Magna Carta was the beginning. The birth, growth and maturity of the English democracy is a legend for altruists of justice in the political record. No wonder Bacon describes such revengeful vindication as wild justice recognizes all men as equal in basic humanity, and nothing can better express this sense than law. We have many instances of this type in justice through law, such as polygamy, which is unjust to woman. Similarly, Hindu property law describes a cult of discrimination against women. The law is not enough and such laws need to be examined and revised to ensure the rights of all persons, with the consciousness of the sense of justice allowing us to move into the next phase of advancement.

A Slave in Your Own House

The altruists of justice are best expressed in the opening words of Rousseau's immortal work Social Contract: 'Man is born free but he is everywhere in chains.' The contribution of the altruists is to give eyes and light to society to make it see how its social, political, economic, religious and educational structures divide its members into masters and slaves, which is outrageously unjust. All institutions and laws that operate in these fields—social, political, religious, educational and personal—must be revised so that man who is born free remains free until the ashes of his cremated body mingle with the elements of Nature. We must now move out of the darkness of the slavery to authority into the light of freedom for individuality. No man has the right to keep another man under his physical authority enforced by law.

There was a long tradition of negro slavery across the world. What was most wicked about the institution of slavery was not the ill-treatment of slaves by the masters, but by the institution itself. Abraham Lincoln, who ordered the emancipation of all slaves in America, asserted: "As I would not be a slave, I would not be a master." The individual is sacred and his freedom is an inalienable right and duty; however, freedom is divided by some authority.

There are no appreciable differences between man and woman in terms of intelligence, abilities and aptitudes. The same false distinction is responsible for discrimination against women in the material field, for example, in denying a woman the right to remarry. In general, the social emancipation of women took the form of revolt against enforced widowhood, denial of education, the right to a vocation and freedom, economic inferiority in matter of share of property and marital inequality in the form of polygamy and divorce. Rousseau in France and Froebel in Germany became the spearheads of this movement of the emancipation of the child. What is 'right' is not what God commands. How do we know that what God commands is right? Real morality is the life of reason.

Devatma worked hard to deliver man of his low-loves and low-hates, which lead him to be unjust to other existences and to himself. The ethical consciousness is decorated by an uncompromising reverence for the individual.

The altruists of fulfillment focus on the facts and examine the problem, which concerns renovating the techniques and objectives of social control. The altruists of fulfillment hold that it is not enough for a just society to remove the obstacles of law and social prejudices in the way of individual progress, but also to bring about positive laws and customs. In general, the altruists of fulfillment have tended to be the socialists in different countries.

Values and Social Control

The regulation of mutual relations by tradition, convention, customs or law, i.e., by some social technique which operates above the immediate impulses or passions of the persons covered by it and binds them to respect it, is a step in the evolution of just conduct. The truth of this statement is expressed in the common sense observation that it is better to have a bad law than no law, bad government than no government. Because even a bad law put some check on the arbitrariness or impulsiveness of even those whose vested interest it happens to serve. In the absence of a law, there is nothing to checkmate the arbitrariness of those in power and advantage. The worst enemy of justice is arbitrariness. A law, however bad it may be, prevents arbitrary behaviour from those in power, and thus, serves justice. Hence, the remedy against a bad law is not to cut out all laws, but better laws in general. The elimination of elements of injustice in the social techniques of law, custom, convention and traditions in all areas of life, political, social, religious and cultural by eliminating discrimination based on arbitrariness of distinctions, such as power, position, wealth, colours, caste, sex and age.

However, the moral perception of the altruists of freedom has exceeded the line of truth in advocating no social control or social influence in the life of an individual. It is true that in customs and laws, which are the technique of social control, there are elements of an arbitrary authoritativeness, pinpointed by the altruists of freedom and which their efforts help to eliminate. The altruists of fulfillment focus on these facts and see that the problem concerns renovating the techniques and objectives of social control. They point out that altruists of well have removed the arbitrary authoritativeness in laws and conventions in social customs, practices and educational systems.

The altruist of fulfillment works to see that the municipality, the state and the central government have welfare departments, which provide the conditions of health of the unborn child from the day of his conception. For example, the health visitor visits the pregnant mother, takes care of her health problems and provides for her proper nourishment. Also, the school provides a free school uniform, free books, free stationery and free lunch for the poor children in common social life. The altruists of fulfillment work to bring women at par with life and destiny.

The Problem of Measurement

We have examined a historical study of the various forms in which altruism of justice has manifested itself. The first expression of altruism of justice was shown by those who fought to substitute the rule of law in place of the arbitrary rule of an individual. Without law, there can be no justice, for law puts a check on the arbitrariness of individuals and thus calls halt to the passions and powers of the individuals in authority.

In the twentieth century, we had another class of altruists of justice. They were inspired by the light of truth, meaning that individual freedom must be dove-tailed to consciousness of social good. The problem of justice faces the problem of measurement in simple and complex, situations of life.

However, those who practice the new methods of examination know how they fall short of the just assessment of the individual, even when the operation of the subjective element is reduced. Ignorance blocks the way of human good will to find the most reliable examination techniques.

There has been another development to assess the intelligence, aptitude, interests, motor skills, motivation and total personality pattern. The history of test psychology throughout the world is an earnest of human effort to be just to individuals and many testers have been faced with tremendous difficulties at each step in their test construction.

From Social Exploitation to Enlightenment

The exploitation for which a person seeks a guru is social. Gurus enjoy a great prestige and dignity in all societies of the world. The history of religion stands as witness to the motivation of social exploitation. Gurus appear and disappear with the knowledge of bygone ages, and every new guru achieves their basic recruitment from the lowest social strata, as is the tale of every religion, old or new! Every religion cherishes the guru's enhancement and the guru's outlook is always well respected. Further, it is a fact that both gurus and religion in general enjoy a number of distinguished personalities. On the other hand, science has its own domain that exists outside of hypocritical religion. Our thinking varies from person to person in the maze of prestige, honour and financial matters. Undoubtedly, religion as a life occupation is a pillar of life, and life celebrates a far more social honour.

Social welfare is possible in the lap of selfless service only. In education and profession, there is a need to enhance young talents towards altruism. Out and out religious missionaries are serviceable only if they enhance greater social reforms. As such, social prestige should be lesser than 'altruism'.

From Political Exploitation to Enlightenment

If frustration drives some millions to seek spiritual geniuses or Gurus, exploitation attracts other millions to do the same. It has its own spheres and exploitation is the second major motive in establishing a relationship with a Master. Exploitation is dipped in selfishness; henceforth, through and through, all selfish relations are the cases of exploitation. This is similar in the case of institution, selfish teaching, profession and political exploitation. Political parties misuse their power to gain votes and salute their Gurus. Thus, politics and religion should not be used in combination with each other as many different religious institutions have evil mindsets, and overall, politics and religion end up fighting for the position of authority and power. Gladstone and Disraeli were great political contemporaries who both occupied the most powerful position of Prime Minister of Great Britain. However, the lower forces dress themselves in acceptable fashion and betray the individual. In fact, attaining moral or spiritual idealism is the most difficult challenge to overcome. All this drama is a mouse trap scene in the guise of lust of power. Fake spiritual exercises, the acceptance of the Guru and extra-spiritual wishes satisfying of the Guru are false circuits of the lust of power.

From Ethical Exploitation
to Enlightenment

We can distinguish biological ethics, social ethics and personality ethics. There are certain good and bad practices that affect our biological survival. However, physical health is not the only moral ground for temperance in food and sex. Intemperance may involve expense, which the person may not be able to afford. When we wish to avoid over-indulgence in food, drinks and sex for reasons of biological survival or economy, we are at the level of biological ethics.

Dev Samaj has an atmosphere that helps one to give up drinking, smoking, a non-vegetarian diet and adultery. This aspect of Dev Samaj's service is appreciated. So many parents send their children to Dev Samaj institutions and Dev Samaj meetings to safeguard them against developing habits of drinks and adultery. Dev Samaj's social ethics are supremely appreciable. Dev Samaj propagates all healthy human relations. Some seek Dev Samaj for personal ethics and wish to be altruistic, with many accepting Dev Samaj without any selfishness.

In contrast, religion and ethics are different. A good man of transparent valuations may not be religious at all, for a good man of transparent virtues may not be religious at all. For a good man to be religious, he must have faith and love in a belief, which is regarded as the highest religious life (sublime life) and not a life of love for a great cause or even the greatest cause.

Hypocrisy, myth and falsehood corrupted all religions; thus, the golden religious life connotes a faith and love of the Master and it strives for faith in or a love of altruistic life. When the twin ladders are present in a person, he is religious. In spite of low hate and low love, the highest value for humans is to involve the highest love of the Divine Being; however, it should be noted that the arena of faith and love of divine is too comprehensive to describe. To service all four kingdoms is to enable us to be serviceable to all existences. The crown or glory of such salvation and evolution is that it opens the gates to being in love with the Master as an affectionate disciple. This condition is essential for a disciple – if he is devoid of aforesaid affection, he is not accepted, even he is free from all eight of the gross sins. Altruistic gratitude is what Devatma cherishes.

Know How to Live

We can be appreciative of others if we avoid judging others by their motives and accepting that different people have different ways of working. We carry a mixed bag of motives, and every human has their own brain-wind. Thus, the rightness of an action is judged by the consequences it produces, which depends on circumstances. Different people have different set of working of the mind. A man given to service of a great cause is accused of some unworthy motives. One contemplation is set in the sphere of the parent-child. In fact, the blessing of birth is downgraded by attributing an unworthy motive to parents and invaluable service and concern given by them is considered a bargain for old age. In the decorative frame of service, as given by parents (i.e. birth, physical, mental, moral and spiritual culture is incomparable). Parents love to serve their children and are anxious for their entire welfare.

Unmistakably, love is never a selfish act, as it may be limited in object or objective.

Great mindsets offer us a wealth of information to learn from. Moral psychologist Kant said, "Who knows whether one's 'little self' plays a part in one's most exalted action of duty!" As such, great action dazzles us to the extent that we forget about motives. However, we downgrade our fellow men by concentrating more on their motives than on the rightness of their action. In fact, our lack of appreciation of others' actions and life is due to our love of self. Therefore, we need the virtue of mudita (i.e, the feeling of being happy at others' excellence). Further, we need to efface jealously for the dear ones, while we should also develop the culture of the feeling of Mudita to be sweet to others and joy for ourselves 'in full swing.'

Dance in Ecstasy Before the Beauty

There is only one condition in which the accounts can be balanced. For example, when the debtor develops love for his benefactor, his services are no longer motivated by the benefits received. He or she serves out of love, and they do not love their benefactor because of what they means to them, but rather, what he or she is in themselves. The devotee is at the level of gratitude in relation to his Master, for he works for a very humble devotion. Thinking of a master as a "protector, preserver and evolver of spiritual life in us" is to gaze at him only in the aspect of what he means to us and not at what he is. Undoubtedly, we tend to view the master in his or her utility to humankind and the other three kingdoms of Nature.

Devotion to Devatma cannot be measured in terms of the level of gratitude, love, affection, service and freedom from low-love and low-hate. In fact, it is the attraction of a moth to a star and is the mad delight of a devotee to dance in ecstasy before the beauty of the Master until the last unit of heat in his body is exhausted.

The Best, Liberated and Fully Evolved Man

It is not good behaviour that matters, but rather the courage that we bring to it. A good man is at their lowest when his good behaviour is 'fear inspired'. However, goodness in the grip of fear or cowardice can never be benevolent – it is dusty and garbage. A man who openly commits crime when he transforms can be of strength to the cause of goodness. Goodness must be positively founded, cowardice is the worst foundation and courage is the highest foundation.

Freedom from the low-loves of money, sex, ease, place, wife, children, vanity etc., will allow someone to achieve great success if he has a positive love for goodness. Therefore, there is no comparison between the miserly sacrifice to the good men for goodness and the unlimited abundance of sacrifice of the evil men for evil, as Goodness yearns for the day when man will show the same dare-evilness and martyrdom; then and then alone will man be at his best, liberated and fully evolved. Secondly, if he develops a vision and love for such sublime life, who is an out-and-out lover of truth and goodness and a hater of untruth, evil, and injustice, etc., then man will be good at his best.

Seek Truth Unconditionally

Devatma had developed in his life love to seek truth unconditionally. Dev Dharma would go to science not so much for support, but more for the beliefs it holds and to discover any element of untruth in it. A ruthless subjection of all beliefs to the scrutiny of reason and scientific method was his life's characteristic – a scientific field related to seeing goodness and evil as a condition from evil life and his destiny of salvation and sattvic life. According to Dev Dharma, their solutions are under science. The human personality, both body and soul, is biological in origin and under the natural laws of life and death. It is, among others, an object of nature related to scientific laws. Hence, there is no conflict between the religion of Dev Dharma and science in terms of method for knowledge, for it does not ask for the 'privileged status' for the soul capable of supernatural communication.

The Future Belongs to
the Altruistic Man

- A person has altruistic feelings if he serves some existences with whom he is not bound by ties of low-loves or undue attachment. A person can do altruistic service to his own children if he is motivated in his service by the sole motive of their good. Again, a person may develop undue attachment with some orphan children, for example, and hence his service may not be altruistic. A person is altruistic if it is to the good of the other, which is the sufficient motive of his doing service to the other.

- The acuity of an altruistic feelings in a person opens his eyes to some evil in the society or raises his gaze to higher vision of the society. It is these exceptionally gifted altruists who awaken and develop the altruistic capacity of the less-gifted in society who come to share their insight into some evil or vision of good.

- A person with an altruistic feeling experiences, to some degree, the suffering of the victim of that evil, or imaginatively lives through the thrill of the satisfaction that would come to others when the visional good is brought in their lives. It is altruists of compassion who experience the suffering of the down-trodden in society. It is altruists of the future who are full of joy for their new vision of interpersonal relations, for which they live and labour.

- Some people feel inspired to engage themselves in altruistic work by removing some suffering or doing some constructive work to rebuild society. However, their low-loves are too powerful and would not allow their altruistic feeling to have its way. A person can be an altruist only if his feeling of altruism is strong enough to overcome the opposition of his low-loves.

- Unless an altruistic feeling becomes the character of a person, he cannot claim to be an altruist. An altruist is a person who lives altruism every minute of his life, in the same way as a greedy man is one who lives for wealth, even in his dreams.

- Satisfaction in one's altruistic work is an indication that the altruistic feeling has become his character. Unless a person finds pleasure in his altruistic work, he is an altruist, though he does altruistic work. To do altruistic work is not to be altruist, though it is a step towards being an altruist.

- If the enthusiasm for the altruistic work does not grow with time, it means that it is infected by low-loves and low-hates. This is an alarm-bell for the altruist to safeguard his altruistic feeling from the evil influence of low-loves and low-hates. If he is not conscious of what is happening to his altruistic feeling, he may lose it altogether.

- An altruist does not spare himself in his work for a good cause. One must be whole-heartedly devoted to the work at hand. Without the gift of being able to forget oneself in a great task, an altruist fails in his vocation. There can be no half-heartedness for an artist, neither relaxation of effort nor surrender to laziness. He is so full of what he is called upon to do by his insight and vision that every other thing sinks before it. His altruistic feeling taps the last ounce of energy from him. Death alone can spare him from his constant commitment to his self-chosen service of a great cause.

- An altruist never despairs of his great cause, even in the most non-co-operative and inimical conditions in the social and nature world. An altruist is inspired by faith for the victory of his or her great cause to which they serve. This feeling of altruism is like a lighthouse to him, for it is an unfailing light that cuts through the darkness of opposition that surrounds him. He is able to direct the ship to his cause in spite of the storms that toss his ship, for he has the lighthouse of altruistic feeling in him, and this light gives him the faith to rise above despair.

- An altruist has invincible faith in the victory of their good cause. This unconquerable faith and identity with the good cause makes it impossible for them to give up, as the altruist and the good cause are not two but one. The altruist would prefer to give up their life, but not their good cause, for their knows their cause to be a far more excellent thing than themselves.

- One who has not the character to meet the challenge of circumstances, to exert a greater effort to overcome obstacles, and thus have the character of invincibility – all non-moral qualities – cannot be altruist. A great cause throws up great challenges to the courage, resourcefulness, energy, intelligence, perseverance, patience, faith, or an altruist. Without these non-moral qualities in greater abundance, he cannot stay an altruist of first importance.

- An altruist seeks no return for the service he or she renders to society, and seeks no praise, title or reward. Satisfaction in the accomplishment of removing suffering or bringing good in even only a few lives is so valuable that the altruist finds every other satisfaction relatively insignificant. An altruistic feeling gives eyes to the altruist to see the intrinsic value of his work of removing some suffering and ushering in some good, and he feels all sufficient satisfaction in working for it.

When one expects a return for his service to a great cause, here and hereafter, he is not an altruist. What motivates his altruistic work is not altruism, but the desire for name and fame, power and position, possessions and pleasures. Hence, this type of human is anything but an altruist, and their altruistic services will also cease if they fail to get praise or reward, for it is for their satisfaction that they do altruistic work.

When one's life is characterized by the above excellences, he or she can be said to be an altruist.

Pearls of Thought

(New light on Altruistic Life)

Altruistic motivation and conduct are variegated in human beings. One may take to altruistic conduct to promote the health, strength and happiness of one's soul. Another may take to altruistic conduct in view of his consciousness of the innumerable services received from society. Still another man may be inspired to altruistic conduct from the sense of justice. Some others may take to altruistic conduct out of desires to reduce misery of the less-placed in life or help the progress and happiness of normal fellow human beings.

There is another species of altruistic motivation, i.e. to share life with the humblest, to love man as man, as distinct from men of one's social group, community or religion.

(1)

Exploitation is to use other people as a mere means to an end. It is always bad, even if there is a positive result. For example, if a person demands more work than initially bargained for, it is bad, even if he is working for a charitable institution.

Some men engaged in great causes show great cruelty to those who work under them in the interest of their cause. Again, all selfish relations are cases of exploitation, for in all selfishness, others are used as a mere means to one's advantage.

We exploit an institution when we join it without the proper aptitude and abilities for it and work in it for ends outside the interests of the institution. For example, when a person joins education when he has no liking for teaching, no love for the young and no ability to teach, but he works in it for his livelihood or for the case and comfort of the profession, he exploits education.

Thus, exploitation is misuse. We misuse a person when we cease to treat him as an end himself. We misuse an institution when we satisfy through it those interests that lie outside the purposes of the institution.

(2)

Social exploitation explains the change of religion by those among the better class people. The history of religion stands as witness to this motivation. Every new spiritual master gets its main new recruitment from men of the lowest social strata.

(3)

When we wish to avoid over-indulgence in food, drinks, and sex for reasons of biological survival or economy, we are at the level of biological ethics.

We ought to be free from low-loves and low-hates and cultivate altruistic feelings, for this helps us to keep out of harm's way to the humblest existence in the four kingdoms and makes us serviceable to all existences in hundreds of ways. However, this is not all. The crown, or glory, of such moksha and vikas is that it opens the way for being in love with the master, to be Anuraagi Shishya.

(4)

A devotee is at his best when he develops from the level of gratitude to the level of love in relation to all existences.

If we feel a closeness with Devatma for our own advantage, the relationship is thus conditional and ego-centric. The basis of such a devotion is our ego interests, even though these interests happen to be spiritual.

A devotee rises from this ego-centric relationship when he loves Devatma as a result of appreciating his sublime life. It is not gratitude-born love, but rather a love born of an appreciation of the sublime life. Such love cancels ego-centrism and makes the devotion to Devatma as he is in himself. Devatma's clear vision basks in the beauty of the master, with the last traces of egoism cancelled out, with unconditional love pouring out of one's soul. Like the attraction of a moth to a star, it is the mad delight of a devotee to dance in ecstasy before the beauty of the master until the last unit of heat in his body is exhausted.

(5)

A good human is at their lowest when his or her good behaviour is 'fear inspired'. Goodness inspired by fear or cowardice can never rise beyond its dust level. An evil man who openly does evil can still be courageous, because evil is condemned by society. Such a man, when converted, can be a source of strength to the cause of goodness.

Goodness awaits and yearns for the day when man will show the same dare-devil and martyrdom on its behalf. Then and then alone will humans reach their peak – liberated and fully evolved. Secondly, if one develops vision and love for such sublime life, becoming a lover of truth and goodness and a hater of untruth, evil, and injustice, etc., humans can reach their full potential.

(6)

A right action must have the right content and right motivation. This can happen when the motive is free from the last trace of ego attachments and the personality completely surrenders itself at the altar of truth that the right action shines with the glow of holiness.

The highest level of motivation gives us the cue of which motives should inspire our actions. We must be inspired in our right actions by the spirit of the surrender of the best in us, even our soul, in order to strengthen and contribute to the evolutionary process. The highest motivation is self-sacrifice to the evolutionary process. Hence, a right action must become a 'sacrificial' act to the evolutionary process in order to reach its maximum potential.

(7)

This is the lowest level of relation, for I seek my master for his utility for my own gain. The master is so excellent in his beauty that we love him for his own sake, to lay all our powers and services at his feet as a token of love. The highest level is the spontaneous uninterrupted love of the master.

A lover does not desire to be the beloved, even if he or she is offered to change their position; he or she wants to remain the lover to his beloved and contemplates on his or her beauty. In the same way, human beings do not want to be identical with their Master, even if they are offered to be him. In this way, a devotee desires nothing from his or her Guru. What he or she desires is to be in the ecstatic love of his Master and to lay everything at his feet, irrespective of what may happen to him.

(8)

It is gratitude that upgrades us into a moral person. It is reverence that wins us the destiny of being a religious person. Man has a destiny to become a religious person and this gratitude cannot do for him. It is reverence that reveals the intrinsic worth of persons and things, clothes them with sacredness and evokes the homage of heart in relation to them. To a man of reverence, an altruistic person is an extraordinary phenomena in human society. He gives such a person a special place in his heart.

The testament of the feeling of reverence can be broken down into six points:

- A person with a feeling of reverence is deeply sensitive and appreciative of the altruistic virtues of the person who is the object of his reverence.
- He considers such a person sacred and feels it a privilege to lay his head at his feet, and thus, brush aside all the arrogance of his own life.
- He seeks his association to the maximum.
- He invites others to appreciate his altruistic virtues.
- He joins him in his work.
- He undergoes a moral and spiritual transformation.

Reverence is appreciative not only of the extraordinary excellences in individuals; rather, it is appreciative of the marvels of the evolutionary process. The evolutionary process of Nature presents itself on a massive scale in a series of great events of immense significance. One of the greatest spectacles of reverence is the emergence of life. In the immeasurable physical universe, under certain chemical conditions, the candle of life emerged as a miracle of miracles. Life signifies the invisible but invisible power of the evolutionary process.

If we revere animal life, we cannot hunt or hurt or kill animals for sport, trade or taste. Therefore, compassion in action must be the way of our life. If we have reverence for man, we cannot exploit him. Without reverence, compassion and disinterested service lack the lustre of full bloom. It is when we found our compassion and disinterested service on reverence that we rise to the level of religion. A religious man's compassion and disinterested service is based on the perception of the immense value of life, as opposed to inanimate things and to other species.

The feeling of reverence for the evolutionary process in Nature not only gives compassion and disinterested service its full bloom but it also transforms the human being. In a chastened human life, he or she will dedicate themselves as a humble helper in the service of this gigantic creative drama of evolution.

(9)

All good etiquette is based on a tender core of the feelings of considerateness, appreciation, gratitude and love. The observation of good etiquette saves us from injuring others in body and mind. No compassion is complete unless one feels pain for the pain caused to the other, and there is a desire to remove the pain of the injured.

The quality of our pain will grade the quality of our compensation. As parents, we can experience a peculiar form of pain when treating our children harshly. If we develop a fellow-feeling for the injured, then our pain for the injury caused to them has the highest quality. Altruistic love for the existences of the four kingdoms of nature gives our pain of reparation the highest quality.

Again, altruistic pain can checkmate the tendency to injure others again. The purification from the disposition of the wrong done does not end with compensating the wronged. Therefore, we must root out the tendency that leads to wrongdoing, and nothing can do this better than altruistic pain, which is the best purgation. Besides this, we need to develop altruistic loves as an aid to reparations. We know how our responsibility to make amends extends to the wrongs done by our parents, brothers and sisters, community, nation and by humankind in general.

We are so situated in life that we depend on destroying life just to live. We can ease the burden of wrongdoing through ceaseless service of the four kingdoms. The development of altruistic loves is the true compensation for the wrongs done by us as individuals and our relatives, as well as our caste, clan, community, class and country.

(10)

When we live with full truth, we cannot think of harmony with any person (except in self-defence), for rarely there is a person who has not some better side to him. To continue to be in harmony is to refuse to identify a person with the evil part in him.

Complete estrangement is based on the half-truth that the other person is identical with his evil part, and nothing is more dangerous than half-truths, for their falsity is so difficult to expose, as a half-truth hides the other part of the truth.

When we fall into disharmony with another, we paint the other all black and deep black, with no relieving features, for they take away our justification for estrangement.

Two lives separated by the untruth that the other is identical with its evil part, were once united in love and understanding. Can there be greater and richer blessing than love and understanding between two human beings?

We need education to make our occasional capacity into character of life. We instantly become cold, indifferent, and non-cooperative as soon as another differs from us, behaves in an unbecoming manner or offends our vanity or denies our selfishness, for we identify his total personality with his part, which has offended us. However, there is no way out of proneness to the state of untruth, and hence, disharmony, except to be superman. The only solution to the problem of harmony between men is for men to be supermen or be in constant communion with the super-human soul or Devatma.

(11)

To be good is to be good to others, and one of the ways to do this is to avoid disharmony with them, for disharmony with someone not only denies us the opportunities of being good to them, but also it perverts our vision, and undeservedly, we talk evil of them, wish them evil, do evil and live in an untruthful relation to them. To avoid disharmony with another person is to avoid causing uncalled for suffering to them, and thus remain in rightful relation to him. We often fall into disharmony with others due to self-love, jealousy and selfishness.

In light of this, if we are resolute in avoiding disharmony with others, we are too over-cautious with our self-love and jealousies, which disrupt human relationships. Therefore, to be good is to seek harmony.

(12)

To seek harmony is to cultivate the whole gamut of altruistic feelings of appreciation, accommodation, gratitude, charitable interpretation and forgiveness, etc. Thus, to seek harmony is to be good.

If we surrender self-love and self-centredness and develop an appreciation of every little or big service that is done to us, we are blessed with the feeling of harmony with the world.

Such a feeling of appreciation opens us up to ever-fresh, new and charming aspects of the world around us. If I am sensitive and responsive, I can rejoice in the new and charming aspects of happenings in the world in a non-stop cinematographic manner. The world is never dull to me, and I am not tired of it, for I am able to appreciate the infinite aspects of its creativity and beauty in every moment of my life.

If we accept others' moral weaknesses as part of the game of interpersonal relationship, we have a feeling of accommodation. If I do not respect others' peculiarities, I lack the spirit of accommodation. We have moral weaknesses in each of us that permeate the differences in our physical, intellectual, social and cultural makeup, meaning that our capacity to be good is limited and we have many weaknesses.

Feelings of gratitude bring us closer to all the four kingdoms of nature, as they reveal the better part of the existents of these kingdoms and it urges us to contribute to their betterment. Even if there is no life after death, the feeling of gratitude would find satisfaction in recalling the benefactors who are no more, and in fulfilling their good wishes.

Every uncharitable interpretation exposes the underlying hatred or disharmony we bear to one another, or at least a lack of mutuality, goodwill and love for fellow human beings. Such uncharitable interpretations act as a warning bell to repair our relationships or, at least, to be critical or cautious about our uncharitable interpretations.

Forgiveness is the capacity to own the other person in spite of all his misdeeds. Whatever the other might do, he does not cease to be a human being, and therefore, does not deserve to be cut out from our concern.

Forgiveness can arise from feelings of compassion, gratitude, reverence or altruistic love. The first stage of forgiveness is preceded by repentance by the wrongdoer. There is a higher stage of forgiveness when one forgives the wrongdoer without any apology. When we develop this disposition of forgiveness, our acuity to the faults and failures of others, as well as their selfishness and swagger, is reduced, and acuity to the good traits of others, or the services rendered by others, is heightened, and the latter dominates our relationships.

Forgiveness makes us forbearing. When forgiveness is a disposition, it helps one to accommodate oneself to the weaknesses of the others to a point of non-observation. The ideal of forgiveness is that we are to cultivate happy and harmonious interpersonal and intergroup relationships.

(13)

When we fail to appreciate our surroundings, we cease to have a living and altruistic harmony with them. To meet people during the day and not feel enthused by the good in them is to be so full of one's own self as to find no place for them. As such, this behaviour demonstrates apathy, indifference, and callousness. The feeling of appreciation is wider than the feeling of gratitude; also, it is more disinterested than the feeling of gratitude. One needs the feeling of appreciation to build up multiple relationships with a benefactor.

Unconditional love opens up a much wider relationship than the feeling of gratitude, for it extends concern for the good of the others who have done no good to us and possess no merit whatsoever and even those who have done wrong to us. Yet, there is still an element of ego-centricity involved in this form of unconditional love. However, the feeling of appreciation is not spoiled – it is free from all ego-centricity and is reflected in the clear glass of the feeling of appreciation.

The feeling of appreciation can rise to the unconditional love for the excellence of the others – this love is called Eros. In such a case, the magnificent splendour of the qualities of the object captures our appreciation; consequently, we come to develop a communion, commitment and dedication to it. Also, the knowledge, beauty, virtues and skills of others shine brightly, to the degree that we have knowledge of them and to the measures of acuity in terms of our feeling of appreciation, which is distinct from our knowledge and other altruistic feelings.

The feeling of appreciation blesses him who feels appreciation. A human with a sense of appreciation is able to see the world in kaleidoscopic beauty, as it were, as compared with a human without a sense of appreciation, who sees the world in black and white, or even worse, in black alone. In contrast, a cynic undervalues, or rather, denigrates the qualities in the other. This type of human being lacks the light of appreciation, and thus, nothing enthuses them – the sunrise and sunset leave him cold, and the great men are seen to have feet of clay. Further, they paint the society in dark colours of selfishness, insincerity and wickedness. He sees only what is foul, evil, and ill-odoured and lacks lustre, beauty and joy in life.

It is when we shed such standards of comparison and see things from their unique standards that we can witness the true excellence of the things and rejoice in our appreciation of them. When we start judging a thing by an abstract standard of perfection, unrelated to it, we switch off the light of appreciation.

To be appreciative, one must recognize the uniqueness of each class of objects or individuals. We are to learn to appreciate and appreciate with enthusiasm whatever good we see in the other things, however humble they may be, and however limited their value may be. It is ecstatic with the thought that the tiny spark of life is the result of billions of years of laborious effort of the trial and error process of evolution.

To be able to see another with their own eyes and appreciate the good in them, one needs imagination and humility. We are so much in love with our own self that our vision is jaundiced with untruth. Our self-love, which comes in the form of selfishness, does not allow us to enthusiastically appreciate the innumerable benefactors of all the four kingdoms of nature. Our selfishness is so pervasive and parasitical that our feeling of gratitude never knows full bloom – it has stunted its growth in the climate and soil of selfishness. The literature of the world contains very little of the lyricism of gratitude towards benefactors in interpersonal and infra-personal relationships!

We are unappreciative and complaining souls, for we condemn the world. We are enriched when we acknowledge the excellences of others, may they be physical, intellectual, moral or spiritual. Our appreciation adds to the total value of the world. The world now has an incalculable value, for the two together – the beautiful world and the aesthetic appreciation of it – fill the whole with value.

There is no greater punishment in life than to be 'left out' or ignored. This is the penalty that practically every great man pays. Thus, a poor society is one in which its altruistic workers are not appreciated. What we need, however, is not only the feeling of appreciation of the excellences of others, but also the feeling of appreciation and enthusiasm for the value of our work. We do ourselves harm when we cease to appreciate what good we do in our life or profession. These altruistic feelings are liable to untruthfulness in their evaluation, and hence, the feelings of appreciation and criticism can both deviate into untruth.

The feeling of appreciation establishes our relation with the other. If we find nothing good in others, we sap our relationship with them.

(14)

We need the cooperation of all altruistic feelings to create sweetness and light in different interpersonal relations. It is this feeling of harmony which helps one to cognize the value of sweetness in mutual relations, which is not merely utilitarian but also intrinsic.

To love something good is to love something in a positive way. The feeling of harmony delights in the beauty of harmonious relationships – it is said that the world loves the lover. Lovers are persons who have achieved a very high degree of harmony. To appreciate the feeling of harmony between lovers is to value harmony, since the harmony between lovers does no great good to the world.

The feeling of harmony cognizes the value of harmony both as a utility and as an intrinsic value and leads to all efforts to create conditions of harmony in inter-personal relationships.

It is the feeling of harmony that has led to the evolution of civil behaviour and which, when taken in the context of social structure and history, may be said to constitute civilization. As civil means polite and obliging, not rude, the genuine feeling of harmony demands the cultivation of polite language.

Good etiquette is meant to create harmony in interpersonal relationships, for it is based on respect for the feelings of others. A man with the feeling of harmony is tolerant of differences. The feeling of harmony makes us accept variety as fundamental to the human situation. It is when we develop a scientific attitude of dialogue with others in political, social, moral and religious fields that we work for a harmonious society.

There is both utility and intrinsic worth in seeking harmony with infra-human worlds. The ecological balance protects human life from ultimate extinction. The presence of a variety of natural environments, plants and animal life duly enriches the human experience. Therefore, to exist is to co-share life in harmony with all the four orders of nature.

(15)

There are two types of interpersonal relationships: of contract and of commitment or unconditional love. The contract relationship is conditional. Here, the relation between the two parties is conditional on the mutual observance of the contract, and its continuation depends on certain conditions being carried out by the persons in that relationship.

The economic relationships are cases of contract. They represent the basic relationships without which society is not possible. What keeps society going is the discharge of functions contracted for by each member in it. The greater the efficiency with which the terms of the contract are carried out, the greater the coherence and satisfaction in the relation between the individuals involved in it. If in an institution, each individual, from the sweeper to the CEO, carries out the functions assigned to him, the institution flourishes.

However, in a contractual relationship, the fulfillment of the agreement condition is conditional on others carrying out the terms of the agreement. As such, a contract means a conditional relationship.

There are other relationships that are not cases of contract but of commitment. The relation of a mother to her child is of commitment, of unconditional love. A mother gives love to her child unconditionally. She does not love the child in expectation of what the child might do for her – even when she expects something, it is not an expression of demand, but a luxury of love.

Love delights in return of the love. It neither notarizes nor depends on the thought of return, and flourishes even when unrequited. A mother does not cease to love her son even when he deserts her. There are numberless mothers who look after their imbecile children. Could such mothers expect their children to look after them in old age?

Parents are good to their child even when the latter is not good to them. They are committed to the child's welfare, however limited and poor their conception of good may be. It is foolish to persuade a mother to worry about her child when she does not care for it because we use a language of contract – not one of self-effacing commitment. If there is one person in the world who would not abandon her child, however low he may be in capacities and character, however hated and abandoned he may be by society, it is the mother. Her relation to her child is one of absolute commitment. All our reasoning against her child fall flat on her. We may call her blind. Yes, she is in a way. But she can also call us blind, too, for she can tell us, "My son does not cease to be my son, because he is wicked, don't you see this! I am committed to my son as son, not as bright or dull, good or wicked!" We can protest thus,

"You should be committed to your own good, not to your son." Her automatic response will be, "You wish to tell me that I should maintain my relation with my son if it is to my own benefit. No! Don't tell me that! If he is ill or immoral, that is all the more reason for him to receive my love. You are not thinking in terms of commitment, but in terms of contract!"

A wife's relationship with her husband is one of commitment in most cultures of the world. This commitment comes not because the husband is good-looking, well-placed, bright, well-mannered or moral, but rather because they share a partnership together and each has their own separate roles. Marital life abounds in the commitment of a woman for a man, and Indian literature has beautiful stories of woman's commitment to love her husband in the characters of Sita, Savitri, Damayanti and Parvati. Marital life abounds in the commitment of woman for man.

The life of commitment is unselfish. It is the business of culture (i.e. our literature, education and religion) to foster the feeling of commitment or unconditional love for the stability and harmony in interpersonal relationships. The life of commitment has a higher level than parental or conjugal – it also pertains to the spiritual level.

However, commitment comes with compensation to some individuals, whereas there is often a lack of commitment to one's organization and its cause. Society is inferior in its excellence, it consists of rank and file and normally degenerates in quality in course of time. Hence, it is much more difficult to show commitment to society.

Religion is a search for Devatma

Faith in and Love for Devatma

The role of religion is vital in the drama of the human race and deeply affects all aspects of human life. The socio-anthropomorphic study of the human race tells us that religion stands as the foundational cornerstone of human civilization. Therefore, man needs religion to protect and perfect himself and his society in the eternal flux of this world process.

There is no doubt that religion has taken many turns and tempests with different human communities over the course of time. Due to the wide range of religious groups, the world has bled and suffered from war for years; even so, true religion can ultimately give meaning to humanity.

The need for religion should bring a devotion to a cause that will consequently give our fragile and fugitive existence significance and value. In the age of science, we need a religion free from incredible dogmas and an uncritical attitude towards life, and furthermore, it must be free from low-loves or low-hates.

The history of religion gave us a noble thinker, who had devoted all his life to finding a scientific religion known as Dev Dharma. In the natural religion of Devatma, we find a scientific philosophy which is altruistic in character and bases itself on the facts and laws of Nature. Scientific knowledge is taken to be the standard of true knowledge of whatever exists.

In religious philosophy, religion and ethics are not the same thing, though they are so intrinsically related. A good man of transparent virtues may not be religious at all. For a good man to be religious, he must have faith and love in a being, which is accepted as the highest. Religious life is not a life of love for a great cause or even the greatest cause – it must be essential to it, and have faith and love for some being – whether human or superhuman. In this book, I have defined religion in such a way that it can be grouped into good and bad religions, while I have also defined it in evolutionary terms. Religious life implies the incomparable elements of faith and love, regardless of whether the subject of worship is a stone, a tree, a statue, or a great man, God or the Devatma. There are also false religions that advocate the faith and love of a being who is either a myth or unworthy in his character.

Let us be clear as to what religious life is – it is the absolute faith in and love of the Master and the strive for altruistic life. When both of these things are present in an individual, he is religious and religious life revolves this axis. The first is peculiar to religion and is its differentia. Even if we are raised by personality ethics (i.e. even if, for argument's sake, we are free from low-loves and low-hates and have developed altruistic loves, we are not religious).

Faith in Devatma is the other requisition for being religious, and is closely related to the development of psychological techniques, which may one day help society to have mature individuals free from passions and lusts, and full of social virtues. Even then, psychology would not have dispensed with religion. The greatest contribution of a religion is its leader who worthy, essentially of faith. Is it the highest development of a personality, to be good, i.e. to be free from low-loves and hates and to be imbued with and immersed in altruistic life? The answer is no. The highest value for man is in love, and the highest love is the love of the Divine Being. In the love of the highest divine being, man touches the peak point of his destiny. Hence, it has been the soundest instinct of mankind and the natural culmination of the highest philosophy to place the highest value as love of the divine being. There have been errors as to the defining characteristics of the divine being, but there has been no error in the intuition of humankind to give the highest value to faith and love of the divine being.

So great and sublime is the experience of the faith and love of the divine being that morality is made secondary to it. We ought to be free from low-loves and low-hates and cultivate altruistic feelings, for this helps us live a safe and humble existence in the four kingdoms, and allows us to be serviceable to all existences in myriad ways. However, of greatest importance is the crown or glory of such moksha and vikas, as attainment is tantamount to being in love with the master, to be Anuraagi Shishya.

If we appreciate that differentia of religion is love of the divine being, it thus becomes clear why Devatma put his faith in him as the first condition of membership of Dev Samaj. This condition is intrinsic to religious life. As per definition, although one may be free from all the eight gross sins, he is not religious, but may be considered altruistic, which is not to be confused with being religious. Despite having gratitude for Devatma, he is not religious. This point finds strength in the historical event membership conditions, which were revised by Dev Samaj. These were disciples with an exceptional gratitude for their master – they had rendered historic services to him. Yet, these grateful disciples failed to pass the set membership criterion, and because the new conditions demanded faith in Devatma, which was wanting in them. This showed their life lacked the differentia of religious life – they had joined religion without being religious.

A Devatma is a soul, which is neither all powerful nor all knowing. Regardless, he is the soul, which is free from all weaknesses of human souls. No evil passion touches his life and conduct, and there is no altruistic feeling lacking in him. He is the soul with a new psychology. His urges are governed by the principles of truth and goodness and every thought and act of his life is processed by these two principles and they bear the charm of unique quality.

439

It is this equipment of an all-sided love of truth and goodness that had made him so completely satisfied with the souls that can open their window of worship to him.

When one opens the window of worship to Devatma, it enjoys the highest illumination and noblest purity of every nook and corner of its being to the limit of its climax.

Goodness awaits and yearns for the day when man will show faith in or love of Devatma. Then and then alone will man be religious, liberated and fully evolved.

And after touching this level, man does not want to be identical with his Master, even if he is offered to be him. The best lover does not desire to be the beloved, even if he or she is offered to change his position. He or she wants to remain the lover to his or her beloved and contemplate on his beauty. So, a best devotee desires nothing from his Master. What he desires is to be in ecstatic love of his Master and to lay everything at his feet, irrespective of what may happen to him.

Devatma: Beyond Experience

In the spiritual world, the personality of Devatma is totally unique. The life which is beyond our understanding rides on the ripple of complete harmony. In the world of the religion, there have been various sorts of religious avatar gurus, peers, prophets and saints. Their intellectual thoughts are related to transcendence or the hyper natural. Their thoughts had accompanied their personality and behaviour in one compound, and their view is related to the thought that the soul of an individual is not the production of a sensual or natural world.

Ancient prophets and seers presented this consciousness in Brahman, thereby enunciating all family bonds. They declared their life's definitive attribute in God as yog or dharm-yog. The eligibility of gurutav (to gain guru) is to fuse in God.

In raising the question as to whether there is a God, we can't deny that there are energetic elements, such as air, water, fire and land. Also, there is the natural world of food, fruits and flowers and the world of animals and birds. There is also the world of individual society, which comprises parents, sisters, brothers, husbands, wives and relatives, castes, countryfolk and companions. If we have the duty to rise and develop a feeling of gratitude towards God, love and meditation, then is it not our duty that in individual society, animal world, natural world and plant world we should have to develop the feeling of appreciation, gratitude and service?

We have an innumerable amount of services from these four worlds. Our knowledge of civilization, art, science, and literature, religion and philosophy are indebted to fellow men. In light of these facts, is it not spiritualism to forget or discard these benevolent individuals?

However, God's disciples, seers, prophets, saints and gurus showed disregard to the framework of developing the feeling of service in the appreciation of these four worlds. They created songs with full enthusiasm, devotion, and devotional feelings towards God's appreciation, but did not create and sing songs in the gratitude of the four worlds. God relates to the Guru in their Samadhi (meditation), which does not take or give place to these four worlds.

They disconnect their relationship to their surrounding existences of four worlds from the world of mind and intellect. They balance their consideration on God's experience only, which may be limited. In Devatma, there is an initiation of new life and personality. From an intellectual perspective, there are various sorts of existences in the world and these are genuine. Every existence also has its different life, in the same way a stone has its own life and we have to realize its truth. If this stone is beautiful, it is our duty to appreciate it. If this stone is a part of the decoration of our courtyard then it is our duty to clean it and to protect it from harm – this is our religion. It is also true to all existences that various existences should be accepted with gratitude and that their debts be paid.

Master Devatma, in his meditation, does not only meditate with the evolutionary part of nature but He deepens his relation with the four worlds to whom He achieved service. In his meditation, Devatma searched for these various existences. His life became filled with those aesthetic heart touching incidents that show how his life relates to the service of the four worlds.

When we consider that God and God alone is truth, then we consider other existences as minor or declared as illusory. The stage of Braham

Gyan is the condition of Nirgun emotion. This emotional condition is the stage of empty unity, which has no place for multi-existences and multi-attributes. In the meditational stage, our God-related disciples, Brahmvadi guru or rishi do not have the nectar and comprehensiveness, completeness, and enhancement for the relation of multi existences' positive attributes. Only that person can take delight in the 'unity in diversity' that accepts and regards the innumerable existences of the world or does service, and he became worried about helping and reforming the disabled, helpless and feeble existences. This personality is our Devatma and it is clear that Devatma has a completely new sort of personality. He has a soul that has comprehensiveness and a supreme relation that is, in the development of Earth, is unique in itself. In Devatma, in relation to the existences of the four worlds, the basis of the service of positive love is unique.

Devatma does not have the tendency of renunciation of truthful sources at any rate for altruistic work. Devatma is the only eligible Sublime-force for the individual creed. With his help, we the soul who has created a link in the existences of these four worlds on the basis of truth and goodness, and in whom the melody of goodness for these existences is in abundance. This evolutionary process is the condition of complete unity. By establishing a bond with them, we gain enthusiasm, light and power for establishing a relation with the four worlds and service.

When I respect animal life and whichever animal is under me, I take care of them and with the outlook of Devatma – the path giver. If I serve my parents, then Devatma's own life is the pinnacle of light. If I wished to be an ideal husband, then Devatma's own life is perfectly enthusiastic. If I wish to serve individuals, then he makes me supremely and eligibly serviceable. If I aspire to the ideal true Master of love, then the light of Devatma's sublime beauty can allow me to reached a higher aspiration of love.

Faith in the Sublime Beauty

When a fit soul basks in the sunshine of the sublime light (Dev Jyoti) of Devatma and understands that by developing love or partisan spirit for falsehoods and evil thoughts and deeds, one degrades his soul and vitiates its constructive power. In addition, by siding with truth and good thoughts and deeds, he increases the spiritual vitality of his soul, and thereby promotes and blesses his soul-life; further, he also comes to realize that the highest sublime life which the Devatma has evolved in his soul by the unfoldment of the forces of complete love of truth and goodness, is one great reality. This reality is above all forms of doubt and can never be questioned or doubted; then, by such a two-fold realization, he awakens an altruistic feeling of true faith in his heart, to which faith directly apprehends the truth and is itself a witness of that truth.

- In the sublime light of the Devatma, it is necessary to see that Nature, which has given birth to Devatma through its evolutionary process, is a great reality, and every existence in nature becomes better and evolves its capacity through assimilating favourable conditions existing in Nature, etc.

- It is essential to realize and put one's faith in the truth that every animate or inanimate object grows comparatively better according to how it participates in the evolutionary process in Nature and grows worse or degrades according to how much it obstructs, opposes or grows hostile to it.

- It is essential to realize this truth in the sublime light of Devatma and strengthen one's faith in it, for love for truth and love for untruth are two contradictory forces and it is essential that the votaries of the two must come into conflict. In this conflict and war, the ultimate victory inevitably lies with the lover of truth and its partisan or supporter.

- It is essential to realize the truth in the sublime light of Devatma and strengthen one's faith in it. In this way, nature's love of goodness and love of evil are two contradictory forces, and the votaries of the two must inevitably, according to the law of Nature, come together, and in this great conflict or war, this is inevitable in consonance with the evolutionary process in nature. This means that the lover of goodness and his co-operators or supporters must ultimately triumph. Now, if a person is unfit to receive Devatma's sublime light, which is necessary to enable him to realize the above truths for establishing faith in their reality, he can never develop the requisite true faith in relation to Devatma.

Religious faith is when one appreciates the spiritual benefits received from his guru, and this develops faith in him.

The feeling of gratitude gives us faith at different levels of benefits. The feeling of gratitude is a feeling that allows us to appreciate a benefactor and therefore strengthen faith in him.

Faith rises to a higher level when we develop reverence for our object of faith. Through feelings of reverence, one appreciates the inner greatness of the Devatma, along with the blessings showered by him. The faith that finds its further foundation in reverence has some light of understanding in it. The devotee understands through his reverence one or another excellence of sublime life, the spiritual journey of Devatma.

As a reverence deepens, the light of understanding brightens. Therefore, the feeling of reverence is a feeling that gives appreciation of the inner greatness of the benefactor, and thus, it further strengths faith and also illumines it.

The feeling of aesthetic love makes us fall in love with the beauty of the inner excellences. Therefore, at this stage, faith is not only the strongest but also the most illumined. At this stage of aesthetic love for the sublime life of Devatma, faith shines as bright as a gem of the rarest and most serene light. Faith is at its best when it is nourished by aesthetic love. Empowered with intellectual brilliance, the devotee, with aesthetic love for Devatma, is beholden to the total panorama of Nature in its kaleidoscopic beauty of the evolutionary process manifesting Devatma and his mission.

A person who has no feeling of gratitude, reverence or love for Devatma has no faith in him. Faith is blind when it does not rest on experience but on social conditioning. To this end, our communion with Devatma is poor and our faith is a matter of social conditioning or routine, however unshakable it may be.

Faith does not mean to accept the teachings of Devatma about nature, the evolutionary process, the manifestation of Devatma, the Dev Jiwan and Deva prabhava and to be convinced of its truth in general, but rather to regulate one's life by it. If I do not allow my concrete present to be qualified by the word of my master, then I have not believed in him. I do not fave faith in Devatma when I only follow him where it is convenient for me. I have faith in him in everyday life, and if I sacrifice my advantages, possessions, success, position, power, victory or risk my all, my life would not be conducted according to the light of his words.

Faith in Devatma is the most difficult relation to Devatma, for it asks us to take all risks in being true to his life and teaching the fierce struggles and temptations of worldly life.

The testament of the Faith can be defined as follows:

The faith of a person is not intellectual acceptance only. It is emotional and behavioural commitment.

- A person full of Faith while losing it, becomes a fish our of water.
- At every moment in solitude he yearns him.
- At the point of meeting he feels himself in Paradise as he gets the wealth of all the world.
- He feels protection and blessed in his company
- He realises the supreme meaning of life in his company.
- He is always in love in his merging.

Reverence for the Sublime Beauty

When any soul that is illumined by the sublime light of Devatma realizes the true sublime beauty of the Devatma and the sublime forces developed in it and by means of that light, on the one hand, they are able to be completely devoid of those sublime forces and completely dominated by various low-loves and their resultant low-hates. Thus, a sufferer from various soul-maladies may find and realize, in the sublime beauty of Devatma, a cure for all the soul-diseases and full and suitable conditions for soul-growth, and then and only then is he able, on the one hand, to directly comprehend the true glory of the sublime beauty of Devatma and his own utter insignificance and Devatma as his only refuge. On the other hand, he becomes desirous of singing the glory of the Devatma or longingly hearing others indulging in the similar melody of song to the glory of the sublime beauty. By awakening such a desire or longing, he spontaneously bursts into singing his praises and listening to songs sung to the glory of the sublime beauty, and by such an experience, derives in his heart higher or altruistic ecstasy or joy. Such a soul-experience or realization is termed altruistic reverence. By the development of this altruistic reverence, the devotee awakens true humility in his heart in Devatma's relation. By the development of this altruistic reverence, the devotee awakens true respect for him in his heart, and is anxious to make that feeling manifest in his relation. In fact, he makes an actual expression of that feeling. It is only when this altruistic feeling is fully developed in a soul that he is able, by means of his inner vision, to see the true glory of the sublime beauty of the

Devatma, and is able to fearlessly and fervently propagate that glory before others.

The testament of the feeling of reverence can be defined as follows:

- A person with the feeling of reverence is deeply sensitive and appreciate of the super-altruistic virtues of the sublime life, which is the object of his reverence.
- He considers the sublime life extremely sacred and feels it is a privilege to lay his head at the feet of the sublime master, and thus, brush aside all the arrogances of his own life.
- He seeks his association to the maximum.
- He invites others to appreciate his sublime life.
- He joins his supreme mission.
- He undergoes a moral and spiritual transformation.

Gratitude for the Sublime Beauty

Any individual charged with the sublime influences ('Dev Prabhavas') of Devatma realizes the various spiritual favours which he has received from him; that is, the various false beliefs from which he has been liberated and the true knowledge about the true religion and soul that has been imparted to him. From the freedom which he has attained from false and harmful rites and rituals, as well as the physical and domestic blessings that he has received and the many debts and obligations, he or she feels an urge to do disinterested service prepares his or her holy wishes to respect those humans, animals and plants, all of which are dependent on the individual and endeavours to serve and protect them, even after his (the Devatma's) departure from this Earth. He feels a similarly strong feeling of proving serviceable to him, and above all, he is ready and fully desirous to sacrifice his mental and bodily energies, such as his wealth, etc., at the altar of his services. Then, and only then, can such a noble feeling of his be called the feeling of gratitude.

The feeling of gratitude, when it is our character, seeks and finds ways to do something for the sublime benefactor. A man of gratitude is never satisfied with what he has done and it would be blasphemous for him to say so. Gratitude is the conscious appreciation of the service of the Master which is being received and conscious desire to make some return to the Master.

When we build our relations with Master Devatma on what He does or can do for us, it is a relation of utility. The lowest ethics that can spring from such basis of relationship is exploitation and hatred. The highest ethics that can flower from it is altruism of gratitude. We generally build our relations with others on utility, whether they are things or persons.

When we treat human beings, as mere objects of utility, our conduct reaches the limit of wickedness. Tragedy deepens to its darkest dye when mere utility is the basis of relation with the dearest.

Let us explicate the gap between the acts of gratitude, the feeling of gratitude, the sentiment of gratitude and the altruism of gratitude.

1.   The Acts of Gratitude-

Acts of gratitude are acts by which we make a return for the benefit received. When a good is done to us and we return this good turn, our action is an act of gratitude. Most of the etiquette and our social duties are acts of gratitude such as the etiquette of mutual gifts and presents. Acts of gratitude may not be due to the feelings of gratitude and if not, then It is morally very inferior.

2.   The feeling of gratitude-

It is only when acts of return are inspired by a pure feeling of gratitude that they have positive moral quality and the acts are real cases of gratitude. When someone does us a favour which we appreciate, we experience a feeling of gratitude for the benefactor. From moral standpoint this spontaneous feeling is more valuable than the offer of a whole universe in an act of gratitude lacking genuine feeling of gratitude. Feeling of gratitude is spontaneous, immediate but short-lived

3.   The sentiment of gratitude-

The spontaneous feeling of gratitude is to be cultivated to become a sentiment for the benefactor through moral education and self-culture.

Sentiment of gratitude is a stable disposition, a character-force which gathers in depth and intensity as ages in time. Devotion of a whole life-time and the martyrdom of Sharavan Kumar traces out the psychological biography of the sentiment of gratitude.

However, sentiment of gratitude is not the whole story of gratitude. Sentiment of gratitude is specific in character. It is in relation to a definite person or persons, things. A Plato's gratitude is attached to a Socrates so that he cannot forget him in the best of his philosophic writings. An Ananda's gratitude is directed to his Buddha. It is a gratitude-for one's Master, for one's Particular society, for one's country, for a particular thinker.

4. The Altruism of gratitude-

When we realize the truth in our life that we are based by our environments—physical, biological, social and cultural. Also we are cared as children by the earth under our feet, by sun over our heads, by the air that blows, by the water flows, by the plants that grow, by the animals that serve us. We are human, because of our human parents, human society and human geniuses. All these factors contribute to build tinniest and the titanic in life. The essence of altruism of gratitude is that since my personality is a contributed existence, I must make my contributions to the whole. It is not limited to the service of particulars from whom the service was and is being received. Its object of service is the unknown existences of all the four orders of the Universe, too.

In whatever stage of development feeling of gratitude exists, either as act of gratitude, sentiment of gratitude or altruism of gratitude, it is characterized by making the other the direct object of service. It is not a case of dynamic gratitude, if my motivation in return of service for the service received is to promote the good of my soul. Such cases of gratitude do not reduce the centrality of self in one's welfare. In pure or unconditional feeling of gratitude, the welfare of the benefactor is the direct object of concern and tends to reduce one's centrality on the stage of life.

Attraction to the Sublime Influences

When any fit person awakens under the rays of Devatma's sublime light, he or she is able to obtain true freedom from the soul maladies, which they have developed from the operation of low-loves, which diseases and degrades his soul and vitiates his constructive power, thus making him a wayfarer on the path of degeneration. He further realizes that it is by these sublime influences alone that he has been able to develop, to some extent, the altruistic forces which help him to establish a heart-communion with the Devatma and awaken the other altruistic forces. These forces can be sustained and stabilized under the same sublime forces, and only then can he develop a desire and wish to imbibe these sublime influences. Such a desire or wish for such sublime influences is known as the feeling of attraction for the sublime influences.

If such an attraction or feeling for assimilating the sublime influences has not awakened in a human, he or she would never perform any religious exercise by themselves to acquire them, nor would he or she be able to acquire them through personal spiritual exercise ('sadhana'). In such a state of his soul, he would not be able to establish any soul-communion with the sublime beauty ('Dev Rup') of the Devatma. Hence, by himself, he will not be able to have the privilege of direct worship of the Devatma.

Survival of the Sublime Species

(The poetry of suffering, agony, torture, and sacrifice)

Thousands of years
Narcissus repents on her blindness,
Through long struggle of centuries
Emerges a 'perfect sublime ablaze'
in the garden house!

Ah!
Enormous commitments in
a short-lived life!
General practitioners who 'came across'
were all deformed!
The repetition of longings at this
condition was vain!
These were circumstances
That could not acknowledge completely
the beauty of sublime life!

They Crucified Him at Every Moment

Suffering is only a contemplation
of positive experience
in the case of achieving
a higher meaning of life.

Suffering and pleasure
are respectively
negative and positive effects,
or hedonic tones,
or valences that psychologists
often identify as an essence
in our emotional lives.
It is a transition of emotions,
Despite its initial disrupting nature,
suffering contributes to the
organization of meaning
in an individual's world and psyche.

In turn,
meaning determines
how individuals
or societies experience
and deal with suffering.

The way of thinking
connotes more things i.e.
Life without anguish
or pain,
without happiness,
without grief exists
only in the imagination.

Whence,
the reality is amalgamation of
the two (happiness
and loneliness).

Concerning suffering,
there are mainly two
fundamental questions.
The first is, what is the
origin of suffering?
and from where does it emerge?
The other is whether agony
and pain are concordant
with the justice and law
of mercy in Nature.

All the religious people of the
world should answer
these two questions.
Yeah!
in full-fledged way,
If God is the Lone Creator
of the world
and the Manifestation
of goodness,
thence,
from where have all these

miseries come from?
Can God of Goodness be
the agent of misery?
and just as He creates, also destroys?

Dilemma! Roundabout!

Acknowledgment of the fact
affirms
If
One God is the sole origin
of all creations—even then
those events that are seemingly
wicked —were enigmatic for masses.
It is an enigma of mind eye!

Significantly,
The reader should understand
that life and teaching of Devatma
is completely scientific.
In science, there is no evidence
Where God does exist,
Therefore, belief is justified and valid
that
Devatma's sufferings are
not because of God.
Therefore,
the questions are meaningless
in our chapter—
Why is there suffering in the world
if God is all powerful and loving?
WHY?
Why doesn't He cease it?
"Can He
Or

Is He weaker than we think?"
May be because of certain
reasons such as
Free will, certainly,
God cannot stop evil and suffering
because He is powerless.

How much evil should be stopped?
For the greater scheme__
Prevention of further evil.
For the greater plan,
For discipline and instruction,
To serve as a warning,
It is the repercussion of sin,
To make a point,
To serve as a means to bring
The similar, so and so on.
Thence,
the initial question-what is the
origin of His suffering
and from where does it emerge?

Either because of His complete
love of truth
and Goodness or something else.

According to Devatma's
pearls of wisdom

"Where is to found
that painful record of
all those long
series of continuous hurts
to my heart
and the injury caused to physique,

through sour opposition
of my Mission
at the hands of deep dyed lovers of evil,
through traitors to my Mission
and the ungrateful,
vindictive and wilfully
malicious persons and even by loyalists
through their dirty and low-feelings."

It is beyond the pen
of man to describe
the intensity of the suffering
of Devatma
to portray
whether it be real or
imaginative sympathy,
_____the spirit
we wish to represent.

From this time forth
the uniqueness of
Revered Devatma
separated him from all human minds,
therefore
the human mind is unable
to reach this state of sympathy,
even in imagination.

Even Devatma handicapped
by human language-
which can describe experiences
of human souls
because
language is the product
of human efforts

to express his thoughts,
emotions,
and feelings-- express his
inability
to describe the intensity
of his sufferings.

Unquestionably,
Tender hearted personality
Cannot endure
Time to time
Afflictions and tortures,
It is
Too hard to describe
this route of deep pain,
Only
Devatma recognizes this unfavourable time.

There is a circuit of various
forms of persecutions
and prosecutions
against Devatma,
just for example:
Devatma has been
'a source of hat redness'

He has been accused of gross vulgarities
and immoral sins.
O this woof!
This blubbering howling!
The leaping sparks of devouring,
destructive fire of vindictiveness
and jealousy,
Oh that all were being emitted
from hundreds of hearts.

O these seeds of infertility!
What an embarrassment!

There was not a single
vulgar adjective
that was not used against him
such as a cheater,
a liar, a criminal, a debauchee,
a hypocrite, murderer,
misappropriate one,
a bad character, female infanticide etc.

O these parching lips of falsehood!
O dead humanity!
There was hardly a crime that
was not knitted on his name.
There was no indecency
From which he was not accused.
These accusations were not merely oral
Henceforth, writings in the form of articles,
in the newspapers, posters and books too.

O inappropriate papers of 'blue inks'!
Wake up! Wake up! Age-long sleepers!
Most degraded people
found great satisfaction to tease
Devatma's disciples on the way-side,
to through dust on them,
to strike them with fists,
to snatch propaganda book
from them,
tear them, to break
the head of some of them
with sticks.
What is the dwelling place of humanity?

Harmony, integration, goodness
and truth are out of order!
What a degradation of judgment call!

Human hatred threw
the accumulated filth
of its wicked hearts
on Devatma
by inappropriate charges,
another many malicious
and degrading forms of
persecutions,
such as creating rowdies
in his meetings,
burning sign boards, throwing
brick-bats etc.
In the teeter evaporation
of low feelings,
Essence of truth vanished.

He was declared as addicted
even to those eight great sins,
Whereof the renunciation is
indispensable condition,
for a disciple of the lowest grade.

Ah! This lowest stage of vulgarity!
In the garb with odious conduct,
When Devatma started his sermons,
they would create novice,
throw stones and break door panes
or even attempt to injure him.
O this criminal personality!
Heart turns into tattering
and shattering condition!

Devatma was tortured
and tormented by the powerful
source of law.

Number of absolutely false law-suits
were filed against Devatma
and his disciples,
this continues up to five years.

What an injustice!
Callous! Fierce views!
Devatma had to pay not
only heavy
fees for legal proceedings
On that account,
Heretofore,
As a repercussion,
but
other expenses of litigation also
which are its necessary course.

Says Devatma, "almost all the accumulated
funds of the infant Samaj,
which were quite meagre,
were spent.

The Samaj press had to be
stopped and sold away.
The staff of the press had
to be dismissed.
Most of the office furniture
such as tables,
chairs and almirahs had
to be sold away.

"A large portion of the headquarters'
buildings
(including Devatma's residential rooms)
were given on rent."

The annoying behaviour of the prosecutor,
Chanda Singh who was blind pleader
in Ferozepur
filed nine false suits
(criminal and civil prosecutions),
was most shocking.

Even the magistrate felt
the behavior of Chanda Singh
so insulting
that he wrote in his judgment
thus:
"Chanda Singh's manner and bearing
is insufferable while in court."

Throughout the case,
his manner has been most
offensive to the accused....

As Chanda Singh is a blind man,
I have shown great forbearance
with him
than I would with any
other person.
"As a result
he has now gone beyond
all bounds."
When these means of persecutions
against him
failed to crush Devatma's Mission

then attempt on his life was also
excited and practiced.
What a conspiracy of thought!
Words are sobbing at the pages
of time.
For instance,
An Arya pamphlet referring
to Devatma said,
"Catch him, bind him, hang him."
Some sent forth the cry,
"Would some Nihang Singh make
an end of Him."

What an inhumanity!
Truth can never be veiled.
Never.
Never.

Writes Devatma,
"They wrote to me letters
threatening me with death.

Through posters
they expressed
the wish: "May some
giant
strangulate him."

This feeling gathered strength
and culminated in actual attack
on Devatma,
when a state ruler found an opportunity
to vent his ill-feeling
by abusing and firing at him
five or six shots

Fortunately,
he missed his aim and most
precious life was rescued.

Devatma had to suffer the
unbearable
shock of the ungrateful deserters
and traitors
who joined persecutors' camp
and are welcomed
and made potent instruments
to harm Devatma.

For example, Dharam Pal
prided himself
that he had circulated
as many as
seventy thousand copies
of his pamphlets and
periodicals
to injure the reputation
of Devatma
and his Dev Samaj.
The black ingratitude of
deserters
and traitors shocked
Devatma beyond measure.
Who will measure
his solitary vein?
Devatma was all alone
among devils.
Writes Devatma,
"Bitter persecutions had already
seriously affected my health
Ergo

These, my kind friends, seemed
determined to blot out my
very existence
by every means.

They could devise and
employ under
the British Raj.
It is not only traitors
that have shocked Devatma
But
even those who remained
with him,
have by their wish of higher
consciousness
been a source of pains to him.
Says Devatma, "During this long time,
this degraded land has failed to give
me a single soul,
in such critical and trying
moment of my life,
to whom
I could count upon as a perfectly
trustworthy
and unfailing friend and
a true well-wisher.
O this wailing!
This land could not produce
'even a single soul of truth'.

"...sometimes their selfish, self-sufficient
and egoistic heartedness
relieved by the presence
of higher feelings,
lead them to such actions

as sorely and
deeply wound my heart
and cause me pain
an anxiety that is
simply indescribable.

Several times their behavior becomes
so extremely shocking
to my highly sensitive higher feelings
that this agony becomes unbearable for me
and on such occasions
sometimes
I have wished that it
would be better
if death may relieve me of this
awful mental
and heart torture
and release me from
such sufferings."

What a bloody humanity!
Heart sinks and sinks........
Again Devatma writes
his memorable article Vilap.
"Alas! How painful is
my condition!
Oh! How painful is my life!
However filled in great sympathy
and solace!
But in this wide world,
is there a single soul,
who can prove a balm to
my bleeding heart
and give relief to my
suffering soul?

Apparently none.
For other apart this,
even those who come in my contact,
are not able to feel and realize
the full measure
of my tribulations.

And when they cannot adequately
realize
my painful position,
their sympathy even if they possess any,
cannot be of any use to me.

I am born to endure all alone
these extraordinary agonies
and certainly
I alone will have to bear them.

Alas!
How solitary do I feel myself
on account of these peculiar troubles!
Alas!
There is none in this world,
whom I can call my own in this respect!
After a long day's hard work
even the most simple labourer,
does at night,
rest in the soothing arms of sleep
which recoups his exhausted energies and
refreshes and revives him
for the next day's work.
But

"I am deprived of even
this gift

of Nature
which is accessible even to
the lowest
sentiment creature
that crawls upon the earth."

What is a life if full of evil?
Humans should have to die?
They have lost their insight
of goodness,
Certainly.
This terrible suffering had been
continuous
for years
and their hurts had shattered not
only Devatma's heart
but body too,
even then Devatma had
immutable faith,
that the Mission is in
accordance with the
laws of Nature,
therefore,
it cannot but progress and spread.
And this was inevitable.

But the tale of the persecution
by the outside world and hurts
from inside ranks daunted him not,
deterred him not,
but determined him
more and more
to work for his Mission
of doing highest spiritual goodness
even to the persecuted humanity.

It is the Rock Strong aim.
In the grip of great agony,
the light house on the shore of
this was not beyond,
though troubles
were still shining bright.

Even in the state of great
predicament,
the light of sublime knowledge
burnt bright
in Devatma,
showing him the path.

There was a special Mission
of Devatma's manifestation
and a special life-vow,
whose fulfilment is imperative
not only for the enhancement
of the country
but for the spiritual welfare
of the mankind.

This Mission and life-vow cannot
attain fulfillment
carrying the burden of all
these pains and tortures.

The Promise of Paradise

The word 'Sacrifices'
sometimes connotes
a psychological
and sometimes
ethical meaning.

Sometimes we speak of a man
sacrificing his honor,
money or his throne for a woman,
In such case,
its mean to give up one or another,
without referring to its ethical value.
But ethical sense of sacrifice
is to give up something lower
for something higher.

Sacrifice is the triumphant choice
of a higher value in comparison
to a lesser one
or an evil done by human will.

Let us see
the gradation of sacrifices
i.e., instrumental, intrinsic
and absolute.

An instrumental sacrifice is a sacrifice
made for the sake of realization
of some good end or ideal.
Apart from the end such sacrifice
loses its goodness.
It has two varieties: inner and outer.

Inner instrumental sacrifices
are necessitated
by individual's own limitations
or weaknesses
but outer by the treatment
of society.
A person is a great person
in comparison with one
who succumbs to home attractions
and sacrifices a great cause.
But
in our enthusiasm of admiration,
we must not forget that such sacrifices
are confessions of limitations
and those
who have combined home-life
with the best service of a great
cause locating
on a much higher ethical ladder
in the scale of values.

Popular imagination frames
fetish of sacrifices
and regards such instrumental
sacrifices
as an end in themselves;
so that a person who
indulges in them,

without regard to their
contribution to human goodness
is generally regarded as worthy
of greater respect
in comparison to one
who makes no such sacrifice.

For instance,
how many admirers of Devatma
have realized their reverence
for Him, qualified
because
He lived in a decent house
fitted with some of the amenities
of modern life
and set with artistic taste!
Such qualification of
praise is stupid,
based as it is, on a complete
misconception
of sacrifice.
Devatma had no need to
make sacrifice of home
and hearth
because far from being
attached to them,
He used them for the
greatest goodness
of mankind.

No moral weakness could
characterize
His soul
and therefore no sacrifice,
which is a confession of some

inner weakness,
could be His.
If we could have true insight
into His sacrifices,
our soul would feel dazzled
before the Himalayan height
of Devatma,
which could combine in
itself all the moral values
in perfect harmony
and hierarchy.

Now let us take
the outer instrumental sacrifice.
We know how inhumanity of society
has imposed on great men
certain tragic sacrifices,
which they have willingly made
rather than given up
what they held to be true and auspicious.

Christ was repaid for his services
by crucifixion.
Giordano Bruno had to stand
the suffering of being burnt alive.

Such sacrifices
are the expression of strength,
for they do not arise out of individual's
inner limitations
and weaknesses.

Devatma had to endure sacrifices
of tremendous character of His unique cause.
He was ignored,

hated, humiliated
and persecuted by those
whom he loved to serve.

His life was framed,
a target of bullets.
He was dragged from court to court.
He was rendered penniless
and he had no place of His own
to put his head on.

The legend of Devatma's sacrifice
is a story of tragic
and terrible sufferings.
However,
we must remember that
it is not necessary
for a man to be great,
that he should be crucified
or burnt alive,
for such a demand would mean
that savagery, inhumanity
and brutality,
nay could utter more
i.e., wanton cruelty, bloodlust,
and atrocity of society should be kept intact
or intensified to make future great men
as great or greater than those
who are gone before.

What is required
to give quality of service to a soul is
that he should have a ready will to
surrender all that is related to him,
including his body and soul
for the great cause he holds dearly.

In this connection, 'ready will'
must not be confused
with wishful thinking.
For example, a person indulges
in wishful thinking
when he toys with the idea
that he can sacrifice this position
or that position,
this or that thing and even
his life when the person's actions
show naked lust for power and possession.

Such is the contemplation
of the political leadership
of the day,
for all are talking of peace
and sacrifice for it,
without the 'ready will'
to sacrifice national selfishness
for international goodness.

In the religious world,
such thinking is moral
and spiritual garbage.

Intrinsic sacrifice:
This is a sacrifice,
which is auspicious in itself
without reference to an end
or ideal.

If we yearn to know
whether a certain thing
is intrinsically in our favor,
we must consider

that thing in isolation
from everything else
and ask ourselves
if its existence,
however short or brief,
is worthwhile even if
nothing else results from it;
for example, is it right for a person
to sacrifice his false beliefs,
even if they lead to his
being blown to pieces
by a bigoted government
and therefore, complete annihilation
of his body and soul?

It is up to point
because we believe that
when existential values
and ethical values fall apart,
it is right to hold the
ethical values,
Hence
what is intrinsically reliable
may also have great
instrumental values
e.g., knowledge is intrinsically good,
it is also instrumentally good.
Sacrifice of false beliefs,
low-loves and low-hates
is intrinsically good,
and it is also instrumentally good
because their sacrifice
strengthen the constructive
power of human soul.

Such sacrifices stand on much
higher ethical ground
than instrumental sacrifice,
for such sacrifices
are good under all conditions.
Again, such sacrifices are more heroic
than the
highest instrumental sacrifices,
for to give up a cherished idea,
is to wrench asunder a part
of one's own soul.

Such sacrifices involve
a much higher moral stamina,
much greater spiritual grit
and special soul gifts;
but this inner drama of human soul,
however magnificent in its grandeur
is not open the view of the
ordinary man and
therefore, its appreciation
is in inversely proportion
to its greatness.

For a human being,
such intrinsic sacrifices
are possible to a limited extend
because
psychologically it is impossible
to sacrifice
all his falsehoods and
low-loves and low-hates.

His sacrifices are limited to giving up
particular false belief only,

but not that part of nature,
which produce falsehood.
Again, human soul can succeed
in freeing him from one or
another of low-loves
but he cannot sacrifices that
part of his nature,
which produces low-loves
and low-hates.

It is only given to Devatma to rise
above all low-loves and low-hates
and He alone has the sublime nature
that can eschew all falsehoods
and all low-loves and low-hates.
Again, the limited extent to which human soul
can make intrinsic sacrifice is marred
by human frailty.
Man has misfortune to transfer
his assets into liabilities.
Every intrinsic sacrifice
successfully made gives pleasure.

Soon the pleasure falls apart from activity
and goads the soul to indulge
in the activity for the sake of pleasure,
e.g., instinct of food when satisfied,
gives pleasure
and then one seeks food for pleasure
even against the survival.

Similarly, intrinsic sacrifice
brings pleasure
with it and such pleasure,
instead of

helping the further evolution of the soul,
generally produces self-love.
And self-love, when unchecked,
is dirge to the soul's inevitable death.
Therefore, human souls need the guidance
of Devatma
if it is to have moral evolution,
Moreover,
It is scientific evolution to behold things
on factual grounds.
Absolute Sacrifice:
All intrinsic sacrifices are not
of equal value;
some of higher values than others.
For instance, intrinsic sacrifice
of giving up
low-love of children is lower in value
than giving up low-love of
selfishness or self-conceit.

Again,
a person who is able to make
two intrinsic sacrifices,
is superior to the one who makes
only one of them.
Absolute sacrifice means
the highest sacrifice,
which a unique soul is capable of.

It is the legend of valor,
Thus,
Absolute sacrifice includes
all intrinsic sacrifices
and sacrifice of determination
by pleasure principle of thoughts,

feelings and actions,
even altruistic thoughts,
feelings and actions
Such an Absolute Sacrifice is
possible only to a soul
who has complete love for
truth and goodness
As well as complete hatred for
untruth and evil.
Such a soul is Devatma.
Let us bask in His light to behold
the glory and grandeur of His
unique absolute Sacrifices!

With
Supreme gratefulness,
Let us
Frame 'an evergreen plant of modest thankfulness'
Towards
Nature for such supreme manifestation,
For such a vision of life.

The Poetry of the Beyond

What an energetic review of life!
After diving deep into the sublime life,
he realizes a living bond among
every compartment of the world.

What a purification of life!
What a transformation!
He seeks a relation with
numerous living
and non-living existences
with higher feelings,
When he beholds
Any living and non-living existence
or non-living matter is in malapropos
Thence
Myself,
Having a bond towards this matter
its harm of this sort creates a feeling
of heart wreck in him
Pushing his heart towards a prison...........
An exile of miseries..............
Whether
Any
Child, any family member performs

any inappropriate activity
for any person, animal, plant,
or any non-living matter
Thence
He feels a torment
Scrutinizing it,
his heart terminates
into numerous pieces
If any person keeps
negative activities
in numerous relations,
Thence he feels an interruption
If he examines things in
a filthy position,
Then he realizes a repentance......

If he sees peering at
himself
and another
in a condition of garbage
whether
clothes, utensils, lamp, books,
pictures, boxes or shoes
Or anybody's anything on a table
In a worse position
Thence
He feels maladjustment ......
If he beholds anything out of place_ splitting
Then he bears tortures to that extent
We can't explain......
We can't estimate.

If he observes any
plant is in need of water
And water is not provided,

The same plant is withering,
This harm hurts him to what level
we can't describe
If he notices
One of his family members does
not show respect
to any other assistant
Or
does not feel torment or pain for him
or not express aesthetic or justice able behavior
Then his heart holds on
If he views
any person making a blunder or
any inappropriate pledge in
the sphere of others,
Or wishes to harm another person,
plant, or animal
Then his
Heart receives wounds to the
supreme extent /level
If he notices
any person does not perform
suitable duty
at appropriate time in his relation
Or any other relation
Then he endures heartaches
If
He makes out any harsh person
establishing tyranny on him
or any other person
Again
If he beholds any of his relative
having ripe eligibility
Does not develop one or another life
or

life protective shield
Then
If he examines
any person keeping mythical
beliefs for his soul life
or any other subject related to propaganda
or
Any mythical view or belief
in the arms of myth
and
he becomes corrupt and harmful in any relation
Then
If
He sees anyone having jealousy or quarrelsome feeling
does any inappropriate harm
Then he is shocked.

If he notices anybody
misusing his money
And anything in a wrong way
Then
He carries worries
If he sees
being impatient any person harms his physical health
Thence
He takes a fever of worries.

Henceforth
These numerous hurts
always motivate him
for the protection of any dependent
or needy persons,
To anyone showing his
guilt for harmful person
Or possibly raises sublime light

towards him,
Framing any essential
higher knowledge,
The souls that have
been devoid
of these above higher values,
They do not feel the hurts
and they
do not protect any wretched
person
By the maiden feeling of splitting
up of the heart
Or do not try to rescue
any person in any condition
They do not develop any higher
transformation
performing this revolution.

Henceforth, in numerous departments
of the world
to bring various benevolent activities,
He arises in eligible souls a higher or
positive feeling
A nectarine brook of altruism.........
therefore
He calls forth a revolution
This feeling is absent in crores of people
What a dearth!
What a meagreness!
There is not a spot here
Henceforth
in the world arising these higher
transformations
the development
the frame work

needs
as he is as it is for him, to
Complete this specific development's
specific aim or pledge
It is essential for it
to endure for him numerous lower forces -
massive tortures and torments
to accept various sacrifices
for deliverance
Paying one's physical,
mental and heartily strength
And sacrifice is also inclined in it.

Any individual, from whichever
feeling
whatever sort of satisfaction,
he feels,
If he does not receive it
Thence, this circumstance,
for him,
is necessarily restless and torridness.

In him, in relation of world's every
department
All sublime feelings are developed
That wish highest force-unity in him
Henceforth, in whatever relation
To whatever reason
The curse is produced
i.e., any possible and desirable
welfare is not possible,
To that, he feel aches
And if this torture is extremely
Powerful,
Thence, tattered with this

He felt heart attacks
But to whom persons, this knowledge
is not developed,
they do not feel pain and restlessness in
Such incidents
To them
In whatever relation
Is not the knowledge of evil
and curse
For it, they do not feel any torture
And not any dispute and sorrow
Henceforth, many people
In the sphere of him and other existences
of various types
Adopting various brands of curses
and evils or lower forces
Do not feel any regret
It does not end here
That they do not feel pain,
But, they live a very quiet and
gleeful life.

As a stone is not influenced by
blood sucking insects,
As the illiterates in any relation
For their inappropriate conduct
Do not realize any pain and disputes
And no any hatred...
Henceforth, the circle of their
innumerous curses
and crimes is equally continuous
And any imaginary Master or deity or
their any giver of mantra guru (guide)
Cannot provide salvation from them.

As the hunger and thirst are essential
for the protection of health
And that person
who feels,
out and out no hunger
and thirst
And does not feel any tension
for not receiving diet
and water
The destruction of his body is certain
Likewise, one side which soul in relation
to its any worldly relative
For his any low force
Does not notice any quarrel and in its relation
produces any inauspiciousness and falsehood
Not feeling any wound,
And on the other side,
he has no ambition to gain
any knowledge
regarding a higher life
His destruction, according to this
law of nature
During some time is certain

Adopting goodness
and inauspiciousness,
truth and untruth
related various sublime knowledge
and with world's every department
with the amalgamation of truth
and auspiciousness
being his soul's evolution
for me
to this world's illiterates
as it is essential to get various

sorts of tortures
sobbing,
in that time or it is requite to be restless
but from this super filament
illiterate one to this
in various conditions
to me from their any low force
are hurting me by wounds
or seeing me crying or restless
due to it
it is not enough
that they are not seeing in me
any treasure house of sublime
knowledge
and by their one or another
crime or curse,
any shock
or quarrel or hatred
hurting me
in spite of it, oppositely
regarding me, they fire one or
other fault/accusation on me
or one or other worst view
doing this they are creating
their heart invariably
more defamed, low, hard and creaky.

Herbert Spenser in his book
"education" writes in one of the place:

"If by any system
of culture
an ideal human being
could be produced,
is it not doubtful

whether
he would be fit
for the world as it now is?

May we
not on the contrary,
suspect that his too
keen sense of rectitude
and too elevated standard
of conduct,
would make life intolerable
or even impossible?"

Herbert Spencer was a
well-known evolutionary.
In a book "education" for man,
he described
high education based method.
And
suddenly seen inside
rising this question,
if any person had been born
among common persons
with huge higher powers.
From that,
he could be an ideal life
lived individual,
from which,
crossing (unto) the high method
of education,
thence,
the condition of common individuals,
as the present condition is,
living among them,
how will he correlate with them?

To answer this question,
he wrote that
he is suspicious
that in this world,
the life of
this ideal man
will be extremely sorrowful
and impossible.

Whole Challenge of Life

In the world for such selfless
altruism transfiguration,
As if there is requirement
for my birth
In the similar module, for me
For the fulfillment
of this aim or
For the requirement
of my necessary,
through and through life vow
It is urgent to endure various
sorts of low forces
and innumerable afflictions
from my various relatives,
It is the call of the moment
To sacrifice myself,
To endure pains, to
bear the burden of my physical health,
for this provision
of my physical, mental
and heartily potential
Is certain
For one word
For their deliverance and

higher development
To sacrifice all and surrender for them
It is uppermost life vow
Day by day
I have to sacrifice
for this super highest penance pious fire
I have to relinquish my
strength's requisite sacrifices
Oh world!
In your higher developmental circuit
You have directed me
for the coverage of this
unique sublime crucifixion
You have blessed me that
sublime powers
While completing the
structure of my soul
That were foremost for
this sublime penance

Had anyone noticed this grand miracle
of the appearance of this sublime aura?
In this visible touchstone
Evolution's incredible but visible rule
Enlightening whatever aestheticism
Is its superior twinkling glimpse attracting,
infatuating anybody's heart?
Oh my unique sacrificial task
O my selfless activity
My surrender
and death are revolution
Is this valuable to anybody's brain?

These are the century's
terrible sacrifices

Whatever fruits
are sprouted due to them
Whatever transmutations
under the souls in men and women
developed,
whatever auspiciousness happened
in families for them
and their offspring,
what sorts of institutions
have been opened
what sorts of books have been written,
essays have been compiled,
truth related religious knowledge
and religion related truth,
whatever has been published
for the arena of soul life,
for soul life's evolution and destruction
in its relation whatever filaments
have been appeared,
there has been modernized
the wisdom
and religious morale,
religious based ignorance
an ill etiquettes,
immodesty has been effaced,
the mystery of imaginary caves,
and mythical views has been revealed,
the enigma of science related authentic
brain power has been appeared
devilish sense has been out of order
and the ray of truth-goodness laid feet.

All and all
Is due to my incredible
life vow

And for the raising glory of this
The unique greatness of my sacrifice
Is this all sacrificial pyre not establish
me on drum beating grandeur?
Certainly it does....

Oh!
in this country
or earth's any other country
Can the footstep of this
penance be recognized?
Is my penance and life vow not unique?
Thence
what elephant - version right of man!
To see and realize the capacity
of the aestheticism
of my prime benevolent penance
and grandeur
of this unique life vow
Having participated in this task
To realize this first-rate
auspiciousness is
Man's prime right
In the fire ground of this penance
To sacrifice treasures, physical
and mental power
And
through and through
With capacity
Relinquishing heartily powers
with the earthen lamp of enlightenment
Of fire
invariably
For the people of this country
How ambitious this is!

this significant yearning!
will raise its feathers to
souls that will gleefully
sacrifice themselves speedily
To that extent
my aim for my birth
will be fulfilled from the world
And the welfare of this country
and earth is certain
To that extent
that is not happened hitherto
My existence,
my life vow,
my sacrifice
and my struggle,
Has been appeared to
whatever evolutionary
certain law of the world,
That was certain in its structure
for the higher transfigurations
in all its departments,
In the same module
according to its unmistakable law
(having bearing the arrows of,
this dark sill
and low force related
thousands souls
who
were my sworn enemy)
Hitherto to
which framework has it
been fructified
All this is the grandeur
of super astonishment
and magnificent blessing.

Dark Pitch of Roundabouts

In me,
in the world's every department's
Various auspicious production
and wisdom's present(ongoing) lane,
whatever evil
persists in whatever relation by
Any reason and if there is delay for
the footsteps of welfare
I felt MYSELF AS A tortured one
and a victim of maladjustment
in that relation
Realizing a pitch of frustration,
having the intensity of this knowledge
From such each to each(routine like)
quarrel and maladjustment,
having an emotion of restlessness to this
vagueness and
Unhappiness
I am deeply shedding my heart......................

Deeply full of scars!
Henceforth,
whoever having lack or
scarcity of this wisdom,

they could not understand the real fact
the tale
does not end here
That they do not perceive any
frustration from it,
from any affection and mishap
Heretofore, having a look at me
do not feel any affliction
What a negligence !!
What a free mindedness
on the cloak of life!!

According to their low pleasure's
low motivation, they consider me
From the insight of defame and hate.

They have deficiency of whatever
relation's whatever evil,
they do not know this devilish task
They do not realize this
fault/WRONGDOING,
there is no possibility IN THEM
Of the knowledge of this fault
CERTAIN AURA OF DECORUM
IS OUT OF ORDER!

MODESTY SLEPT IN DEEPEST
CAVES OF BLACK SILL!!
They do not BEHOLD any deficiency,
henceforth millions of people
what should be UTTERED in my arena
and world's outlook
and in relation of world's other existences,
the curse,
DARK PITCH OF ROUNDABOUTS

of the tale does
not end here
that they do not realize any torture,
heretofore they continue to live
in quietness and happiness...................

As stone does not
RECOGNIZE
the presence
of the blood sucking insect (jok)
Likewise these ignorant ones
in any relation for their
unsuitable morale
do not realize any torture and
quarrel and no hatred for these activities.

When any person due to
his/her ignorance
and absent mindedness
in my elation does not perform
any work at appropriate time
and suitable way and shows in this
work a filth of carelessness
free mindedness,
I realize that MATTER from his behavior
for me
in the MILIEU of worldly
relation
in spite of auspiciousness
THERE IS HUT OF
inauspiciousness
or will be..................
thence for this every mishap,
circumstances
due to my evil like several

intense knowledge,
I noticed frustrated,
such as if anybody ripe wound has been hit
by anybody
AS A REPERCUSSION
this torture and pain he examines
to highest degree
UNMISTAKABLY this pain connotes
as if it may be my condition,
As hunger and thirst are essential
for the protection of body,
similarly who has no feeling
of hunger and thirst,
not getting food and water
at appropriate time,
in total deficiency to
this RECOGNIZES any worseness
and frustration,
the destruction of
his body is essential.
Similarly, inside
whose soul if there
is not a feeling of
any torment in any
relation's sphere
for any low pleasure and he
is not feeling wounds shattering
for the appearance of any inauspiciousness
and injustice
Not examining tiredness and WOES,
thus
the aspiration of life is uncertain..................

Yeah !!
his destruction is certain,

embracing goodness —
inauspiciousness,
truth-untruth related various
knowledge
with world's all departments
domain.........................

By truth and auspiciousness
related adjustment,
developing this all and all,
my soul's all over evolutionary
power got energetic.
It was requisite for me from
world's ignorant relations,
to gain several sorts of tortures
and woeful hurts from these...................
Heart sinks and sinks.......................
Alas!! Alas!!
O ignorant one to this super filament!
O your ignorance and low force!
caused ....
absolutely caused torture to me,
creating a pinch of unhappiness for me
beholding me worried and scornful,
not this only that you are not
reforming yourself,
feeling for me any high wisdom's treasure,
any grandeur and regret for in
one or another crime
or evil's any shock or quarrel !!!
O residents of Wasteland!
You are not purifying yourself !!

Heretofore
Leaving this crime....................

Oppositely in my relation,
carrying the arrows of accusation
in high numbers for me
Taking one or another
conspiracy against me,
You are creating your heart bitter,
defamed, low, vulgar, hard
and devil like(inferno/pandemonium)

Oh!
Religious life is too hard to describe
Too many hardships on this route to present
For a savior of religion,
for an authentic guide
it is too difficult, too precious to find/search
the appearance of any religious
seeker and complete devotee
It is a call
A recall of moments
for a certain devotee

Life is on the Razor's Edge but Still

They lay emphasis
on the adoption of mentioned
fashioned religion,
That science grounded religion,
In its comparison,
They are fiddling with a single ray
of study of the affection
of imaginary views,
do not have a real knowledge
in continual routine
in the domain of life
for the authentic subject of sublime religion
and the saviour of authentic religion,
They have no light
in their deliverance,
no wisdom, no understanding
about life's low–pleasures
How miserable is all this

Henceforth, they realize
they do not have any satisfactory revolution,
struggle for their deliverance
Having no affection
in the sphere of sublime religion,

its sources and sublime society,
not a light of wisdom they identify
that is common to everyone,
that could transform them as 'purified ones'
Having not a knowledge of 'profitable right
Or authority' over other low-pleasures
Continuously
in their relation,
in spite of killing
or effacing their low-values
they could not sprout in themselves
a ray of true devotee
And loyal disciple
This all scene is in front of me
and this is under my discernment from centuries
beholding this scene/viewpoint,
my heart got elephant like attacks
My heart shattered tiny to tiny pieces...............
uncountable filaments
This country, this very country
A tale of tears

Until now
For my unique activities,
This country
could not bless my capable soul,
on the clock of time
and my full-swing,
oceanic strength was destroyed
vanity and deterioration for this.......................
On the moment
Day by day,
I could not console myself
my woeful temperament
Or frustration excavates for the

pearl of certain law/reality?
Am I not the appearance of such religion
whose
all over education of religion all transfigurations
(Related to religion)
and all tasks are unique from the
outlook of its bona fide insight
and brain wind?

At that time
This all,
in the insight of my religious relatives,
so-called religious relatives
Is this ongoing process have been
the object of defame
and embarrassment for me,
Is it all sworn defame for all this
that I did not allot any emphasis
on any imagination, myth, untruth,
any false view in my education,
life and many activities
Is there no one in the world for
the development of my love,
for the authenticity of truth
All and all
The supporter of love of truth
No one there!
Shedding tears
It is a heavy time to toil and struggle
Will be vain? will go to garbage bin??
Will there be no one at this time the
devotee of my work?
Is there no department in this nature
for the success of my incredible and
super benevolent life-vow for
The protection of my aforesaid significant work?

After adopting my life-vow
Till twenty years
For my unique life-vow
My limb to limb sacrifice, all this will be the tale of a moment
A magic-show of mere eyes of the moments
Oh! Oh!! In world's every relation's goodness,
my heart's thick sheet of love, ambition and serious horridness
will all be in vain
Will it be?

No, never
The law of the world's evolution is true and certain
I am beholding that..................
My appearance/footsteps is the fruit of that law
I have been authentic to that
Yeah!! Purely loyal
How can it be mythical for it?
How can it!
Cannot.......can never!!
This boulder strong certain law is spreading
the ripple of amalgamation (correlation) in all
Departments of the world,
Unmistakably, over this earth,
in various relations, certainly,
there are countless evils and maladjustments
Heretofore, above this ladder,
Arriving in higher,
small countries,
From the realization of the law of evolution
there is uniformity
Yeah, concord!
The monarchy of unity among physical,
biological, animal, individual world
and all worlds
I realized this superior filament,

world has produced me with the veins of this magnificent law,
To recite its grandeur,
for its foundation, nurtured me for all struggle
My struggle in this moment/era is grand in all degrees,
Henceforth, for its 'nectarine victory'
For its unquestionable dignity
There is no suspicion left

No suspicion
With the confinements of time
Favourable circumstances
will embrace this soil
Hitherto,
if I could not achieve devoted souls
Thence,
will they never take a ride
Why?
certainly,
I will be blessed
with my heartily yearning,
Completely,
for all worldly auspiciousness,
goodness and welfare
for whichever law's
I have been true
Until now
For the loyalty of that viewpoint,
I have been tortured invariably with super terrible,
untold hatreds by the
Disciples of imaginary views for the loyalty of that belief
I had been a victim
of thousand individual's hatred
and false accusations for whose loyalty,
Pious sheet of truth,
I have noticed myself on this earth always as a 'solitary reaper'

and companionless
Oh these creeping roads of life
The aestheticism of life,
in this unsuitable direction is shedding tears repeatedly
This law
this imperishable law
This pot of life
cannot enunciate me
cannot uproot me
unquestionably,
This over-all contemplation,
according to my unique self-sacrifice and
potential on this earth
In relation to mankind and every world
Will provide evidences
of selfless benevolence,
supreme brightness
of altruism and prime welfare.

The Real Ecstasy

In the arms of tranquil - soul and sublime - ecstasy
In my conduct, soul-quietness and sublime-frenzy

It was uppermost adjuration for me
for the salvation
of the soul,
And the authority over soul's
Over all low force related strength,
in the arms of prime
Potential, quietness
and super ecstatic advancement,
That's why such incredible
and super benevolent peace and such precious
And grand selfless ecstasy I chalked up

Embracing sublime life,
I have been real aspirant for world's
Higher evolution
In the realms in relation to such worldly–benevolence
for its goodness with suitable potential
I enhance/use /my powers appropriately
I endeavoured my best in the arena of
every world to raise these higher
influences to some bit

In every world
I live in whichever place
Each day at dawn, I spread my soul's higher
influences all around
Keeping myself laborious in higher tasks
Heretofore,
my worriment soul gains the
bestowal of higher ecstasy
and sublime—seventh- heaven
And
at any place,
if there is rain in abundance,
in full swing, the same degree earth got wet
that overflow of water
That oceanic ripples
In the same degree,
whichever day whatever
auspicious quietness,
whatever good love and affection
for selfless works
That moment...............................

That day, in my heart,
the nectarine pious sensation maximizes
This glory is not like those such intoxications
that are cumulated in the addiction of poisonous,
harmful drug—addictions,
i.e., bhang, wine, opium, post, chars
and chandu
(all intoxications of carcinogenic poisonous things)

This is out of all things
An uppermost version related to religion's
various higher feelings and affections
This twinkling grace is an immortal nectar

and sublime tranquility
This satisfaction is produced through higher religious life
out of all sorts of poison,
for soul this is equally benevolent
This super flavour is a purified source,
away from all sorts of filth
Deep-seated divinity of the heart,

This taste sensation is a life provider bestowal,
that's why this is called nectar
that is not sprouted in
A heart without effacing low pleasure's (liberation),
cleansing heart and
Breaking the shell of the sense of
Other's curse or back biting in any way
Without these cleansing/refined feeling,
this ambrosia does not open its petals in anyone's heart and
without
Complete deliverance and evolution of
overall limbs of development,
this does not frame its milieu...........
Therefore, having a body filled with complete lethargy,
without diseases and complete structure,
with any part of the body, man does not realize any pain
Similarly,
from any mountain whether any evil person hits
with pebble and hammer
or with big-sworn knife,
Thence, for its pain one feels heartaches
Henceforth, similarly if my soul is away from any disease
and develops evolution in each part,
creates nectar in my heart,
offering me life-lemon, provides me super benevolent peace
and grand-to-grand relish,
thence

In this world's lacs of low-pleasure–people,
while living among them, from their low forces, their pain............
It was essential for me to irritate/get woeful conduct,
and as a world's benevolent and selfless devotee, for me,
enduring these presentiments was essential,
Absolutely, I got shattered with these heart attacks
My assistants
When they perform any inappropriate activity
in my relation or any other...
To whom I wish to behold in developed stages,
in spite of developmental roads,
they enhance feet into
under developmental directions
Thence, for their such activities,
in these circumstances
I perceive hatred and maladjustment
from high or low degrees
Similarly, if my small/tiny/sensitive body
wants to quarrel,
then I examine it thoroughly
Leaving such of these pains
My soul was filled with aforesaid precious quietness
and sublime contentment at many moments
In small worlds of the paradise (invisible world of angels),
the development legged-up in the sphere of religious people,
higher to higher degrees
to that extent these people's physical, visible,
biological, animal, plant
and individual world's relation-related–existence,
those identities' unity's evolution
and mutual adjustment has been established
Henceforth, in many higher worlds
With each world,
every sort of relation has been forever
benevolent and heavenly

There has been no low-pleasurable-life,
no any physical and soul-scar unlike this world
Every relation for everyone has been an
ambrosia of benevolence and gleefulness
There, all existences' all activities have been
evolutionary to each other in the amalgamation of
Mutual uniformity
There is monarchy, unity and development all around
All is aesthetic, graceful, altruistic and soothing
While living here,
I am getting whichever numerous aforesaid
sorrows for the flagging victory of goodness
and struggle against inauspiciousness,
that filaments of afflictions will breath last one day
on the death bed
And filling myself with heavenly grace and quietness,
with complete religious life,
precious and selfless serviceable peace
pouring myself in the nectarine-jiggery-flavored,
complete-selfless- service- of –sublime- contentment,
One day these all modest pearls,
will live in my heart without any obstacle

Blank Walls All Around

Under the deep core of the world
There is mutual correlation
of bad incidences
and circumstances In them,
where there is the circuit of worse circumstances,
one to one adverse happenings
There is plethora of opposite footings

There are threads
of auspicious stages in them also
I realized this factual understanding
This rational wisdom.................
I perceived in my life and other's life
At the time, on the pavement
of higher force,
leaving one or other simple obstacles
I noticed these such
horrible-mishaps on my way
and such hardships and
shocking heartaches
have opened their jaws
in such extent
that from their single reminiscences
heart got severe attacks

Yes, heart breaking rolls
Invariably, at one to another moment,
I examined/perceived as if there might
be no soil under my feet
A fish out of water,
As if tables turned in full strength
And every matter, in my relation
has been in a reverse order
There is no final home for
stumbling hardships
What should I say?
After another problem,
More hurdles appears with fierce eyes

And these all accidents and vicissitudes
have been uttering in a loud pitch/voice:
'there is no gateway of success for you'.

In such a condition, there
has been such visualizations,
such sorts of influences
that are indicating,
for you all around the
roads are blocked.

There is not a ray of
hope for my escape
For my high motive's
'successful – working-highway'
All around is darkness
Tempe tests
Ruinations
Pebbles
Blank walls
All around disappointment
Deterioration

Heretofore,
Among
the appearance of this
prospect of super horrible,
harsh terrible details
the light inside me
was still alive
it cannot 'bade goodbye' to me
This has not left my finger
Even for a moment
and as if in the days of shrawan,
bhadon (seasonal
changes in Hindu calendar),
in this season
All around
There is noticed
Thick-tempest/air bubbles,
Due to earth's darkness
Thundering and speedy
lightening in the sky
Has appeared
It shows its grandeur force
Likewise, invariably,
I see and realized
This filament of higher light
and glare in my heart
while examining myself in
harsh terrible, horrible, afflicted
and disappointed accidents' dark
to dark blockage
and from inward enthusiasm
With my tongue
repeated several times
'all will be right at suitable time'
and this grand to grand-super element

has been proved suitable at the fingertips of time
All and all
the circle of my ill fate/bad fortune
Has started to be tattered
Obstacles deceased
The darkness of terror and woefulness
has begun to be ruined
The sky was full of colour without dirt
And the route of my life has opened
more and more in a clear way
What a benediction of nature
Astonishing! Bewitching!!
Appropriate circumstances
have been developed
and adverse mishaps ruined
My inward light has presented
the glory of victory
over darkness,
triumph of an aspirant
of truth over untruth
and my auspicious feelings'
victory over inauspiciousness
has been visualized
It is such a certain law in
such worldly evolution
as it is the experience of my life,
According to this matchless,
aesthetic
and incredible law,
finally,
forever
a higher-forceful-soul has been
victorious in life's highest motive
and
super most direction.

Ah! My miserable Condition

My condition has continued to be worst
throughout many years
There are the reasons for its deterioration:

In this world,
for me,
in relation to my complete unique life-vow
I have to struggle for basic whatever
super precious elements
invariably for the
Advancement of precious truthful light
for these various sorts of sources
for the beginning
and continuation of propagation
and working methodology,
For this I have to suffer which
stripes of super thick mental ailment,
whatever views, study,
the publication of letters,
sermons and lectures
whatever set of book writings,
I have to perform this all over work
for this,
it was requisite for me to devote

full time in these works
Delving in all these activities,
I secured much work
From my mental powers

For the fulfillment
of my unique life vow
I have to undergo
whatever likes of
ambivalent tribulations
and obstacles
While in their grip,
being a victorious in these clutches,
I have to perform various categories
of super difficult struggles for my success
and among these most difficult struggles/hardships
I did not get any appropriate sympathy,
support and suitable advantage of assistants
These aforesaid difficult and unique works
I could not acquire significant physical material viz.
Means for the appropriate protection of body,
the body needs whichever denomination of diet,
rest, accurate dwelling
place, recreational things and
medical treatment at the time of disease
I did not get it...............

Due to higher consciousness inside my heart,
I have to bear from outside people and my
comrades-social persons,
mixed bags of complete horrible attacks
and innumerable incurable tortures
Gazing at my life-vow
As I can say this without any terror
that in this earth there had been not a person like me

Carrying this super life vow
As if looking at the aura of last reason,
I can pronounce this without any suspicion that I,
in relation of this life-vow
have endured
whatever mishmashes of numerous heart
piercing afflictions,
maladjustments and quarrels
and I am carrying this heavy bundle hitherto
all these have not been suffered by anyone

From time to time
I burdened that rock strong pain,
I cannot describe it in mere words
Inside the core of these such restlessness
At a time
Developed such ferments
that from all these alarms of the reign of terror
my heart does not gain the ambrosia of rest
My heart yearns for this moment
to escape myself from this perplexity
thinking for a long time
in a painful module
catching the threads of depression
recurring:
'from any extent/degree
May I be unconscious!
In the hard knocks of fainting fit
May I feel giddy!'
Henceforth
Oh this infirmity of heavy jumble
I cannot be unconscious
my brain does not receive enough blood
and I feel giddiness
The potential of speech goes in vain

Any work does not get proper response
Heart shrinks works
Heart does not wish anything,
gets the drowsy image of restlessness
Body is under the arrows of evil eye
Heretofore
I cannot do anything
Helpless
Pauper

My own people from their one to another low force,
while developing my skeleton like heart,
as a feeble one,
Does not leave me from the cage of trials
Oh these boulder illness
These heavy heartaches
Heart attacks and grief
The horrible repercussions

Now, what will happen?
That all future will communicate?
Leaving many other people from outside
Who have no sympathy for me
Naturally,
they despise me and variously for my unrest and life-vow
They excavate conspiracy
They find it as a satisfactory level
henceforth
Those hundreds of people that have been
present in sublime society do not
understand my this miserable condition
That those persons who know
me from other's conversation or from
outsider's conversation their
Condition is too normally

not like this that they could realize pain
For me, from contemplation
to what extent I understand
unlike my own ones that have been
assistants to me for some time in reality
and rest of the persons do not care of my pain
Not any small to big level
But among most of them repeatedly
While knowing this or getting the chance
to understand this
That I am highly tortured, they,
with their conduct spread their influence
towards me as they
Do not recognize me as diseased and tortured.

These persons,
full of pride-carelessness
(from the condition of my selfless service)
these harsh persons,
while I have been tortured one
In spite of getting their sympathy
More and more
I received maladjustment,
quarrels, disputes and pain
Receiving all these pains
I considered myself like a helpless one,
like a solitary bird on the branch of lonely tree
and like a person who is burning up with
temperature and alarms of chaos
its estimate one can realize.....................................
On the sublime sheet of moments
It's estimate cannot be
counted on mere fingertips

A Solitary Bird: Anonymous, Ignorant, and Forever Tortured?

I have been a solitary bird, anonymous,
ignorant and tortured one
among my own near and dear ones.

My soul while evolving, complete structure is
quite majestic
among all incomplete structural souls,
its ideal, its ambitions,
Character
and from the view of its forces
because of this indifference,
it has its huge attributes
Henceforth,
it does not correlate among its surroundings
crores of incomplete structured ones
and low force related souls
and due to this natural super
difference, aforesaid suite of persons,
for me,
do not feel any attraction and away from me
Low-force related soul arriving at me cannot fulfill
their any low force related yearnings

Henceforth, instead of being attracted towards me,
attract towards people,
who are similar to their nature,
live among them and live life here

You will have gazed at one to one dog
when sees any anonymous dog and recognizes
him by smelling sensation suddenly
That he is not related to their clan
And, henceforth,
whether he shifts his direction to leave
Him alone or by the feeling of the flames of
excitement of hatred and disputes
attacks him and cause him
harmful woes in various ways
With time,
hundreds of low force related souls
have been behaving like this
These people finding themselves
dissimilar to my nature,
and not seeing any attraction towards me,
inwardly they all have been out of touch

And out of my insight
or by the excitement of their one
or another low feeling start teasing me
And find satisfaction in my quarrels and harmful situations
And search comfort in this contentment
It is the sole reason
from the point of my nature,
if I am selfless well-wisher of all and brother to all
but on this earth,
there is no such person
to whom I could recognize the bond of a complete brotherhood
or friendliness

who has been free from his ego and various lusts
to that extent one has to give full right to me
about himself appropriately

To that extant he has been with me to full extent
While myself,
living with my own family and society persons
Finding myself among them lonely
and anonymous one
What should be said in the sphere of my family and society?

All are unable to see and recognize my sublime aura
And its unique magnificence, according to my position
They do not respect me
but
Repeatedly behave inappropriately,
what should be performed for one to
one courteous super brotherhood- gentleness
who does one gentleman to another
Oppositely
Inside me, for their higher values and nearness
whatever feelings are sprouted in full swing
that do not fulfill to satisfaction
Because they find a very less aspiration
for my nearness and while living at the same place
They are far away from me
I am far away from them
In such a condition for me,
feeling myself lonely among them
anonymous and unknown is natural
And each to each person,
as living among anonymous ones
cannot open his complete heart before them
Likewise, is my condition
Once upon a time,

I was at my birth place where I was living my family
and clan relatives
And different many other anonymous people
but among themselves,
everyone present there
I was feeling anonymous
there was no one appropriate
to my internal condition
I cannot communicate hearts' main
conversations in front of anyone
Therefore, one day,
at night hours,
my heart was harshly tormented
and full of unrest,
looking at sky
And pronouncing those twinkling stars in English
I started to recite my tale of terror
and for a long time kept on reciting
before stars
After this,
my heart got relief to small extent
Myself, having complete religious life certainly
Searched myself in knitted threads with all over cover
As all would be my own
I want to know their condition
and keep capability to understand them
In that relation, I fulfill my responsibilities
But
They, being devoid of numerous essential religious feelings,
do not keep with me that lived/alive relation
as I have with them
Therefore, while living among them, in their company,
I am feeling them as my own
As they are my dear ones
Where getting a wave of loneliness

from them
I notice a pinch of loneliness
when living among them
I receive inappropriate conduct from them
instead of appropriate behaviour
i.e., love, devotion, and sympathy
thence
my heart shattered to the core
Crying and screaming
That among my own near and dear ones
I am unknown and ignorant
and when from my own dear ones
from their scarcity of the reason of various religious feelings
And from them previously whatever disputes and tortures
I received and I am still a victim of these wounds
And from outsiders whatever harsh terrors I have to suffer
I notice these woes
Thence, I examine myself not as an anonymous and ignorant one
But wounded and tortured in the reign of disease of plague

After the Dark Night Is Dawn

My disputes, afflictions and their final stage
I wish to classify
that in
My present condition I get whatever quarrels and sorrows
Whatever clans of various wounds
Why all these 'on the way'
My present quarrels and afflictions can be divided
into whichever mountainous parts
These are:
That quarrels and tortures
whose reasons are physical disease
That quarrels or pains
whose reasons are in reverse order
That heartily quarrels or pain
that's reason is people's tyranny towards me
that heartily quarrels and tortures
that's reason towards individuals etc.
is my intense sympathy and my intense feeling of goodness

My physical health suffered a lot
I was on my deathbed
Filthy interplay of moments

In the relation of body naturally

I have been in 'the circle of one or another complaint'
Henceforth
Whilst/ till time
there has not been any harsh or harsh pain,
till that time/ moment
from 'whose clutch' I have been out of reach i.e.,
I was feeling unrest
heretofore
Lives in a quiet condition
henceforth, invariably,
for the presence of one or another problem
Others do not realize that clod
when myself, at such of that time,
with common problems
have been occupied in my
Any higher and good work or writing,
studying, conversation and propagation
Then
Myself too, do not have its knowledge
at any extent and myself
In quiet mind, with melodious
quietness and comfort
Kept on doing my work
But, from 'mishap circuit'
if any incident had been unbearable, then
According to its intensity
Certainly, I achieved quarrels and pain
In stomach spine-like pain,

Ear pain, jaws pain, joint pain, head pain, chest pain
Problem in the blockage of breathing activity and cough
From this, invariably, I endured time to time
Whatever unbearable and heart piercing pain
I know this only
Nobody can understand these arrows

Describing it,
I cannot enlighten/reveal it to others
but in relation of
My body from auspicious prayers
and sources of the strength of will
Such unbearable tortures had been
produced from some time
In the circuit of physical quarrels
I consider it significant to pronounce
that I live in what sort of patience and fulfill
My work with 'roll of punctual system'
In relation of diet and for the reason for
keeping myself safe from their harmful influences'
Sources related appropriate
various ways
I perceive for this all things suitably
I have been protected
from 'most of maladjustments'
In the season of summer, for me,
some months have been certainly
painful and harmful
The days of harsh heat
These days are like burning and burning
Unbearable! Highest flames of perspirations!!
those days, for me
Have been very hard

It seems to me that in these days
I should have to voyage at any rate
from ground dwelling place to mountain area
I have to live in cold
I am realizing this big place, then
my life can escape from another side.

I can perform my life-vow related huge prime benevolent

Higher activity
That I cannot perform while living in hot place
I am realizing this big obstacle for many years
But there could not find any satisfactory remedy
Hitherto, to protect myself from it
Among my relatives there is not such a person
who wishes to devote his all............
And all strength wholeheartedly to remove this problem
Yes, now those individuals' life
In that condition, while living there
for them
it is very difficult for them to notice any
of my such problematic or essential need
In European people there are some people
except many individuals
for one to one plant
they have 'such intense relation,'

while seeing this, one can observe
this is a wonderful trait
What a scenery of life
Full of benevolence
an attribute of humanity
Stunning
Miraculous
Heart touching
What a feeling
Europeans have such feelings for their plants

These plant pots did not demand
any appeal to their real relative for
transmuting them to mountain
Or in that topic
to contemplate and adopt any remedy
they cannot appeal such a request

But inside their real relative, for them,
whatever love was present in him, for them
That itself embraced in his heart
that feeling
fulfilled
and aforesaid task has been performed
in spite of this aesthetic love, nobody
can create love to anybody
In the teaching of Dev Dharma (sublime religion),
not only this positive feeling is taught
But for the protection from destruction
many other higher feelings and loves,
ripples for man have been considered essential.

My heart tortures are innumerous,
my heart has been above
than all sorts of tortures
what low forces related soul
intertwined physically,
due to their low force
in a
visible view,
The patients of jealousy for their low force
burn in the flame of that
horrible force
servant of ego due to their ego's
various low forces
got various suites of afflictions and quarrels
Except others,
seeing their one to one selfless benevolent
in antagonist view,
people are filling with jealousy
towards them creating bad feeling,
Enduring huge heartily
torments and afflictions,

crores of people
While the destruction of assets, land
and worldly low relatives got huge
various inappropriate quarrels
Impatient and crime ridden soul
in spite of the destruction of their soul
by one or another vulgarity
Have been 'on death bed' with many
types of horrible quarrels
Immodest souls,
due to their ill etiquettes,
misguided by various suites of tyrannical ways,
ill-bad tempered soul due to their sickness
Are suffering numerous filaments of torments
The hunger of name or prestige,
in the clutch of the assistance
of ill-traditions is
Transforming man
into boundless brands of temperature etc.
I am above these slices of
low force related uncountable unrest,
Because, over me, there is no
right of any low love,
Being Devatma,
gaining soul's complete
structure and advantage,
having various sublime-Higher feelings
and sublime loves
During my days in this death,
till some time
it is essential for me to gain various low-forced
related soul's ill behaviour,
heartily scars
And disputes
Henceforth, myself from such persons,

though they are my near to near relatives
I thought
From far away relatives, in the course of life,
I was tortured equally
Unmistakably, equal arrows of death
From them,
I have been pieced time to time
That unbearable and thick pain that
cannot be described
When, at what time, I am on this earth,
I am in a bond with various breeds of
individuals in one or another relation
While living among them tried
for various struggles
And selfless services
To that extent it is
essential for me to gain scars?
to have a bond with earthly persons,
a feeling with them
inappropriately
I suffered their ill-behaviors
and ill-temperatures
in the range of
'maximum or minor tortures
and quarrels' time to time
I noticed this ....

Thence, in my heart among world's four clans
i.e., individuals, animals, plants
and inanimate world
to what extent is possible the colours
of sympathy and goodness
to that extent seeing their any quarrel
and dispute
Seeing and hearing their harms

I felt torments and got quarrels and
unrest invariably,
it seems that me, among whatever souls
who are not seeing any higher
transformation,
observing them in
the 'state of underdevelopment'
I am screaming............

They are ignorant to themselves,
To the knowledge of such condition,
they do not feel
any pain and they, being ignorant
spent a 'life of roses',
Myself, except many persons,
In the arena of harsh-bad condition
of animals and plants
(This state disturbs me)
And
torture-ridden many inanimate things
all provided me tortures
I find myself in world's higher parts
With various threads of bonds
and heretofore
Naturally, for them in one or another way,
I feel in many of the conditions
They do not feel any pain wherever is it
and knowledge for myself
because of my understanding in their relation,
I feel sometimes
Sympathy, mercy, depression etc.
And get the dispute of one or another type.

These all disputes raise my consideration towards them
In many of the relations, with high pitch, they do this

Myself, raised by them for their goodness
or reformation or their protection whatever can I do
I do
For this I try a lot
If outwardly there is no assistance
thence from my inward potentials
I provide them help and henceforth
With my capacity doing their goodness
in world's higher development
I have been evolved
due to the reason for this earth and its
individuals' huge minor condition
and
it was essential for me to gain aforesaid
various afflictions for some time but one day
enthusiastically, renouncing this earth,
all pain of this earth and quarrels will be here only
These all will not 'voyage along with me'
they will leave me and I will leave them too
One day, this all will be 'like a dream'
'like a fragment of transience'

Therefore,
the higher evolution will be enlightened
to the greatest degrees
and its 'twinkling magnificence'
will be like 'priceless diamonds'
that will be
illuminating its 'precious -grandeur-victory'
throughout the world.

Alone! Long Waiting and Wailing!

O villainous hotchpotch of moments!!
I have been accused for titanic crimes,
Degraded with incalculable
names i.e. liar, cheater, hypocrite
And a misappropriate......
O harsh moments
I have been advertised
An adulterer and characterless......

Naught! naught!
I am broken into tiny fragments......
When I lost my infant daughter
Thence
I was cursed as a murderer and assassin
Who committed many crimes.....
I have also been tagged as 'a betrayal' and most
Disloyal for the community and the country...
By all hook and crook
I have been crushed under sharp-edged heels
However, these accusations were merely oral
For unspeakable years...
Suddenly tables turned
These accusations 'knitted' against me in writing forms
i.e., articles in newspapers in the form of

'anonymous elephantine posters' on the highways
Through books in various languages...

What deterioration this is

I was degraded with committing some
Of ten sins which a person had to abjure
in order to be initiated as member of the lowest
grade in my society (of Dev Samaj)............
oh! this baleful tale of heart-attacks!
Too piercing to describe

Except of these line-to line repetition of
such false accusations and propaganda of hatreds,
if some persons were drawn towards me by
the influence of my spiritual power,
he was as encircled by these opponents
as vultures do around a dead body
there was no need of sermons
among deaf and dumb

if they gaze at me
to salute spiritual lighthouse inside me
next moment
under the clutch of antagonists
they got transformed and frightened
maintaining distance from me
they are instances of double-panorama......
in these circumstances i.e.,
amusement and deep-seated melancholy...
noticing the miserable stage of such persons
in 'dilemma'........
I am beneath a barrage of tears.....

Some such persons, due to my influences

had salvaged from certain sins,
and had become better persons,
heretofore,
as soon as adversaries dinned false propaganda
in their ears, they left me like the *brahmin*
who left his goat in the *Hitopdesha*
In the *Hitopdesha* a *brahmin* is shown
leading a goat in a jungle
Several 'temptations' appeared
one after another
communicating
to the *Brahmin*:
"the animal
he was leading was not a goat but a dog"
He was taken in by their statements
and left his goat......
It is over and all
The conspiracy of superstitions
In which
"all myths are dancing".......

Believing it to be a dog
Several of my run-away disciples
have believed against their own direct experiences,
the false propaganda of my enemies
sided them and deprived themselves
of their own goodness and their benefactor...

In a country where people have been saturated
in mythical beliefs for thousands of years,
it is no astonishment if some among them
believe in the false propaganda against their
own truthful direct experience
Undoubtedly
"Birds of the same feathers flock together".......

If I forget run-sways for a while
there was another category of deserters
who became disciples at one or another time,
when their altruistic disposition was aroused in them,
therefore,
did not continue to stay with me
as they did not find satisfaction of one or another of their
low passions, and deserted me...
Among them are those who lacked the feeling
of gratitude and were dominated by the feeling
of vindictiveness joined my enemies
and became far more ungrateful and inimical to me......
"this seed of prejudice plants ungratefulness'"

My enemies used them well
and under their cover they got occasion
to inflict terrible sufferings and tortures on me
It is not possible to describe the injuries I experienced
by their evil dispositions and the terrible anguish
undergone by me by their most degraded character
and conduct......
They
who were with me
alone understand to some extent,
how 'opponents' were cruel and unbearable
to me
how their attacks had caused various terrible illnesses
to me and the pathetic condition to which my
body was reduced for months on a deathbed....
The
tale goes on and on....
I used to organize sermons and anniversaries
of my society at my ashram........

They came there and at times

exhibited such filthy behaviour which showed:
"they are motivated by their evil passions,
did not care even for the criminal law of the state".....

It was an ordinary practice for them
to break benches
and lamps, at times to set certain things
on fire, sometimes to indulge in throwing stones,
shouting obscene abuses, and to
talk in a rubbish way......

They found great satisfaction to tease my
disciples on the way-side,
to throw dust at them,
to strike them with fists,
to snatch propaganda books from them,
and tear them,
to break the head of some of them with sticks......
Oh!
In fact, it was hard for them to recognize
my 'sublime wisdom'
With the amalgamation of white,
we can transform any colour
Therefore,
With millions of endeavours
We cannot transmute white colour
By all means...............
They could not understand my 'sublime glory'
They wrote me letters threatening
me with death.....
Through posters, they expressed
deadly- wish: 'May some
giants strangulate him'.

The Cry of Shrill Words

Oh! How painful is my plight!
Ah me!
Have mercy and warmth
On the scissor's edge
Is there anyone in the world
who can be a 'sharer' of the pain in
my heart and stand in sympathy with me
in this state of helplessness and suffering?
Apparently, there is no such person
Even
my ache is not properly appreciated
by those who stay near to me
whether they cannot appreciate my suffering,
how can I get sympathy from them,
even if they possess it.......
what is this?
this carcinogenic –bloodthirsty
maladjustment of brain-wind!!!!!!!!!
Therefore, I am lone to suffer this
unique crucifixion.....
I have to inhale it certainly and silently.......

Alas!
How much am I rendered lonely

by this unmatched crucifixion?
Ah me!
There is none with me in this world!!
I am 'solitary reaper' on
this wasteland......

After a whole day's labor, even
the most sinful labourer
has sound sleep.........

After rest, he becomes capable for next day's activity.......
Therefore, several times, I do not get even
that rest in the night.......
Ah me! I am deprived of that necessary
comfort which is available to the meanest
creature of this world.

From where I get this heart-breaking
suffering, this crucifixion?

Is it the consequence of some evil done by me?
Not at all, for my soul is liberal from evil.
Is it due to the excessive indulgence of some
bodily urge, appetite or passion?
Not at all....
There is no bodily urge, appetite or passion
which can dominate me
.........is not under the control of the
sublime forces in me...
Where is the abode of this suffering
and torture undergone by me?
Where is their dwelling place?
Undoubtedly,
its source is in the evil-life of
those persons

for whom I have accepted the
burden of deliverance and evolution....
Due to their prejudices
for their vulgar life
they find their satisfaction in inflicting,
consciously or unconsciously, several varieties
of tortures on me.......
In a way, whatever hurts me, provides pleasure to them.
They are worshippers of pandemonium........

These terrible sufferings
one must bear with a stoic heart.
This terrible suffering has been
continuous for years and their hurts have
shattered not only my heart but
my body too.
Due to these hurts I have for several
years past, lost my
physical health.
There are certain bodily ills that have transmuted into
Chronic ones
especially pain of joints gave me a lot of trouble........

My mind has been severely
affected by the stress.

What physical state is this
Without rest and response ?

The body is not at rest, the brain is not at peace...
When the enemies of my sublime mission hurt
me for a while,
they damage my unique sensitive heart so much
......that on some occasions my heart and body
recognize woes to shattered pieces.......

When they cause some serious hurt to me,
it causes such deep and unbearable pain and suffering
that no one else can possibly
experience it......
When a clod is thrown on a dune,
its particles spread to a limited extent......
heretofore,
when the same clod
is thrown in a pool of water,
it produces ripples
whose circle goes on expanding and growing larger
and larger...............
Similar is the condition of my
sensitive heart...........
Many sinners experience no pain or a
nominal pain when a fellow sinner does
something wrong,
but in my case, when some
sinners indulge in some mean attack or when
similar sinners with whom I am concerned to
render spiritual assistance,
show any undesirable conduct,
thence,
the suffering in my heart spreads so widely
......the same experience hurts me
so badly that I alone can understand.

Why do I receive all these immense sufferings?
why does my heart feel
so much afflictions?
it is because my soul is not similar
to the souls of the world-worshippers and sinners,
but is entirely unique from them.
From
the point of view of sublime forces,

my soul is as different and unique in
excellences as is the difference and uniqueness
of my entire life from their life…..
My soul is hyper-sensitive
with strong and superior sublime feelings
…….. it gets hurt according to this equipment
by one or another low and sinful conduct of
other persons…..

How remorseful!
How calamitous and malevolent

Even those well-wishers
and so-called companions
through their negligence or foolishness,
cause me the painful hurts
hurled by the enemies…….

If some stone of accusation came flying,
they by their foolishness, became
agents to divert it to me!

Henceforth,
Where I might go
Wherever I like or stay
I was the victim of
these troubles and tortures
these villains would ordinarily
never leave me……..

who was there to be a witness
of how much I had been
Injured on various occasions…………..
No one can even estimate the tale
of cannibalistic conspiracies……..
No one!

how much suffering and damage those
hurts had caused to my body,
brain and heart, at the hands of
deep-dyed lovers of darkness,
deserters and traitors of my
mission and by vindictive
and ungrateful persons
and even by loyalist supporters
through their dirty
and low feelings…
no one can imagine………………..

A lover of ancient Indian religious
philosophy of our country can ask
me:
When you are liberal from
every low attachment to the world,
and are not one among the people of the
world in terms of your life and character,
then why do you stay amidst them
and serve them and consequently suffering year
after year, terrible tortures and extraordinary pains
from them?
Why don't you stay away from those
who are the cause of all your pains and tortures?'

In a warm reply,
I can only vocalize,
There lies a special mission
of my manifestation
and a glorious life-vow too,
whose fulfilment is imperative not only for
the advancement of my country
but for the spiritual
welfare of mankind….

This mission and life-vow
cannot enhance towards fruition
without carrying
the burden of all these pains
and tortures for myself.......

Answer Me: Oh Heaven, Oh Earth

Due to on-going persecutions
my body was in a state
of 'terrible- illness' and weakness….
My heart was broken
I was filled
with intense pain and disappointments……
My eyes were wet with tears……
The yacht
of my life-vow on which flew the flag
of my mission was tossing in the ocean of misfortunes…
There was pitch- dark and drought
all around me….
I was in the grip of demonic- agony……
However, in this state of
double-edged predicament,
the light -house on the shore of this sea of troubles
was still shining bright……
The rainbow of sublime knowledge
burnt rightfully in my soul,
showing me the route…..
Inspired by this light inside me,
I wrote out with the
emotional -fullness of my heart
the following lines
at the final stage of my *'Vilaap'*

Will this terrible pain and torture of my
innocent soul go in vain?
Through repeated calamities and sufferings
I have set feet on the brink of
death from which if so desired,
I could have saved myself.......
Therefore, I did not desire
to avoid these cruel sufferings
due to my loyalty
and commitment to
my Mission.......

I have sacrificed 'each and every inch of my life'
for years on end for
the spiritual reformation, welfare of others
and these great tortures I
have been getting on occasions,

in this drawn out suffering
there is no comparison of this.....
with momentary suffering of crucifixion....
It is not a game of a day

Will all these
unbearable sufferings and passage through scathing
fire bear no fruits?
Will all my great efforts for my life-vow go in vain?
Will my manifestation in Nature prove abortive?
Will no one awake to the glory
of my Mission?
Will the world always remain unavailable
to me and hold me as an object to despise?

Will all my tears shed in the hours of loneliness
and stillness, go waste?

Will my lamentations bear no fruit?
Will the seed of sublime life
which I have sown, dry into death?
Will no one soothe my suffering heart
by undergoing similar sacrifices?
Will there no one be true lover and disciple of mine
in this world of 'Pishachatva' (evil world)?

Will not some others dedicate their lives
inspired by love for me
with my instance of complete surrender
at the altar of sacrifice?
Will not hundreds of men rise to sacrifice themselves
completely for the great and glorious cause (of Dev Dharma)
for which I have martyred myself?
Will they not, for whom I have sacrificed myself,
be salvaged and reformed and their life enriched by
the nectar of my divinity and the heavenly- fruits
of this
Divine life?

Will not more and more souls come forward day by day to continue,
swell and spread the brook of sublimity
set in motion by me?
Is my mission not in accordance with the laws of Nature?
Can this mission of mine ever meet death?
Can it stay away from growth and expansion?
Oh Heaven, answer me! Oh Earth, speak your mind!
These were not just utterances of my lips....
They were the echoes of the unique sublime feelings
of my soul which overwhelmed me at that time....
When the chaste Sita was brought from the Ashram
of Balmiki to the court of Ram Chandra
and false accusations were made against her chastity,
she was heart-broken

by the shock of this false accusation…
She was besides herself with pain…..
With tears in her eyes
Oh this helpless
but chaste woman,
looked to the ground and motivated by
her feelings of chastity addressed the earth thus:
"If I am a chaste woman, oh Earth, open wide through
the power of my chastity, so that I may take to
eternal samadhi in your lap"…
(As I write these lines about Sita;
a stream of tears is tricking from my eyes.)

At the time of my extreme painful lamentation,
I called upon, out of my most agitated heart
and in restless pain in piteous words,
not only on earth but heaven too,
to bear witness to me and my mission thus:

Is not my mission in accordance with the laws of Nature?
Can it ever disappear?
Can it stay away from progress and
expansion?
Oh Heaven, tell me!
Oh Earth, bear witness for me!"
On these words charged with my spiritual strength,
earth shook and the heaven
trembled
suddenly, in response to my queries,
these words resounded in the auditorium of my mind:
Certainly, your mission is in accordance with
the laws of Nature.
Be patient.

Be assured that this mission
cannot but progress
and spread....
Both Earth and Heaven
bear true witness to this!

Pain Within Pain

What a conflagration!
What a wildfire!
Pain within pain
oh this affliction of perceptions!
What a dilemma!
What a tragic episode of brain wave!
Will I always be a solitary
reaper in this emotional hut?

Sometimes,
when there is a 'violent tempest',
enormous dust from all
sides.......... rises towards the sky,
covers it and
as a consequence
it gets so dark that for sometimes
nothing was visible...
But gradually as the storm subsides
and the sky is
cleared of the dust,
the things are seen as they are......
At the time,
when the enemies of my mission raised a great
storm of opposition to persecute me,

some persons noticed nothing
but darkness all around....
Those who had raised this dark thunder-light,
were happy over it in various ways....
But
those who know the nature of such stormy persecutions
look at things in a different glory.....
They realize
whenever a great soul appears and attacks
some evils in the structure and life of society
to bring about 'some special change' in it,
his evil opponents indulge in persecuting
him.
It is the dilemma of centuries...
During such stormy oppositions by
vulgar opponents,
several times happens that some
persons who get benefitted by
this great soul and who also join him
in work with him for some time,
leave him to join his opponents
due to certain
wicked- weaknesses and passions in them
and they give active support to intensify
the storm of oppositions......

But the 'people of wisdom' know
.... such stormy opposition is inevitable
against any such reformation....
As the cause of the great soul progresses,
there is still,
greater and greater opposition to it for
a longtime to emerge...
It appears as if it is inevitable
for a violent storm

of opposition to 'wake up' against any new mission
or ideal
and perhaps it is part of the scheme
of things for the fulfillment of the purpose
for which a mission comes into being!
Thus, those who understand this law of social
Transmutation
who are able to understand the unparalleled
significance of the mission of Dev Dharma
and the manifestation of the Founder of the Dev Dharma
they should not feel
a horror by the extraordinary violence
of the storms raised by the opponents
of the mission these days......
They should know that although great difficulties
and troubles necessarily appear in the wake of such
stormy opposition (and these difficulties and troubles
affect different persons differently
according to their heart-wind)
yet, by facing these with patience,
confidence, and courage, storms disappear
during the course
of time
Surely, there are superior repercussions.
which would have never been
possible without
such unfavourable circumstances.

No Hope of My Survival

Harsh! Harsh!
How gloomy and remorseful
is my stage!
How much my life is resplendent
with compassion and kindness!
Who on this comprehensive
world will grasp
my finger in the guise of compassion
and pious emotions
in this vague and tragic situation?
No one?

Wailing pearls of mine will not be
praised by near and dear ones
in their hearts, ripe fruit of appreciation
cannot rise.

Too dilemma! Too mercy!
Alas!
The attacks by the opponents
continued 'at full swing'
And intensity
Last many years,
among the run-away

and ungrateful disciples of mine,
brought out a publication against me
and several others wrote in journals,
articles comprehensively
of false accusations.......
Through such publications
the flames of hatred
and enmity flared up against me.
It was the forest of deterioration
without any aspiration........

People
who according to their own
statements, had joined me as 'disciples'
under the command of Almighty
now stood on
the platform in the very presence of their same God,
to offer devotional prayer for
my premature death and early widowhood of
my wife!

The foolishness of myths
How far their omnipotent and
all-compassionate
God has complied with their wishes,
is not for me to communicate.......
Even though I considered their activities as
most sinful,
still on several occasions,
I wished for the welfare of
these 'ungrateful disciples'
and other great enemies of mine,
in my spiritual
exercises of prayers......
Besides the aforesaid nefarious activities,

these enemies of my mission adopted
various suits of wicked activities which
their God-intoxicated heart urged them to
perform.......

In a law court
even the greatest criminal
gets a chance to defend himself...
But
Whence
after two days of this public meeting,
I announced a public meeting in my own
Ashram, in an attempt to defend myself
this I wished to decode
my troubles and illness,
heretofore,
these devotees of just God,
out of the fear of exposure of their falsehoods,
they did not allow the meeting to be held by
creating terrible -noise and
confusion..........
If my 'protective forces' had not
come to my aid
and if the
police and others had not
been with me,
they would have crushed me and
if possible put me to death
and thus, satisfied themselves....

This meeting
arranged by me
could not be held and my
nervous system was already
defective...

my ailing body suffered a
complete breakdown
due to the shocks
received in 'time to time mazes'
through their devilish activities…..
I got seriously ill….
My illness grew like 'incurable wound'
day by day………
and I set toes
in a soil
in which
there was no hope of my survival………….
It was the cave of
Pandemonium (satanic-abode)……………

Tragedy Deepens to its Darkest Dye

It was night.
There was stillness all around.

Unconsciously,
I took shelter
Those who surrounded me
Were deep in thought…………..
I could not survive the night….
I did not excavate a myself
Where I was: But in this critical stage
some of the inhabitants of Parloka
were present and were
using all their spiritual powers
to rescue me………
There was struggle between
life and death…………..
Ultimately the spiritual powers triumphed…..
Death was declined…………..
I became conscious………

My illness, grew less and less
in the next
few months, I was on my feet again…………
When the continuous persecution

in the court persisted,
I had very wide difficulty to
secure the services
of an advocate
while my opponents had a number
of advocates to work for
them free of all charges...............

It was a terrible time for me,
for I had no companion to help me
except three or four disciples of mine................
On our side, we had no experience
of court procedure...........
We were not trained hitherto...................
On the opponents' side,
there were lawyers,
who were rich and were friends of top officers
and well-versed in procedures of law................
Apart from my three or four disciples, there
Was no one prepared to appear as true witness........
for me so much
so that even those who had at one
or another time benefitted from me were
not willing to pronounce
true evidence for me..................
We had emerged in a state of utter helplessness...........

There was no dearth of devotees of God
and shouters of
"Satya Mev Jaitey" (Truth alone triumphs)
but none of them
was prepared to be a comrade of truth................
On the contrary hearts of several
of them bounced with
enthusiasm to assist our opponents.

They helped them in all possible ways.
By creating this new painful method of
Persecution
these opponents had played the last
throw of the dice………….

On perceiving my state
of suffering and helplessness
they had come to
believe that these court entanglements
of mine
would sound the death knell
of my life-vow,
and myself.
The chief persecutor used to assert
in the open court:
"It is my object in life to destroy
the Dev Dharma Mission."

He also proclaimed,
"I will have his Ashram
Auctioned,
I will behold to it
that this man is compelled to leave Punjab."

My persecution through litigation dragged
on for years and all these
years the opponents tried to torture me
and harm the work as far as it was
possible.
I had an insight into the Minds
of the devotees of Almighty to an
extent which I had never known before.
Due to my helplessness,
it was

natural for my persecutors to believe
that my mission would soon breathe last...........
This belief was widely announced and thousands
of people found
such announcements palatable to them.
In this
Miserable struggle,
it is true
that my body was completely shattered...........
I became a permanent invalid.
I sustained lot of monetary losses.

I had to close down my press and my mission-work
was very much hindered
but ultimately the truth triumphed over untruth
and the aphorism: "Yato Dharmah tato jaiyab"
(The side that holds to truth, triumphs),
proved true...........
Ten years after my commitment
to my life-vow
and on the occasion
of my birthday celebrations,
my disciples presented me
with an address in which they narrated
the 'life and death'
persecutions, the great sacrifices,
the intense pains
and the heroic struggles
I had undergone for the spiritual
welfare of others.................

I reproduce below a portion of what I said in reply
to this address:
Ten years ago when in opposition to public opinion,

I fully resolved
to devote myself entirely to the spiritual service
of mankind,
I had fears of certain inconveniences,
troubles, and difficulties..........
But I had little idea
That
with the passage of time, and growth of my
spiritual life, I would have to
undergo increasing persecutions
and tortures from those for whose spiritual service
I had dedicated my life...........
The troubles and tortures you have mentioned
in your address merely touch the fringe of
what I have suffered.
At that time and thereafter also,
the spiritual principle that was operative in my life
.... has dominated me to date was that
I should be true to lit a light...........
I should always be ready to follow the path in
the manner I am directed by my spiritual light.
Due to the hold of this principle in my life
I have never given it up even when I saw various
troubles and sufferings in store for me......................

I have repeatedly impressed on you
that even if the whole world
goes on receding from me, even then.............
I would try to remain true to myself and
I would follow whatever direction
I get for serving
my ideal mission.
I cannot remain unchanged because there
is the law of change all around us..........
Being under the law of transformation
it is inevitable for me to change...........

Because
I must change, why should I transmute
for the worse?
I should accept the direction of the light
which has illuminated before me,
my true ideal and the power which has enabled me
so far to follow this light...........
here lies my spiritual welfare and the spiritual welfare
of those who have true spiritual communion with me,
follow me, walk in my foot steps and accept me
as their true benefactor...........
Thus, in order to remain true to my ideal
I have not counted the cost of worldly deprivations
which ordinary people do and which even
the so-called religious people, (due to their low nature)
feel concerned with and even consider necessary......
Yes, it was not possible
for me to care for these deprivations and-sufferings.........
I was so built by the spiritual heredity
I was endowed with,
and the events of life which shaped me............
It was natural for me
To carry these sacrifices...............
One can understand well my unique spiritual
nature and the operation of the above-mentioned law
in me by a study of my past life,
my sayings and my articles..........
Those who possessed nature contrary to mine
could not be friends to me
and thousands among them became my persecutors...........

In accordance with the Hindu tradition
I could have lived, like a
sadhu or a rishi, in solitude
and in complete isolation

from other people.
I could have pleased those who visited me
by speaking to them some
pleasing aphorisms
In this way, I could have kept relations
with those who came in contact with me
and thus, I could have gained
in popular esteem.
But I could not do all this
due to my special spiritual inbuilt.
I have considered my life to be a life
of struggles and war against
forces of evil and untruth.

There is and can be war only between people of
opposite ideals of life, not between people
of the same ideal..........

Nature had selected me and kept me ready
for war against forces of evil and untruth and so
it became imperative for me to live a life
of war (against forces of evil and untruth).
No one can feel and know the terrible struggles through
which I have passed my last ten years and the
crucifying and torturing events through which my
soul has suffered. He alone can know all this who has
a nature identical with mine. ....
Therefore, even those persons who have established
relation with me and benefitted in higher life from me,
show lack of appreciation for
what I have suffered and do not know the tell-tale of my heart........

These last ten years have a strange history.
Every succeeding year
has proved more terrible and varied in its troubles and difficulties.

The continuous cataract of terrible tortures
undergone by me has put me in a frame of mind
as to suspect if still worse agony of death is in store for me......
It is not possible for me or for you to clear this suspicion.
I feel at this moment that the condition
under which I took my birth and the
condition under which I have been called upon
to wage war against the forces of evil
and untruth gives me a unique position in history.........

I have developed such tender sensitivity
that when I see some event or situation
offensive to any one of my higher senses
I get terrible hurt and it continues for so
long and is so painful that sometimes
I am not able to bear it and suppress it.........
I start asking myself whether a day will
come in my life when I will be surrounded
by pure and high-soiled persons, life amongst
whom will exclude the
possibility of such kinds of torments and tortures for me.
I do not consider that such a blessed state
of things is impossible.
In the destruction of evil and the evolution
of Devatva,
I see the vision of the world of people
who are loving, useful, loyal, and trustworthy
to one another.
I consider it a supreme ideal of my unique life
to bring about that day, and to produce men of
very high character who can prove a leaven to
raise their own countrymen to spread untold
blessings for them and for other kingdoms of Nature.

I wish to produce heaven on earth.
I want to herald a religion on this earth
which will destroy all sins and evil
and which will produce men of trust and character
through whom human relations will be
in all respects sweet and blessed.
I want to establish a religion which
blesses true moksha/salvation
to human souls and so fashions high character
in them that they prove a complete blessing
not only for fellow human beings
but for all living beings with whom
they have beneficial relationship........
If such high-spirited men are evolved and their
noble life becomes a creative and dynamic tradition,
thence
not only my mission in life will be fructified
but it will also establish its own uniqueness.

A Priceless Nectarine

If I have remained true to the
ideal of my mission,
without caring for
worldly and second-rated persons;
and struggled to wage war to 'bring about'
triumph for divine life in accordance with my mission;
if I have attacked
with all my strength the 'forces of vulgarity'
and borne all the possible
sufferings and tortures from the partisans of evil;
if I have performed it to show
that
if there are partisans of evil there is at least
one in me who is loyal to
the life of Devatma.
If only through the successive
triumph of Devatma
(though there is torture for me at each step in
working for its victory) my
countrymen are infused with new life
and strength to gain high spiritual
achievements and also form themselves into a grand
and superior nation,
then who else except myself

would be ready to bear the agony and tortures to bring
about these blessings of the sublime life
It is not natural for man to desire for pain and suffering.
No man likes them for himself for a day........
Man is thirsty for pleasure................
He is so attached to pleasure that he does not
hesitate to misbehave even towards his own children
and other relatives for his personal comfort
and benefit......
A sensible person can easily understand
the uniqueness of my nature when he understands
how
in this 'war between Devatma (good) and Pishachatva (evil)'
I have borne suffering and torture,
not only for days or months
but for 'full ten years.'
What a dirty scenario of discernment!

I have never deprived another of his dues because
of my strong sense of justice
thence, on the contrary
I have utilized my various energies in the service of others........
It is a thousand pities that the more
I have waged war against Pishachatva (evil) and untruth
for establishing Devatma and
the more I have
harnessed my powers in the service of others,
the more I have been subjected to tortures........
Had my soul and my mission not been unique,
how could have it been possible for me,
...... that an average man cheats even his
kith and kin
deprives them of their
rights,
not just for one year

but…….
For a
'full ten years' at full swing
from those 'very persons' for
whose welfare I have
ceaselessly worked!'

Gems of sublime vision

- It is imperative for me to stand by Truth and silently fade away. I cannot be disloyal to my love of Truth. I cannot show my back in this battle. Though unknown, ignored, disrespected, and hated, I can die in peace only if I remain loyal to my life-vow and die struggling for it.

- Yeah …even if my physical death proves the end of my individual entity, I cannot go astray from the path of my life mission. This life is a continuous continual struggle!

- O man! Thee not only body but soul too; Do not waste your time pursuing material things.

- I am a tree of divine life which produces blessed fruits. He, who gets associated with me, like a branch is to a tree, not only avoids harm to himself and others but also produces blessed fruits in his own life and in the life of others.

- I am ship of hope for the souls drowning in the ocean of evil life. I am like yeast for saving, improving and bettering the fallen communities and nations. I consider it a supreme ideal of my unique life to bring about the day, and to produce men of very high character who can prove a leaven to raise their own countrymen to spread untold blessings for them and for other kingdoms of Nature.

- I want to herald a religion on this earth which will be destructive of all sins and evils and which will produce men of trust and character through whom human relations will be in all respects sweet and blessed. I want to establish a religion which gives true moksha to human souls and fashions high character in them that they prove a complete blessing for all living beings.

- On being free from the influence of every evil-prone motive and on being equipped with every higher-feeling-constituting complete religious life, it was to be inevitable for me to enjoy the state of highest peace and highest bliss. I did attain to such absolutely valuable and most beneficial peace and such absolutely valuable and most useful bliss.

- On being in the state of sublime life I am truly desirous of higher evolution of every order of Nature. On establishing beneficial relation with every order of Nature, I use my energies for its good. I take to the spiritual exercises to reach my higher influences in less or more degree to every order of Nature. I keep engaged in higher thought and higher conduct. Therefore, there descend in me higher "RAS" and sublime bliss.

- Just as the earth becomes more and more wet as it rains, so the more I engage myself in noble thought, higher love, and higher conduct; there is greater and greater production of divine satisfaction. This ecstasy is not that kind of intoxication which is produced by taking of harmful poisonous things like hemp (bhang), wine, or opium. This ecstasy is produced by religious life. It is free from all elements of poison and is all beneficial for the soul. This higher "RUS" is clear of all impurities. It is life-giving relish and therefore it is called nectar. This sector does not sprout in any heart without deliverance from one's evil feelings, without gaining purity and innocence of heart and without engagement in one or another altruistic activity. It does not grow into full bloom without complete deliverance from evil dispositions and development of all-sided religious life.

- I cannot deviate even to the infinitesimal extent from following the evolutionary laws of Nature, in my soul, even though this earth of ours may shatter into pieces or our sun may set for ever.

- Our sun may stop shedding its light or our earth may give way under our feet and breaks into pieces, but I being a complete lover of truth, come what may, can never, trample upon any truth, which alone dawns upon me, and being a complete lover of goodness, can never go astray from the path of goodness and betterment.

- You cannot degrade me by your constant viciousness. I cannot be influenced by you despite remaining with you. You must flee from me, after tormenting me and harming yourself one day.

- To fight on, to fight on for my unique mission has been a life principal with me, even at the point of perishing.

- Exerting constantly for the realization of my unique supreme goal or my life vow, even at the point of death, has remained my foremost aim. Hold on, hold on is the whisper that I hear from within and certainly, I will hold on. Weeping and wailing and struggling I will hold on.

- I am not bound with any man or any other existence. I am only a complete lover of truth and goodness, and my relationship with all is primarily based on truth and goodness.

- The life force which does not do any constructive work is bound to die.

- The only two things humans should love in this world are Devatma and selfless service to others.

- The manifestation of Dev Dharma or divinity has not taken place in a stone or a tree but in my soul and all its higher excellences are in my soul.

- Foolish are they who seek the manifestation and the excellence and blessings of the sublime life in sources other than me.

- I have appeared as a special manifestation for those persons who on being given to self-will and lost in soul-ignorance are destroying themselves through engaging themselves in worldly ambitions and sins. I want to disengage them from the worldly life and put them in commune with me so as to save them from death and to make them heir to superior and pure life and its blissful fruits.

- Due to terribly stormy opposition by my opponents, my nervous system got shattered by their inflicting horrible and painful sufferings. I was on death bed due to severe illness but ultimately when I recovered from my serious illness, my inner spiritual light shone with greater illumination. On the one hand, I saw and felt sympathy for, the pitiable state of millions of people, bereft of this light, living an ugly life of spiritual ignorance and on the other hand I realized the excellence of the nature of the light in me. During this time, I felt a strong urge to say something about this light and inspired by this thought, I had the following sentences taken down by a disciple of mine:

- I have in me a new light for you. Commune with me and get the light that is in me.

- Only through communion with me and by getting my light, you can see and realize all those truths that pertain to Dev Dharma or true divine life.

- Are there not some among you who have obtained my light and are able to see and realize more or less my teachings?

- Do not forget that the light that you have obtained so far is meagre and so in that little light you are able to see very little. Apart from some elementary truths you are able to see the subtle truths of divine life only dimly and that also occasionally.

- The more my light enters your soul, the more you will be able to see clearly and vividly the truths of divine life. The more this light grows bright and stable in you, the more you will be able to get rid of your low life which, instead of exposing you to spiritual light, keeps you in the darkness of appetites and passions.

- The more you get my light, the more you will be in a position to enlighten others who are comparatively in greater darkness than you.

- In the spiritual darkness, a soul is led astray from the spiritual path and goes the way of death. My light takes a soul out of darkness, puts him on the spiritual path and delivers it from death, unto life.

- Remember, it is not the sound of my words which carries light to your soul. It is through your communion with me that you are illumined with my light.

- Give up all forms of your disloyalty to me and commune with me with all your heart so that my light may illumine you more and more.

- The light I have received is not meant for me only but it is for others also. In fact, it is for all.

- The souls should receive from me the light which has been given to me for their welfare. They should not deprive themselves of its life-giving blessings through disloyalty to me due to some evil passion.

- Blessed are those souls who rise above their undue attachment to ego or evil relatives who increase their spiritual darkness or the worldly opinion and come or want to come under my light which delivers them from spiritual darkness and death.

- Every soul who unites with me in love and surrenders to my influences, gives up his past evil and gains a new, pure, and noble life.

- The extent to which a soul assimilates my higher influences, through communion with me, to that extent he is illumined by that new light by which he is enabled to see and realize more and more the reality and the laws of spiritual life.

- The extent to which a soul assimilates higher influences through communion with me, to that extent he develops love for such virtues and blessings of divine life and its laws for which he has developed capacity to know and realize the truth.

- The extent to which a soul assimilates higher influences through communion with me, to that extent he shapes himself into divine life of which I am the ideal manifestation.

- The extent to which a soul assimilates my higher influences through communion with me, to that extent he develops hatred for all those sins for which I have hatred.

- The extent to which a soul assimilates my higher influences through communion with me, to that extent he develops love for the four fundamental truths about my divine life, namely, Eternity, Truth, Justice, and Goodness.

- The extent to which a soul assimilates my higher influences through communion with me, to that extent he develops pain for his evil thoughts and actions.

- The power of divine life which is like leaven in me, demolishes and destroys evil. So, this power is spiritual means for the reformation and betterment of sin-sodden and suffering souls.

- There is no soul who has not become comparatively better and nobler after uniting with me, even if he has communed with me in the least degree provided he has surrendered his self-will.

- A branch which is grafted to a thorn apple (Dhatura) produces poisonous fruits and a branch which is grafted to a grape vine produces grapes. In the same way, a soul who associates with an evil soul produces poisonous and destructive fruits for others but a soul who associates with me obtains spiritual nourishment of divine life and produces pure and higher changes in others.

- Just as a branch of a poisonous plant can be known by its characteristics, so a soul united with me, like a branch grafted with a life-giving tree, can be known by life-giving characteristics of divinity which have manifested in me.

- I am a tree of divine life which produces blessed fruits. He who gets associated with me, like a branch is to a tree, not only avoids harm to himself and others but also produces blessed fruits in his own life and in the life of others.

- A cow on being hungry does not avoid taking grass in the jungle out of fear that some leaves of the grass maybe dusty. A man who is hungry does not avoid taking wheat loaves (chapaties) out of fear that there may be some particle of sand etc. in it. A soul who is hungry for life-giving blessings of divine life does not avoid communion with me out of some imaginary reason against me, for he who eats, lives and be who does not eat, dies.

- He who acknowledges the good tidings of my manifestation, surrenders his self-will, gives me hold on his life day by day, gives up his evil life and seeks unity with my sublime life (Dev Jiwan), like a branch does to a tree, belongs to me and my mission and he alone can benefit from my manifestation.

- Those who are ignorant of the life-giving and destructive conditions of soul-life or the laws of life and death of the soul and are not only slaves of evil life but are also partial to and in love with it, cannot realize the truths pertaining to the truth and importance of my manifestation, the truth of the need of uniting with me and the life-giving blessings of such union, unless they get rid of their evil life. Such souls in their present sorry state in many cases have hated and hurt me to an extent which no one else could.

- To the extent a soul gains intimacy with me through communion, to that extent he is absolutely different from every other person given to worldliness and evil, in his intrinsic worth and style of life.

- To the extent to which a soul, is different from the worldly and evil persons in intrinsic worth and style of life, to that extent the evil persons, finding him different and opposed to their way of life, will hate him and find pleasure in harming and hurting him.

- Blessed is the soul who feels closer to sublime life (Dev Jiwan) and different from the lovers of evil life to the degree they ill-treat him, for he thereby remains protected from their evil influences.

- The extent of the depth to which a soul unites with me, to that extent it becomes imperative for him to respect and love all those who are united with me and are under my influences. He feels he belongs to them and they belong to him. He who does not show this conduct does not belong to me.

- It is imperative for those who have offered their lives for my mission and vowed themselves to spread the good tidings of my manifestation, and unite souls with me for their betterment, to achieve complete freedom from their past moral distortions and impurities of the soul and give evidence, through all their conduct, that they give the highest place to me in their hearts next to God. After that they love all my missionaries and show no jealousy or vindictiveness towards them and do not squirm when they discover some one of their fellow missionaries are making better progress but rejoice in it. They do not harm the true glory of the mission or prove a hindrance in the discipline of the mission due to attachment to name, position, or comfort.

Books I Have Loved

1. Dev Shastra volume I
2. Dev Shastra volume II
3. Dev Shastra volume III
4. Dev Shastra volume IV
5. Four Fundamental Truths about Human Soul
6. The Fundamental Distinction Between the Believers in True Religion and Those of False Ones
7. Fundamentals of Philosophy
8. Scientific Philosophy
9. Freedom from Spiritual Slavery and Higher Evolution of Man
10. False Belief in God and its most Baneful Results
11. Evolution and Dissolution—the Two eternal Laws
12. On Good Manners
13. Mujh mein Dev Jiwan Ka Vikas (The evolution of Divine life in Devatma)—Volume I And Volume II
14. Aduti-Tiyaag (Volume I to VII)
15. Atam Katha—A brief autobiographical sketch
16. Dev Atma
17. Fundamentals of Moral and Spiritual Life
18. Dev Dharma in the Service of Man
19. Revolution in Religion
20. A Short Catechism on the life and Philosophy of Devatma
21. Moral and Spiritual order in the Universe
22. What works these Miracles

Works Cited List

Sublime Journey Untouched by Time

Prof. Kanal, S.P.; 1. Four Fundamental Truths about Human -Soul; Preface;

2. Naturalism in Dev Dharma, (1) (1984)
3. Why do we not believe in God (2), (1984)
4. Can Humanism Be a Substitute for Religion? (3) (1984)
5. What Can take the Place of God in Religion? (4) (1984)
6. What Makes Dev Dharma a True Religion? (5) (1984)
7. The Basis of Morality & Religion (6) (1984)
8. The meaning of life (7) (1984)
9. Unity of Religion (8) (1984)
10. The Future of Religion (9) (1984)
11. The concept of Ideal Man in Religion (10) (1982)
12. Dev Dharma in the Service of New Society (11) (1984)
13. Religion and Human Relations (12) (1984)
14. Religion in the service of Education (13) (1984)
15. The Challenge of Suffering in Human Life (14) (1984)
16. The world of Religious Experience (17) (1984)
17. Glimpses of Beauty Sublime
18. The Chandelier of Altruism
19. www.Devatma.org

What Type of Heaven Is This

1. AGNIHOTRI, SHREE SATYANAND; Dev Shastra volume I-Nature-Tattwa
2. AGNIHOTRI, SHREE SATYANAND; Dev Shastra volume I- Nature of the Universe; Published by Prof. Kanal S.P.
3. Ibid; "The good wishes of the Author:
4. www.Devatma.org

A Glipmses of Your Own Future

1. AGNIHOTRI, SHREE SATYANAND; Atma Katha: An Autibiographical Sketch of the FOUNDER OF DEV SAMAJ (1985); Translated by Principal Kanal P.V.
2. AGNIHOTRI, SHREE SATYANAND; Mujh mein Dev Jiwan Ka Vikas-volume 1;
3. AGNIHOTRI, SHREE SATYANAND; The evolution of Divine life in me part-1 Translated by Prof. Kanal S.P.
4. Ibid chapter 25; My persecution consequent on my commitment to my life vow,
5. www.Devatma.org

A Sunrise That Never Sets

1. AGNIHOTRI, SHREE SATYANAND; Dev Shastra volume I-Nature-Tattwa
2. AGNIHOTRI, SHREE SATYANAND; Dev Shastra volume III-Manush Tattwa'
3. AGNIHOTRI, SHREE SATYANAND Dev Shastra volume III- Philosophy of Man; Translated by Prof. S.P. Kanal
4. Bhalla Yashpal; Vigyan Moolak Dharam & Dev Samaj Ke sansthapak Param Punjia Bhagwan Devatma ka adutiya Avirbhav aur Mujh Tuchh ko unkii Aduti Den-Part-I

The Secrets of the Evolutionary Process

1. AGNIHOTRI, SHREE SATYANAND; Dev Shastra volume I-Nature-Tattwa
2. AGNIHOTRI, SHREE SATYANAND; Dev Shastra volume I- Nature of the Universe published by Prof. Kanal S.P.
3. Ibid (7) The Advent of Devatma in the Course of Human evolution

A Great Longing For The Master

1. Bhalla Yashpal; Vigyan Moolak Dharam & Dev Samaj Ke sansthapak Param Punjia Bhagwan Devatma ka adutiya Avirbhav aur Mujh Tuchh ko unkii Aduti Den-Part-I
2. Ibid; Vikhyat jano ki Aashaye Aur Bhavisya Vani (Page 8)
3. www.Devatma.org

Master Born Before His Time

1. AGNIHOTRI, SHREE SATYANAND; Dev Shastra volume I-Nature-Tattwa
2. AGNIHOTRI, SHREE SATYANAND; Dev Shastra volume III-Manush Tattwa
3. AGNIHOTRI, SHREE SATYANAND; Dev Shastra volume III- Philosophy of Man; Translated by Prof. S.P. Kanal
4. AGNIHOTRI, SHREE SATYANAND; Mujh mein Dev Jiwan Ka Vikas-volume 1;

5. Bhalla Yashpal; Vigyan Moolak Dharam & Dev Samaj Ke sansthapak Param Punjia Bhagwan Devatma ka adutiya Avirbhav aur Mujh Tuchh ko unkii Aduti Den-Part-I

Opening the Doors of Light and Beyond

1. Dev Shastra volume III-Manush Tattwa 'SHREE SATYANAND AGNIHOTRI'
2. Dev Shastra volume III- Philosophy of Man 'SHREE SATYANAND AGNIHOTRI; Translated by Prof. Kanal, S.P.
3. Ibid; The Emergence of Devatma fit Bringing in a New Era, chapter 39.

Fountain Head of a sublime Lighthouse

1. AGNIHOTRI, SHREE SATYANAND; Dev Shastra volume I-Nature-Tattwa
2. AGNIHOTRI, SHREE SATYANAND; Dev Shastra volume III-Manush Tattwa
3. AGNIHOTRI, SHREE SATYANAND; Dev Shastra volume III- Philosophy of Man; Translated by Prof. Kanal, S.P.
4. Ibid; chapter 3. The Emergence of the Spiritual evolutes, Devatma, in Fulfilment of the laws of Nature, in order to Remove the Most Injurious Soul Ignorance of Fit ('Adhikaari') Persons and to Bring About Higher Changes in Them.

A Blissful Milieu-The Unknown Life of Master

1. AGNIHOTRI, SHREE SATYANAND; Dev Shastra volume I-Nature-Tattwa
2. AGNIHOTRI, SHREE SATYANAND; Dev Shastra volume I- Nature of the Universe; Published by Prof. Kanal, S.P. 1976
3. AGNIHOTRI, SHREE SATYANAND; Dev Shastra volume III- Philosophy of Man; Translated by Prof. Kanal, S.P.

The great Secret with a question Mark (?)

1. AGNIHOTRI, SHREE SATYANAND; Mujh mein Dev Jiwan Ka Vikas-volume 1;
2. AGNIHOTRI, SHREE SATYANAND; 'The evolution of Divine life in me' volume—I; Translated by Prof. Kanal, S.P.
3. Ibid; chapter 3; "The Need for Special Emotional & Intellectual Equipment for Development of Love of Truth"

Psychology of Goodness

1. AGNIHOTRI, SHREE SATYANAND; Mujh mein Dev Jiwan Ka Vikas-volume—II;
2. AGNIHOTRI, SHREE SATYANAND; 'The evolution of Divine life in me' volume—II; Translated by Prof. Kanal S.P.
3. Prof. Kanal, S.P. To Be Good (1988);

Psychology of Love of Truth

1. AGNIHOTRI, SHREE SATYANAND;; Mujh mein Dev Jiwan Ka Vikas-volume 1;
2. AGNIHOTRI, SHREE SATYANAND; 'The evolution of Divine life in me' volume—I; Translated by Prof. Kanal S.P.
3. Prof. Kanal, S.P. Glimpses of Beauty Sublime' chapter 4.

Psychology of Beauty

1. AGNIHOTRI, SHREE SATYANAND; Mujh mein Dev Jiwan Ka Vikas-volume 1;
2. AGNIHOTRI, SHREE SATYANAND; 'The evolution of Divine life in me' volume—I; Translated by Prof. Kanal S.P.
3. Prof. Kanal, S.P. Glimpses of Beauty Sublime' In the Service of Beautiful; (chapter 20);

Psychology of Altruism

1. Prof. Kanal, S.P. The Chandelier of Altruism; The Altruists for the process of Evolution; (chapter 11);
2. Prof. Kanal, S.P. Devatma Ka parichey;
3. www.Devatma.org

Psychology of Love

1. Prof. Kanal, S.P. The Chandelier of Altruism; Motivation of Love; chapter (7);
2. Prof. Kanal, S.P. Devatma Ka parichey;
3. www.Devatma.org

Psychology of Virtue

1. Prof. Kanal, S.P. Ethics of Devatma; The Dimensions of Human Nature; chapter (29);
2. Prof. Kanal, S. P. Glimpses of Beauty Sublime' The Master On Himself; chapter (1);
3. www.devatma.org

The Psychology of Man

1. AGNIHOTRI, SHREE SATYANAND; Dev Shastra volume III-Manush Tattwa
2. AGNIHOTRI, SHREE SATYANAND;; Dev Shastra volume III- Philosophy of Man; Translated by Prof. Kanal S.P.
3. www.devatma.org

Psychology of Sublime life

1. AGNIHOTRI, SHREE SATYANAND; Mujh mein Dev Jiwan Ka Vikas-volume 1;
2. AGNIHOTRI, SHREE SATYANAND; 'The evolution of Divine life in me' volume—I; Translated by Prof. Kanal S.P.
3. Ibid; What is sublime life; chapter 1;
4. www.Devatma.org

The House where Nobody lives

1. AGNIHOTRI, SHREE SATYANAND; 'The evolution of Divine life in me' volume—I; Translated by Prof. Kanal S.P.
2. Ibid; Preface by the Translator; Prof. Kanal S.P.
3. www.devatma.org

For the Sake of Evolution and Harmony

1. Prof. Kanal, S. P. Glimpses of Beauty Sublime' The Mission of My Master; Chapter 16;
2. AGNIHOTRI, SHREE SATYANAND; 'The evolution of Divine life in me' volume—I; Translated by Prof. Kanal S.P.
3. www.Devatma.org

The Message: A Matter of Life and Death

1. Prof. Kanal, S. P. Glimpses of Beauty Sublime' The Message of My Master; Chapter 18;
2. www.devatma.org

Wonder of Wonders

1. Prof. Kanal, S. P. Glimpses of Beauty Sublime' Miracle of My Master; Chapter 19;
2. www.devatma.org

Schedule of a New Species with New Vision

1. AGNIHOTRI, SHREE SATYANAND; Atam Parichey, First Part;
2. Ibid; Mein Kaya Karta Rahta Huin;

The fire Test of Piousness

1. Prof. Kanal, S. P. Devatma Ka Parichey;
2. Prof. Kanal, S. P. Introduction to Devatma, Translated By Dr. Kaur Ramanpreet;
3. Ibid; Disparity in piousness

The Only Holy Approach: Completeness

1. Prof. Kanal, S. P. Devatma Ka Parichey;
2. Prof. Kanal, S. P. Introduction to Devatma, Translated By Dr. Kaur Ramanpreet;
3. Ibid; Disparity in Completeness

The Door to Bliss and Beauty

1. Prof. Kanal, S. P. Devatma Ka Parichey;
2. Prof. Kanal, S. P. Introduction to Devatma, Translated By Dr. Kaur Ramanpreet;
3. Ibid; Disparity in Beauty;

The Pulse of the Foundation

1. Prof. Kanal, S. P. Devatma Ka Parichey;
2. Prof. Kanal, S. P. Introduction to Devatma, Translated By Dr. Kaur Ramanpreet;
3. Ibid; Disparity in Foundation;

From the wave to the Cosmic Ocean: Subjectivity

1. Prof. Kanal, S. P. Devatma Ka Parichey;
2. Prof. Kanal, S. P. Introduction to Devatma, Translated By Dr. Kaur Ramanpreet;
3. Ibid; Disparity in Subjectivity;

Truth: The Ultimate Value

1. Prof. Kanal, S. P. Devatma Ka Parichey;
2. Prof. Kanal, S. P. Introduction to Devatma, Translated By Dr. Kaur Ramanpreet;
3. Ibid; Disparity in Truth

Wings for the Truthful Knowledge

1. Prof. Kanal, S. P. Devatma Ka Parichey;
2. Prof. Kanal, S. P. Introduction to Devatma, Translated By Dr. Kaur Ramanpreet;
3. Ibid; Disparity in Truthful Knowledge

The Value of Scientific Knowledge

1. Prof. Kanal, S. P. Devatma Ka Parichey;
2. Prof. Kanal, S. P. Introduction to Devatma, Translated By Dr. Kaur Ramanpreet;
3. Ibid; Disparity in Scientific Knowledge;

The Highest Phenomenon on the Earth: Devatma and Fools

1. AGNIHOTRI, SHREE SATYANAND; Dev Shastra volume III-Manush Tattwa
2. AGNIHOTRI, SHREE SATYANAND; Dev Shastra volume III- Philosophy of Man; Translated by Prof. Kanal, S.P.
3. Ibid; chapter 10; The Emergence of Devatma Has the Purpose of Ridding Mankind of all Those Various Kind of Completely False and Most Harmful Teachings About Soul, Propagated in the Name of Religion and Based on the Ideal of Pleasure and Pain

The Secret Taste of Honey on the Tongue

1. Prof. Kanal, S. P. The Chandelier of Altruism;
2. www.devatma.org

The Last Milestone: Philosophy of Truth

1. Prof. Kanal, S. P. Glimpses of Beauty Sublime' On Truth; Chapter 3;
2. www.devatma.org

The Natures of The Universe-Ontology

1. Dr. Mittal, K. K. Perspectives of the Philosophy of Devatma;
2. AGNIHOTRI, SHREE SATYANAND; Dev Shastra volume I-Nature-Tattwa
3. AGNIHOTRI, SHREE SATYANAND; Dev Shastra volume I- Nature of the Universe; Published by Prof. Kanal, S.P.
4. Ethics of Devatma; Prof. Kanal, S.P.
5. www.Devatma.org

Nature Alone is a source of all Knowledge

1. Dr. Mittal, K. K. Perspectives of the Philosophy of Devatma;
2. AGNIHOTRI, SHREE SATYANAND;; Dev Shastra volume I-Nature-Tattwa
3. AGNIHOTRI, SHREE SATYANAND; Dev Shastra volume I- Nature of the Universe Published by Prof. Kanal, S.P.
4. Prof. Kanal, S.P. Ethics of Devatma;
5. www.Devatma.org

Truth Cannot Be Lost: Evolution

1. Dr. Mittal, K. K. Perspectives of the Philosophy of Devatma;
2. AGNIHOTRI, SHREE SATYANAND; Dev Shastra volume I-Nature-Tattwa
3. AGNIHOTRI, SHREE SATYANAND; Dev Shastra volume I- Nature of the Universe; Published by Prof. Kanal, S.P.

4.   Ethics of Devatma; Prof. Kanal, S.P.

5.   www.Devatma.org

Evolutionary Naturalism in Devatma

1.   Dr. Mittal, K. K. Perspectives of the Philosophy of Devatma;

2.   AGNIHOTRI, SHREE SATYANAND; Dev Shastra volume I-Nature-Tattwa;

3.   AGNIHOTRI, SHREE SATYANAND; Dev Shastra volume I- Nature of the Universe; Published by Prof. Kanal, S.P.

4.   Ethics of Devatma; Prof. Kanal, S.P.

5.   www.Devatma.org

Keep The Doors Open: The Human Evolution

1.   AGNIHOTRI, SHREE SATYANAND; Dev Shastra volume I-Nature-Tattwa

2.   AGNIHOTRI, SHREE SATYANAND; Dev Shastra volume I- Nature of the Universe; Published by Prof. Kanal, S.P.

3.   Ethics of Devatma; Prof. Kanal, S.P.

4.   Ibid; The Human Evolution; chapter 32;

5.   www.Devatma.org

Always On the Funeral Pyre— Human Altruistic Personality

1.   AGNIHOTRI, SHREE SATYANAND; Dev Shastra volume I-Nature-Tattwa

2.   AGNIHOTRI, SHREE SATYANAND; Dev Shastra volume I- Nature of the Universe; Published by Prof. Kanal, S.P.

3.   Ethics of Devatma; Prof. Kanal, S.P.

4.   Ibid; The Limits of Human Evolution; chapter 36;

5.   www.Devatma.org

The Great Love Affair with the Universe

1.   AGNIHOTRI, SHREE SATYANAND; Dev Shastra volume I-Nature-Tattwa

2.   AGNIHOTRI, SHREE SATYANAND; Dev Shastra volume I- Nature of the Universe; Published by Prof. Kanal, S.P.

3.   AGNIHOTRI, SHREE SATYANAND; Mujh Mein Dev Jiwan Ka Vikas-vol. 1;

4.   AGNIHOTRI, SHREE SATYANAND 'The evolution of Divine life in me' volume—I; Published by Prof. Kanal, S.P.

5.   Ibid; True Principles of Scientific Philosophy; chapter 45;

The Philosophy Whose Time Has Come

1.   AGNIHOTRI, SHREE SATYANAND; Dev Shastra volume I-Nature-Tattwa

2. AGNIHOTRI, SHREE SATYANAND; Dev Shastra volume I- Nature of the Universe; Published by Prof. Kanal, S.P.
3. AGNIHOTRI, SHREE SATYANAND; Mujh mein Dev Jiwan Ka Vikas-volume 1; Chapter 46
4. 'The evolution of Divine life in me' volume—I; 'SHREE SATYANAND AGNIHOTRI; Published by Prof. Kanal, S.P.
5. Ibid; True Principles of Scientific Philosophy; chapter 46;

Journey From Fiction to Reality

1. AGNIHOTRI, SHREE SATYANAND; Mujh Mein Dev Jiwan Ka Vikas-vol. 1; Chapter 47
2. AGNIHOTRI, SHREE SATYANAND; 'The evolution of Divine life in me' volume—I; Published by Prof. Kanal, S.P.
3. Ibid; True Principles of Scientific Philosophy; chapter 47;

Skies Beyond Skies

1. AGNIHOTRI, SHREE SATYANAND; Mujh Mein Dev Jiwan Ka Vikas-vol. 1;Chapter 49;
2. AGNIHOTRI, SHREE SATYANAND; 'The evolution of Divine life in me' volume—I; Published by Prof. Kanal, S.P.
3. Ibid; Fundamental Principles of Dev Samaj; chapter 49;

A Journey without End

1. AGNIHOTRI, SHREE SATYANAND; Mujh Mein Dev Jiwan Ka Vikas-vol. 1; Chapter 48;
2. AGNIHOTRI, SHREE SATYANAND; 'The evolution of Divine life in me' volume—I; Published by Prof. Kanal, S.P.
3. Ibid; True Principles of Scientific Philosophy; chapter 48;

This is the Whole world

1. AGNIHOTRI, SHREE SATYANAND; Mujh Mein Dev Jiwan Ka Vikas-vol. 1; Chapter 50;
2. AGNIHOTRI, SHREE SATYANAND; 'The evolution of Divine life in me' volume—I; Translated by Prof. Kanal, S.P.
3. Ibid; True Principles of Scientific Philosophy; chapter 50;

Human Soul: Unknown to Yourself

1. AGNIHOTRI, SHREE SATYANAND; Dev Shastra volume III-Manush Tattwa
2. AGNIHOTRI, SHREE SATYANAND; Dev Shastra volume III- Philosophy of Man; Translated by Prof. Kanal, S.P.

3. Ethics of Devatma; Prof. Kanal, S.P.
4. Ibid; Human Soul is Born; chapter 10;
5. www.devatma.org

The Book Of Secrets: Embodied Soul

1. AGNIHOTRI, SHREE SATYANAND; Dev Shastra volume III-Manush Tattwa;
2. AGNIHOTRI, SHREE SATYANAND; Dev Shastra volume III- Philosophy of Man; Translated by Prof. Kanal, S.P.
3. Ethics of Devatma; Prof. Kanal, S.P.
4. Ibid; Can Soul Be Disembodied; chapter 11;
5. www.devatma.org

In Search of a Lost Treasure

1. AGNIHOTRI, SHREE SATYANAND; Dev Shastra volume III-Manush Tattwa
2. AGNIHOTRI, SHREE SATYANAND; Dev Shastra volume III- Philosophy of Man; Translated by Prof. Kanal, S.P.
3. Ethics of Devatma; Prof. Kanal, S.P.
4. Ibid; Are Human Souls One or Many; chapter 12;
5. www.devatma.org

You cannot Escape Change

1. AGNIHOTRI, SHREE SATYANAND; Dev Shastra volume III-Manush Tattwa;
2. AGNIHOTRI, SHREE SATYANAND;Dev Shastra volume III- Philosophy of Man; Translated by Prof. Kanal, S.P.
3. Ethics of Devatma; Prof. Kanal, S.P.
4. Ibid; Can Human soul Escape Change; chapter 13;
5. www.devatma.org

A Small Candle is Enough

1. AGNIHOTRI, SHREE SATYANAND; Dev Shastra volume III-Manush Tattwa;
2. AGNIHOTRI, SHREE SATYANAND; Dev Shastra volume III- Philosophy of Man; Translated by Prof. Kanal, S.P.
3. Ethics of Devatma; Prof. Kanal, S.P.
4. Ibid; Is Human Soul the Doer; chapter 14;

You are not Immortal

1. AGNIHOTRI, SHREE SATYANAND; Dev Shastra volume III-Manush Tattwa;
2. AGNIHOTRI, SHREE SATYANAND; Dev Shastra volume III- Philosophy of Man; Translated by Prof. Kanal, S.P.
3. Prof. Kanal, S.P. Ethics of Devatma;

4. Ibid; Is Human Soul Immortal; chapter 15;
5. www.devatma.org

A Little Taste of Human Life-Force

1. AGNIHOTRI, SHREE SATYANAND; Dev Shastra volume III-Manush Tattwa
2. AGNIHOTRI, SHREE SATYANAND; Dev Shastra volume III- Philosophy of Man; Translated by Prof. Kanal, S.P.
3. www.devatma.org

Education for Life before permanent Death

1. AGNIHOTRI, SHREE SATYANAND; Dev Shastra volume II-Satya our Mithya Tattwa
2. AGNIHOTRI, SHREE SATYANAND; Dev Shastra volume III- Nature of Knowledge; Translated by Prof. Kanal, S.P.
3. Prof. Kanal, S.P. Ethics of Devatma;
4. Ibid; What Can the Human Soul Know; chapter 17;
5. bid; What does the Human Soul Know; chapter 18;
6. www.devatma.org

The Light-The Gateway of Devatma

1. AGNIHOTRI, SHREE SATYANAND; Dev Shastra volume III-Manush Tattwa;
2. AGNIHOTRI, SHREE SATYANAND; Dev Shastra volume III- Philosophy of Man; Translated by Prof. Kanal, S.P.
3. www.devatma.org

Ethics and Laws of soul

1. AGNIHOTRI, SHREE SATYANAND; Dev Shastra volume III-Manush Tattwa;
2. AGNIHOTRI, SHREE SATYANAND; Dev Shastra volume III- Philosophy of Man; Translated by Prof. Kanal, S.P.
3. Prof. Kanal, S.P. Ethics of Devatma;
4. Ibid; The category of His Ethics; chapter 20;
5. www.devatma.org

Ethics with a Difference

1. AGNIHOTRI, SHREE SATYANAND; Dev Shastra volume III-Manush Tattwa;
2. AGNIHOTRI, SHREE SATYANAND; Dev Shastra volume III- Philosophy of Man; Translated by Prof. Kanal, S.P.
3. Prof. Kanal, S.P. Ethics of Devatma;
4. Ibid; The Empirical Method of His Ethics; chapter 21;
5. www.devatma.org

The Root Problems of All Problems

1. AGNIHOTRI, SHREE SATYANAND; Dev Shastra volume III-Manush Tattwa;
2. AGNIHOTRI, SHREE SATYANAND; Dev Shastra volume III- Philosophy of Man; Translated by Prof. Kanal, S.P.
3. Ibid; chapter2; Love of Low Pleasure in Man is Root Cause of His Most Deplorable Ignorance about His Soul
4. Prof. Kanal, S.P. Ethics of Devatma;
5. Ibid; Four Philosophies of Pleasure; chapter 25;
6. www.devatma.org

Dark Slavery of Human Bondage

1. AGNIHOTRI, SHREE SATYANAND; Dev Shastra volume III-Manush Tattwa;
2. AGNIHOTRI, SHREE SATYANAND; Dev Shastra volume III- Philosophy of Man; Translated by Prof. Kanal, S.P.
3. Ibid; chapter 11; Love for Various Kind of Pleasure in the Human World
4. Prof. Kanal, S.P. Ethics of Devatma;
5. Ibid; Nature of Human Bondage; chapter 26;
6. www.devatma.org

Fallen a Prey to Bondage

1. AGNIHOTRI, SHREE SATYANAND; Dev Shastra volume III-Manush Tattwa;
2. AGNIHOTRI, SHREE SATYANAND; Dev Shastra volume III- Philosophy of Man; Translated by Prof. Kanal, S.P.
3. Ibid; chapter 11, 12, 13, 14, 15, 16, 17, 18, 19; Love for Various Kind of Pleasure in the Human World
4. Prof. Kanal, S.P. Ethics of Devatma;
5. Ibid; The Sphere of Human Bondage—Low-Loves; chapter 27;
6. www.devatma.org

The Inferno of Low-hates

1. AGNIHOTRI, SHREE SATYANAND; Dev Shastra volume III-Manush Tattwa
2. AGNIHOTRI, SHREE SATYANAND; Dev Shastra volume III- Philosophy of Man; Translated by Prof. Kanal, S.P.
3. Ibid; chapter 20; Various Kinds of Pleasure-Giving Low-Hatred in the Organism of Human Soul
4. Prof. Kanal, S.P. Ethics of Devatma;
5. Ibid; The Sphere of Human Bondage—Low-hates; chapter 28;
6. www.devatma.org

The Range of Human Bondage

1. AGNIHOTRI, SHREE SATYANAND; Dev Shastra volume III-Manush Tattwa
2. AGNIHOTRI, SHREE SATYANAND; Dev Shastra volume III- Philosophy of Man; Translated by Prof. Kanal, S.P.
3. Ibid; chapter 20; Degradation of Human Soul
4. Prof. Kanal, S.P. Ethics of Devatma;
5. Ibid; The Dimensions of Human Bondage; chapter 29;
6. www.devatma.org

The Crucial Symptoms of Human Bondage

1. AGNIHOTRI, SHREE SATYANAND; Dev Shastra volume III-Manush Tattwa
2. AGNIHOTRI, SHREE SATYANAND; Dev Shastra volume III- Philosophy of Man; Translated by Prof. Kanal, S.P.
3. Ibid; chapter 20; The Chief Symptoms of the Degradation of Human Soul.
4. Prof. Kanal, S.P. Ethics of Devatma;
5. Ibid; The Symptoms of Human Bondage; chapter 30;
6. www.devatma.org

From Human Bondage to Freedom

1. AGNIHOTRI, SHREE SATYANAND; Dev Shastra volume III-Manush Tattwa
2. AGNIHOTRI, SHREE SATYANAND; Dev Shastra volume III- Philosophy of Man; Translated by Prof. Kanal, S.P.
3. Ibid; chapter 20; The Chief Symptoms of the Degradation of Human Soul.
4. Prof. Kanal, S.P. Ethics of Devatma;
5. Ibid; Moksha of Human Bondage; chapter 31;
6. www.devatma.org

Health, Strength and Growth of Soul

1. AGNIHOTRI, SHREE SATYANAND; Dev Shastra volume III-Manush Tattwa
2. AGNIHOTRI, SHREE SATYANAND; Dev Shastra volume III- Philosophy of Man; Translated by Prof. Kanal, S.P.
3. Ibid; chapter 20; The Chief Symptoms of the Degradation of Human Soul.
4. Prof. Kanal, S.P. Ethics of Devatma;
5. Ibid; The Sphere of Human Evolution-Higher Loves; chapter 33;
6. www.devatma.org

Higher Hates are Dynamic Motives

1. AGNIHOTRI, SHREE SATYANAND; Dev Shastra volume III-Manush Tattwa;
2. AGNIHOTRI, SHREE SATYANAND; Dev Shastra volume III- Philosophy of Man; Translated by Prof. S.P. Kanal;

3. Ibid; chapter 20; The Chief Symptoms of the Degradation of Human Soul.
4. Prof. Kanal, S.P. Ethics of Devatma;
5. Ibid; The Sphere of Human Evolution-Higher Hates; chapter 34;
6. www.devatma.org

Universal Agreement Remains Untouched

1. Prof. Kanal, S.P. Humanistic Meditation
2. Ibid; Meditation on Moral Culture;
3. www.devatma.org

Applied Ethics: Each Relations is a Mirror

1. AGNIHOTRI, SHREE SATYANAND; Dev Shastra volume IV-Sambandh Tattwa;
2. AGNIHOTRI, SHREE SATYANAND; Dev Shastra volume IV- Duties and Prohibitions in Sixteen Different Interpersonal and infra Relation; Translated by Prof. Kanal, S.P.
3. Ibid; chapter 20; The Chief Symptoms of the Degradation of Human Soul.
4. Prof. Kanal, S.P. Ethics of Devatma;
5. Ibid; Texture of Altruistic life; chapter 35;
6. www.devatma.org

New Frontier— from the Limitations to Limitless

1. AGNIHOTRI, SHREE SATYANAND; Dev Shastra volume III-Manush Tattwa;
2. AGNIHOTRI, SHREE SATYANAND; Dev Shastra volume III- Philosophy of Man; Translated by Prof. Kanal, S.P.
3. Ibid; chapter 20; The Chief Symptoms of the Degradation of Human Soul.
4. Prof. Kanal, S.P. Ethics of Devatma;
5. Ibid; New Frontiers of Moksha and Vikas; chapter 37;
6. www.devatma.org

Freedom: The Source of Truth and Goodness

1. Prof. Kanal, Chandelier of Altruism;
2. Ibid; Altruism of Freedom; chapter 18;
3. www.devatma.org

Humanism: A New Direction

1. Dr. Mittal, K. K. Perspectives of the Philosophy of Devatma;
2. Prof. Kanal, S.P. Philosophy of Religion;
3. www.devatma.org

Discover Your Face

1. Prof. Kanal, S.P. Gems of Thought;
2. Ibid; Checks-Ups to know if We are Altruists; chapter 14;
3. www.devatma.org

A Synthesis of Truth, Goodness and Beauty

1. Prof. Kanal, S.P. Devatma Ka Parichey;
2. Ibid; Uniqueness of Sublime life;
3. www.devatma.org

The Door From Impulsive Level to Freedom

1. Prof. Kanal, S.P. Gems of Thought;
2. Ibid; Levels of Behaviours; chapter 15;
3. www.devatma.org

The Purpose of Life is Life Itself

1. Prof. Kanal, S.P. Ethics of Devatma;
2. Ibid; The Unexamined life is not worth living; chapter 24;
3. www.devatma.org

In the service of Past

1. Prof. Kanal S.P. The Chandelier of Altruism;
2. Ibid; chapter 12; The Altruism of the Past
3. www.devatma.org

In the Service of Present

1. Prof. Kanal S.P. The Chandelier of Altruism;
2. Ibid; chapter 13; The Altruism of the Present;
3. www.devatma.org

In the Service of Future

1. Prof. Kanal S.P. The Chandelier of Altruism;
2. Ibid; chapter 14; The Altruism of the Future;
3. www.devatma.org

The Sweet Taste of Altruism: The Future

1. Prof. Kanal S.P. The Chandelier of Altruism;
2. Ibid; chapter 15; Altruism of the Future—Its Relation to the Present and the Past;
3. www.devatma.org

Future: Crucifixion and Deliverance

1. Prof. Kanal S.P. The Chandelier of Altruism;
2. Ibid; chapter 16; The Altruists for the Future—Their Crucifixion and Deliverance;
3. www.devatma.org

Law is not Enough

1. Prof. Kanal S.P. The Chandelier of Altruism;
2. Ibid; chapter 17; The Altruists of Law;
3. www.devatma.org

A Slave in Your own House

1. Prof. Kanal S.P. The Chandelier of Altruism;
2. Ibid; chapter 18; The Altruists of Freedom;
3. www.devatma.org

Values and Social Control

1. Prof. Kanal S.P. The Chandelier of Altruism;
2. Ibid; chapter 19; The Altruists of the Fulfillment;
3. www.devatma.org

The Problem of Measurement

1. Prof. Kanal S.P. The Chandelier of Altruism;
2. Ibid; chapter 20; The Altruists of the Measurement;
3. www.devatma.org

From Social Exploitation to Enlightenment

1. Prof. Kanal S.P. Glimpses of Beauty Sublime;
2. Ibid; chapter 9; Social Exploitation;
3. www.devatma.org

From Political Exploitation to Enlightenment

1. Prof. Kanal S.P. Glimpses of Beauty Sublime;
2. Ibid; chapter 10; Political Exploitation;
3. www.devatma.org

From Ethical Exploitation to Enlightenment

1. Prof. Kanal S.P. Glimpses of Beauty Sublime;
2. Ibid; chapter 12; Ethical Exploitation;
3. www.devatma.org

Know How to Live

1. Prof. Kanal S.P. Gems of Thought;
2. Ibid; chapter 3; How We can be Sweet to Others;
3. www.devatma.org

Dance In Ecstasy Before the Beauty

1. Prof. Kanal S.P. Glimpses of Beauty Sublime;
2. Ibid; chapter 24; When is a Devotee at His Best?
3. www.devatma.org

The Best, Liberated and Fully Evolved Man

1. Prof. Kanal S.P. Glimpses of Beauty Sublime;
2. Ibid; chapter 23; When is a good Man at His Best?
3. www.devatma.org

Seek Truth Unconditionally

1. www.devatma.org

The Future Belongs to the Altruistic Man

1. Prof. Kanal S.P. Ethics of Devatma;
2. Ibid; Human Evolution; chapter 32;
3. www.devatma.org

Pearls of Thought

1. Prof. Kanal, S.P. To Be Good;
2. Prof. Kanal, S.P. Glimpses of Beauty Sublime;

3.   www.devatma.org

Faith in and Love for Devatma

1.   AGNIHOTRI, SHREE SATYANAND Dev; Shastra volume III-Manush Tattwa;
2.   AGNIHOTRI, SHREE SATYANAND; Dev Shastra volume III- Philosophy of Man; Translated by Prof. Kanal S.P.
3.   Ibid; chapter 27; The True Method of Communion with the Devatma.
4.   www.devatma.org

Devatma: Beyond Experience

1.   Prof. Kanal S.P. Devatma Ka Parichey;
2.   Prof. Kanal S.P. Introduction to Devama; Translated by Dr. Kaur Ramanpreet
3.   Ibid; Uniqueness of Sublime life

Faith in the Sublime Beauty

1.   AGNIHOTRI, SHREE SATYANAND; Dev Shastra volume III-Manush Tattwa;
2.   AGNIHOTRI, SHREE SATYANAND; Dev Shastra volume III- Philosophy of Man; Translated by Prof. Kanal S.P.
3.   Ibid; chapter 28; The True & Unshakable Faith in the Sublime Beauty ('Dev Rup') of Devatma.
4.   www.devatma.org

Reverence for the Sublime Beauty

1.   AGNIHOTRI, SHREE SATYANAND; Dev Shastra volume III-Manush Tattwa;
2.   AGNIHOTRI, SHREE SATYANAND; Dev Shastra volume III- Philosophy of Man; Translated by Prof. Kanal S.P.
3.   Ibid; chapter 29; The True & unshakable feeling of reverence for the Sublime Beauty ('Dev Rup') of Devatma.
4.   www.devatma.org

Gratitude for the Sublime Beauty

1.   AGNIHOTRI, SHREE SATYANAND; Dev Shastra volume III-Manush Tattwa;
2.   AGNIHOTRI, SHREE SATYANAND; Dev Shastra volume III- Philosophy of Man; Translated by Prof. Kanal S.P.
3.   Ibid; chapter 30; The True & unshakable feeling of Gratitude for the Sublime Beauty ('Dev Rup') of Devatma
4.   www.devatma.org

Attraction For the Sublime Beauty

1. AGNIHOTRI, SHREE SATYANAND; Dev Shastra volume III-Manush Tattwa;
2. AGNIHOTRI, SHREE SATYANAND; Dev Shastra volume III- Philosophy of Man; Translated by Prof. Kanal S.P.
3. Ibid; Chapter 31; The feeling of Attraction for the Sublime Influences ('Dev Prabhavas') of Devatma.
4. www.devatma.org

They Crucified Him Every Moment

1. AGNIHOTRI, SHREE SATYANAND; Aduti Tiyag Volume I, II, III, IV;
2. Glimpses of Beauty Sublime;
3. Ibid; Chapter 20; Persecution of My Master
4. www.devatma.org

The Promise of Paradise

1. AGNIHOTRI, SHREE SATYANAND' Aduti Tiyag Volume I, II, III, IV;
2. Glimpses of Beauty Sublime;
3. Ibid; Chapter 21; Sacrifice—Human & Divine
4. www.devatma.org

The Poetry of the Beyond

1. AGNIHOTRI, SHREE SATYANAND; Aduti Tiyag Volume 1;
2. Ibid; Chapter 1; Introduction;

Whole Challenge of Life

1. AGNIHOTRI, SHREE SATYANAND; Aatam Parichey-volume 1;
2. Ibid; Chapter 2; Mera Aavirbhav Aur Mera Jiwan Brat

Dark Pitch of Roundabouts

1. AGNIHOTRI, SHREE SATYANAND; Aatam Parichey-volume 1;
2. Ibid; Chapter 3; Uch Bodhh-Janit meri Becheini vaa viakulta;

Life is on the Razor's Edge But Still

1. AGNIHOTRI, SHREE SATYANAND; Aatam Parichey-volume 1;
2. Ibid; Chapter 4; Mere Sambandhio ki Vartmaan Avastha aur Mein;

The Real Ecstasy

1. AGNIHOTRI, SHREE SATYANAND; Aatam Parichey-volume 1;
2. Ibid; Chapter 5; Mujh mein Aatmic Shanti aur Devanand;

Blank Walls All Around

1. AGNIHOTRI, SHREE SATYANAND; Aatam Parichey-volume 1;
2. Ibid; Chapter 6; Naana Durghatnao se meri Aantric Avasatha;

Ah! My Miserable Conditions

1. AGNIHOTRI, SHREE SATYANAND; Aatam Parichey-volume 1;
2. Ibid; Chapter 7; Meri Aasahee Avasthaa;

A Solitary Bird: Anonymus, Ignorant and Forever Tortured?

1. AGNIHOTRI, SHREE SATYANAND; Aatam Parichey-volume 1;
2. Ibid; Chapter 8; Mein Appne janno mein bhi rahker Akela, Aprichit, upekshit, aur utpidit raha huin;

After The Dark Night is Dawn

1. AGNIHOTRI, SHREE SATYANAND; Aatam Paricheyvolume 1;
2. Ibid; Chapter 10; Mere Kallesh aur Dukh aur unka Antt;

Alone! Long Waiting and Wailing!

1. AGNIHOTRI, SHREE SATYANAND; Mujh Mein Dev Jiwan Ka Vikas-vol. I;
2. AGNIHOTRI, SHREE SATYANAND; 'The evolution of Divine life in me' volume—I; Translated by Prof. Kanal S.P. (1994)
3. Ibid; Chapter 25; My Persecution Consequent on My Commitment to my Life-Vow;

The Cry of Shrill Words

1. AGNIHOTRI, SHREE SATYANAND; Mujh Mein Dev Jiwan Ka Vikas-vol. I;
1. AGNIHOTRI, SHREE SATYANAND; 'The evolution of Divine life in me' volume—I; Translated by Prof. Kanal S.P. (1994)
1. Ibid; Chapter 25; My Persecution Consequent on My Commitment to my Life-Vow;

Answer Me: Oh Heaven! Oh Earth!!

1. AGNIHOTRI, SHREE SATYANAND; Mujh Mein Dev Jiwan Ka Vikas-vol. I;

2. AGNIHOTRI, SHREE SATYANAND; 'The evolution of Divine life in me' volume—I; Translated by Prof. Kanal S.P. (1994)
3. Ibid; Chapter 25; My Persecution Consequent on My Commitment to my Life-Vow;

Pain Within Pain

1. AGNIHOTRI, SHREE SATYANAND; Mujh Mein Dev Jiwan Ka Vikas-vol. I;
2. AGNIHOTRI, SHREE SATYANAND; 'The evolution of Divine life in me' volume—I; Translated by Prof. Kanal S.P. (1994)
3. Ibid; Chapter 25; My Persecution Consequent on My Commitment to my Life-Vow;

No Hope of My Survival

1. AGNIHOTRI, SHREE SATYANAND; Mujh Mein Dev Jiwan Ka Vikas-vol. I;
2. AGNIHOTRI, SHREE SATYANAND; 'The evolution of Divine life in me' volume—I; Translated by Prof. Kanal S.P. (1994)
3. Ibid; Chapter 25; My Persecution Consequent on My Commitment to my Life-Vow;

Acceptance of the Peaks and the Valleys

1. AGNIHOTRI, SHREE SATYANAND; Mujh Mein Dev Jiwan Ka Vikas-vol. I;
2. AGNIHOTRI, SHREE SATYANAND; 'The evolution of Divine life in me' volume—I; Translated by Prof. Kanal S.P. (1994)
3. Ibid; Chapter 25; My Persecution Consequent on My Commitment to my Life-Vow;

A Priceless Nectarine

1. AGNIHOTRI, SHREE SATYANAND; Mujh Mein Dev Jiwan Ka Vikas-vol. I;
2. AGNIHOTRI, SHREE SATYANAND; 'The evolution of Divine life in me' volume—I; Translated by Prof. Kanal S.P. (1994)
3. Ibid; Chapter 25; My Persecution Consequent on My Commitment to my Life-Vow;

Gems of Sublime Vision

1. AGNIHOTRI, SHREE SATYANAND; Mujh Mein Dev Jiwan Ka Vikas-vol. I;
2. AGNIHOTRI, SHREE SATYANAND; 'The evolution of Divine life in me' volume—I; Translated by Prof. Kanal S.P. (1994)
3. Ibid; Chapter 18; My Great Struggle in the Most Difficult Task of Research;
4. Illuminated Truths (Dictums of Bhagwan Devatma); Shriman Baldev Singh Ji; Dev-Dharam Publication
5. www.devatma.org

Index

615

620

Author Biography

Sukhdev Singh
Director of Devatma organisation (U.K.)

Presenting a word on philosophy has ever been a challenging task then what to say of a philosophical work and that too of such an unconventional school of thoughts. When something qualitative of higher level comes across, it results into treaties and commentries. This is the fragrance of the life and the philosophy of Devatma that has evolved in this text. The author has successfully attempted to encompass all the possible aspects of philosophy in this single volume. Altogether an excellent way to lighten the darkest part of the life of Devatma on the part of the present author is capable of unfolding the gates of thoughtfulness. During the course of his discourse Devatma had to suffer from great opposition from various quarters but without being affected from those miseries he continued to engage himself devotedly to his mission, to found forth the ultimate boundless ethical standards that are next to impossible in the history of humans. None before or even after him could touch the milestone as established by Devatma. There has been a general principle of achievements in this universe that greatness awaits only the consistency of positivity who can continue his onward journey even through frustrations to fruitify the proverb that one is great only if he can rise again after every fall and who can always remain awake and active for the attainment of its goal whether or not he receives recognition or applause. An important lesson is evident here that those who complain of non-recognition and applause at unfavorable circumstances, whose eyes are set on problems rather than on opportunities can never attain the attainable in their life. "THE HIGHEST MEANING OF LIFE" is not merely the collection of five words but the height of the meaningness in the life. The author has not left any stone unturned to make the text more and more appealing by mixing prose and poetry appropriately. The contents are land marked and the language is appealing. In my view, this book will play the role of the enlightening torch to the scholars who aspire to go ahead in the field of the natural philosophy, particularly that of Devatma. Best of wishes on your well deserved effort!

- Dr. R.k. Satyashree, Ph.D on Devatma.

Sukhdev Singh, director of Devatma Organization U.K., presents the principles of Dev-Dharma in this shelf-bending offering.

This belief system, founded by an Indian man known as Devatma, uses "scientific methods to discover human nature and its destiny." It teaches that the soul is biological in origin and that evolution allows man to pursue Dev-Dharma's highest values of Truth, Goodness, and Beauty. On this evolutionary path, man struggles to subdue "low-loves and low-hates" in order to replace them with "high loves and high hates." When man has attained this purification, he achieves a state of altruism, "true harmony with existence in nature." Nature is made of "four kingdoms... humans, animals, plants, and the physical worlds," and the perfect man lives in service to them.

These basics are made reasonably clear in the Foreword and first chapter. The vast majority of the remaining book is a re-iteration and expansion of these principles in the form of poems, short, numbered paragraphs, and lists of bullet points.

- BlueInk Review

An attempt to capture the nature of the human soul in a grand synthesis of religious and scientific ideas.

Debut author Singh ambitiously aims to provide a comprehensive account of Devatma, a religion that portrays itself as the only truly scientific account of man's spiritual life. The faith was founded in India in 1887 by Bhagwan Devatma, who was inspired by the theoretical innovations of Charles Darwin and Herbert Spencer. He also made evolution the centerpiece of his own worldview, applying it to the human soul. The author contends that the soul is purely biological and should be understood in relentlessly empirical terms as an "organized life-force." Unlike other faiths, Devatma rejects supernatural metaphysics, preferring to ground its perspective in nature, and unlike scientific evolutionary theory, it purports to explain not only the factual aspects of the world, but also the gradual emergence and meaning of human values. The evolutionary pinnacle, the author asserts, is overcoming egoistic pleasure—manifested in "low-loves" and "low-hates"—for the sake of altruism, culminating in selfless service to mankind. As the director of Devatma Organization U.K., his knowledge of the religion is expert, and his rendering of it is impressively exhaustive. He also helpfully discusses the ways in which he feels Devatma is inclusive of but ultimately completes the history of philosophical humanism. However, for a book that constantly touts Devatma's scientific superiority over other religions, ...

- Kirkus Indie Review

Life is a strange quest, and Sukhdev Singh wants to help others reach the ultimate conclusions about its purpose. The Highest Meaning of Life is Singh's literary roadmap to life, and in its density and difficulty, it parallels the whole bizarre trip.

This extensive tome presents multiple faces. First it focuses on "the Master," a hypothetical philosophical adept whom all should aspire to be like: a being without the fears, worries, and hang-ups that obscure the ultimate truth. The Master is not concerned about time or expediency; the Master only has love for the truth. The book suggests that anyone, if they follow the path of enlightenment and knowledge, can become the Master.

But in order to become a Master, the book argues, one must first study, analyze, and adopt certain precepts. As such, this is also a rule book concerned with the ethical, spiritual, and philosophical rules that must be followed by those seeking a path to the sublime.

This secondary "rules" portion of the work is its best. It includes reminders that change is unavoidable, that emotional bondage is personal slavery, and that the "beyond" is a space where human reasoning fails. Whereas other portions of the text can be hard to digest or even to contemplate, the "rules" portion is straightforward and clear.

The book draws on a literary tradition with its roots in Buddhism, Hinduism, and other Eastern religious philosophies. This text is also part of Devatma, another esoteric religious philosophy. Devatma, as is this book, is concerned with accepting life's amorphous mosaic rather than with trying to bring order to the cosmos. Singh's literary approach to this complex topic is at times hard to follow, though for those interested in Devatma, this is an excellent place to start.

With its emphasis on enlightenment, this book is so daunting that it is almost Herculean; it taxes patience with its meandering and flowery prose. Almost every paragraph works to unlock higher truths.

This style at times feels a little maddening, with an overemphasis on rhetorical questions. Those more familiar with Western traditions of logic, rationality, and empiricism might be put off by the somewhat supernatural, or at least extraordinary, themes at play here.

More a textbook than a pleasure read, and more a gospel than it is a polemic or an extended essay, this is a work for serious students with strong intellectual bents; it should be approached with the necessary earnestness. If tackled from a specific mindset, The Highest Meaning of Life will be an enjoyable and fulfilling work, possibly offering highly sought-after spiritual truth.

- Foreword Clarion Review

Lightning Source UK Ltd.
Milton Keynes UK
UKHW02f1221290618
324968UK00002B/26/P